AF322587

THE THIN PLACE

THE THIN PLACE

RODNEY PEAVY

Gospelfoot Publishing

This book is dedicated to my soulmate, Beverly...
Thank you for always steadying me...

Jesus answered and said unto him,
If a man loves me, he will keep my words:
and my Father will love him,
and we will come unto him,
and make our abode with him.
-John 14:23

Contents

Preface

In January 2010, I started what would be for me a great adventure. I began a very small and humble web ministry called Burning Bones Ministries or www.burning-bones.com. It was so named after the Bible verse Jeremiah 20:9, which speaks of God's Word becoming like a fire burning in my bones should I try to hold it in. This theme mirrored the enthusiasm I was feeling at this point in my spiritual life. I was seeking a way to further express that enthusiasm. Thus burning bones was born.

Sadly, this web ministry no longer exists. It would only last for a few years and would consist mainly of a daily devotional that I had written with a few other writing and teaching projects made available as I wrote them. It was in the early days of social media and my web designing skills were very basic. I was not trying to earn a living with my writing or really even trying to reach beyond my circle of friends. It was primarily just to supplement the pastoral ministry of which I served at the time. However, the Lord blessed my efforts and I developed a very generous mailing list for my daily devotionals, which came in the form of emails to your inbox instead of posts or tweets. At least, I think it was generous for someone of my experience. It would eventually become the catalyst to the release of my first book, *Filling the Quiver: Is Adoption God's Will for My Life?*. Nevertheless, as life often does, things became really busy and Burning Bones web ministry had to be pushed aside.

Still, I would like to think that God used these daily devotions to touch many hearts. I miss the many interactions I had with readers and subscribers during that period of my ministry. I often found myself joyfully surprised by just how God would use certain daily readings to speak to others. My heart was enriched with the conversations they would initiate. While I would like to think that I was able to help others deepen their relationship with the Lord through this ministry, it was probably myself that grew the most I do believe. God used his word and His creativity within my heart to mold and shape me during this period of my life. I do not wish for that work and time to have been in vain or forgotten. It is for this reason that I now seek another method of sharing this short period of my personal life with anyone that might be seeking a closer relationship with the Lord. This book is an extension of that early ministry.

This book is a collection of those daily devotionals from years ago with changes made where contemporary context was necessary. They are not meant to be a substitute for daily Bible reading or personal bible study or group study. On the contrary, if anything, I hope they will only lead you to desire more of the milk and meat of God's treasured word. Some of the daily readings are very personal in nature and others are more general. Some might even be humorous. But regardless of the style, hopefully you will find all of them to be based on Biblical truth and sound theological teaching. And prayerfully, God will use them to guide your heart. Perhaps, His word will become like a "burning fire shut up in your bones" as it was for me at the time of writing.

It is with great humility and overwhelming gratitude that I accept the trust you have placed in me by reading these devotionals. May God bless you as you read these pages...

-Rev. Rodney Peavy

Introduction

What is the thin place?

It is a place where heaven and earth touch. At least that is one of the many definitions I have encountered.

It can refer to an actual literal physical place or locale or to a more symbolic state of mind or meditation. The terminology "thin place" is often used as a metaphor to describe an intimate spiritual event or encounter, an event where the earthy encounters the Divine. It has so many different interpretations, some of which are unfortunately tied to mysticism and other new age beliefs, such that many Christians stay away from the use of the terminology. In those contexts, they are right to do so. It is nonetheless beginning to find common use among many Christians, as the many articles and writings on the subject will attest. While we can argue whether or not that is good or bad, in proper theological context, the idea of finding a "thin place" is one that all believers should be striving for, regardless of what you wish to call it.

The concept of a thin place is most often attributed as being a product of the Celtic spirituality of Ireland and Scotland of the fourth and fifth centuries A. D. In recent years, there has been a revival of interest in this period of history in the west, in particular in the area of Celtic Christianity and its practices. As evidence, you see the symbols of that period in jewelry and artwork everywhere you look. You may not have known what you were looking at, but you have most certainly seen the Celtic Cross, the Celtic Tree of Life, The Trinity Knot, etc... in the form of jewelry, bumper stickers, tattoos or in more serious artwork and architecture. These symbols are filled with imagery and are an expression of the early Celtic Christian teachings. Many believe them to be connected to the deep tie with nature that the ancient pre-Christian Celtic mystics followed. When Christianity came into the land, that deep cultural connection with nature and creation was still part of their early practices as does the artwork and artifacts of that day reveal. The name "thin place" or "thin space" is part of that rich tradition.

In regard to that pre-Christian Celtic tradition, the thin place was considered a literal place, where it was thought that one might more easily encounter something sacred. The belief was that there was something special about the actual location. It was special; in that, it was believed the barriers that often keep us from encountering the divine were "thinner" at these locations. Thus, the name "thin place". Therefore, in a thin place, we are thought to be closer to the divine and more apt to have a spiritual experience. Altars were often built, and people would travel many miles on pilgrimages for meditation and prayer to these places, all in the hopes of one of these encounters. Once Celtic Christianity became dominant, the thin place concept would abandon the pagan beliefs and begin to be thought of as a place you could instead go to encounter the true and living God of the Bible, often the place of some Christian event or of significant church beginnings. The Island of Iona is still referred to as a thin place for Christians of that region of the world, and a place of pilgrimage for many. Iona is thought of as the birthplace of Christianity in Scotland and would be the launching point of missionaries into Northern Britain, forever changing the region. It is just one example.

However, a very basic research on the subject will reveal that there are those that would argue that the concept of a thin place has always existed and predates Celtic spirituality. They would argue that the name thin place was only adopted from the Celt's to try to describe intimate encounters with God and the places where they occur. For example, if the thin place is a place created for man to have closer more intimate access to his Creator, then the thin place must be traced back all the way to Eden.

What was Eden after all, if not a place for close communion with God? In the garden, there was nothing separating mankind from his Creator. The barriers between us and God were as thin as it could get. Unfortunately, due to the fall, this thin place became closed to mankind. Ironically, it was man's "thick-headedness" that led to the separation and dissolution of this thin place.

The same argument would continue and say that ancient Biblical history is filled with what could be called thin places. Mt. Sinai, that holy ground where Moses shed his shoes is sometimes referred to as a thin place. In the Old Testament, each time God would speak and instruct the Old Testament patriarch or prophet to build an altar in remembrance of some occurrence or miracle, he was marking a thin place, a place where God and man had communed. Even the tabernacle and later the temple have been referred to as thin places, places specifically designated by God as a place for spiritual communion. Even the ordinances of Baptism and the Lord's supper table of the New Testament itself is often referred to as a thin place.

In a more modern and down to earth interpretation (forgive the pun), often people familiar with the terminology use it to refer to places of a more personal significance. For example, one might refer to the time and place of their acceptance of the Lord as personal savior as their thin place. It might also be a favorite place of retreat they refer to as a thin place. Perhaps they went there for a spiritual renewal conference or meeting and while there it seemed as if God was speaking more clearly to them than at home; therefore, it become a thin place in their mind. I have one of those. In fact, I have several of those. In fact, in that context, one could say that church itself is meant to be a thin place.

My first one occurred as a teenager. It was not at church. It was on a beach. I finally, in a time of prayer and meditation, surrendered to God's call to vocational ministry in Panama City Beach, Florida. I was attending a summer youth camp. For me, that beach will always have a special place in my heart. It is hard to explain, but for me, I could hear God's voice more clearly that morning on that beach than ever before. But to most, that beach is a place of partying spring breakers and sunburns, not a place of spiritual renewal and divine encounters. You see, that thin place moment I had that day was because of the condition of my heart at that particular moment more than the physical location, as beautiful as it might have been.

With that in mind, if the concept of the thin place is biblical and can be traced all the way back to Eden, then let's follow it to the natural conclusion. From Eden we go to the Old Testament altars. From there we go to the tabernacle and then later to the temple. From the temple we go to the ultimate thin place of Bethlehem and to the actual Immanuel, "God with Us" being born like us and walking among us. Then we follow him all the way to the cross and ultimately to the empty tomb and ascension. Then on Pentecost, the Holy Spirit came and now indwells all believers.

Listen to what Paul says in 1 Corinthians 3: 16-18:

> ¹⁶ Do you not know that you are a temple of God and
> *that* the Spirit of God dwells in you?
> ¹⁷ If any man destroys the temple of God, God will destroy him,
> for the temple of God is holy, and that is what you are.

We are the temple of the Holy Spirit. God indwells his children. We no longer have to go to an altar or tabernacle or temple to encounter God. He lives within us. Pilgrimages, though enriching and enjoyable, are no longer necessary. When that temple veil was torn upon the crucifixion of Jesus, traveling to specific places to encounter God became needless. When that veil was torn, we became the thin place. We are the thin place! I need only go as far as my own heart in prayer and meditation to encounter the true and living God. Jesus is my high priest and mediator, and the Holy Spirit indwells my very own heart.

Are there special places where you can feel the presence of God easier than in other places? Perhaps. But it is not because there is anything special about the physical atmosphere or "energy" in that place. That is mystical nonsense. It is because we go there in expectation of hearing from God. It is because we have most likely prepared our hearts ahead of time in such a way as to initiate communion with God. Even the communion table itself is just a table made of wood. It is the reverence and prayerful attitude we take with us as we approach it that makes us tremble when we go to it.

Those Old Testament thin place locations were no different. There was nothing special about the specific geographical location. In fact, for many of those spots today, we are unsure of exactly where they were located. So, obviously it was not the coordinates that we should be seeking. It was never about pinpointing the location. If we did know for sure, we might only find a stack of rocks. It was the heart of the person involved in those stories that God was aiming at and exemplifying for us, not some point on a map. It's our heart condition, not the location that brings us into communication with God.

There are a couple more of what some would call thin places that I personally frequent. They are both on our family property. One is deep in the woods behind my house, on top of a tall hill. From there I have beautiful views of sky and trees and sunsets. I built myself a bench and lugged it all the way up that small mountain and strategically placed it so that my views are optimal. I often take my Bible and go there for times of prayer and meditation. I have truly encountered God on that hillside.

The other is at the opposite end of our property. It is in the valley. (There has to be a sermon illustration in there somewhere.) In this valley we have a beautiful flowing creek. I have some rocks I often recline upon as I watch and listen to the babbling water. From time to time and weather permitting, I may even stick my toes into the refreshing water. I also often take my Bible and descend to the creek for times of prayer and meditation. Likewise, I have often heard God's still small voice very clearly in this, my personal thin place.

However, there is nothing special about those places beyond the significance I place upon them. They are beautiful natural locations. Don't get me wrong, I love them! I find great moments of relaxation and escape when I go there. I can even act like a little boy when no one is watching and play barefoot in the water. But the fact that I hear God's voice when I go there is because I am going there to hear God's voice. There is nothing mystical or supernatural going on in my thin places. It has nothing to do with the trees or the water or the "energy" in the atmosphere. It is not like God is waiting on me in those places. I am hearing from God better when I go there because I am intentionally trying to hear from Him and have already prepared my heart to do so before I even arrive. I have intentionally removed myself from my personal distractions and am actively seeking to hear from God. But the truth is that I don't have to go to the creek to do that. I can do it in my bed, in my car, or in my study. In fact, I can even do it while working, cooking or even on the back of my lawn mower. The thin place is not a place, as much as it is a mindset.

You see, we don't go to the thin place. We are the thin place. It goes with us.

That is, it goes with us, if like the ancient Celt's we have no barriers between us and the divine. The barriers we might have include unrepented sin, pride, jealousy, lack of knowledge of God's word and truth, and especially a complacent spirit. If we want to encounter God on a daily basis, then we must be intentional about trying to keep these hindrances thin. The thicker they grow, the harder it is to hear from God.

God is His wisdom and love has given us the means to create in ourselves a thin space of communion with Him. He gave us his Holy Spirit to teach us and guide us. Through the Holy Spirit, we feel conviction of our sins, of our barriers to the divine and the means of which to ask for forgiveness leading to repentance. Through the Holy Spirit we also have guidance in our seeking asking and knocking (Matthew 7:7-8). Along with this support, we also have His inspired Word to teach us and guide us. Put simply, we have everything we need in order to create in ourselves a thin space of personal daily encounters with God Almighty.

God is not hiding is some mystical locale or place, hoping that you might one day stumble upon his presence during a pilgrimage. From the garden of Eden until present day, He has been making a way for us to get our thin place of Eden back. More than anything, God longs to have communion with you. In evangelical circles we call it a personal relationship with God. That is exactly what it is. He wants to spend time with you today. The thin place is where heaven touches earth. He wants to be that close to you. You can have that thin place experience every day. He wants you to live in a state of perpetual thinness or closeness with Him. It's not a place or an event, it's a state of being that every believer should long for....an ever growing closer and closer communion with God.

This book is merely a beginning step in having that type of encounter with him on a daily basis. Along with scripture readings, you will read a devotion that will help lead you to your thin place. Call it your daily quiet time or daily devotional. It does not matter. There is nothing special about this book. It is the attitude and desire you have within your own heart that creates the thin place living. Let the Holy Spirit guide you.

Each daily reading will begin with a section titled **From Above**. This is suggested readings from God's inspired Word. This is God's word to you from above. Next is the section titled **Here Below**. This section is my devotional interpretation of that passage. While I do pray it is helpful, it is not inspired. It is my attempt to help you hear the message God has for you from His word and is meant only to get your heart and mind open to the voice of God and whatever message He has for you. Lastly, the final section is **The Thin Place**. This is where heaven touches earth, where truth meets application. This is the goal and purpose of the daily devotional. This is where you take what you have read and basically ask the question "What is God telling me personally?" Then you apply it to your life. It is the point of prayer, introspection, and application. It might even be a point of conviction and repentance, a point of thinning out those spiritual barriers between yourself and God. Put simply, it is where things happen. It is the thin place. Prayerfully, it will begin to be your consistent mindset in all things.

Do you long for that thin place in your daily life? Do you want to be known to be like old Enoch of the Old Testament, of whom it is said that he "walked with God"? Like many others, he was a living thinking breathing walking thin place. His heart was a place where heaven and earth came together in perfect communion and fellowship, a sacred meeting space. He was not alone. Biblical history is filled with such believers. You can be one too. God wants it. The question is... do you? Let this book help you find it.

Let's go to the thin place...

1

January

January 1
A Daily Grace!

<u>From Above</u>: John 3:1-5, Luke 9:23, Psalm 30:5

Focal Passage: *In reply Jesus declared, "I tell you the truth, no one can see the kingdom of God unless he is born again." -John 3:3*

<u>Here Below</u>:

Most of us can agree on the overwhelming significance of the words first spoken by Jesus to Nicodemus on that dark night of questions. The implications of this conversation would literally change hearts and souls of men for millennia to come. Though not used as it once was, the phrase "born again" is the heart of the salvation message taught by Jesus. But I say it reaches even deeper than our need for a saving grace. It reveals a need for a daily grace.

Jesus was revealing to us through His words a truth of God's nature. The necessity of being "born again" implies that God is a God of second chances, of starting over, of new beginnings. While salvation is once and forever, our need for starting over comes daily. God, in His love for us, has seen that need and met that need. This morning, when you wrestled yourself out of bed, it was in essence a new day for you to live for the Lord. It is a new opportunity to surrender your will to that of God.

Yesterday is what it is, good or bad. Recognize it. Learn from it. Use it. Repent of it. Then let it go.

Today is your chance to make those needed changes. With a time of daily repentance comes a gift of daily grace. With a gift of daily grace comes a blessing of daily joy.

So you need to start over today? Good! God seems to be okay with that... In fact, He desires it.

Why not take Him up on His offer of a brand new beginning?

The Thin Place: Ask, Answer, Pray and Apply.

What areas of my life need a new beginning?

What in my life have I not truly surrendered to the Lord?

What can I do differently today that might help bring about the needed change?

January 2
Higher Than I

From Above: Psalm 61, Psalm 34:8, Luke 11:9-13

Focal Passage: *From the ends of the earth I call to you, I call as my heart grows faint; lead me to the rock that is higher than I. —Psalm 61:2*

Here Below:

In this beautiful song, David acknowledges a simple and profound truth that we would be smart to apply to our own lives. He needed a God that is bigger than himself. Keep in mind; most believe that as David was singing these words, he was indeed the King. He was the most powerful man in his part of the world, if not the whole world. Yet, he was praying that He might be led to a rock higher than himself. He needed a God bigger than the king.

Does your life reflect that type of humility? Does your life reflect your need for something or someone bigger? You might say, of course it does. But how many times do we only consult the Lord when all other options have failed? How many times do we seek His involvement in our crises only when we are facing defeat? These are tough questions. Too often we pride ourselves on our own resourcefulness and strength too greatly to admit our need for help.

Let's consider the logic of this way of thinking. We would be quick to say that God is the all-powerful all-knowing creator of all that exists. We would also be quick to say that nothing catches God by surprise. Right? Then why do we only seek his help and guidance when all other options have disappointed us? As a child of God, we have access to someone who not only knows everything and has power over everything; this same person loves us above all things! David recognized that even his power as king was nothing compared to God's vision and strength. He also recognized that God only desires the best for His children.

So, why not seek the Lord first? After all, it only makes good common sense. God is higher, bigger and wiser than even your best efforts.

<u>The Thin Place</u>: Ask, Answer, Pray and Apply.

Has there been a time when you tried to do things on your own strength before turning to God, only to fail?

Is there a situation in your life right now in which you need guidance from someone higher than yourself?

How can you approach this differently than in the past?

January 3
In the Way

<u>From Above</u>: 2 Timothy 2:19-22, Romans 5:1-2

Focal **Passage**: *If a man cleanses himself from the latter, he will be an instrument for noble purposes, made holy, useful to the Master and prepared to do any good work. -2 Timothy 2:21*

<u>Here Below</u>:

There was a song released several years back by a contemporary Christian musician named Grover Levy called "If You Want To Lead Me To Jesus " which contains these words:

If you want to lead me to Jesus
You better find a better way
Cause your life is speaking so loud
I can't even hear a word you say...

These words are very cutting and at the same time very revealing. Too often there seems to be a disconnection between what we say we believe and what our lives profess. While our intent may be well, a profession of a deep life-changing faith in Jesus Christ while living in opposition to those words is more damaging to the cause of Christianity than saying nothing at all. The world needs to see genuine faith at work in our lives. Lord, help me to never get in the way!

But it really goes deeper even than our testimony to others and the effect it will have upon them. There is a certain restlessness that we will personally experience which comes as the result of a disjointed life. Call it conviction. Call it guilt. Call it whatever you want. The outcome is the same. When you lead a life of spiritual polarization, the result is a lack of peace. This is not God's will. His will for us is peace.

Now this doesn't mean we must obtain some form of sinless perfection in order to obtain peace and be a proper witness. It will never happen this side of Heaven. Nevertheless, we are to strive be Christlike in our witness. That is why God introduced grace into the world. Without grace, we are at best in a struggle. To believe and profess otherwise is to be spiritually dishonest. Peace comes when we embrace grace in our efforts to be an effective witness. We live by grace! Thanks be to God for His grace and mercy!

The Thin Place: Ask, Answer, Pray, and Apply.

Can you relate to this idea of a spiritual restlessness? Can you identify the cause?

What can you do differently to bring peace to this restless situation?

What opportunities will you have this week to be a living testimony to the benefits of a life of faith?

January 4
The Good Life

From Above: I Timothy 6:17-19, Matthew 6:19-20

Focal Passage: *In this way they will lay up treasure for themselves as a firm foundation for the coming age, so that they may take hold of the life that is truly life. –I Timothy 6:19*

Here Below:

It never ceases to amaze how the men and women of the early church seemed to have a grasp of life that we seem to miss so often in our day. We see this especially in the life of the Apostle Paul. In this letter to Timothy, he is basically instructing this young pastor to lead his flock to an understanding of what adds real value to life. Real value is not in riches or fame, but in our relationship with the Lord. Wealth and fame is uncertain at best, God is not.

Every day we see this truth displayed almost *ad nauseum*. One can't turn on the television, radio or log onto the internet without seeing another story of how someone famous has messed up their life. It is an endless barrage of rehabs, DUI's, arrests, affairs, bankruptcies, lawsuits and the like. Why? These people are usually those whom we would assume have it all. They have disposable wealth. They have fame. They have beauty. They have fans. They have education. Yet, more times than not, their lives are a wreck. Again, why? Because most of them do not understand what the Apostle Paul knew to be true.

Real life can only be found in relationship with the Giver of all life. Keep in mind, Paul was a prisoner and eventually a martyr. Yet, no one would question Paul's grasp of the good life. He had it. He could have kept his mouth shut and probably have been freed to pursue another course. Yet, he knew his rewards were not here, but to come. He knew this was "truly life".

One doesn't have to be rich and famous to put the loves of this world before our relationship with the Lord. It can happen even to us "ordinary Joes". Our desire for more of the world is often greater than our desire for more of God. Yet, what was true for Timothy's flock is enduringly true for us today as well, perhaps even more so. A house is only as strong as it's foundation. Why not take hold of the life that is truly life?

__The Thin Place__: Ask, Answer, Pray, and Apply.
Take an honest inventory of your life. Where do your treasure's lie?
What priorities in your life have a lasting eternal significance?
How might I reorganize my life so that God's purposes might come first?

January 5
The Simple Things

__From Above:__ John 10:9-10, Psalm 65, John 1:1-4
Focal Passage: *The thief comes only to steal and kill and destroy; I have come that they may have life, and have it to the full.-John 10: 10*
__Here Below:__
Friends and loved ones often share a private giggle over a saying or a phrase that is special to the two of them alone which might not have meaning for others. One of the somewhat private expressions that my wife and I share is the following statement: "It's the simple things in life that give me pleasure." This statement delivered with my "expert" comedic timing, following a silly word or action from one of our kids or following the carrying out of some mundane household chore or the sneaking of some private pleasure, will always bring a smile to our face and warmth to our hearts. I know it is corny and may not speak to you, but to our household, it brings joy.

As cheesy as this phrase might seem, there is I believe an undeniable truth hidden within. How many times have we longed for the simpler days of childhood? Have you ever longed for days of running barefoot through fresh cut grass, playing for hours in a sandbox, catching a jar full of fireflies or maybe just spending great quantities of time searching for just the right stone to skip across a still pond? And have you ever taken a spoon and eaten peanut butter straight from the jar? Oh, how I've longed for those simpler times...

I believe God designed His world in this manner on purpose. First of all, God does nothing by accident. Second, He had mankind in mind when He created this world. Logically speaking then, the reason we find such pleasure in nature and the "simpler" things in life must be by His design. He wants us to enjoy life. The burdens and troubles of life were not His creation, but ours. When sin entered the world, so did stress. This was never God's intent. This then leads us to God's grace and forgiveness, available to all. The cross is God's answer to our anxiety.

Sure, there are manmade pleasures in this life. Technology can be fun and stimulating. But let's be honest, does anything compare with the enjoyment of God's presence in the everyday aspects of His creation? Not in my opinion. Simply put, sometimes we just need to "chill out". So with this said; sometime today, take off your shoes and walk in the grass. Then go into your kitchen and pick up a spoon, open a jar of peanut butter and enjoy the abundant life God has given you!

The Thin Place: Ask, Answer, Pray and Apply.

What are some of your normal daily activities in which you find pleasure?
How could God be using these activities to speak to you or strengthen you?
Have you thanked God for those activities that bring you pleasure?

January 6

Are You Hungry?

From Above: John 4:31-35, Luke 4:3-4, Psalm 34:8

Focal Passage: *"My food," said Jesus, "is to do the will of him who sent me and to finish his work." –John 4:34*

<u>Here Below:</u>

There is probably no more enjoyable undertaking than to sit down to a great meal. Delicious food accompanied by engaging fellowship is the canvas on which many great relationships begin and grow. Perhaps even now, you can remember a special dinner in which a close relationship began for you as well. Let's face it...most of us enjoy a good meal perhaps a little too much. Most of us have never felt genuine hunger pains in modern day America to say the least. Yet, there is something even more important than food for the body; that is, food for the soul.

In this passage of scripture, the disciples of Jesus, out of love for Him, openly acknowledge the fact that He had not eaten and must be hungry. They were, I believe, out of genuine concern for Jesus' physical wellbeing, looking out for their Lord. With all the people vying for His attention, I imagine Jesus at this point in His ministry did find it difficult to even take time to eat. After all, there were no drive through windows to approach and no microwave meals available! So, His disciples were doing what loved ones do in such times. I am reminded of my grandmother as I was growing up, who never seemed to be satisfied that I had eaten enough. "You haven't eaten enough to keep a kitten alive!" she would say to me, even though I was stuffed.

Yet, that day the disciples would receive a truth from Jesus that would be more filling than any meal. He basically told them that His food was living for the Lord. Even simpler, there are things more important than our physical needs, urges and pains. By His words, Jesus was teaching you and I that being in the center of God's will is more satisfying and more rewarding than any meal. Was He telling us to ignore the physical needs and aspects of this world in exchange for the spiritual? Of course not. He was teaching us that if we are to be Christlike, there needs to be a hunger for God's will in our lives and a hunger to see it accomplished. This is a hunger that should supersede all others

Are you hungry today? Well, what do you do when you are physically hungry? You get something to eat. So, what do you do when spiritually hungry? Simple. You just taste and see. Mmmm, Mmmm... Good.

The Thin Place: Ask, Answer, Pray and Apply.
What do you hunger for the most in your life?
Upon what do you spend the majority of your effort, time and resources?
How do these things fit into the will of God for your life?

January 7
Eat The Word!

From Above: Ezekiel 2, 3: 1-4, Psalm 119: 9-16
Focal Passage: *"And he said to me, 'Son of man, eat this scroll I am giving you and fill your stomach with it.' So I ate it, and it tasted as sweet as honey in my mouth." –Ezekiel 3:3*
Here Below:
The prophecies of Ezekiel are filled with dramatic imagery and metaphors. These illustrations were used of God and the prophet to drive home a point of importance to the onlookers and listeners in Israel. They were an often-stubborn people, who at times also seemed a little hard of hearing. Not only hearing challenged, but they seemed to also have difficulty applying lessons learned from past mistakes to current decisions. Does this behavior sound familiar?

One thing that constantly amazes me is the consistency of mankind in the repeating of past mistakes. It seems we haven't changed very much over the millennia when it comes to application of God's truth to our lives. Put simply, we are still making the same mistakes people were making back in the days of the prophets and even further beyond. Why is that? Even on a more personal level, why do we sometimes repeat ourselves even to the point of our own demise?

Could it be that an understanding of God's ways is more than just knowing the words?

God was sending Ezekiel to carry out an overwhelming task. He was leading him to preach a message of repentance to His wayward children. This message would require more than just an intellectual understanding of God's word. It would require digesting God's word. He told him to eat the word. Think about it. When we digest food, what happens? Those foods are broken down molecule by molecule. Then our body processes the nutrients received and distributes them as needed throughout our bodies. They then provide us with nourishment, strength and protection.

The same is true of God's word. It is not enough to just know it, so that we might be able to "spit" it back out. We are to digest it, especially those words which due to our current circumstances might be a little hard for us swallow. We are to take it into our innermost selves, break it down and apply it to our spiritual lives. In return we receive nourishment, strength and protection. It then becomes to us as "sweet as honey". This digestion of God's word then equips us to make better decisions and to prevent the repetition of past mistakes. So don't just nibble! Take a big bite. Eat the word

The Thin Place: Ask, Answer, Pray and Apply.

How have you failed to learn from past lessons?

What does God's word teach about those lessons and how might a genuine application have changed the outcome?

What can I do to improve my spiritual "dieting" practices?

January 8
The God of the U-turn

From Above: Matthew 3:1-3, 4:17, Acts 2:36-38

Focal Passage: *From that time on Jesus began to preach, "Repent, for the kingdom of heaven is near."–Matthew 4:17*

<u>Here Below:</u>

It was around 10 o'clock pm. I had been preaching at a youth revival in the southern part of our state and tomorrow was to be the first day of my spring break. My plans were to leave the church that night and travel over five hours to my home and spend a week with family. However, as often occurs, my plans did not proceed as expected. From the time I left the church driveway, I was driving in the wrong direction. In the days before cell phones and GPS systems, I was on my own in a place I did not recognize. I couldn't make sense of the map and I just would not stop and ask for directions. So, for nearly two hours I drove on in the wrong direction. Finally, tired, exasperated and beaten, I turned around. Hours later I found myself right back where I started.

Oh, how simpler that night might have been had I just turned around sooner! Had I only turned around when I first realized I was going in the wrong direction! Perhaps I would have made it home the same day I left! Yet, in stubbornness, I pressed on in futility. If only I had made a u-turn sooner.

That is the definition of repentance. It is a spiritual u-turn. It is recognizing the wrong direction and choosing to go in a different direction. With some sin it can also mean a literal turning around. It is no coincidence that the very first recorded sermon of Jesus was a message of repentance. He was simply taking the message that John the Baptist had been preaching and giving it new life. Later, in the infant church, we would see Peter preaching the same message and literally thousands coming to faith in Christ. This message was and is the heart of the Gospel. It was and is the heart of the Christian life. It was true then as it is true now. A repentant spirit is a necessity.

We only grow in faith when we regularly repent of our sinfulness. More than just feeling shame or sorrow over our sin, repentance is agreeing with God that our sin is leading us in a path of destruction. It is then choosing His path over our own. Not only does it make the journey more pleasant for us, but it is also a commandment by Jesus himself. Isn't it wonderful to know that we serve a God that allows u-turns? In fact, he desires them. The sooner we make the u-turn, the better the drive.

The Thin Place: Ask, Answer, Pray and Apply.

Do you have any unrepented sins that are standing in the way of your relationship with God?

Can you remember joy experienced in the past as a result of true heartfelt repentance?

What is stopping you right now from repenting and experiencing that freedom and joy again?

January 9
Not So Small

From Above: Leviticus 26:11-12, Psalm 139, John 1:1-14

Focal Passage: *"Where can I go from your Spirit? Where can I flee from your presence?"*- Psalm 139:7

Here Below:

The January midnight sky is perhaps the most awe-inspiring element of all God's creation. Gazing into it, one can't help but be reminded of our tiny place in the endless cosmos in which our God exists. Some often decry these overwhelming feelings of insignificance as they star gaze, thinking only of our small corporeal existence relative to the vastness of the universe. On the contrary, the cool night air and crystal-clear starlight should instead serve as nightly reminder to us of our great significance; that is, our great significance in the eyes and heart of God. Perhaps we are not so small after all.

How can that be? Well, with the entire universe at his disposal, God chose to indwell <u>us</u> with His Holy Spirit. With the cosmos as a playground, God chose to live inside you and me. Wow! We are His preferred dwelling place. From the Garden of Eden forward through the cross and beyond, God's plan has always been fellowship with His children. His desire has always been to dwell among us and have His presence known in our lives. As immense and awesome as our God is, He chooses to be present in the lives of His creation. It is mind staggering to say the least. Yet it is nonetheless true.

The incarnation of Jesus proves this point. Jesus gave up the glories of Heaven to dwell among us. In so doing, He took upon himself the hurts and struggles of the human experience. Then when His earthly ministry was complete, He left us a Comforter to guide and direct our steps. At no point since the time of creation, has the created been left alone by the creator. At no point have we been forsaken. His presence is forever with us.

Now this can be a comforting thought and it can be a frightening thought. It is comforting; in that, we know God is watching over us as a protective parent. It can also be frightening; in that, we know God is watching over us as a protective parent. Nothing goes unseen. But isn't that love as well? We would frown upon an inattentive or uninterested parent, would we not? We might even call it abuse! Yet, we can know with certainty that God is never inattentive or uninterested. We are always the center of His attention. What a great love He has for us!

So, with that said, go outside tonight and cast your gaze into the eternal night sky. Take it in. Know that as overpoweringly beautiful as it may be, God chose to be with you.

The Thin Place: Ask, Answer, Pray and Apply.

When do you feel the presence of God the deepest? Why then?

If God desires fellowship with you as scripture teaches, what can keep it from happening?

What can you do in your life to invite the presence of God daily?

January 10
Prerequisite Praise

From Above: Psalm 30, Psalm 63 ,Luke 19:17-40,

Focal Passage: *"I tell you," he replied, "if they keep quiet, the stones will cry out."-Luke 19:40*

<u>Here Below:</u>

There are times when I am ashamed to have anyone enter my home office for fear that they might see my music collection. It really has grown to the point of excess and embarrassment. Over the years I have collected a gargantuan amount of music in various formats. I have everything from the old cassette tapes to CDs and of course now I've gone digital. It is an eclectic collection of music. I have collected everything from hard rock and alternative rock to classical and jazz. I have even been known to enjoy Gregorian chants. I started this collection as an early teen and have never discarded a single piece of music purchased. Over the years I have given some away only to replace it later with another copy. However, I am glad to say that out of the thousands of pieces of music I own, all but a handful, are what I would consider "Christian" music. To say the least, this form of praise has always been an integral part of my everyday life.

Isn't that the way it is supposed to be? I am not talking about purchasing and listening to large amounts of Christian music. I am however saying that praise itself is to be a vital piece of our everyday lives. The Bible teaches us so. It is no coincidence that the largest book of the Bible, the book of Psalms, is itself a collection of praise and worship music. We often forget as we read the beautiful language of the Psalms that it was at first intended on being sung, not spoken. They are songs. Not only are they songs, but look at the content of the text. Often, these praises were being expressed in times of great trial and distress, especially in the case of David. Some of the most beautiful were written when he was in hiding, fearing for his very life. Yet, in those times he, a man after God's own heart, saw fit to offer praise to God. In other words, it is always time to praise God, regardless of our circumstances. God is worthy of it and God desires it. I believe that in those times of praise, David found a strength that all the self-motivation and positive thinking in the world could not offer. In praising

God, he was reminded of His relationship with the Almighty Creator of all. There he found comfort, strength, and reassurance. Praise is a must if we are to have that peace.

In listening to and singing along with my music collection, I have found some of the peace that David found. However, praise is more than music. Music, as good as it might be, is not necessarily praise. Praise happens when we in our hearts acknowledge our love and adoration for One that words cannot adequately describe. It happens when we sing, when we pray, and it happens in our thoughts and actions. It is possible to praise Him with our lips and not with our deeds. So today, let praise be on the tip of your tongue, and most importantly let it be in the center of your heart.

The Thin Place: Ask, Answer, Pray and Apply.

How often do you simply praise God for His greatness?

In your prayer life, how much of your time is spent praising God versus asking Him for something?

What actions can you take today to reflect an attitude of praise?

January 11
Living in Denial

From Above: Matthew 10:32-40, Matthew 16:24-26, 2 Corinthians 12: 9-10

Focal Passage: *"Then Jesus said to his disciples, "If anyone would come after me, he must deny himself and take up his cross and follow me. "-* Matthew 16:24

Here Below:

Probably one of the most misunderstood practices of our day is this idea of denying self. We live in a world in which it is more common to live lives of excess and overindulgence. The idea of holding back just isn't in our mindset much these days. We want what we want, and we want it when we want it and how we want it. Among other things, this includes money, food, influence, and respect. The list goes on. Yet, at the very heart of the teachings of Jesus is this fundamental principle of self-denial. "He must" Jesus says. A true disciple is one that has denied self, taken up a cross and followed His example.

Now what does this "denying self" really mean? As with most Biblical truths, we must be careful not to become too legalistic in our interpretation. Is Jesus saying in the above passages that we are to truly deny ourselves the common comforts of society? In Matthew, when He refers to loving our family, is He saying that as disciples there really is no room for looking back? Is he saying the opinion of others doesn't matter? I don't think so.

However, there is a point to be made here. He was instructing us in the attitude of self-denial as a warning. A truly sold-out disciple of Christ is going to face opposition in this world. There is going to be others that simply will not understand your desire for righteousness and Christlikeness in your life. There may even be times when those closest to you may oppose you because of your faith. Likewise, there may also be times when you may be called upon to go against even your own human and sinful nature in order to please God. In that instance, denying yourself will be your challenge. Again, there is a very fine line here. It is a line that can only be seen through the eyes of God's grace. Only by His grace and our surrendering of self can we finish the race a winner.

Put simply, the Christian life is not for wimps! It will be necessary to stand strong from time to time. The key is knowing from where your strength really comes. Denying self means knowing that at times there may be difficult decisions to be made. Denying self means understanding that the opinion of others, well though it may be, is not nearly as important as God's opinion. Denying self and taking up a cross means coming to the point in your life where you realize all these truths and you are okay with them. That is when we are most likely to be used of God. That is when we can follow in Jesus' example as a true disciple. It's not always going to be easy, but it will always be worth it.

<u>**The Thin Place**</u>: Ask, Answer, Pray and Apply.

Has there ever been a time in your life when you were called upon to deny self in order to be faithful?

Were you concerned about what others thought?

What evidence is there in your life that God's opinion takes priority over others? Can you improve this?

January 12
Your Very Own Floyd

<u>**From Above:**</u> Psalm 19:12-14, Proverbs 18:1-8, 20-21, Philippians 2:1-2

Focal Passage: *"The tongue has the power of life and death, and those who love it will eat its fruit. "*-Proverbs 18:21

<u>**Here Below:**</u>

His name is Floyd. He would come into the store in which I worked in college day after day. Each day he would walk by without speaking, making little to no eye contact. At first, I purposely avoided him due to the rumors circulating among coworkers of his abrasiveness and irritability. However, one day something told me to speak to him and to attempt to engage him in conversation. As he entered the store, I approached him and enthusiastically greeted him. "How are you today?" I gleefully asked, very proud of my kind gesture. I did not get the response I had expected.

"Why don't you just mind your own business!" He snarled as he stomped away.

Wow! The rumors were true. This guy was a real crank. Yet something still would not let me leave Him alone. I decided that day to get to know Floyd. Each day he would enter, and I would say something kind or make some joke in an attempt to break the ice. Finally, after weeks of pursuing the matter, the ice thawed, and he actually spoke to me in a common and polite manner. Before long we were talking daily and in just a short while we became good friends. I discovered that he was not the abrasive brute that most had made him out to be. In fact, he had lived a very interesting life. He had been a P.O.W. in WWII. He was a decorated war hero. Through our conversations, I had opportunities to speak with him of the Lord. I discovered that as grumpy as he was, he did have a saving faith in Jesus Christ. One day, months after I had moved hundreds of miles away to another state, I received a phone call. It was Floyd. He was just calling to ask how I was doing. To this day we are friends.

As I think of Floyd, I am reminded of a spiritual truth found in the above passage of scripture. Within our words lies the power of life and death. With a simple kind word, we can reach even the hardest hearts. Think of your own life to a time when the right word spoken at just the right time brought you from the brink of depression to a place of joy. With our words we can tear down an individual or build an individual up. With our words, we can destroy a person, or we can rescue a person. With our words, we can show the love of Christ, or we can destroy our testimony.

I thank God for Floyd, because this simple grump of an old man reminded me of the power of my words. Perhaps you have a Floyd in your own life that could use some encouragement right now. Ask God to show you your very own Floyd today. Share some encouragement. You will be blessed beyond words.

The Thin Place: Ask, Answer, Pray and Apply.

Would you say that the majority of your words are positive In nature or negative? Be honest.

When has someone given you encouragement with their kind words? To what effect?

What opportunities will you have today to show kindness to someone?

January 13
Home Sweet Home

From Above: Matthew 22: 35-40, John 14:19-24, Romans 8:13-17

Focal Passage: *"Jesus replied, "If anyone loves me, he will obey my teaching. My Father will love him, and we will come to him and make our home with him. "*-John 14:23

Here Below:

In the above passage of scripture, Jesus gives us a promise of tremendous worth. When asked by Judas, not Iscariot, concerning His revelation of Himself to the world, Jesus promises that God will make a home in the heart of a believer. It would no longer be necessary to commute periodically to the temple to worship and offer sacrifices. God's dwelling place would no longer be a room tucked away in a large stone building where only the privileged few could come and experience the presence of God. God was going to make His home with His children. Because of the sacrifice that Jesus was about to offer, you and I would have daily access to God through prayer and through His Holy Spirit. No appointment would be necessary. The invitation would always be open. After all, one doesn't need an invitation to visit someone with whom they dwell. When you share the same home, fellowship is inevitable. At least it is supposed to be.

But notice one thing about Jesus' words. There is a condition. "If anyone loves me..." Jesus said. If we love Him, we will obey Him. It is then that God the Father will return the love He already feels for each of us and will come and live with us. Again, we see in these words that our God is a real gentleman. He never forces Himself upon anyone. It is our choice to love Him and accept what it is He is offering. But consider the conditions He mentions here. All we are asked to do is to love Him, listen to Him and to obey Him. Isn't that what family is supposed to be? Isn't that what Jesus is saying here when He speaks of making His home with us? He wants to be in a relationship like that of a close family member, specifically our Father. Consider the security that comes with this type of relationship. Having God at home in our heart provides a sense of refuge that no other relationship in this world may give.

Not only that, but those with whom you dwell see your home as is. There is no mad dash to straighten it up with them as you would for impending guests. Those who live with us see the daily messes we make. They see the dirty dishes on the counter and the laundry on the floor. They see your daily life as is and to them it doesn't matter. What matters is simply being at home with you. I think that is what Jesus is teaching us here. He is more concerned with having a place to dwell than with a clean house. Besides, He alone can clean up our spiritual homes as needed. That is His desire. Today, do you know that His desire is to be at home in your heart? Is He welcome? Welcome Him today. Love Him. Listen to Him. Obey Him.

The Thin Place: Ask, Answer, Pray and Apply.

Are you in need of some spiritual housecleaning today?

Have you tried to straighten up your spiritual home before on your own only to fail?

How can you help God to feel welcome and at home in your heart?

January 14
Drive By Theology

From Above: Ecclesiastes 5:10-11, Matthew 6:19-34, I Timothy 6:9-14

Focal Passage: *"But seek first his kingdom and his righteousness, and all these things will be given to you as well. "*-Matthew 6:33

Here Below:

The other day I was intrigued by a transfer truck on the interstate and it left me scratching my head as it passed. It was a very nice and apparently new looking truck. It seemed to have all the amenities including all sorts of fancy chrome trim and a large sleeper compartment. It was obviously a very expensive vehicle. The thing that captured my attention the most was the message this truck was sending those it passed. Across the back of that sleeper compartment were painted in fancy white script the words "Addicted 2 Money". The interesting thing about this message was what was on the tag at the rear of the truck. This tag had the words "Truly Blessed" right beside a pair of praying hands, all embossed in a gold finish. Is it possible to be addicted to money and be truly blessed at the same time? I couldn't help but laugh, all the while knowing this trucker was not alone in this mindset.

All too often we judge our blessings by the state of our material possessions. We also are quick to perceive our blessings in relation to that of others. We forget that financial prosperity may not be a God given blessing at all. It could simply be a result of some wise financial decisions and maybe even some questionable ones. Sometimes it may be a result of pure luck. But it is not always a blessing. In fact, some of the most content and happiest people I have met had very little materially speaking and they would be quick to tell you of their blessings. I wonder if that truck driver would still consider himself "Truly Blessed" had he been driving an older truck without the fancy paint job and the shiny chrome. I wonder if he would consider himself "Truly Blessed" if he were unable to drive a truck at all! Only heaven knows...

The reality is that we are blessed whether we have great financial and material possessions or not. Granted, financial success may very well be one way in which God chooses to bless. It is however not the end all to God's blessings. In fact, I would say it is far down the list if we were to rank our blessings according to their importance. Family, friends, health, and joy would definitely come before money in my list of blessings. Among them, salvation through faith in Christ is the first and most important blessing of all. None of those things have anything to do with money. In fact, the Bible is clear about what being "addicted 2 money" will do for you. The love of money is the root of evil. This truth can definitely be seen in our day. How many homes struggle or even break apart due to a misplaced love of money? It only causes stress and grief. It is only when we see where our true wealth lies that we understand our blessings. The peace that comes with that is something that money can never buy. So, if you ever see that truck on the highway, blow your horn, wave and then count your blessings...

The Thin Place: Ask, Answer, Pray and Apply.

Are you guilty of placing too much emphasis on wealth?

Have you ever felt "less blessed" because of financial struggles?

Where does your real wealth lie today? Take time to thank God for your true blessings today?

January 15
From Wreck to Reconciled

From Above: 2 Corinthians 5:17-21, Ephesians 2:1-5, Colossians 1:19-29

Focal Passage: *"For God was pleased to have all his fullness dwell in him, and through him to reconcile to himself all things, whether things on earth or things in heaven, by making peace through his blood, shed on the cross.*"-Colossians 1:19-20

Here Below:

"But this is just the way I am..." she said. "Well, I wasn't raised that way..." he responded. For nearly two hours of a marriage counseling session, these types of comments were passed back and forth between the two troubled spouses. They seemed to be desperate for reconciliation; yet both were unwilling to admit any personal fault and unwilling to make necessary changes. Both were standing firm on the fact that this is how they have always been, and change was not likely in the future. Unfortunately, they were probably right. However, it is not supposed to be that way.

As hard as it might be for us to accept sometimes, the Christian life is all about change. We are to be in a constant state of growth.

And guess what? Growth is change. Change doesn't have to be an ugly word. On the contrary, it is a beautiful thing. The change that has been wrought in us as children of God is the Holy Spirit reconciling us to Himself. It is God making His "peace" with each of us.

Just like the above-mentioned couple, true reconciliation could not be achieved between God and man until at least one of us changed our ways. Unfortunately, the ability to change is limited to for man. We are sinful by nature and set in our ways. That is why we have such a difficult time with change in our lives. Yet, God's love for us was such that He found a way for reconciliation to take place. He didn't need to change. He was never at fault. The only other answer was for change to be created in us. So, God made a way for that to happen. It happened through the shed blood of His Son.

So, the next time you are tempted to say "Well, I have always been this way...!", ...just stop! Don't say it! God is not interested in the way you have always been! He is more interested in what you can be! Besides, as a believer in Jesus, you are not who or what you used to be. You are a new creation. You have been transformed from a spiritual wreck to a reconciled child of God. God went to great lengths to make that reconciliation possible. Don't take it for granted and never ignore it. In fact, nurture that growth and you will be amazed at the changes God can bring forth in your life. You will be amazed at the peace that can be yours. God is big enough and strong enough to take you from where you were to where He wants you to be.

<u>**The Thin Place**</u>: Ask, Answer, Pray and Apply.

Have you ever thought to yourself that personal change is impossible? Why?

When you pray, do you pray for God to bring about necessary changes in your life?

When do you feel most at peace with God? Why then? How can you make this occur more often?

January 16

Do You Praise Your Father With That Mouth?

<u>**From Above:**</u> Proverbs 26: 18-21, Romans 1:28-32, James 3

Focal Passage: *"With the tongue we praise our Lord and Father, and with it we curse men, who have been made in God's likeness. Out of the same mouth come praise and cursing. My brothers, this should not be. "*-James 3:9-10

<u>**Here Below:**</u>

We are often quick to label sins as being more severe or more "sinful" than others. Perhaps we do this to help us feel better about those sins with which we ourselves struggle. At least we are not as bad as so and so...! Well, as you study the Word of God you will quickly learn that these labels are misleading to say the least. In fact, in the above passages, you will see a particular sin that most of us write off as not being all that bad. That sin is the sin of gossip. Yet if you notice the first chapter of Romans, you will see that the sin of gossip is listed right alongside some pretty heinous sins. It is right there with murder, depravity, malice and more. In fact, if you read a few verses prior you will see that the sin of gossip is in company with even sexual perversion. Wow! Is it really that bad? The bible says yes.

Gossip is probably more damaging to the cause of Christ than any other sin, due to the fact that gossip is rarely grounded in truth, and it hurts all involved. With all sins, there are consequences. Unfortunately, we can suffer the consequences of the sins of others. But with gossip, the consequences are often more severe for the victim than for the one who is actually committing the sin. Unfortunately, once the words are spoken, they can't be taken back. The damage is done. Likewise, gossip is probably the most widespread and widely accepted sin of all. After all, who hasn't been a part of a conversation that began with the words "Listen to what I have heard...." Or "Don't tell anyone where you heard this, but..."? How many individuals have been hurt from conversations such as these, which might have even begun with good intentions? How many churches have lost impact in their community due to the sin of gossip? It is a tool of the devil himself.

In James 3:9-10 he tells us straight (as he often does) that we use the same mouth to praise God and then we turn around and use it to curse someone made in the image of God. I remember asking a foul-mouthed person one time if they kissed their mother with the same mouth in which they were spouting profanities? (Granted, that was probably not the right approach to the problem.) But isn't that what James is asking? Running down an image of God is to God no different than running Him down. So, the next time you are tempted to be drawn into a conversation grounded in gossip, just walk away. Don't participate. Use your mouth for what it was intended. Use it to praise God. Also remember, one who gossips to you, will most likely gossip about you. Choose your conversations and your friends with godly wisdom.

The Thin Place: Ask, Answer, Pray and Apply.

Do you struggle with the sin of gossip? Be honest.

Are there certain people in your life with whom you struggle more often with the temptation to gossip?

What steps can you take to avoid the sin of gossip and its damaging effects?

January 17
Oh, Brother!

From Above: I Samuel 18:1-5, 19:1-7, Proverbs 17:17, 18:24

Focal Passage: *"A man of many companions may come to ruin, but there is a friend who sticks closer than a brother."*-Proverbs 18:24

Here Below:

Friendship is one of those defining possessions in life. He who has friends has great wealth. Likewise, one without friends is poor to say the least. Yet, true friendship is something that cannot be bought, sold or traded. It is a gift from God Himself. Friendship is a tool that God uses to help us through the troubles and trials that inevitably come in this thing called the human experience. To face them friendless is to face a battle unequipped for the fight.

One of the most famous friendships of all history is that of David and Jonathan. Their friendship withstood personal, family and even political pressure. A covenant existed between these two that was deeper than even their own dreams and aspirations. This friendship kept and protected these two and was unmistakably an instrument used by God to fulfill His will for the people of Israel. All of this came to be because these two vowed to put each other first. That is friendship. Hasn't that always been the message? We all need a Jonathan in our life from time to time. That friend may be a spouse, a buddy from school or a relative. Whoever it may be, the necessity is the same. We all need someone to lean upon when we are weak. We all need someone to listen to us when we feel we can't be heard. We all need someone to run to when we are scared. I pray you have such a friend in your life.

As essential as these types of human relationships might be, we have a friendship that is even greater. Being an only child, I am only now learning with my own children what exactly is meant in the above Proverb when it refers to "a friend that sticks closer than a brother". There is typically a bond between siblings that is uniquely strong. It is usually unconditional and lasting. I have seen my kids fight with one another and insult one another only to turn on others when they do the same. That is "brotherly" love. Yet, the Word tells us that there is a friend that is closer than that. Wow! As Solomon wrote these words, I don't think he was just talking about friendships like that of his father and Jonathan. He was talking about the Lord. As great and necessary as your earthly friendships can be, there is one relationship more important. Friends can let us down. Brothers can fail to watch our back. Not so with this friend. God will never leave us or forsake us. He will never choose someone else's side over yours. He will always put you first. That is His way. That is who He is. He is your friend. Base your human friendships on that kind of love and you will never be in want. You will be wealthy indeed.

The Thin Place: Ask, Answer, Pray and Apply.

Who would you consider to be your best friend? Why?

Has there even been a time in which a friend came to your rescue?

What steps can you take to cultivate godly friendships and perhaps even start some new ones?

January 18
The Easy Way Out

From Above: 2 Samuel 24:17-25, Romans 12:1-3, Ephesians 5:1-2,

Focal Passage: *But the king replied to Araunah, "No, I insist on paying you for it. I will not sacrifice to the Lord my God burnt offerings that cost me nothing."-2 Samuel 24:24a*

Here Below:

Who among us has never taken the easy way out at least one time in our lives? I would say that probably we all have at least once and perhaps multiple times. After all, why not? Doesn't it make sense that we would want to go the way of least friction and complication? Well, that may be perfectly acceptable and proper for some things in life, but when it comes to the things that matter the most, the easy way usually leads to the less favorable outcome. Put simply, when it comes to the important matters in life, especially matters of faith; we get out of it what we put into it.

In the above Biblical account of an event in the life of King David, we see that he understood the importance of giving God our best and not our leftovers. David, having seen the need to offer a sacrifice of repentance to the Lord, had an opportunity to do it the easy way. Araunah, either out of fear or reverence for his earthly king, offered to give David the supplies he would need for his sacrifice. David's response is timeless and powerful. He was not willing to offer a sacrifice to God that he didn't pay for himself. You see, he understood that a sacrifice that cost nothing wasn't really a sacrifice at all. The whole concept of sacrifice includes a genuine giving of oneself for the benefit of another.

While as Christians, we are no longer bound by the sacrificial system of David's Old Testament, there are still times when we will be called upon to make sacrifices. We are asked to give of ourselves for others. We are called to take up our cross. We are called to offer ourselves as living sacrifices. For this to be a true sacrifice, we must conclude that there is going to be a time when we are going to be called upon to give in one way while our natural human and worldly instincts might be leading us to go in a different direction. While our salvation is not dependent upon such sacrifices of will and self, our growth most certainly is. David understood that. It wasn't until he gave some of himself that God would be able to use him. The easy way would have been for him to just use this other man's supplies and offer the sacrifice, but it would mean nothing. God deserved David's best. But he did use the same supplies, after he paid for them. What is the difference? The difference is that now it was truly David's offering. God, out of His love for us, has offered us salvation, mercy, and grace. What can we give of ourselves to show Him our appreciation? The giving of oneself is worship in its purest form. Don't sell God or yourself short by giving less than your best, as difficult as it might be. Give Him your best this day.

The Thin Place: Ask, Answer, Pray and Apply.

Have you ever been tempted to take the easy way out as opposed to carrying out God's perceived will?

What has been the result of taking the easy way out in spiritual matters in your life?

Do you believe that God can give you the strength to make the necessary sacrifices of will and self?

January 19
Leave Me Alone!

From Above: Psalm 46, Luke 5:15-16, I Peter 2:1-5

Focal Passage: *"But Jesus often withdrew to lonely places and prayed."*-Luke 5:16

Here Below:

One of the most vital of the spiritual disciplines taught by Jesus and perhaps the least practiced is the discipline of solitude. We live in a time when our lives are so filled with "going" and "doing" that we rarely have time to just be alone. Then when or if we do have spare time, we fill it with the noise of television, social media and other forms of entertaining clutter. While there is not necessarily anything wrong with these enjoyable distractions, we need to be equally eager for time alone. If our engines never stop to be refueled, sooner or later we run out of gas; or worse yet, we burn up.

Jesus taught this discipline not so much with His words, but with His example. In Luke 5 we are told that Jesus regularly found time alone to pray and meditate. If you notice in the gospel accounts, these times alone often preceded or followed an "extra" significant event in the earthly ministry of Jesus. Even though Jesus was God incarnate, His body grew weary. Not only His body, I imagine that His spirit grew weary as well, especially in the height of His popularity. It seems He was always giving, giving, giving of himself. While this was His driving purpose, He still needed times of refreshment. He occasionally needed to get away from the crowds and the noise. These times refreshed Him from the tasks behind and strengthened Him for the tasks ahead. It was in these times that we were told that He also prayed. So, in a sense, He was not alone in His times of solitude. Neither are we.

Psalm 46 tells us to be still. It is then that we can see God at work. So many in our day bemoan the notion that they cannot see God at work in their lives; however, I wonder how many times they can't see

Him is because they simply don't take time to watch for Him and to listen to Him. How many times do we pray and the second we say "Amen" we rush off to another task, not waiting and listening for an answer? Solitude provides us with the opportunity to do just that! If Jesus needed it, then we most certainly do. It is in times of solitude that we not only see and hear God more clearly, but we also see ourselves more clearly. When we are left alone with ourselves, we see ourselves for what we really are.

Sometimes, as I well know, the family life can make this discipline very difficult to achieve. Life can be hectic. It is in those times that we need solitude the most. We must be intentional when it comes to the spiritual disciplines, especially this one. That is why they are called "disciplines". Solitude will not just happen on its own. We must make it happen. We must set aside time and guard it. As hard as it may be sometimes, we may just need to say "leave me alone" to the world around us. Make time today to get to know yourself and most importantly to get to know God just a little bit better.

The Thin Place: Ask, Answer, Pray and Apply.

Do you find it difficult to find daily times of solitude? When is a good time?

Can you remember a still quite time in which you know God was present and speaking?

What changes can you practically make in your daily schedule to assure moments of solitude?

January 20
The Successful Failure

From Above: Matthew 7:7-11, Matthew 17:20, Ephesians 3
Focal Passage: *"Now to him who is able to do immeasurably more than all we ask or imagine, according to his power that is at work within us, to*

him be glory in the church and in Christ Jesus throughout all generations, forever and ever! Amen."-Ephesians 3:20-21

Here Below:

1831 failed in business; 1832 defeated for state legislature; 1833 failed in business again; 1835 sweetheart died; 1836 had nervous breakdown; 1838 defeated for speaker; 1840 defeated for elector; 1843 defeated for Congress; 1848 defeated for Congress; 1855 defeated for Senate; 1856 defeated for Vice President; 1858 defeated for Senate; 1860 ELECTED PRESIDENT; Name –Abraham Lincoln.

We have all felt the sting of defeat and setbacks in our lives. It is part of the human experience. The difference between those whom we would consider "successful" and those who fail is how they deal with those setbacks. Invariably, it also depends upon your definition of success. Success in the Christian's life should not necessarily be measured by outcome or results. Sometimes there is success in failure. Huh? How can that be?

Well, consider this fact. If we are pursuing the will of God for our lives and striving to see it to fruition, it doesn't guarantee that those around us are doing the same. We still live in a fallen world and therefore we do sometimes face roadblocks to God's will. Being fallen as well, we ourselves do still sometimes mess up, even though our intentions may be admirable. But is not God pleased with our attempts? If so, are we not therefore successful? In fact, God desires to use our failures at times to build us into the people he would have us to be. The scriptures are filled with accounts of humans who failed according to the world's standards. Yet, we know God saw them differently. He saw great heroes of the faith.

We must also remember that nothing is impossible with our God. According to His own word, He is able to do more than we can even imagine. I am not sure about you, but I have a pretty good imagination. Well guess what? God can do even more than I can imagine with a heart that is totally and completely surrendered to Him. Therefore we must look at our failures as teachable moments in our lives. We must learn from them, seek God's hand at work in them, and pray for guidance through them. While there is no guarantee that things will always go our way, we do have a guarantee that if our will is in agreement with God's will, there is nothing that can't be accomplished. Do you believe that today? You see, success is not about what we can do on our own strength, but what God can do in us by His. That means the sky is the limit! Or is it? Not with my God! Trust Him with your dreams today.

The Thin Place: Ask, Answer, Pray and Apply.

Has there ever been a time in your life when you just felt as if life would be simpler if you just gave up?

Are you in danger right now of giving up on your God given dreams and aspirations?

Does your life reflect a belief that God is able to do more than you can ask or imagine?

January 21
Blind Ambition

From Above: 2 Kings 22, I Corinthians 9:24-27, Hebrews 12:1-2

Focal Passage: *"He did what was right in the eyes of the LORD and walked in all the ways of his father David, not turning aside to the right or to the left."*-2 Kings 22:2

Here Below:

Hidden within the annals of the Kings of Israel is the story of one King that contains many spiritual treasures of which we can learn and apply. His name is Josiah. Only eight years old when he became King, he was following a legacy of malevolence and idolatry. His father and grandfather before him were some of the most evil and corrupt kings the nation had ever seen. They had systematically tried to wipe out the existing copies of God's word. They had set up altars to false pagan gods within God's own temple. They also had mountain altars erected to worship these abominations. Human sacrifice was even part of their worship. Put simply, they had done their best to abolish the worship of the one true God. Their lives ended in violence and murder. Now, with this evil heritage, this boy king would step onto the scene. But there was something very interesting about this new king. The Bible tells us that he did not look to the right or left. Instead, he did what was right in the eyes of the Lord. What a testimony!

Through Josiah's faithfulness, the Word of God was rediscovered, and proper temple worship was restored. The altars in the high places were destroyed and once again God relented from judgment and Israel was restored to a proper relationship with Him. Revival took place. This story is a one of grace, restoration, and commitment. It is also a testimony to the importance of being blinded to the world's ambitions and keeping your eyes on the things of God.

Racehorses often wear blinders that keep them from seeing the horses next to them. Instead, all they can see is what is ahead, specifically the finish line. Wouldn't it be nice if we had some sort of spiritual blinders? Wouldn't it be nice if we had some tool that would help us to see only the direction God would have us to go, to see His finish line? Well, we do in a sense. We have that in God's Word. We also have it in the direction of His Holy Spirit. Unfortunately, we can still be distracted by forces around us that would love to guide us in their direction. Like Josiah, it may be family, friends, circumstances, and it may be the status quo. Whatever the distraction, we must keep our eyes straight ahead.

Josiah wasn't perfect, but the legacy he left behind was far better than the one left to him. Wouldn't it be nice to have said of us postmortem, "Here is a person who did not look to the right or left, but kept their eyes on God."? What an epitaph! It can be yours. With God's help and through His strength we can be like Josiah. Keep your eyes ahead. Don't look back. Don't look to the side. Look ahead.

The Thin Place: Ask, Answer, Pray and Apply.

Has there ever been a time in your life when you gave in to the influences of outside negative forces?

If so, what was the outcome of that compromise?

What changes can you make in your life that will aid you in avoiding spiritual distractions?

January 22
Coming Clean

From Above: Psalm 19, Psalm 103:8-14, I John 1:5-10

Focal Passage: *"The fear of the LORD is pure, enduring forever. The ordinances of the LORD are sure and altogether righteous."*-Psalm 19:9

Here Below:

One of my favorite Psalms is Psalm 19. I especially like verse 9, where it speaks of "The fear of the Lord is pure...". In the King James version the word translated "pure" in the NIV is translated "clean". I like that. While it is basically saying the same thing, there is something so right about feeling clean. There is nothing like the feelings one has when stepping out of the shower, having washed all the dirt and grime of the day down the drain. And how about slipping into bed between two crisp freshly cleaned sheets? It is one of those simple yet life affirming pleasures. Likewise, in our spiritual lives we can experience that same sense of cleanliness. How is the fear of God clean?

If you read on down in this Psalm, you will see that David, like all of us, did struggle from time to time with feelings of spiritual inadequacy. He at times felt spiritually dirty, and I might add rightfully so. Yet, we also see in this very intimate prayer song the solution. The solution comes in understanding the forgiveness of God. David acknowledges very matter-of-factly that he doesn't understand even his own sinfulness at times. Sometimes it is unintentional. Sometimes it is intentional. Sometimes it is blatantly open. Sometimes it is hidden. Yet, the result is the same. It leaves one feeling dirty. Yet we also see that the answer to this problem, like all others is beyond human control. The answer can only be found in a proper fear of the Lord. In the fear of the Lord there is purity. Having a healthy fear of the Lord means understanding God's rule and power is greater than our own. So is His forgiveness.

Have you ever failed to forgive yourself for past mistakes? This is a question I am confronted with regularly in counseling conversations. Too often we have a hard time forgiving ourselves for mistakes for which according to God's own Word we have already been forgiven. In reality, when we do that, we are saying that our standards are greater than that of God himself. God's Word is clear. If we are truly repentant and truly confessional, then because of <u>His</u> righteousness, <u>His</u> faithfulness and <u>His</u> trustworthiness, our sins are forgiven. "As far as the east is from the west" His word says. You can't get any cleaner than that! That is why understanding His heart and His desire to grant forgiveness is so vital. It is only through Him that we can truly feel clean and pure. Thank you, God, that it is not by my own strength! You can scrub and scrub all you want on your own strength, and you will never feel clean. However, one shower of God's grace and forgiveness and you are white as snow. So, stop trying to come clean on your own power. It is futile at best. Confess, repent, and trust God with the cleaning.

<u>The Thin Place</u>: Ask, Answer, Pray and Apply.

Is there a mistake from your past of which you are just having a hard time letting go?

How is holding on to this guilt hampering your spiritual life in the present?

Do you believe God's word is true concerning His forgiveness? Can you then accept it and move on?

January 23
The Saddest Verse in the Bible

<u>From Above:</u> Judges 16, Hebrews 13:5 , 2 Timothy 2:11-15

Focal Passage: *"Then she called, "Samson, the Philistines are upon you!" He awoke from his sleep and thought, "I'll go out as before and shake myself free." But he did not know that the LORD had left him."* -Judges 16:20

<u>Here Below:</u>

Probably the saddest verse in the Bible would have to be the one above. The last part is what makes it so sad. Samson did not even know that the Lord had left him. Samson, a man whose life had been dedicated to the Lord from the time of his birth, a man so devoted to the things of God that he had taken the Nazaritic vow, had neglected his spiritual life to the point that he didn't even notice the absence of God in his life. Notice the lifestyle he was now living. It was one of prostitutes, violence, and decadence. How did he get from extreme dedication to extreme debauchery? Did it happen all at once? Was it a conscious decision? Probably not. That is how sin works and why it is so dangerous.

Unfortunately, if we are not careful, we may find ourselves like Samson, apathetic and alone. Now let me make something clear. As believers in Jesus Christ, we are promised in His word that we will never be left alone nor forsaken. When I speak of being alone, I am referring to being left to our own devices and therefore facing the consequences thereof. It is a choice we ourselves make when we compromise on the will of God. When Samson chose to break his vow to God, he chose to face the world on his own strength. Yet, God still had a purpose for him. It wouldn't be until Samson repented and turned back to the Lord that God would be able to use him again. Again, this doesn't always happen all at once. I doubt Samson woke up one morning and said "Today, I am going to break my vow!". It starts with a little compromise here and a little flirt with sin there. Before you know it, you find yourself like Samson, so accustomed to your sin and so used to God's absence in your everyday life that He is not even missed;

that is, until we find ourselves in a bind. Then we cry for help. We must not let that happen.

We must guard our spiritual lives as if everything depended upon it, because it does. Again, God is never going to leave us. He did not really leave Samson. Samson left Him. God, gentleman that He is, will not force His will where His will is not sought. Therefore, we must make a conscious effort to protect our spiritual selves from this destructive form of apathy. We do that by staying grounded in His Word, by renewing our vows regularly, by repenting of our sins daily and by purposely creating for ourselves an environment that encourages development. We must surround ourselves with the things of God and seek some form of accountability. Put simply, we must continually grow in our faith. If we are not growing, we are dying. Don't let the saddest verse in all of scripture become your life verse.

The Thin Place: Ask, Answer, Pray and Apply.

Are you in danger of becoming apathetic when it comes to spiritual matters in your life?

Do you agree that God's word teaches that even though we fail, as did Samson, God still loves us?

What steps can you purposely take today to help you avoid spiritual apathy?

January 24
Oh Lord, Please Don't Let Me Be Misunderstood!

From Above: Isaiah 51:7-8, Matthew 5:1-12, John 15:17-21

Focal Passage: *"Blessed are you when people insult you, persecute you and falsely say all kinds of evil against you because of me. Rejoice and be glad, because great is your reward in heaven, for in the same way they persecuted the prophets who were before you." –Matthew 5:11-12*

Here Below:

There was a song made popular by Elvis Costello years ago called "Please Don't Let Me Be Misunderstood". It was remade more than once, even by one Christian band. The lyrics and tune are addictive. After trying to explain his particular position, the songwriter expresses his frustration in the chorus, which says "I'm just a soul whose intentions are good...Oh Lord, please don't let me be misunderstood!". Who hasn't felt that way at one time or another? Those are words we can all sing.

The need for acceptance and understanding is a need that we all have too one degree. However, being accepted or understood is not always going to occur. In fact, scripture is clear concerning this in a life of faith. If we are truly living for the Lord, there are going to be times when those around us simply will not understand our actions or our inactions. In fact, they may even misread your intentions or perhaps even dislike you due to your beliefs. That is why words such as "aliens" and "strangers" are often used to describe the child of God. This flies in the face of what so many teach and preach in our day, which might explain the weak influence of the church today. We are told by many that once you come to faith, all your problems will disappear. You can have a stress free, problem free life right now, if you have enough faith. This kind of teaching leads to disillusioned and doubtful converts. Nowhere in scripture are we taught that the Christian life is a carefree life. I wonder what the early church leaders, most of whom lost their lives due to their faith, think about this prosperity gospel. The example given us by Jesus Himself is one of sacrifice and surrender, not satisfaction and success. The difference is in how we view success in light of God's will and calling in our lives.

Put simply, we should strive to be more interested in pleasing God than in pleasing man. It means accepting the fact that we may not always be understood or appreciated by men. Instead, it could mean you are doing everything right. I have come to see it like this. One of the greatest compliments I can receive is to be insulted because of my faith. One of the greatest achievements I can reach is to be misunderstood by the lost world. Does that make it easy? Of course not! Truly grasp this concept in your heart and you will know what Jesus meant in the Beatitudes when He said we are "blessed" when we are persecuted. So don't lose heart if the words to that song above are yours! In fact, gain strength in knowing you are making a difference. By the way, you are understood. Jesus understands perfectly.

<u>**The Thin Place**</u>: Ask, Answer, Pray and Apply.

How important is the opinion of others to you? Why?

Has there ever been a time when you let the opinion of others keep you from being a witness?

How important is pleasing God in your life versus pleasing man?

January 25
The God of the Belly Laugh

<u>**From Above:**</u> Psalm 126, Proverbs 17:22, Proverbs 15:30

Focal Passage: *"A cheerful heart is good medicine, but a crushed spirit dries up the bones."* –Proverbs 17:22

<u>**Here Below:**</u>

It was after what had been an extra stressful day that I found the truth of the above verse so relevant. It had been a day of work-related stress, chores and children bickering with one another. This kind of anxiety can be as crippling as any disease to the body, as my headache had proven. Then it happened. My angst was interrupted with joy. Deciding to go out to dinner, all six of us were packed into our SUV. Something was said that I found amusing. I can't even remember what it was now, but at the time I found it very funny. It was so funny in fact that I broke into a pretty significant belly laugh. Then one of the kids remarked to my somewhat goofy laughter and it sent me even deeper into this laugh. Before you knew it, the laughter had a contagious cascade effect and we were all laughing, I almost to the point of suffocation and crying. We literally had to pull over until we had it out of our systems. It had been a long time since I had experienced that kind of laughter and joy. Almost instantly, the headache disappeared along with the worries of the troublesome day. What was a day I wished to forget turned into a family memory that I will cherish forever. Proverbs 17:22 is wisdom, timeless and ever so true.

We all have days when we find it difficult to be cheerful; yet, it is a state of mind that has healing qualities. If we can find something to be cheerful about, then those things we worry about tend to lose their hold on us. It doesn't have to be anything major. An out of the way humorous comment or a simple goof or spill when carrying out a daily chore can turn what could be a difficult time into a time of joy. Perhaps we need to purposefully seek reasons for cheer. Perhaps we need to look for humor and fun in ordinary things. After all, life can be humorous at times and most definitely fun. We should also remember that the same God that created the belly also created the belly laugh! So, take your medicine!

I have often wondered why so many Christians more times than not look as if they have swallowed a lemon, even in times of worship. If anything, Christians should be the first to show expressions of joy and cheer. Of all creation, we have the greatest reason to be cheerful. While a life of faith is not a guarantee that things will always go our way, we do have assurance that no matter what happens, we will overcome. Eternal life awaits the believer. That alone is reason to be cheerful. Not only that, but cheerfulness is contagious. It spreads like wildfire. With a cheerful spirit, you have the ability to be an encouragement. It is not unspiritual to laugh and have a good time. Faith is not always about being solemn or still. The expression of cheer despite circumstances can be an act of worship itself. It is in essence an acknowledgment that life with God is good. If that is not worship, I don't know what is....

The Thin Place: Ask, Answer, Pray and Apply.

Would you say that you are a cheerful person? Would others agree with you?

Do you believe that you have a reason today to be cheerful?
How can you be a cheerful encourager and witness to someone else today?

January 26
Rethinking Your Serve

From Above: Matthew 10:37-42, Matthew 25:31-46, Philippians 2:1-8

Focal Passage: *"And if anyone gives even a cup of cold water to one of these little ones because he is my disciple, I tell you the truth, he will certainly not lose his reward."*–Matthew 10:42

Here Below:

There is no such thing as a tiny act of service. Anything done for or in the name of the Lord has the potential to be a life changing and world changing event. We see this truth illustrated by Jesus. Giving someone a cup of cold water may not seem like a big deal. However, if you are the one that is thirsty, a cup of cold water at just the moment of need can make a major impact. It could be the difference between life and death. A simple act of service may very well be the catalyst for a life altering change.

The reality is that we may never know the extent of the good wrought by our acts of service. We do not always see the fruit right away. In fact, we may never see it ourselves. This fact doesn't affect our call to serve. True service is not about results. It's all about the serve. We must leave the results to God. We are simply called to be obedient and submissive to His will. For the believer, the rewards come later, as Jesus reminds us in this passage of scripture.

Too many of us like to classify our acts of service as being more or less important than others. This is unfortunate. Each act of service rendered unto God is of equal importance. We each probably need to rethink what service really means. Serving God is more than just church attendance and church work. That is most definitely service, but it is not the end all to service. Offering a word of encouragement, sharing a time of prayer, and even providing a meal can be an act of service unto God. Just as with a giving a cup of cold water, you may never know how thirsty someone might be for a shoulder to cry on. We have no way of knowing just how desperate someone may be for a word of encouragement. That is why we must simply obey when the Holy Spirit is leading us to serve. We have all been there. We all know what it is like to have someone call at just the right time. Again, it can mean the difference between life and death. That is why we must never think of our acts of service as little acts of service. Everything we do for the Lord has eternal significance, especially if it done by His leading.

Some of the most effective saints of God that I have encountered in my lifetime are not what you might expect. Their names were never engraved on a plaque of appreciation. Their names will not be found on a manmade list of "Who's Who". Yet, their acts of service, as unglamorous and discreet as they might have been, had a lasting and eternal effect. That is the humble serving spirit that is exemplified in our Savior. No task is too small to be seen by our great God. He knows your heart. He knows your serve.

The Thin Place: Ask, Answer, Pray and Apply.

What are some things you do as an act of service unto the Lord?

Have you ever felt as if your acts of service aren't as important as others?

Here is the real question. Would you still do these things if no one but you ever knew about it?

January 27
Scared with a College Education

From Above: Psalm 27, Matthew 10:28-31, Mark 4:35-41

Focal Passage: *"He said to his disciples, "Why are you so afraid? Do you still have no faith?"* –Mark 4:40

<u>Here Below:</u>

The great thinker and philosopher Larry Fine of *The Three Stooges* once said, "I'm not scared. I'm just apprehensive." When asked by one of his buddies for the meaning of the word apprehensive, he responded by saying "That's scared with a college education." I must admit, there have been times in my life when I could relate to what Larry was saying. I have been apprehensive. Ok...I was scared. Who hasn't been at one time in their lives? Fear is universal.

I feel I must preface my thoughts on fear with this statement. Fear in some respects is not a bad thing. It can be a mechanism that I believe God instilled in our hearts to keep us from doing reckless things. For example, because of fear, I will not pick up a rattlesnake. Due to fear, I will not stand too close to the edge of a cliff. Fear can be a good thing. It can protect us from ourselves and our own foolishness. This can also apply to impulse decision making as well. However, fear can also be very destructive.

Many times in scripture, the Lord would introduce Himself with the words "fear not". Why? He knew that it is human nature to be afraid of what we do not understand and what we cannot explain away. I am not talking about the boogeyman hiding under our bed. I am talking about the uncertainty of the future and the uncertainty of surrendering ourselves to the Lord. An uncertain future, both immediate and long-term, can be a frightening concept. As a result, fear can paralyze us. It can be the one obstacle that keeps us from reaching our potential in Christ. This is where our faith must overcome our fear.

Jesus raises a very cutting question in the above passage. "Do you still have no faith?" he asked. Wow! That question must have been like a slap in the face for those disciples, a loving slap in the face. He was basically reminding them that they had already seen Him and His power many times before; therefore, they had no reason to fear. This loving rebuke was as much for us as for the men in that boat that day. We have seen God work in our lives already. Why should we worry about what we can't yet see? He has taken care of us thus far. Will he not continue? That is faith. Part of faith is knowing that God is bigger and stronger than any boogeyman of uncertain times ahead. Faith is knowing that while it may be uncertain for us, for God it is written. We can't see it, but He can. Don't let your fear keep you from taking the next step in your realization of God's will in your life! Fear fulfilled today leads to regrets tomorrow. "What if...?" is not a question I want to ask myself one day. Don't be apprehensive! Trust in the one who commands even the wind and waves.

The Thin Place: Ask, Answer, Pray and Apply.

Is there something in your life right now that you are afraid to face or accept?

Thinking of your past, has God ever failed you?

Is there any reason to believe that God will not protect your future if your truly surrender it to Him?

January 28
The Glory Days

From Above: Deuteronomy 4:9, Isaiah 43:16-19, Ephesians 2:1-13

Focal Passage: *"Only be careful, and watch yourselves closely so that you do not forget the things your eyes have seen or let them slip from your heart as long as you live. Teach them to your children and to their children after them. "* –Deuteronomy 4:9

Here Below:

The Christian life is all about looking ahead. It is about growth, development and obtaining increasingly more and more of the mind of Christ. Yet, with that mandate, we are told over and over in scripture to remember days gone by. We are told to never forget what God has done in the past and to teach it to our children. Moses told the children of Israel repeatedly to remember. Why? Why was remembering such a necessity? Why all the Old Testament rituals and New Testament ordinances to remind us of historical and spiritual truths? Well, because God knows His children. He knows how soon we forget.

This forgetfulness is best illustrated in the up and down way we so often travel spiritually. One day we are on a mountaintop and the next day we are in a valley. It often takes only a little trouble to send us to that valley. Why? Because we forget how God has worked in our past. We focus on the now instead of focusing on the faithfulness of God. This is why it is so important to remember both the accomplishments and the failures of the past. In both, God was faithful.

Now there is a difference between remembering the past works of God and settling for the past works of God. There are many churches in our day that speak of the good old days when they were really reaching their communities and making a difference. They become so enamored with the way things used to be that they fail to change with the times and become stagnant and Ineffective. The same is true of us as individuals. We can content ourselves on past spiritual victories and fail to grow in the present. Nothing is sadder than someone trying to live life as they once did in their glory days. It's almost like the high school football star still wearing his letterman jacket ten years after he graduated. What once was enviable has now become pitiable. It is great that God has done big things in your past, but He wants to do something bigger in your present. When God commands us to remember the past, it is so that we might see even greater things in the future. The same God who led Moses and the children of Israel through the Red Sea is the same God that wants to lead you ultimately through your own Red Sea. He did it then and he can do it now. It also helps to remember that without Him, we were at one time lost in our sin. This kind of remembering keeps us humble. It is in this humility that we are best able to be used of God. So, remember the past, learn from the past, but look to the future.

<u>The Thin Place</u>: Ask, Answer, Pray and Apply.

How has God worked in your past? Where were you spiritually at the time?

Do you ever consider those past accomplishments when you are facing a decision today?

How can you apply your past to what you would like to see happen in your future?

January 29
The Trouble with Time Machines

From Above: Ecclesiastes 3:1-11, 12:9-14, Romans 11:33-36

Focal Passage: *"He has made everything beautiful in its time. He has also set eternity in the hearts of men; yet they cannot fathom what God has done from beginning to end. "* –Ecclesiastes 3:11

Here Below:

Being somewhat of a science fiction fan, I have always dreamed of how nice it would be if I had a time machine. If we had some device that would allow us to travel backwards and forwards in time, it would enable us to fix problems from the past and predict the uncertain future. We could erase misspoken words and stop conflicts before they even begin. Not only that, but there would be no more wasted time. If we needed more time to complete something in our lives, we could just hop in our time machine, put it in reverse and give ourselves a few more hours, days or even years. Nothing would be left undone. Unfortunately, there is no such thing as a time machine; and besides, it never worked in all the old sci-fi movies anyway. It always led to further complications. We simply cannot undo what has been done. That is the true nature of time and our place within its boundaries. We are only given so many hours in a day and once they pass, they are no longer editable. We can find forgiveness for and freedom from the past, but we are still unable to buy back lost time.

Unlike God, who has always been and will always be, there was a time in which I did not exist. However, being created in His image, there will never be a time from the point of my conception forward in which I will not exist. We are eternal beings. In fact, we are told in the above passage that God set eternity in our hearts. This reality explains why cultures all over the world, even those furthest removed from Christian influence still seek an explanation for life after physical death. God created us for eternity. It is in our design. However, due to our fallen nature, we often struggle with the fleeting nature of our earthly lives. Time seems to pass at breakneck speeds, and we are left feeling helpless to its passing. Therefore we must grasp every moment and live our lives as if all eternity depended upon it.

The Teacher of Ecclesiastes understood the value of the moment. After experiencing all that the world offered and realizing the transitory nature of time, he came to this conclusion. All that really matters is what we do for God. Life is a precious gift of God; therefore, we must utilize every moment we are given for the glory of His kingdom and our eternal home. So much of our time is spent on things that have absolutely no eternal significance. What a waste! The seventy or eighty years we are given, if we are so blessed, are but an instance in the scope of eternity. Why waste our most precious commodity on the temporary, when we could be focused on the eternal? Application of this principle leads to a life of fewer regrets and less need for a time machine. Live each moment as if it matters to God, because it does. It is a gift we can return to Him only once. Make the most of this day.

<u>**The Thin Place**</u>: Ask, Answer, Pray and Apply.

Do you have any wasted time in your past that you wish you could live through again?

How much of your daily schedule is spent on things that have no eternal significance?

In relation, how much of your time is invested in things of eternal importance?

January 30
Not For Sale

<u>From Above:</u> Psalm 119:1-12, Proverbs 23:23, John 14:6, 18:33-40

Focal Passage: *"Buy the truth and do not sell it; get wisdom, discipline and understanding. "* –Proverbs 23:23

<u>Here Below:</u>

There are some things in life that simply are not for sale. We all have cherished keepsakes with which we have such a deep emotional attachment that we would never consider selling them, regardless of the offer. To us, their value is such that no offer would be sufficient. Sometimes these items are tangible, other times they are philosophical in nature. Often, these intangible things are more valuable than all our earthly possessions combined. A list of these valuables might include our love, our relationships, our dignity, our reputation, our self-respect and especially our faith. Among these protected treasures should be included one more item of significance. That item is truth. I am not referring to our meager understanding of what is true, but to God's infallible truth. The above Proverb gives us some pretty specific instructions concerning the truth of God. We are to buy it and never sell it.

God's truth is revealed to us in many ways. The two primary ways His truth is revealed to us is through His Word and through His Holy Spirit. Through a regular discipline of prayer and meditation on the Word, we are exposed to the truth. Probably, we can all agree to everything said to this point. We all know God's Word is truth and we all know the importance of remembering that fact. Yet, I think the writer of this Proverb was implying that we need more than just an intellectual understanding of the truth of God. The directions he gives us are evidence to this fact. We are to hold on to the truth so that we might get wisdom, discipline and understanding. It is not enough to know God's Word and will. We must apply it with wisdom to our own lives. We must discipline our actions with the truth of God. In other words, His truth is not just something we know, it is something we live each day.

So many of us are guilty of doing just what the Proverb is warning us to avoid. We buy the truth. We acknowledge the truth. Then the pressure of Christian living in a non-Christian world sets in and we sell it for something more convenient. We sell it for something maybe less noticeable. We sell it for something easier. Put simply, we often exchange God's truth for a cheap generic version that the world offers. In the end we find that the world does not have our best intentions in mind, to say the least. God's truth always does. Why? It is because His truth is Truth. For man, truth often depends upon circumstances. This is relativism. God's truth doesn't change with the tides. That is why we can trust God. He doesn't change with current trends. His love and wisdom is constant and forever. Jesus said "I am the Truth". Don't trust your understanding to a generic truth. Buy God's truth and never let it go.

The Thin Place: Ask, Answer, Pray and Apply.

Has there ever been a time in your life when you listened to bad advice instead of heeding God's truth?

In retrospect, how different might the outcome have been had you followed God's instruction?

What habits can you develop that will strengthen your understanding of God's truth?

January 31
Rest in Peace

From Above: Isaiah 26:3-4, John 14:23-31, Philippians 4:4-8

Focal Passage: *"And the peace of God, which transcends all understanding, will guard your hearts and your minds in Christ Jesus. "*–Philippians 4:7

Here Below:

One of the most beautiful words of the English language is the word "peace". It is a word that has many connotations. While the idea of political peace is comforting, I am not referring to peace in this social respect. I am however speaking of a peace that according to the Apostle Paul goes beyond human understanding or description. It is a peace that can only be found in one place. It can't be found in selfhelp books or in any psychological counsel or word play. It is a peace that comes only from God Himself. This concept of peace is one that many souls in our day long to discover. You cannot turn on the television without seeing another advertisement for some new sleep aid or some new pillow or mattress that is supposed to once and for all help us get a good night's rest. Now sure, sometimes we struggle with insomnia for medical reasons, but more often than not it could probably be accredited to a restless spirit in need of peace. We live in restless and anxious times.

The peace of God that the Apostle Paul is referring to in the above passage goes beyond just a good night's sleep or a clean conscious. I don't think he is talking about a simple feeling of absolution that comes with a repentant spirit, though there is definitely a place for that. He is referring to a peace that goes beyond even the freedom found in forgiveness. He is talking about an assurance that comes with trusting in God. When we fully grasp the power and the love of God, then His peace naturally follows. It is a peace that knows full well that whatever the weather, God will care for His child.

Jesus told His followers, which included each of us, that He was leaving us with His peace. Did He mean by those words that to trust in Him was some sort of guarantee against the perils of life? By no means did he mean that. In fact, He assured us that life would always be filled with troubles and trials. He just wanted us to know that we could have His peace as we encountered these crises. We could face them knowing that God still has our back. This attitude explains the Beatitudes. It also explains the rest of the New Testament which was largely written from within prison walls or under persecution. Yet, those words are filled with hope and yes, peace. Peace doesn't come from being free from life's problems and it doesn't come from having a better under standing of life. It comes from a better understanding of God and His love for you and I. So do not fret if life makes you feel restless. Instead, try to focus not so much on life as on the giver of Life. Rest easy tonight knowing your heart is guarded by God himself.

The Thin Place: Ask, Answer, Pray and Apply.

Would you say that you sometimes struggle with a sort of spiritual restlessness?

How distracting is this restlessness in your life?

What steps can you take to deepen your understanding of God's love and power in your life?

2

February

February 1
Hide and Seeker Friendly

<u>**From Above**</u>: Isaiah 65:1-2, Matthew 7:7-11, James 1:5

Focal Passage: *"I revealed myself to those who did not ask for me; I was found by those who did not seek me. To a nation that did not call on my name, I said, 'Here am I, here am I. "*–Isaiah 65:1

<u>**Here Below**</u>:

It was a favorite game of my children. Our two oldest children were four and three years old at the time. As we had done many times before, my wife and I each chose a partner and turned off the lights, taking turns finding the other two in our own family version of hide and seek. As my oldest son and I searched for my wife and three year old, we stumbled through the dark to the room in which I could hear giggling coming from the closet. I could hear my wife trying to silence the eager little boy as we approached the closet door. I opened the door and did my best to pretend to not know that they were in there, in an attempt to heighten his enjoyment of the hiding experience. I felt all around the clothes hamper where he was hiding, commenting on my difficulty in finding him. "Where can he be?" I would ask. Finally, when he could stand it no longer, the silence was broken with his high pitched three year old voice, so desperate to be found. "Here me is!!!..." he squealed into the darkness. He so wanted to be discovered. What a memory! Perhaps you have a similar recollection with your own family experience or childhood.

Many times I have encountered individuals whom seem to believe that the spiritual life is like playing a game of hide and seek. I am not talking about a childhood game. I am referring to a game that is not enjoyable and can be worrisome to say the least. The conversation begins with a statement such as "I wish I knew what God's will is..." or "I wish God would tell me what to do next...". Understand, there is nothing wrong with asking these questions. On the contrary, it reveals a desire to know God's will for your life. This is good. However, many seem to believe that God's will is hidden from us and part of our purpose in life is to seek it out. God's will by definition is what God wants for us. It doesn't make sense that He would hide something from us that he wants us to have so earnestly. God's will is not some mystical truth that is revealed to us when we finally reach a level of spiritual maturity and understanding. It is what he wants us to see right now.

The above passage from Isaiah is an interesting passage. God is saying through His prophet in this passage that He even reveals Himself to those who do not ask for it. He stands before even them, like my son in our game of hide and seek, saying "Here I am, Here I am!". He wants to be found. He wants His will revealed in your life. If He would do this for someone who doesn't even seek Him, how much more will he do it for one who does? The lesson for us is simple. Do not complicate God's will for your life. Most of it is already revealed in His word. The rest is just a matter of asking and believing.

<u>The Thin Place</u>: Ask, Answer, Pray.

Is there a specific area of your life in which you need to discover God's will?

What does His word already say about this particular need and your attitude concerning it?

Is it possible that God has answered you already and you are waiting for a more agreeable option?

February 2
The Mandate to Meditate

<u>**From Above**</u>: Psalm 1, Psalm 119:15-20, 97-106

Focal Passage: *"Blessed is the man who does not walk in the counsel of the wicked or stand in the way of sinners or sit in the seat of mockers. But his delight is in the law of the LORD, and on his law he meditates day and night. "*–Psalm 1:1-2

<u>**Here Below**</u>:

When we hear the word meditate, we often have images of a transcendental nature come to mind. In our mind's eye, we may see someone sitting in a "criss-cross applesauce" formation on the floor with their eyes shut and hands in the air facing upward as if they are trying to catch the rain, all the while waiting for some new age revelation. Likewise, we may picture some monk in a monastery or some long bearded guru on top of a mountain with wisdom available for anyone who might traverse the mountain in search of it. These stereotypical thoughts concerning meditation are unfortunate. They paint a very false picture of Biblical meditation. After all, God's word is filled with the mandate to meditate; therefore, it should be a very prominent part of the life of a child of God. Meditation is vital.

Meditation is more than just reading and studying His word. Meditation is taking it one step further. It is asking the question "What does this word say to me today?" It is reading and then allowing the Holy Spirit to knead the word into your heart. I study the word daily. That is good. I memorize scripture. That is also good. However, it is when I meditate on the word that I experience the greatest times of spiritual growth and development. I take the biggest steps toward becoming what God wants me to be when I stop and listen. Meditation means coming to a word from God and then waiting for God to reveal the meaning to you in a very real and sometimes practical way. Sometimes it happens quickly, other times it may take days or even weeks or longer. But know this; if it is a word from God, it is not a secret. He wants you to know it. He wants you to meditate upon it. He has something to say to you.

Recently, this has become increasingly clear to me. There was a particular verse that I kept running into everywhere I looked. I was thumbing randomly through my Bible one day. There it was. The very next day, I heard it on the radio. A day or two later I came across the verse in a book I was reading. Over and over again this verse kept appearing. I was reading it. I understood it. I was not however meditating on it. Finally one day I began to see that God was probably showing me this particular word for a reason. So I went back to it and prayed. Within a deeper look at the verse I began to see that it held an answer to a prayer that I had been praying for weeks. I had not seen it, because I had not meditated upon it. It wasn't until I slowed down and in silence just allowed the Holy Spirit to expound it for me that I found my answer. Oh how often we complicate matters? Who would have thought that by doing <u>less</u> (on my own strength) I would actually receive <u>more</u> understanding? Be still. Be quiet. Listen. Meditate.

<u>The Thin Place</u>: Ask, Answer, Pray.

Are you ever guilty of reading and studying God's word, but not meditating upon it?

Is there a particular passage of scripture that God keeps bringing back to you?

What habits can you change that might make meditation a more prominent part of your life?

February 3
Tattle Tale Theology

From Above: 2 Corinthians 3:1-5, Ephesians 3:12, Hebrews 10:19-23

Focal Passage: *"Let us draw near to God with a sincere heart in full assurance of faith, having our hearts sprinkled to cleanse us from a guilty conscience and having our bodies washed with pure water. "*–Hebrews 10:22

Here Below:

"Daddy, he hit me back! He hit me back!..." she came tattling. In her eagerness to get her brother in trouble for hitting her, she was totally unaware of her own guilt. Her four year old conscious was not yet able to discern blame. To her it was simple. She had been hit (back) and she wanted justice. Of course, what she quickly learned was that justice isn't always what we want. Mercy is much better. Why? Because like my daughter, we are all guilty. It wouldn't be long before she would be able to distinguish her own guilt and blame from that of others. It is part of maturing and growing and it is not necessarily a pleasant concept to grasp. How many of us struggle with guilt? Too many I'm afraid.

However, in one sense, feelings of guilt can be both good for us and bad for us. They can be good; in that, these feelings can lead us to repentance, which in turn sets us free. They can be bad; in that, unattended they can cause us to think so little of ourselves that we feel that God could never forgive us, which is unbiblical. We in turn carry a burden that we were never intended to carry. Guilt can be a joy stealer. It can rob us of the life that God desires. Remember too that our conscious can fail us. God's Holy Spirit will not. This is why it is so important to deal with guilt head on. We cannot ignore it or underestimate its power to influence our decisions. So how do we deal with guilt?

The writer of Hebrews refers to being cleansed of a guilty conscious. Sounds good, huh? Well notice the steps we must take. First, we are told to draw near to God. In other words, turn to God. There is no freedom from guilt found anywhere else. Most psychological counseling of our day teaches us how to live with our guilt. God is all about erasing it all together. Second, when we come to him, we must come with a sincere heart. Be honest! It never ceases to amaze me how we fail to bring things to God out of shame or guilt, all the while forgetting that He already knows it anyway! Nothing you have ever done is going shock God. He knows. So just be honest about your sins and you are one step closer to being guilt free. Third, remember your faith. Understand your faith. Remember the cross. Remember the sacrifice. Remember the sin debt, yes your sin debt, which has been paid and paid in full. In other words, when God looks at your heart, he doesn't see your guilt. He sees the shed blood of His son that was shed once and for all. Being free from a guilty conscious has nothing to do with having confidence in yourself, it is about having assurance in Christ. A clear conscious doesn't come from being a better person. It comes from a relationship with a God who loves you anyway. Do your best, but trust in God.

The Thin Place: Ask, Answer, Pray.

Can you tell the difference between your conscious and Holy Spirit conviction?

Would you say that you have a clean conscious?

What steps do you need to take to find release from a guilty conscious?

February 4
Band-Aid Belief

From Above: Malachi 4:2, Matthew 4:23-25, Mark 2:1-12,

Focal Passage: *"When Jesus saw their faith, he said to the paralytic, "Son, your sins are forgiven." –Mark 2:5*

Here Below:

Aside from a mother's kiss, there is probably nothing else in existence that has the healing qualities of a band-aid. A band-aid has the ability to dry crying eyes and pacify even the most distressed child. It can almost instantly soothe the skinned knee or the bruised elbow. It is almost magical in its powers. Yet, the older we get, the bigger and more expensive the band-aids get, the less pacifying they become. It could be due to the fact that our injuries are also more complicated. Sometimes they are physical. Sometimes they are emotional. Whatever, the injury, we have all been in need of a spiritual band-aid.

As a pastor, I have had the privilege of standing by many a sick bed and more than my share of what would become a death bed. I have heard and offered the prayer for healing, only to see it often go unanswered. Perhaps unanswered is not the right word. Perhaps it was answered, just not in the fashion which we would have preferred. That is the funny thing about healing. It is not always what we might expect. For the child of God, death is in a sense a healing. In fact, it is healing in the most perfect sense of the word. There will be no more tears and no more sorrows. It is truly a healing of the soul. I believe God's word teaches us that healing is more than just a release from physical ailments. It is a release for the soul and spirit. It is a freedom to live for God unshackled by the world.

Take for example the miracle that took place in the story above taken from Mark's gospel. Notice, Jesus didn't immediately heal the man from his physical infirmities. This must imply that Jesus saw the greatest need being forgiveness from his sins. The physical healing came second as a demonstration of His power. This was not unusual. In almost every miracle of healing we see Jesus perform, there was without exception another more important miracle that occurred. In every account we see someone coming to faith in Christ. In fact, it was due to their faith that the physical healing was even able to happen. This tells me that there are more pressing needs in life than to be physically healed. It is not that God is dispassionate. It could be that He wants something even better for us. It could be that he desires to teach us something through our situation, whether it be physical or spiritual in nature. It could be that He wants to do more than just give us a spiritual "band-aid" for the moment. Maybe He wants to give us something more permanent and lasting, something that might just help us avoid injuries in the future. Pray for healing, but be willing to accept it in whatever form it may come.

The Thin Place: Ask, Answer, Pray.

Have you ever thought of your prayers for healing as being unanswered?

Do you or someone you love stand in need of healing right now, physical or spiritual?

What miracles has God performed in your life up to this point?

February 5
A Myth Understanding

From Above: Psalm 119:151-152, John 8:30-36, Hebrews 4:12-13

Focal Passage: *"Then you will know the truth, and the truth will set you free."* –John 8:32

Here Below:

I remember in college taking a required class in mythology. In this class, we discussed everything from Greek mythology to Homer's *Iliad*. We even discussed the mythology of George Lucas' *Star Wars*, which I might add, I enjoyed thoroughly. It was a very educational class and I do not regret taking it. However, within our curriculum was one topic that I found disturbing and as I recall I even voiced my objection to my somewhat secular professor and class. Within the discussion of the myth types was included a discussion of the Holy Bible. Now in one sense, this was good; in that, this may have been the only time some of these students have ever read any of the Bible. In another sense it was bad; in that, it placed the Bible in the same category with all these mythological stories and ultimately called into question its divine inspiration and purpose.

Now the purpose of this today is not apologetic in nature. While there is much evidence for its inerrancy and infallibility and much that could be said as to why the Bible is not like other writings, there is one reason in my opinion that overrides them all. God's word is alive and it has the ability to change lives. While I understand the intellectual importance of studying mythological types and the understanding of good versus evil in a mythological context, I also recognize that God's word is not myth. Why? Too many lives have been forever altered by the simple reading of the word. All the intellectual discussion in the world can't explain how lives can be turned around by reading a book. Sure, there are writings out there that influence us, that may even help us, but only the word of God has the power to lead us from death to life. *The Iliad and the Odyssey* has never done for anyone what the Bible has done, nor has *Star Wars* for that matter. As enjoyable and well written as they may be, they are just stories. The Bible is more than just a collection of good stories. It is God's truth, will and ways revealed to mankind.

One of the unique qualities of scripture is its intimacy. A book written over a period of thousands of years and thousands of years ago is about <u>me</u> in the here and now. Now it is not arrogant or prideful to say that. It is simply the truth. God's word is about <u>you</u> as well. When we go to it with an open heart and a heart that is willing to receive, God will use it to reveal the inmost parts of your intellect and your soul. No other writing can say that. That is why we are told that God's word is alive. It has the ability to cut to the heart. God uses it in very specific ways to reach your very specific needs. It is His truth and His truth sets people free. No other writing will set you free. So when you go to His word today, remember it is not a myth, it is instead a love letter from God written specifically for you. Read. Enjoy your freedom.

<u>The Thin Place</u>: Ask, Answer, Pray.

Have you ever doubted the truth and divine inspiration of the Bible?

Is there a particular passage of scripture that God has used to speak to you recently?

Do you ask "What are you saying to me, Lord?" when you read the Bible?

February 6
Kicking the Habit

<u>From Above</u>: Psalm 51:1-7, Romans 7:15-25, Galatians 5:22-26

Focal Passage: *"So I find this law at work: When I want to do good, evil is right there with me."* –Romans 7:21

<u>Here Below</u>:

"How come I keep doing things that I know I shouldn't do? I pray for forgiveness, promise to never do it again and then before you know it, I am right there doing it all over again..." Have you ever said that? Be honest. We all have. Why can't we stop doing things that we know are bad for us and perhaps even sinful? Why can't we kick our bad habits? This is a question that is as old as man and common to all. In fact, one thing that I have always found comforting is the fact that the apostle Paul had the same struggles as you and I. Now, don't get me wrong. I am not boasting in the fact that Paul obviously struggled with some sin or temptation. I just find reassurance in the fact that even a spiritual giant such as the apostle Paul had bad habits. I am not making light of habitual sin either. It can ruin our witness and hurt the cause of Christ, all the while bringing on such intense feelings of guilt and shame that a child of God can become disheartened to the point of just giving up. When our intent is right and we still fail, we can feel like there is no point in trying anymore. This can lead to spiritual despondency. What do we do then? Well, to break our bad habits, we must grasp what Paul knew to be true.

First, if we are to kick a habit, we must first acknowledge why we do it in the first place. We are fallen. From the very beginning of creation, we have been doing things that are bad for us. It doesn't make sense, but it is the truth. Human nature is to do just the opposite of what we need to do. Paul understood this. He decried the fact that he just kept doing what in his heart he didn't even want to do. In other words, he was admitting that he knew better. He just couldn't help himself. Now this doesn't release him or us from responsibility. It just acknowledges what happens when we let the ever present evil influence us. Understanding this also means recognizing that God knows this about His creation. If it were not so, then there would have been no need for the cross of Jesus. God knows you are not perfect and loves you anyway. It is by the righteousness of Christ that we are saved, not our own.

Second, we must understand that we can't break a bad habit on our own strength. Making promises over and over only to break them is futile and self-defeating at best. While God may honor your intent, it is only by His strength that you will ever have final victory over your habit. It is a spirit filled life that conquers habits, not hard work and noble intent. Think about it. One of the least talked about fruits of the spirit is the last one listed in Galatians 5. It is the gift of self control. If we allow the Spirit to fill us and lead us, over time self control will defeat the habit. Isn't it ironic that self control comes not from our selves, but from God? Repent and then ask Him to fill you daily and in time you'll kick it.

The Thin Place: Ask, Answer, Pray.

Do you struggle with a specific habitual sin? Are you disheartened by an inability to break it?

Do you feel as if you need a greater Holy Spirit presence in your life?

Do you pray to that end, asking specifically for the gift of self control?

February 7
What's That Smell?

From Above: I Corinthians 1:18, 2 Corinthians 2:14-17, Ephesians 2:10

Focal Passage: *"For we are to God the aroma of Christ among those who are being saved and those who are perishing. To the one we are the smell of death; to the other, the fragrance of life."* –2 Corinthians 2:15-16

Here Below:

Smell is one of the most powerful senses the human body possesses. It can bring us great pleasure and can most definitely bring us great discomfort. It can be enchanting, it can be repulsive. The sense of smell can also be one of the strongest memory stimulants in the world. Oftentimes we may encounter a particular fragrance and immediately our minds race back to memory from our past in which that smell was present. There is a certain sweet aroma that I have encountered that immediately brings to mind fond memories of walking along a path of Sweetshrub and Honeysuckle in my grandparent's woodland as a child. Likewise, an antique handmade quilt I possess still smells like my grandmother and her home even though she died years ago. When I am near it, I am reminded of her. Smell has the ability to take us to another time and another place, at least for a moment.

Well according to God's word, we are the aroma of Christ. The passage from 2 Corinthians tells us that we are to carry the fragrance of Christ throughout the world. This passage of course is figurative. Paul is using the illustration of smell to drive home a point. Smell is very unique. You would never confuse a rose with a fish. They are very different. While other aromas may be similar, there are still tiny differences. As wonderful as they both smell, even a rose and a gardenia are easily set apart. Likewise, we are to be distinguishable from those without Christ. We are to have the same effect as my grandmother's quilt on those around us. When they encounter our "aroma" they are to be reminded of Jesus. Sometimes we do this with words. Sometimes we do it with our actions. The love, compassion and mercy of Christ should so permeate our being that people are taken to another time and another place in our presence. They should see the mind and heart of Christ.

Unfortunately, not everyone translates a fragrance the same way. What smells like heaven to me might just smell like a musty old quilt to someone else. Likewise, Paul teaches us that to some we will be the fragrance of life and to others the smell of death. In other words, not everyone is going to appreciate our smelling like Jesus. Some may figuratively hold their nose in your presence. Not everyone will understand or appreciate your Christian witness. It has always been that way and it will always be that way. It is not our calling to be pleasing to all, but to smell pleasant to God. So the real challenge for us is to smell less like the world and more like Jesus. Which do you smell more like today?

The Thin Place: Ask, Answer, Pray.

Would you say that your life radiates the mind of Christ?

Would you say that your life is easily distinguishable from those around you?

What changes can you make that might serve to make your life more distinguishable?

February 8
Killing My Old Man

From Above: Romans 6:6-7, Ephesians 4:21-24, Colossians 3:7-10

Focal Passage: *"For we know that our old self was crucified with him so that the body of sin might be done away with, that we should no longer be slaves to sin-- because anyone who has died has been freed from sin..."* –Romans 6:6-7

Here Below:

"I've really got to find a way ...Of taking care of him for good
I know he'd kill me if he could...So I'll nail him to the wood
Killing my old man...You may not understand
He's a terrible man...Got to make a stand and kill the old man..."

These are the lyrics to a somewhat controversial song from years ago performed by the pioneer and now classic Christian rock band Petra. It was controversial due to the title of the song which was simply called "Killing My Old Man". It is easy to see how some might have misunderstood the meaning of the title and the words. However, the message of the song is very Biblical. It is a message of sanctification.

The word sanctification is a word that we hear often in church circles, yet most would be hard pressed to define. Sanctification is simply the process by which we become more like Christ. It doesn't happen all at once. It takes a lifetime. Put simply, it is Christian growth and it begins at the point of our rebirth. At that point, we begin the lifelong process of maturing in our faith and developing into a disciple of Christ that is pleasing to God. At least that is what is supposed to happen. Many things can happen to us along the way that may hinder our development. Sometimes <u>we</u> get in the way. As Paul states in Romans 6 and other passages and as Petra sings in their aforementioned rock ballad, the old self occasionally rears its ugly head and cause us to stumble. We revert to our old way of doing things. We backslide. For this reason we must remember that our old man has been crucified. We are to leave him on his cross and pick up a new cross, one that more readily resembles Jesus.

Again, this is not something that happens all at once. We don't instantly become great heroes of the faith at the point of conversion. We are still sinners. Yet the difference between the born again man and the old man is that the new man is a sinner saved by grace. As Paul tells us above, we are no longer slaves to our sin. It no longer has mastery over us. With the help of God and the grace of God we can crucify the old self and walk in freedom and with confidence. In time, if you take up your cross <u>daily</u> and seek Holy Spirit guidance, the old man will show his face less and less. So don't let the old man win. Take a stand. Leave him on his cross today. With each day comes a chance to walk as a new creation.

<u>The Thin Place</u>: Ask, Answer, Pray.

Does your old man ever show up?

If so, why do you think you struggle so with the "old way" of doing things?

Looking back, can you see that you have made progress in dealing with the old self? If not, why?

February 9
Lord, Help Me Be a Troublemaker!

From Above: Matthew 5:13-17, Matthew 10:32-36, Acts 17:1-7,
Focal Passage: *"But when they did not find them, they dragged Jason and some other brothers before the city officials, shouting: "These men who have caused trouble all over the world have now come here,*
and Jason has welcomed them into his house. They are all defying Caesar's decrees, saying that there is another king, one called Jesus."" –Acts 17:6-7
Here Below:

In the above passage of scripture, the early disciples of Christ are basically being referred to as troublemakers. The King James Version refers to them as "these that have turned the world upside down..." What a description! What a compliment! They were being called out because they were living their lives in such a way as to be noticed by the non-believers with which they associated. In fact, they were living in such a way as to become an irritation to those around them that did not agree with their theology. As a result, they turned the world upside down. I believe this is an example for us to follow. Now please do not misunderstand what I am saying here. I do not believe that we are to "annoy" people with the gospel message. On the contrary, our lives should be such that people notice the difference and are forced to search their own hearts for the reason as to why. The result however may be that this difference may disturb others. That's ok. In fact, it may mean you are doing something right. It is when there is no distinguishable difference from the lost that we have a problem.

Consider the example we have in Christ. Nearly everywhere Jesus went he encountered people that either loved Him or else they hated Him. There were those people ready to fall at His feet in worship and those ready to stone Him. Rest assured though, he never went unnoticed. In a very real and positive sense, Jesus was a troublemaker. He was a rebel. Why? Because the message He was teaching was one so totally in opposition to the ways of the world. He talked about such radical concepts as loving your enemies, forgiving those who have wronged you and salvation by grace through faith. These and others were radical views then and now. Little has changed in two thousand years when it comes to mankind's view of His truth. As a Disciple of Christ, we are still called to be different. Not different in the sense that we are perceived as being "weirdo's" or "freaks", but different in the sense that people will question the reason for our joy, peace and confidence. The early Christians knew this to be true and it was their difference that drew others to them and their cause. In fact, their difference was the catalyst God used to spread the Church and the Gospel throughout the world. He uses the same method today. Lord, help me to be different! Lord, help me to be a troublemaker!

The Thin Place: Ask, Answer, Pray.

Which is more important to you, being accepted by others or being in center of God's will? Be honest.

What distinguishable differences are there between you and those with whom you have daily contact?

Are you willing to be used of God even if others may not understand your motives?

February 10
Who Are You Calling a Kid?

From Above: Psalm 8, Matthew 19: 13-15, Matthew 21:14-17

Focal Passage: *"Do you hear what these children are saying?" they asked him. "Yes," replied Jesus, "have you never read, "'From the lips of children and infants you have ordained praise'?"* –Matthew 21:16

Here Below:

I love the above passages of scripture from Matthew's Gospel. I love it because in it we see a side of Jesus that many don't often associate with Him. He loved children. Sure, we all know this. We sing about this love in the songs of our childhood. Yet, it is rare that we think of the disciples of Jesus being children. Yet, on more than one occasion we see Jesus surrounded by groups of loving and adoring children. This tells us a great deal about our Savior. How so? Well, children for the most part are not attracted to stuffy long faced individuals. On the contrary, they are drawn to loving, fun and perhaps even goofy acting at times kind of people. Well, in our quest for Christian propriety, it may cause us to wince thinking of Jesus in this manner, yet we know for a fact that children were drawn to Him. Not only does this tell us something about our Savior, but it tells us something about ourselves.

Jesus uses the presence of these children as a teachable moment for the other followers, including ourselves. What was a nuisance to the more "spiritual" people in the crowd was what Jesus saw as the model of praise and adoration. The children had figured out what those with all their religious background and theological training couldn't comprehend. Jesus even pointed this out using scripture from the Old Testament as proof. What these children were doing was praise and worship in its purest form. There were no self imposed rituals. There were no manmade traditions constricting their worship. They were just praising the Lord. They just wanted to be near Jesus. Isn't that the definition of worship? Jesus had even said earlier that these children were closer to understanding the Kingdom of God than the religious leaders. Again, it was purity of their hearts that perfected their praise. Being with Jesus was their only motive.

The same purity of heart and motive should drive our worship. In fact, I would go so far as to say that if your motive is not to be in the presence of God, you are not worshiping. You are just going through the motions. Children want to be with those that they love simply because they love them. How many times have you seen a child jump to their feet and run to the arms of a returning parent or friend? Spiritually speaking, our worship should be the same. We are entering the presence of God. Just as a child can't squelch that enthusiasm, neither should we try. Worship and praise doesn't have to be overly pious! It just needs to be honest with nothing held back. We can learn a lot from Jesus' kids. Maybe we could all stand to be a little more childlike in our worship. Be a kid. Run to Jesus today.

The Thin Place: Ask, Answer, Pray.

Would you say that you are totally free and open in personal worship or do you hold back?

What are some motives that might cause one to censor their worship?

What changes can you make personally to help you become more childlike in your praise and worship?

February 11
Uncross Your Fingers

From Above: Matthew 19:25-30, Romans 5:1-8, Hebrews 3:1-6

Focal Passage: *"And hope does not disappoint us, because God has poured out his love into our hearts by the Holy Spirit, whom he has given us." –Ro-mans 5:5*

Here Below:

Have you ever hoped for something specific to happen only to be disappointed? As a child, I had hoped to be an athlete as I grew older. It did not happen. Instead I became a skinny and awkward klutz with bad eyesight. As a teenager, I had hoped to be the most popular guy in school. Again, most people never even noticed me. As an adult, I had hoped to have fame and fortune. It has not happened. Too many times we hope for things that will probably never come to be and become disenchanted as a result. So what did Paul mean in the above passage of scripture concerning a hope that does not leave us disappointed? First we must understand what hope is and what hope is not.

Of all our prized possessions, perhaps the most valuable is the pos-session of hope. The hope Paul is referring to is more than just wishful thinking and daydreaming. It is more than just saying "I sure hope that one day this or that happens..." Hope is trusting that God can and will bring His will to pass, even when it may seem unlikely and then working to that end. Hope is recognizing that we are never out of God's reach or mind and that nothing is beyond Him. Think about the New Testament believers for example. Nearly all of the Epistles were written in a time in which Christians were literally in mortal danger and even imprisoned. Yet, we do not read letters of discouragement and despair as one might expect from such people. Instead we hear about a hope that doesn't disappoint. How? Well, our faithful predecessors understood what we so often forget. If we set our minds on the things of God and hope for those things, it will happen. Now God's will is not always easy nor is it what we might choose for ourselves. Nevertheless, His will is always what is best for us, and I have yet to meet anyone who was at the center of God's will in their lives that wished that they were somewhere else. The center of God's will is always the best place to be and it's always hopeful.

With that understanding, we can have hope in any circumstance. Hope can bring light into a situation that seems to only be growing darker and darker. It has the ability to lift a person from the depths of despair to the heights of joy. Hope is something that the storms of life cannot destroy. Hope is not facing the day with our spiritual fingers crossed. Hope is resting assured that God will prevail. Never underestimate the ability of an all knowing and all powerful God to surprise you at just the right moment in your life. So uncross your fingers and trust in God. Place your hope in Him today. You will not be disappointed.

The Thin Place: Ask, Answer, Pray.

Have you ever had to deal with overwhelming disappointment?

Did you trust in God to get you through that time in your life or did you face it on your own strength?

Most importantly, has God ever given you reason to lose hope?

February 12
Grabbed by God

From Above: Romans 5:7-8, I Peter 3:18-22, I John 3:16

Focal Passage: *"Very rarely will anyone die for a righteous man, though for a good man someone might possibly dare to die. But God demonstrates his own love for us in this: While we were still sinners, Christ died for us. "*
–Romans 5:7-8

Here Below:

If you awoke to find your house on fire, after assuring the safety of your family, what possessions would you scramble to save from the flames? My guess is that it would not be your television, stereo or computer. Probably you would be grasping for those things which are irreplaceable. You would probably grab family photos and other special memorabilia. You would grab that special gift given to you by that someone special in your life, a special friend or family member. You would grab that family heirloom that you had planned to pass on to your children. Granted, these things might not be financially as valuable as your flat screen television or your computer, but their worth to you is not measured in dollar amounts. You can buy another television. You can't buy your family photos. You can't buy another child's first work of art. True worth then must be measured from the perspective of the owner. What might be insignificant to you, might very well be my most prized treasure.

With this said, what then is your worth? There are many in our day who struggle with this question. It is so easy to base our worth on what we think to be successes and failures. We are quick to also view our worth by what we think other people think of us. Neither of these views is appropriate if we are to appraise our actual worth. Again, <u>true</u> worth must be measured from the perspective of the owner. In other words, your owner, your Creator, your Father, is the one to give us an accurate appraisal of your worth. Our worth is determined from God's perspective. While it is impossible to truly see ourselves from God's perspective, His word and His history do teach us about our worth. Figuratively speaking, with His creation in danger of being consumed by the flames, what did God grab on His way out of the door? Well, He rescued us. He did not even spare His own Son. Instead, he let Jesus go so that we might be saved. That tells me that I am of great worth and so are you.

Understanding this affects everything. It affects our view of ourselves and it should affect our view of others. For example, that person at work or school that annoys you and that you wish you never had to see again is of great worth to God. God loved that person enough to allow His own Son to die in his or her place. Do not allow your actions to say that one life might be of more value than another. God loves us each equally. His love is not based on our sinfulness or righteousness. His love is just that, His love. It's not determined by any outside perspective. So when you begin to think that your life is insignificant, remember that God grabbed you on the way out the door. You are of great worth.

The Thin Place: Ask, Answer, Pray.

Are there times when you feel as if your life doesn't matter or that you are not worth anything?

Do you sometimes place value on others based upon what you personally think of them?

What can you do differently daily to remind yourself of your great worth to God?

February 13
My Daddy Can Beat Up Your Daddy!

From Above: John 1:12-13, Romans 8:15-16, I John 3:1-3

Focal Passage: *"How great is the love the Father has lavished on us, that we should be called children of God! And that is what we are! The reason the world does not know us is that it did not know him. " –I John 3:1*

<u>Here Below</u>:

What an exclamation! In the above passage of scripture we see a thought which always seemed to me to be more of an uncontainable outburst rather than a thought out and calculated verse written for an epistle. "What a love!" John is saying with enthusiasm. Now if anyone should know about the love of God, it should be this disciple. We know from scripture that He and Jesus had a very special relationship. John was often referred to as the "one whom Jesus loved". Now our first instinct may be to question that description of John. It could be mistakenly taken to imply that Jesus had favorites. This is of course not true. I have always believed that it was due to the fact that John simply understood Jesus perhaps a little more than the others. Therefore, they were naturally close. John's writings in the New Testament would seem to support this theory. They are filled with beautiful language and imagery all pointing to God's love. Take the most famous verse of all for example, John 3:16. Nevertheless, this unique relationship doesn't imply that Jesus loved any of the others any less. We all have people like John in our lives, people that we are just naturally more comfortable being around. This is natural. Notice however that you never hear John exclaiming his joy over being the disciple "whom Jesus loved". Why? Because He knew that God loves us all equally, as his writings attest.

In fact, this is why he is speaking with such emphasis here. There is no greater love than the one lavished on us by God. God has made us His children. We are the children of the God of the universe, and as two kids on the playground might argue, there is no Dad bigger than ours. Think about this parent child imagery for a moment. There is perhaps no greater bond than that of a parent and a child. Granted, we are a fallen people and it doesn't always happen that way earthly speaking. However, under normal and healthy circumstances, this bond is impenetrable. You can pretty much bank on the fact that while others may turn on you, your parents will usually love you no matter what. They also often have a blind spot to your weaknesses and shortcomings. For example, my mother probably thinks I am the greatest preacher that ever lived. The same is true of my father. You see, that is a parent's love. In that type of love relationship is a very special and a privileged place to be. John knew this and that is why he is shouting. Wow! God loves me enough to consider me a child!? You bet He does. And guess what...you too are also "one whom Jesus loves". What a Savior! What a Father! What a love!

The Thin Place: Ask, Answer, Pray.

How is a parent's love unlike other kinds of love? How about in your family specifically?

How is your relationship with God like that of a parent and child?

What responsibilities do we have as God's children in this relationship?

February 14
My Favorite Valentine

From Above: Matthew 22:35-40, I Corinthians 8:1-3, Ephesians 3:16-21

Focal Passage: *"Jesus replied: "Love the Lord your God with all your heart and with all your soul and with all your mind. This is the first and greatest commandment. And the second is like it: 'Love your neighbor as yourself." –Matthew 22:37-39*

Here Below:

Perhaps you can remember this routine or at least one similar from your own past. Every year in Flowery Branch Elementary School, our class would exchange Valentine cards and then we would stuff our faces with sugary sweets. At the end of the day, we would board our school bus for the ride home, all hyped up on sugar, for what must have been the bus driver's least favorite day of the year. During the frenzied ride home, we would all compare our Valentine's Day take with that of our buddies. In all honesty, the cards were usually meaningless store bought cartoon character cards which our mothers had bought and signed. The moms were always careful to see that no one was left out, even those kids we didn't really like. Well, one Valentine's Day was different. I and others had received a very special card that day that would forever impact me. It was not the usual meaningless store bought card. In fact, it was homemade. A young girl in my class had made this card herself. She had taken index cards and written messages on them for each student. She had then placed a sticker for decoration that she had taken from one of those mail order magazine subscription ads that would come periodically in the mail in those days. You see, it was all she had. She was from a very poor family and one that quite frankly was probably not emotionally healthy, to say the least. She had done all she could for our Valentine's Day party. I remember kids making fun of her card and I can't help but think how hurt she must have been. The irony of it is that of all the cards given that day, hers was the most thoughtful. She had given of herself.

I tell this story because I believe there is a truth here that is undeniable. Much could be said of her treatment that day, but I am thinking more of *her* motives. She wanted to give us each something. She gave of herself. That is real love. It is something that is so fundamental to our faith and yet so often missed. True love is expressed when we give of ourselves to others. Take these two most important commandments. Love God. Love your neighbor as yourself. There is nothing in there about receiving anything. It's about putting God and others first. Also, notice the order of these two commandments. This is no coincidence. If we first have a love for God, then loving others comes much easier. Why? Because the basic starting point in a relationship with God is understanding that we do not deserve His love. Our salvation is a gift from His heart. It is not until we are in right relationship with Him that we can truly love others as we should. So today instead of asking "Will you be my Valentine?", ask "What can I give of myself for you?" I promise you, this approach will never leave your Valentine disappointed.

The Thin Place: Ask, Answer, Pray.

Would you say that your relationship with God comes first in your life?

How does your faith affect your relationships with others, especially those closest to you?

Is there someone special today in your life that could benefit from your giving something of yourself?

February 15
Bitter Free Believers

From Above: Deuteronomy 29:18-19, Romans 8:26-28, Hebrews 12:9-15,

Focal Passage: *"See to it that no one misses the grace of God and that no bitter root grows up to cause trouble and defile many."* –Hebrews 12:15

Here Below:

Have you ever met a bitter person? I am talking about a person whose heart is literally driven by a bitter attitude? Better yet, have you ever been that person? Well if you are not sure, let me help you. A bitter person is easy to spot. They are angered very easily, often over situations that would most would overlook. Along with being irritable, they are never satisfied. Nothing ever seems to suit their tastes and they never have anything good to say about anything or anyone. Everyone is out to get them and they trust no one. While it may sound like I am describing someone with deep psychological problems, I am not. This could very easily be you or me.

In fact, I believe this attitude can effortlessly grow in anyone who allows their heart to go unchecked. I would venture to say that most bitter people do not know of this transformation until they are well within its grasp. It doesn't happen all at once. It happens over a period of time. When you witness true bitterness, you will recognize it. In the heart where a bitter root grows, joy struggles to survive. Its manifestations are sometimes even beyond spiritual. Sometimes you can even see it in the physical person. Bitterness wears us down. It is destructive. It ages us unnaturally. It steals our smile.

This is exactly what we are warned about in the above passages of scripture. We are told by the writer of Hebrews to watch out for any bitter root that might be sprouting. Notice what else it says. This bitterness can "cause trouble and defile many." In other words, our bitterness doesn't only bring ourselves down; it can affect others as well. Let's face it, bitterness is contagious. If you are around bitterness for very long with an unguarded heart, you too will be tempted to become cynical and bitter. This is why we must be prudent when it comes to our spiritual heart condition. We can let situations that inevitably occur feed bitterness or we can starve the bitterness by allowing God to use the circumstance for good. It is a choice. It is not an easy choice; but nevertheless, it is a choice. God's desire for each of us is that we might become bitter free believers, in spite of our setbacks. Our witness depends upon it and our relationships with others depend upon it. Let's be honest, no one likes to be around a bitter person. More importantly, our relationship with God depends upon it. Don't let bitterness wear you down. Surrender it to the Lord today. By refusing to let go of yesterday's problems, we make them tomorrow's problems. By holding on to past hurts, we only give them life and room to grow. Let the Holy Spirit of God empower you to overcome your bitterness before it takes root.

The Thin Place: Ask, Answer, Pray.

Is there a particular subject in which you struggle with a bitter attitude?

Do you know anyone that you would consider a bitter person?

What steps can you take in your own life to prevent that from happening to you?

February 16
Imagine That!

From Above: 2 Corinthians 9:6-15, Ephesians 3:14-21, Philippians 4:13

Focal Passage: *"Now to him who is able to do immeasurably more than all we ask or imagine, according to his power that is at work within us..."* –Ephesians 3:20

Here Below:

As a child, I once slew a three headed dragon with my bare hands to rescue my beautiful damsel in distress. I also captained the very first intergalactic starship and rescued the planet earth from certain annihilation from our reptile-like extraterrestrial enemies. Oh did I mention that I also possess the ability to converse with animals? Do you find this a little hard to believe? Well, in my world it was part of everyday life. I guess you could say that as a child I had a very vivid imagination. It made for an adventuresome playtime. Oh how I miss those adventures! As adults we often forget about the power of the imagination. Our epic quests are swallowed up by the daily grind of simply living. It does not have to be that way. In fact, I believe God desires for us to use our imaginations, especially in serving Him. I don't mean in the sense of dreaming of the incredible such as the fore mentioned fantasies. I am talking about the dreams that the Holy Spirit of God may plant in our minds. I wonder, how many times do we limit what God wants to do in us and through us because of our own lack of imagination?

I love the above passage of scripture. Again, I feel as if I have always had a pretty strong imagination. Well, according to the Apostle Paul, God is able to accomplish immeasurably more than I can even imagine. That is saying something, because I can imagine plenty. What about you? Too often we have our own preconceived notions of what can happen and what should happen. We develop this mindset to the detriment of what God would do in our lives. Think about the Bible adventures we all love so much. I would say without exception that in each great story God performed over and above what the people involved anticipated. Why should we expect that He is any different today? Is He not the same God today that Paul was writing about above? Unfortunately, we put God in a box. We limit what God will do by placing our boundaries on His power. How can we do that? Well, just as God's power hasn't changed over the centuries, neither has His gentle nature. He has never nor will He ever force Himself upon anyone. Therefore, He chooses to move only as far as we allow. Even in those great stories of the Bible, God was able to go above and beyond because the characters involved had faith in His ability and strength. They were also in perfect agreement with His will and were willing to do their part to see it happen. God used them and He wants to do the same with us as well. Imagine how different the church might be if God's children all understood this concept. Imagine how different the world might be if we dreamed bigger and greater than ourselves and our present realities. Imagine how different our lives might be if we simply let God out of the box! Simply put, you can't out dream God's ability and strength. Go ahead and try. Use your imagination. God is daring you to try.

The Thin Place: Ask, Answer, Pray.

Has there ever been a time in your life when God answered your prayers in a way greater than expected?

Looking back, do you think there have been times when you settled for less that God's best?

What can you do differently in the present and future to keep that from happening again?

February 17
Down Goes The Day

From Above: Proverbs 15:1-4, Ephesians 4: 22-27, Hebrews 3:12-14,

Focal Passage: *"But encourage one another daily, as long as it is called Today, so that none of you may be hardened by sin's deceitfulness."* –Hebrews 3:13

<u>Here Below</u>:

Perhaps you have had a night like the one I am about to describe. It is well past your usual bedtime and yet you are still wide awake. You have tried everything short of counting sheep to help you go to sleep, but gnawing away at your mind is the inescapable feeling that something has gone undone in the course of your day. You can't quite put your finger on it, but this feeling has left you in an epic struggle with the sandman and you aren't winning. Mixed among this feeling of something gone undone is the reality of the next day growing closer and closer and your sleep time growing shorter and shorter. It is a miserable feeling. Sometimes this form of insomnia is brought about by something neglected and other times it is something that we did during the day that we wish we could erase and do differently. An inventory of the day often leaves us with the awareness of missed opportunities and words misspoken. It is not a pleasant way to end a day. For this reason we are warned in God's word concerning the missed opportunities of the present day.

We are given some very helpful instructions that if applied will help ward off the tossing and turning that follows a day of regrets. It seems among the most important things to guard throughout the course of the day is our relationships. We are taught to use our time wisely, making sure that we invest it in others. The writer of Hebrews exhorts us to use our time for encouraging others "while it is still called today". In Ephesians we are told to deal with our anger before the sun goes down. In each instance, the urgency has to do with our relationship with others. We are to use our time in mending tears in our relationships as well as building others up. Too often we say to ourselves "Well, there is always tomorrow. I can talk to them tomorrow. I'll apologize then." Unfortunately, I imagine there has never been a person that died that didn't believe that they had at least one more day. I do not wish to be morbid on this subject. It is simply the reality in which we all live. We are not guaranteed a tomorrow. This is what these biblical writers knew while writing these instructions. Therefore, the best day to mend, build and encourage is always <u>today</u>! In doing this, you not only help others, but you help yourself. We must also keep in mind that this restlessness we are talking about here is not always due to some fault of our own. It can sometimes be due to someone else's misspoken word or carelessness. Forgiving the sin of others is an equally important part of the peace that we should seek before the sun goes down. God wants us to have true rest. Only when we apply His principles to our relationships will we find the rest we desire. Use your time wisely. Say what needs to be said before the day goes down!

<u>**The Thin Place**</u>: Ask, Answer, Pray.

Do you take a spiritual inventory at the closing of your day?

Do you ever find yourself wishing that you could start the day over knowing what you know now?

What can you do differently tomorrow to help avoid the same feeling of regret at the end of the day?

February 18
99 Reasons Why My Life Matters

<u>**From Above**</u>: Luke 15:1-33

Focal Passage: *"I tell you that in the same way there will be more rejoicing in heaven over one sinner who repents than over ninety-nine righteous persons who do not need to repent."* –Luke 15:7

<u>**Here Below**</u>:

There was a pastor friend of mine that once had a picture hanging in his office of a small child with a dirty face and torn clothes. This kid looked as if he had really had a fun day. He was a mess. What I remember most about the picture though is the words beneath the picture. Underneath that rascally looking child was the words "God Don't Make No Junk!" What a simplistic and at the same time life changing message within those words, regardless of the grammar. It was a gentle and somewhat humorous reminder to us that we are God's children; therefore, our life matters, if for no other reason than we matter to Him. What a beautiful and true sentiment! Too many times though, I have encountered individuals that felt just the opposite. For whatever reason, they had bought into the lie that their life really doesn't amount to much in the grand scheme of things. They feel dirty or broken and therefore assume that God is not interested in them. This is unbiblical and untrue.

Take for example the Parable of the Lost Sheep in Luke chapter 15. Right there in that beautiful story, Jesus gives us 99 reasons why our life is special to our God. What do I mean? Well, Jesus refers to the rejoicing that occurs when even one disobedient sheep among a hundred is returned to the flock. He is talking about you and me. There is rejoicing in Heaven when even one of us comes to the Lord or returns to the Lord. Why would the shepherd in that parable and why would the Great Shepherd chase after one stray when he still had ninety-nine obedient sheep for which to care? Well, because that one means as much to Him as the other 99. With 99 still faithful, out of love He would still go after the one lost. Now to leave the others in order to find the one speaks volumes to the value of the one. Now this doesn't exactly make sense in the natural economy in which we value things, but it makes perfect sense to God. You see, you belong to Him. You are His creation. You are His child. What parent would not go searching for the one lost child even if it was only one child among a hundred? A parent's love doesn't see us as being more or less important than another. A parent's value system is based simply upon their love for us. The same is true of God. He doesn't see us for what we are but for what we could become if only we surrendered ourselves to Him. He doesn't see disposable people. He doesn't see junk. He doesn't even see the dirty face little boy with the torn clothes. He sees His beloved. He sees His child. He sees his eventual masterpiece. Now when we can grasp the fact that we do not belong to ourselves but to him, our lives take on a whole new meaning. We treat ourselves better and we treat others better. I thank God for the other 99. In them I see *my* value. God came after me. I am not junk.

The Thin Place: Ask, Answer, Pray.

Have you ever questioned your worth?

Why is it that we often try to place value on ourselves based upon what we and others see as important?

What does the Cross tell you about your value?

February 19
God's Stimulus Package

From Above: Romans 7:6-7, Ephesians 2:14-15, Colossians 2

Focal Passage: *"He forgave us all our sins, having canceled the written code, with its regulations, that was against us and that stood opposed to us; he took it away, nailing it to the cross."* –Colossians 2:14

Here Below:

One cannot turn on the television or radio lately without hearing about the pitiful state of our economy. Job loss is at an all time high. Debt is at an all time high. The result is that morale seems to be at an all time low, leaving no one unaffected. Probably the most disheartening aspect of it all is that those in power seem to believe that the answer to the debt and financial struggles is simply to throw more money and more debt in its direction. I am not a financial expert, but I think it is easy to see that spending more money when you are already in the hole, so to speak, is never going to work. We don't need more debt. We need our debt erased. This principle has always been true. However, the purpose of this today is not a political commentary. On the contrary, the principle of debt forgiveness is a spiritual matter. I am not talking about financial debt, though it can very well be a symptom of a bigger problem. I am referring to the debt of sin with which we must all deal with eventually.

As Paul was addressing the church at Colossae, he was confronting a problem that plagued the New Testament Church and I believe still today. It was legalism. Legalism is basically the philosophy that salvation comes through following the rule of law. Put simply, if you are a good enough person, you may get into heaven. For the early church, it meant keeping the law and observing all the manmade traditions associated with the law. This meant keeping all the rituals, abstaining from certain foods and drink and removing oneself from contamination from the world. The problem with legalism is that it is impossible to keep the law perfectly. We are sinners by nature. The law has a purpose though. It was given by God to reveal to us our sin and our need for grace. The problem is in man's handling of the law. It leaves us with a debt that we can never repay and a burden we on our own can never rid ourselves.

In the above passage, Paul speaks of Jesus' cancellation of the written code. I like the translation in the Holman Christian Standard version. It says that God "erased the certificate of debt". You see our problem today with sin is that we try cope with it, leaving us still with a debt. Counselors try to help us live with sin instead of trying to eradicate it. God on the other hand has erased the debt completely through the cross. Real growth in our faith only comes when we understand God's work and grace in our lives. True stimulus comes not from adding to the debt, but erasing it. Thanks be to God that he has nailed my debt to the cross. This in no way contradicts His holiness; in fact, it reassures us of it. Only a Holy and righteous God could offer His sinless Son as a sacrifice for our sin. He didn't just erase the debt. He paid it himself. Accept God's forgiveness today. Accept God's stimulus package of Grace.

The Thin Place: Ask, Answer, Pray.

Have you ever struggled with the idea that God will accept you if you are only good enough?

How does that leave you feeling when you mess up, as we all inevitably do?

How can the understanding of God's grace allow you to live a life of freedom?

February 20
Watch Your Mouth!

From Above: Proverbs 10:18-21, Matthew 12:33-37, James 1:26

Focal Passage: *"For out of the overflow of the heart the mouth speaks."* –Matthew 12:34b

Here Below:

One of the guilty pleasures I have as a minister is watching people stumble all over themselves apologizing for their use of distasteful language in my presence, especially if they didn't at first know that I am a minister. It is as if the fact that I am a preacher makes foul language somehow more sinful or something. I guess they apologize out of respect for my position. More times than not though I think it is just out of plain embarrassment. Once they realize their blunder, the fun for me begins. They will usually say something like "I'm sorry preacher...I don't usually use those words..." or "I don't know what I was thinking...I don't talk like that" Yeah, right! I have found that I often don't have to say a word in response and the less I do say in response, the more frustrated they seem to be with themselves. My comeback is usually a simple assurance that they do not owe me an apology, but that they might owe someone else one. First, the truth is that if you can't say it in front of a preacher, you probably have no business saying it at all. Second, these words don't just spill out of our mouths by accident.

Notice the words in red from Matthew chapter 12, especially verse 34. Jesus himself dispels the myth that words can appear out of nowhere. He very clearly teaches that our words originate from the overflow of our heart. In other words, if you don't have them in your heart, then you don't have to worry about them coming out of your mouth just because you stubbed your toe or hit your thumb with a hammer. James, who is careful to never mince words, tells us very clearly in more than one place that a Christian that can't control his tongue is lying to himself. He and Jesus were saying the same thing. Basically, you either control your tongue or it controls you. We must keep a "tight rein" on it or it may just get away from us. This can be very damaging to others and to our own Christian witness.

How then do we remedy this problem? After all, who hasn't at one time let their tongue get away? I have. We all have. Our speech like all human struggles must be handled with grace. In other words, don't condemn someone for an occasional slip. Acknowledge it. Encourage them. Pray for them. It is when it is not merely an occasional slip of the tongue that we should really worry. If someone constantly uses profane or even negative speech, it is symptomatic of a greater and deeper problem. Address it with that understanding. It is a heart problem. As far as our own speech goes, we must see that our heart is filled with God's goodness instead of the world's negativity. As with most habitual sins, the answer is simple, though not effortless. We must make a conscious effort to be filled with the Holy Spirit of God. Then there is no room for foulness. Our overflow is then godly, not destructive.

__The Thin Place__: Ask, Answer, Pray.

Do you sometimes let your tongue get away from you with negative or even profane language?

Are you in close contact with others that regularly use distasteful speech? What can you do about it?

What steps can you take to avoid your witness being damaged by your own tongue?

February 21
A Jealous God

__From Above__: Exodus 20:1-6, Psalm 78:58, I Corinthians 10:21-24

Focal Passage: *"You shall not make for yourself an idol in the form of anything in heaven above or on the earth beneath or in the waters below. You shall not bow down to them or worship them; for I, the LORD your God, am a jealous God..."* –Exodus 20:4-5

<u>Here Below</u>:

When we hear the word jealousy, we often associate it with sinful behavior and attitudes. Indeed it can be. Anyone with multiple children within their home can see the sin of jealousy played out every day. It is an ugly sin. It is also not limited to children's behavior! How then do we reconcile God's own words in referring to Himself as a jealous God? God is without sin. How can He be jealous? It is quite simple actually. With you and I it is sinful, because jealousy is rooted in pride. We want to be the center of attention. We want our way. With God however it is not pride; it is fact. He is worthy of our full attention; therefore, it is not prideful or selfish for Him to expect to be at the center of our awareness and existence. He alone deserves it. This is why idol worship must be God's most despised sin.

We often think that idol worship does not apply to modern times. After all, it is doubtful that any of us have fetishes or totem poles set up in our homes to which we pray or bow down. We do not go to altars in the high places. Unfortunately, idol worship is perhaps more prevalent today than ever before. You see, idol worship is not simply praying to graven images of pagan gods. Idol worship is placing anything in our lives in a place that belongs only to God. It can be something as simple and harmless as a hobby or a relationship. While these things may be positive in one sense, they can also take a place of priority that was intended for the Lord Himself. For example, there are many in our day that would surrender their regular worship long before they would consider giving up their favorite sport! Does that mean sports or hobbies are bad? Of course not! In fact they can be very healthy and spiritually stimulating in the right context; that is, in God's context. You see, God is not going to be happy with anything in your life becoming more important than your relationship with Him, however well intended. In fact, if you read the second part of Exodus 20:5 you will see just how serious God takes this subject. The punishment for idol worship extended for generations. Now much could be said about the language of this verse and what is meant by this idea of generational punishment and Old Testament law versus New Testament grace. However, I believe the principle God was teaching is that idol worship affects family and friends for years to come. If your family sees you putting something in God's designated place in your life, it will affect their spiritual lives in the future, and so on and so on... Simply put, God doesn't fool around when it comes to idol worship; therefore, we should not make light of it either. Nothing should come between you and your loving, merciful, gracious, awesome and <u>jealous</u> God.

<u>**The Thin Place**</u>: Ask, Answer, Pray.

While observing you, what would others see as the most important thing in your life?

What does the actual amount of time and energy spent in your life reflect as being of most importance?

Is there an interest in your life that you would not give up if God required it of you? Why not?

February 22
The Difference a Day Can Make

<u>**From Above**</u>: Psalm 30, Jeremiah 29:11-13, 2 Corinthians 4:16-18

Focal Passage: *"For his anger lasts only a moment, but his favor lasts a lifetime; weeping may remain for a night, but rejoicing comes in the morning."* –Psalm 30:5

<u>**Here Below**</u>:

I love the humanity of David. In his songs, such as the one above, we see that he was very much like you and I. He had days of spiritual highs and days of overwhelming lows. In fact, David's lows were pretty extreme compared to what most of us go through these days. He had enemies and friends at various times trying to kill him. He even had his own son trying to overthrow him and ultimately murder him. So I think it is perfectly reasonable to say that David understood lows. Yet during those lows we see arguably some of the most beautiful songs ever penned. While I pray that I and no one I know ever experiences the same lows as David, I do believe we can learn something from this man who was known as being "a man after God's own heart".

David understood the nature of the lows. They sometimes occur as a result of our own sinfulness and shortsightedness. In other words, sometimes it is our own fault that we find ourselves in a well of trouble. Likewise, we can find ourselves in lows as a result of the sin of others and at no real fault of our own. Further, in other times it is simply part of the human condition and nobody is at fault. It is possible to do everything right and still have trouble. Sometimes troubles happen "just because". Finally, there is one more possibility. Sometimes our lows could be due to the chastening of a loving Heavenly Father for his children. God does at times need to discipline His children. He usually does this by letting us face the natural consequences of our own rebellion.

While understanding the nature of lows, David also grasped the nature of hope. Whatever the reason for our time of difficulties, tomorrow is a new day. When trusting in God for our strength, our sorrows are only temporary. Many times throughout scripture, morning is equated with a fresh start or a new beginning. That is the hope we have in a relationship with God. His love outlasts any hardship or discipline we may encounter. He is the God of fresh starts.

Whatever you may be facing today, remember that morning will come. God desires for you to experience the sunrise with Him. Don't lose heart in the darkness of the passing day. Instead, warm yourself in His mercy, grace and forgiveness that arrives with each new morning. Wake up. Wipe yesterday from your face. Look into the joy of this day. You will be surprised the difference a day can make in your outlook.

<u>The Thin Place</u>: Ask, Answer, Pray.

Would say that you are in a time of spiritual high, low or somewhere in between right now?

Have there been times in your past in which you had difficulties breaking free from a low time?

How has God been faithful in your past and what does that tell you about tomorrow?

February 23
A Controlled Burn

<u>From Above</u>: Ephesians 4:28-32, I Thessalonians 4:7, I Peter 1:13-16

Focal Passage: *"For God did not call us to be impure, but to live a holy life"* –I Thessalonians 4:7

<u>Here Below</u>:

Once my wife and I, while still newlyweds, decided to go on a weekend camping excursion. We had very little camping gear at the time, but we didn't mind roughing it as long as we were together. So we set out for a state park not too far away and set up our meager campsite. It was a beautiful night. The stars were shining. The crickets serenaded us to sleep that night with their hypnotic singing. It was an almost picture perfect night. We were sure the next day of hiking and exploring nature would be no different. We had been very careful to check the weather forecast, so we knew tomorrow would be great as well. We were wrong. Early the next morning a park ranger came knocking at our tent door to warn us about a controlled burn that was going to take place in the park. We were warned that the area in which we were camping soon would be filled with smoke from the burning. The concept of a controlled burn was then explained to us. This occurs when a fire is started and allowed to burn in a controlled environment in such a way as to burn away any underbrush or other unwanted plant life that might be choking the trees and generally making the grounds look messy. In other words, they are burning up all the unwanted trash so that the growth which is wanted is free to flourish. This is a common practice in state wildlife parks. It is also practiced on farmland. It makes for a more fertile ground in which to grow. However, it made for some terrible camping conditions. We had to pack up and move out to avoid the smoke.

Now I share this story because I feel there is a spiritual principle from which we can learn. Sometimes in order to flourish, we need to institute a controlled spiritual burn in our lives. In other words, there are things in our lives that may very well be hindering our growth. It is necessary from time to time to remove those things. It may be an easy burn, it may not be. Nevertheless, it is necessary to remove the briars and creeping vines from our lives from time to time. We must remember that ultimately we are called to a life of holiness. Holiness does not mean a life of perfection as most commonly believed. Holiness simply refers to being set apart or designated for a specific purpose. For the child of God, living a life of holiness means setting our life apart for the purpose of finding and fulfilling God's will and design. It means allowing ourselves to be used of God. In order for this to happen we must fill our lives with that which pleases God. Anything offensive to God is only going to limit our growth. Hence the need exists for the occasional controlled burn. We are given multiple lists of attitudes in scripture which are offensive to God. We are also reminded of our need for God's strength to remove them. It is not a matter of just striking a match, but a matter of prayer and humility and even at times fasting. God will honor the effort and the result of the burn will be green and healthy growth.

The Thin Place: Ask, Answer, Pray.

What attitudes do you exhibit that might not be favorable for spiritual growth?

What attitudes do you exhibit that are favorable for spiritual growth?

Do you think it is time for a controlled spiritual burn in your life?

February 24
Chasing Dead Snakes

<u>**From Above**</u>: Romans 12:21, 14:7-12, Ephesians 4:31-32
Focal Passage: *"Do not be overcome by evil, but overcome evil with good."*
–Romans 12:21
<u>**Here Below**</u>:

At a pastor's fellowship one day, I asked a pastor friend of mine about his activities of the morning. He responded by saying "I've been chasing dead snakes all morning." He then went on to explain his comment. He had been making phone calls all morning in an attempt to reconcile an issue that had come up the day before at church. It seemed as if there had been a falling out between some of his congregation over something that would in time be considered trivial and probably forgotten. He had been in contact with the parties involved in what seemed to him a futile attempt to make peace and keep harmony within the church. It was an all too familiar story and one to which any pastor can relate. What surprised me about the situation was the somewhat jovial attitude he had toward the situation. At the time I probably would have responded with feelings of frustration and perhaps even anger. After all, these type disagreements often stand in the way of what we are supposed to be about as a church. I think this is what he was implying with the "dead snakes" comment. Yet, his attitude seemed untouched by the situation. He was just laughing about the petty nature of the dispute. He had found a way to separate himself from the negative attitudes of those around him and was therefore better equipped to solve the problem. This is a positive way to deal with strife and I believe a Biblical way.

The fact of the matter is that we will all encounter attitudes that are hard pressed to ever see anything positive taking place in the world. There are those in our church, place of employment and even in our families that will always see the glass as half empty. There will always be those that are going to voice that negativity and ultimately cause division with their words. This is the reality of being part of a larger community. There will be disagreements. The key is to keep oneself from being pulled into these conflicts. We have a mandate as children of God to be a Christ like example in trying times. Paul tells us that we are to overcome evil with good. Instead of responding with more negativity, respond with words of life. This also means understanding that we are all on different spiritual maturity levels. Being in church and being a Christian for decades does not guarantee maturity. We must keep this in mind and be an example of peace and patience all the while remembering that the "dead snakes" may be just what the name suggests, spiritually dead. We must also remember that we are not immune to this selfishness common to all people. God has been patient with us. We are to do the same with others. Only God can change the snakes. It is up to us to simply love them. Look at their good qualities and build upon those. Your attitude is the only attitude you can control and the one to which you must focus your attention. So if you have been chasing dead snakes in your own life...just keep chasing and keep smiling. This is one way to overcome evil with good and one that will not soon be forgotten.

The Thin Place: Ask, Answer, Pray.

Do you tend to the see the glass as half empty or half full?

How do you respond when things don't go your way? Be honest.

Would you say that your life reflects an attitude of hope and joy or an attitude of negativity?

February 25
Monkey on the Menu

From Above: Matthew 7:15-20; I Timothy 4:7-11; I John 4:1-3

Focal Passage: *"Have nothing to do with godless myths and old wives' tales; rather, train yourself to be godly."* –I Timothy 4:7

<u>Here Below</u>:

I'll never forget one family dinner that my family and I enjoyed. We had decided to go out for Chinese cuisine one evening and we went to a restaurant to which our children had never been. It was nicer than most of the Chinese buffets we often frequent. This restaurant was decorated with all forms of traditional Chinese cultural rudiments. There were marble carvings of dragons everywhere along with glass panels on the ceiling with beautiful goldfish engravings. In the background was the hypnotic sound of traditional Chinese flute and harp. The atmosphere was quite breathtaking, especially for my children who had never seen anything like it before. As we took our seats, I watched as the kids looked over their souvenir paper place mat with pictures from the Chinese zodiac calendar. Around the edge were pictures of dragons, monkeys, roosters, boars, rats and other exotic creatures. Each animal had the corresponding years listed from the Zodiac calendar with an analogous description of one born in that year. My oldest son gazed shockingly at the place mat, tossed it aside and said very matter of factly "Dad, if you think I am eating here, you are crazy!" You see, he had mistaken the zodiac calendar for a menu! The idea of monkey or rat on the menu was not at all appetizing to him! Needless to say, we had a good laugh. I tried to explain to him what it meant, but he just thought it was silly. He was right.

What was for us a subject of humor is unfortunately to many a guide by which they try to live their lives. It is always puzzling to me how so many in our day believe what is so obviously a spiritual scam. The same ones that might be quick to dismiss God's Word as myth are often the same ones who are quick to believe in horoscopes and fortune tellers. This is nothing new. People have been fooled by these godless myths for millennia and will continue until Christ's return. Why is it that we are so easily fooled by what scripture teaches us is a trick of the devil? Well, it is because he knows just where to hit us. Being made in the image of God, we are spiritual beings. If we refuse to accept God's truth, we will look for spirituality in other places. Now keep in mind, I am not just talking about those in the world we might consider pagans. It can happen even to those born again. I have had more than one counseling session as a pastor with someone who has fallen victim to some godless myth or teaching. It starts with a neglect of the Bible. When we figuratively push the Bible aside in our lives and reject godliness, we make ourselves vulnerable to lies. God's word is the standard we have to reveal lies for what they are, silly myths. If I believed what that place mat said about me, I would have to divorce my wife and move away, forsaking my family and career. Thank God for His truth! Cling to it! I wasn't born in the year of the boar. I was born right when and where God desired. He is the only One that holds my future.

The Thin Place: Ask, Answer, Pray.

Have you ever been a victim of a spiritual scam? When and why?

How important is the reading and application of God's word to you?

What steps can you take to increase your love for God's word and truth?

February 26
The Best Defense

From Above: Isaiah 51:7-8; Titus 2; James 1:21-27

Focal Passage: *"Do not merely listen to the word, and so deceive yourselves. Do what it says."* –James 1:27

Here Below:

There is an old saying which teaches that the best defense is a good offense. While this is usually applied to sports endeavors and military strategies, it can accurately be applied to Christian living as well. It is no secret that we live in times in which God's truth is coming under fire more and more. In fact, the Bible is being attacked from every angle, including from without and *within* the church. The accuracy and inspiration of the Bible is being called into question with ferocious intensity. It is more important than ever that we do our part to defend the word. However, the best defense of scripture is not what you might think. It is not accomplished in debate or in intellectual wordplay. We do not defend the Bible as we might defend a philosophy or ideal. We defend God's truth by example.

Please do not misunderstand what I am saying. There is definitely a time and place for intellectual debate and we should be mentally prepared for such encounters. However, it has been my experience that winning a debate may cause someone to question their own faulty reasoning, which is good; but, it rarely convinces a soul to pattern their lives after God's Word. It is not enough to prove historically and academically the accuracy of the Bible. We must confirm the spiritual applications of scripture with our own lives. Put simply, it is one thing to tell someone it is true, it is quite another to show them. That is something that agnostics cannot dispute. The open successful application of God's Word is the strongest undisputable form of apologetics and it does not take a PhD to accomplish it.

In Titus 2, we are told to live by a certain pattern laid out by God Himself in His word so that God's word will not be maligned. James basically tells us the same thing with his command. We are not to just read it and even believe it. We are to do God's Word. In doing this, we not only provide a defense of His truth, but it takes the intellectual heat off of us to find the right pattern of living. Think about it. If you are simply trusting and following God's direction, it places the burden of proof (or disproof) on the back of those who might disagree. In other words, God can defend Himself. It is just our task to trust and obey. So if you feel overwhelmed by opposing Biblical views of friends, family or coworkers, don't lose heart and never consider yourself intellectually outmatched! Remember, you have the Holy Spirit of God on your side! Their prowess with words can't hold a match to a living Biblical spirit filled example. Live God's truth unashamedly in front of them and I promise you, truth will ultimately win out.

The Thin Place: Ask, Answer, Pray.

Do you have friends, family or associates with opposing Biblical views?

Are you comfortable debating the accuracy and inspiration of the Bible? If not, why?

What changes can you make in your life that will help better defend the truth of scripture?

February 27
How Many Fingers Am I Holding Up?

From Above: Proverbs 29:18; Psalm 37:3-5; Matthew 6:25-34

Focal Passage: *"Where there is no vision, the people perish: but he that keepeth the law, happy is he."* –Proverbs 29:18 (King James Version)

Here Below:

Recently, as my son was being fitted with his first pair of eyeglasses, I was reminded of when I first received mine. I hated them. They were thick and heavy on my nose and very uncomfortable. To make the experience even more troublesome, they were not very flattering. There weren't as many choices then as we have today. My son had many trendy frames from which to choose. I think I had maybe a dozen and each pair assured my "nerd" classification within the social hierarchy of my schoolmates. Unlike my son whom seemed excited about receiving glasses, I was dreading the experience; that is, until I walked outside of the doctor's office. All of a sudden I was in a whole new world. I could see things that I am not sure I had ever seen before. I could see the leaves at the tops of the trees. I could see birds flying in the air above me. In the background I could make out all the puffy details of the clouds. It was beautiful. With my vision corrected, I could see the world as it was intended. I was still a nerd, but I could see! It was quite overwhelming. In fact, with the danger of sounding of a little "new age", it was more or less a spiritual experience for me. I will never forget my first day of 20/20 vision.

Likewise, 20/20 vision can totally change one's spiritual landscape as well. I am obviously not speaking of physical eyesight, but our spiritual eyesight. Just as with our physical eyes, to see the world as it was intended, we must have 20/20 spiritual vision. Now what do we mean by vision? Well, first of all I think that the verse above taken from Proverbs is often taken out of context. We often use it as an inspirational verse for church growth or a new building fund or whenever we are taking on some new personal task or goal. While it could definitely be applied to those times in our lives, it is actually saying much more than that. This is not simply a verse extolling the value of goal setting. In fact, the NIV version reads "where there is no revelation". The writer is referring to guidance and directions received from God himself. In other words, the warning given here is that when we stop listening to God, we perish. All of the goal setting and striving in the world will not amount to anything if God is not involved in the process. So vision is more than just looking ahead and dreaming big, even though that is good. Vision is trusting in God's direction for tomorrow. It is also knowing that He is capable of seeing and doing more than we can even imagine. Logically speaking, this approach takes some of the pressure off of us as we look into the unknown. Why? Because God's vision is better than 20/20! He sees what we need more than we do. Seeing the world as best as possible through His eyes will open up a whole new world. You can see possibilities never seen before. Surrendering yourself to God brings clarity and purpose to an otherwise blurry landscape. Get your vision checked today! Trust the God who sees.

The Thin Place: Ask, Answer, Pray.

When it comes to looking ahead, does your landscape look a little blurry right now? Or is it clear?

Has there ever been a time when your lack of God given vision caused problems for you?

What can you do differently in your life to help prevent vision loss?

February 28
The Devil is in the Details

<u>**From Above**</u>: Matthew 7:1-5; Romans 14:1-12; Galatians 2:18-21

Focal Passage: *"For none of us lives to himself alone and none of us dies to himself alone."* –Romans 14:7

<u>**Here Below**</u>:

The above passage of scripture contains some very complex principles. It is near impossible to expound upon this verse adequately in only a few short paragraphs, but nevertheless important. It contains a truth that many of us struggle with daily. It is a reminder of God's grace. Oftentimes this passage is mistakenly identified with John Donne's "No man is an island" quotation. While it sounds very similar and could definitely be applied to his very Christian ideal of interpersonal relationships, it does not exactly mean the same. Like all scripture, it must be taken in context for an honest evaluation. In the prior verses we see passages about eating vegetables, judging another man's servant and the Sabbath. Huh? I believe these subjects have more to do with our relationship with God than with others. You see, the implications are there concerning the fact that we have a spiritual responsibility to others, but the emphasis lies primarily in our responsibility to Christ.

Paul was facing a trend toward legalism when he wrote this epistle. He was fighting a form of legalism that still exists today. People were accepting of others based upon their keeping the Jewish laws, specifically concerning what foods they should eat and how they observed the Sabbath. He was fighting tradition. The problem was in the fact that these people were not Jewish. Paul's statement above was a reminder to all that it is not man that we should be trying to please, but God. In fact, from God's perspective we are all in the same category. We are His children. The people were missing this point and failing to rejoice in the building of the Church because they were getting tangled up in the details, details that probably didn't matter much to God in the eternal view of things. There are many things in life that the Bible clearly identifies as sinful and there are other sins not specifically named. There are also things that are morally neutral that can become sinful if the wrong emphasis is placed on them in our lives. We often confuse manmade traditions for God given mandates. What we eat and wear and what time we meet for church are some prime examples, which is exactly what Paul was writing about. Put simply, Paul was reminding us that it is the job of the Holy Spirit of God to convict souls of sin, not ourselves. It is not our calling to "judge another man's servant". Leave that to God. Our job is to try to please God with our own lives, all the while remembering that we all stand in need of God's grace. We are not alone; in that, we all struggle and we all fall occasionally. And we all will eventually answer to God for the use of <u>our</u> time on earth. Meanwhile, we are to simply love God and others sincerely. Leave the details to Him. This simplifies life and frees us to concentrate on our own spiritual growth.

<u>**The Thin Place**</u>: Ask, Answer, Pray.

Has there ever been a time when you tried to place your convictions on someone else? Or vice versa?

What are some convictions you have that might honestly be considered morally and spiritually neutral?

How does the study and application of God's Word keep one from misplacing their convictions?

3

March

March 1
Taking No For An Answer

From Above: Daniel 3:13-30, Matthew 16:24-27

Focal Passage: *"If we are thrown into the blazing furnace, the God we serve is able to save us from it, and he will rescue us from your hand, O king. But even if he does not, we want you to know, O king, that we will not serve your gods or worship the image of gold you have set up"* –Daniel 3:17-18

Here Below:

In the above scripture, we see one of our favorite Old Testament stories. It is an adventure story, a drama, a story of political intrigue and a story of great faith all rolled up into one. It would make for a great motion picture. The epic quality of the story is matched only by the spiritual worth hidden within the account. There is one statement in particular that is perhaps one of the greatest statements of faith ever recorded. It begins with the words "But even if He does not..." Wow! What faith these three young men were expressing with this statement! Facing sure death, in one of the most miserable and cruel ways imaginable, they proclaim their undying devotion to God. They were basically telling old Nebuchadnezzar to do what he must, but to understand that it wouldn't change a thing. They were not going to bow to any idol that day or any day, even if God chose not to deliver them. I am certain that they did not want to burn to death. I imagine they were praying for deliverance. The extraordinary faith being exposed was in the fact that they were prepared to take no for an answer to their prayer.

Many times we forget that God has several options when it comes to how He answers our prayers; at least, our attitudes reflect that we have forgotten. God can say yes to requests. God can say not yet to requests. God can even say no to requests, regardless of the sincerity of the petition. The bottom line is that God, being who He is, can answer our prayers any way He chooses. Not only that, but He owes us no explanation. Too often we seem to approach prayer as if it is some way of manipulating the will of God. Now the Bible is clear that we are to be persistent and sincere in our prayers and petitions. Nevertheless, we should always approach prayer with a seeking attitude and not a demanding attitude. There are those in our day that teach that once certain requirements are met, it is almost as if God is obligated to give us that for which we ask. This "name it and claim it" approach is not Biblical and only leads to disappointment. On the other hand, if we approach God with our needs understanding and acknowledging that <u>He</u> knows what is best for us, our prayers will be answered. The answers may vary, but His nature is constant. The three above mentioned heroes understood that sometimes God says no. That reality didn't change their love for Him one bit. This just meant that He probably had another plan. Boy did He have another plan! As always, His plan was much better than just having them released! His purpose and plan is always better. His "no" is better than my own "yes". Trust the God of the fiery furnace. Trust that His "no" is always for your best.

<u>**The Thin Place**</u>: Ask, Answer, Pray.

How well do you take "no" for an answer when it comes to your prayers? Why?

Have you ever taken matters into your own hands when God didn't answer as you thought He would?

Has God ever used negative circumstances in your life to help you to grow in your faith? How?

March 2
Ambushed!

<u>**From Above**</u>: Luke 11:24-26; 2 Peter 3:17-18; I John 5:1-5

Focal Passage: *"When an evil spirit comes out of a man, it goes through arid places seeking rest and does not find it. Then it says, 'I will return to the house I left."* –Luke 11:24

<u>**Here Below**</u>:

Confidence can be an admirable quality. However, we must be careful to not misplace that confidence. Too often we instead place an unjust amount of confidence in our *own* abilities and strength, especially when it comes to dealing with sin. If not careful, this misplaced self-assurance can lead to a spiritual ambush of sorts. What do I mean by this? Well think about it. How many times has this happened to you? You are struggling with an indwelling sin. This besetting sin is one that you feel definite conviction over and so you become determined to have victory over it. Sounds good so far, huh? Well, you pray and pray and work hard to make necessary changes in your in your life so that you may conquer this sin. Then one day you find that the struggle seems to be gone. You have won. You pat yourself on the back and then forget about it. Time passes. You drop your guard and before you know it, you are right back in the middle of it all over again. You've been ambushed. This leaves you feeling whipped and discouraged. How come we keep coming back to the same sin? This is a question common to us all.

First, we must understand the nature of sin in our lives. As born again believers we have been set free from our sin, yet we must still deal with a sin nature. Paul understood this principle. Even when he wanted to do good, evil was always there trying to trip him up (Romans 7). Even Paul! Well, it must be no different for us. This is why Jesus told us time and again to guard our hearts. We must never drop our guard against indwelling sin. Now don't misunderstand what I am saying! We are no longer slaves to sin. In other words, we can as a believer with the Holy Spirit's help, conquer any sin that weighs us down. It is our choice to either fight it or surrender to it. But it is the nature of sin and evil to always war against the Spirit. This has always been and will always be. Therefore, we must always be on guard. We need never believe that we have arrived at a point of spiritual maturity such that we are no longer in danger of falling victim to sinful desires. If we develop that kind of over self confidence and pride, we are setting ourselves up for another ambush.

Second, we must seek God's help in guarding our hearts. We can only guard it to a certain point and then we are helpless. God on the other hand has endless resources. He alone can subdue sin. He alone can fully protect us and enable us to have victory. In faith in Him we find victory. The guarding of the heart is a never-ending task, but it is one that can sidetrack any ambush. It doesn't just happen. We must be intentional. So stand firm and protect yourself. Guard your heart against the enemy within.

<u>The Thin Place</u>: Ask, Answer, Pray.

Has spiritual complacency ever led to an ambush in your life experiences?

Why do you think we are prone to drop our guards in spiritual matters?

What can you differently to help guard against the return of a besetting sin?

March 3
"I See!" said the Blind Man

<u>From Above</u>: John 9, 20:29

Focal Passage: *"He replied, "Whether he is a sinner or not, I don't know. One thing I do know. I was blind but now I see!"* –John 9:25

<u>Here Below</u>:

The above-mentioned story is perhaps my favorite of all the miracles performed by Christ during His earthly ministry. It is my favorite due to the utter simplicity of it all and the degree to which this simplicity frustrated those who doubted Jesus. By the way, He still has that effect on people today. Here we see a man blind since birth given his sight. Now you would think that everyone would be rejoicing for this man. They all knew him and his family. They had seen him around town many times. They had seen the desperate situation in which he lived. Yet, in spite of the obvious miracle, here comes the Pharisees to throw a spiritual wet blanket on the whole proceeding. It did not work.

I love the simplicity of the blind man's responses to his naysayers. If I didn't know better, I would say that you can almost pick up a hint of sarcasm in his words. When asked to identify Jesus, he basically says "Look, I don't know who He is....All I know is once I couldn't see and now I can!" For Him it was as simple as that. I think there is a lesson to be learned there for us as well. Too often we try to complicate matters of faith. Many of us are like the Pharisees, we need an explanation and we need one that fits our way of thinking. The problem with this is that faith is not about getting an explanation. Faith is about accepting what you cannot explain away with human reasoning. If everything about Jesus could be explained with human intellect and reasoning, then we would not need faith in order to believe. In essence, we would not be trusting in the Lord. We would simply be understanding Him. Faith is about believing in what might seem unbelievable and trusting what might seem unreasonable. God wants more from us that just understanding. God deserves more from us. He wants us take Him at His word, even when we may not understand.

More than one miracle took place that day. More than just this man's eyesight was restored. He found salvation and he found a reason to worship (verse38). It was not because he was trained in theology. It was because he simply believed. His trusting nature allowed Jesus to do something amazing in his life. The same applies to us. Maybe we would see more miracles take place in our lives if we stopped trying to explain everything and just accepted God's works and words by faith. I don't know about you, but I am thankful that my God can't be explained away with human analysis. He is too big and too powerful for that. His words are too mysterious to be written in a text book. They must be written on our hearts. Simply trust and believe and a door will open for God to work a miracle in your life.

The Thin Place: Ask, Answer, Pray.

Do you sometimes require evidence in order to believe in things of a spiritual nature? Why?

Has there ever been a time when you stepped out in faith and received a blessing as a result?

If so, is there any reason to believe that God will not respond to your faith in like manner again?

March 4
Courage at the Crossroads

From Above: Psalm 102:24-27; Jeremiah 6:16; Hebrews 13:7-8
Focal Passage: *This is what the LORD says: "Stand at the crossroads and look; ask for the ancient paths, ask where the good way is, and walk in it, and you will find rest for your souls." –Jeremiah 6:16*

Here Below:

Sooner or later we all come to one. It is inevitable. We can face them with full confidence or we can allow them to bring our life to a spiritual standstill. But accept this as fact; eventually, you will come to a crossroads in your life. We face a crossroads when we find ourselves up against another one of life's inevitable challenges, change. Changing circumstances will eventually force us to make decisions concerning our future. Do we simply accept the change and try to go with the flow? Or do we fight the changes? Do we go this way or that? Sometimes these changes are good, sometimes they are not so good. Nevertheless, they can leave us standing confused in the figurative fork of a road scratching our chin in need of directions. It is an uncomfortable place to be. The change of the day along with the uncertainty of the future is a constant struggle for each of us. Yet, we are not completely unequipped to face the life changing crossroads decisions.

Notice the directions given by God to us in Jeremiah 6:16. The prophet was addressing a people who were definitely at a crossroads in their existence. They were being called back to obedience in the following of the Lord. Their crossroads choice was to follow God or not. But notice the help He provides. He instructs them to look to the "ancient paths". In other words, look to their past. They were to remember the faithfulness of God in their history and apply that faithfulness to their present and future. He understood that in the sea of unending change, there is one rock with which we can tie our boat that does not change with the tide. God is the same today as He was thousands of years ago. Likewise, thousands of years from now, He will be the same as He is today. God's nature never changes. He is the one constant we can depend upon. His faithfulness in our past is an assurance of His faithfulness in the future. Thus believing, we are better equipped to make God honoring decisions at the crossroads points in our life.

There is one danger however. We are to learn from the past, but not to dwell there. Notice the verse above. Look back. Find the good way and then walk in it in the here and now. In other words, a strong past is for nothing if we do not apply the truths learned there to our present. Too often we dwell too long in the past, I believe because of the certainty of it all. It is safe. We know the outcome. The mystery is gone. However, we cannot live there and expect to grow. God's desire is to guide us into our future. So don't fear the crossroad. Try to see the uncertainty of life as an adventure instead of a reason to fear. Seek

His direction at the crossroads and God will be faithful to the adventurer.

The Thin Place: Ask, Answer, Pray.

Do you often find crossroad decisions hard to make?

Has there ever been a time when God's past faithfulness guided your present decisions?

Is it possible to place too much emphasis on your past victories? How so?

March 5
Go To Your Room!

From Above: Psalm 55:17; Matthew 6:1-18; I John 5:14-15

Focal Passage: "But when you pray, go into your room, close the door and pray to your Father, who is unseen. Then your Father, who sees what is done in secret, will reward you." –Matthew 6:6

Here Below:

There was a time in my life in which I would go to the woods behind my house to find solace. In college, it was a specific patch of grass next to the pond behind my dorm. If weather didn't permit, it was simply locked inside my bathroom. As unappealing as that might seem, it was the one place I could escape the frenzied dorm living. I don't think God minded. As a husband and father of four young kids, I now find the back patio to be the most effective place, again when weather permits. During my pastoral office hours, I steal away to the eerie quietness of a deserted church auditorium. These places comprise for me what I believe Jesus is referring to in the above scripture. They are my secret sanctuaries.

In the King James Version of the above passage, we are told to "enter into thy closet" to pray. I like that. Both translations are of course telling us the same thing. Whether we are going to our closet or our room, we are to have a special place set aside in which we can the escape the distractions of the world in order to pray unhindered. I believe this is a passage that can be properly interpreted both literally and figuratively. How? Well, we can pray anywhere and anytime. A private sanctuary is not necessary for communion with God. Our prayer connection to Him is not limited by space and time. His ears are always open to our prayers. However, we live in a world that fights against our prayer life. Put simply, we must be intentional with our prayer lives or else they will be neglected. In a very practical way, by appointing a special place as your prayer closet, you are attempting to shield yourself from the distractions of the world. It may not always work, but it definitely helps and God will honor the attempt.

There is also symbolic importance to having a designated prayer room in your life. By taking the initiative to find a place where you and God can be alone, you are surrendering the next few moments of your life to God. By leaving the hectic nature of life to find a place to pray, you are basically saying to God that communicating with Him is more important than anything else, at least for that moment. It is one small way to express your desire for God's will to take a place of prominence in your life. It is as if you are saying to God "Ok, now I am all yours...!" From experience I can say that God speaks to us anywhere we might be; however, it is those times in my secret places that God's voice has been the clearest. If you do not have one yet, find a peaceful place and designate it as your prayer room or closet. Going there is surrender and worship in the simplest and purest form. You are designating that time and place for God. He longs for time alone with you today! Will you join Him? Go to your room.

The Thin Place: Ask, Answer, Pray.

Do you have a prayer room or closet that you go to regularly?

What distractions do you face when you are trying to have time alone with God?

Looking back, where were you when God's voice has been the clearest?

March 6
WARNING! DO NOT PRAY THIS PRAYER!

<u>**From Above**</u>: Matthew 5:1-16; John 15:1-5; 2 Peter 1:1-8

Focal Passage: *"For if you possess these qualities in increasing measure, they will keep you from being ineffective and unproductive in your knowledge of our Lord Jesus Christ."* –2 Peter 1:8

<u>**Here Below**</u>:

One of the most frightening possibilities of human existence is the thought that at the end of our lives we might look back at the 60, 70 or 80 years we are given and see a life that has not quite lived up to expectations. To see years wasted on things that have no real eternal significance is a prospect that should cause us all to seek preventative alternatives in the here and now. The Christian life is meant to be a life of fruit bearing. Granted, we do not always see the fruit. Sometimes it may be years before the seeds we have planted come to fruition. Nevertheless, we do know in our own hearts if we have attempted to sow fruit bearing seeds in the course of our lifetime or whether we have passed up precious opportunities to plant. I am not sure if anything is sadder than looking back on missed opportunities of usefulness. For this reason we must strive to be daily used of God.

"Use Me!" This is perhaps the most dangerous prayer a person can pray. It is a good prayer and a prayer that God will honor and answer if it is sincere. Nevertheless, it is dangerous and should not be prayed until all the ramifications have been considered. What do I mean by this? Well, being used of God is not always a simple or painless experience. We often aspire to be used of God just as the great heroes of the Bible were used. Consider the disciples for a moment. We would all agree that to be used as they were used is a worthy objective, wouldn't we? Well, just remember that eleven of the twelve disciples were martyred. They were killed as a result of their work. The one that wasn't killed, John, spent most of his days imprisoned on an island. Yet, we would all agree that they were used mightily and were great spiritual successes. You see, being used of God sometimes means allowing Him to work through both pleasant and unpleasant circumstances in your life. In order to bear fruit, God may sometimes have to till our soil a little. I imagine that not one of those early martyrs regret allowing God to use them as He did. Their fruit production is beyond measure. This is not meant to scare you out of serving God, but to encourage you. Don't let circumstances lead you to believe that God is not using you! Time will tell. Your job is to simply be faithful in serving God now. For fruit to grow there is some preparation that must take place. If we are to be used of God and if we want a productive significant life to look back upon, then we must do our part as well. In 2 Peter, the fisherman gives us some insight. We are to fill our lives with things such as faith, goodness, knowledge, self-control, perseverance, godliness, brotherly kindness and love. These ideals put us in a position to be used of God. They are also a preventative to a life of regrets. Are you ready to be used? Are you ready to pray that prayer? Be careful. You never know how God might choose to use you. But know this, you will not regret it.

The Thin Place: Ask, Answer, Pray.

Would you say that that you have planted spiritual seeds in your lifetime?

Would you agree that as long as we have breath, we have opportunities to make a difference?

Are you willing to be used of God, no matter the cost?

March 7
Honest To God...

From Above: Psalm 34:18; Psalm 51; Matthew 9:9-13

Focal Passage: *"Surely you desire truth in the inner parts; you teach me wisdom in the inmost place."* –Psalm 51:6

Here Below:

As I stuck my head in through the bathroom door, I could see my two sons playing in the bathtub, blissfully unaware of my presence. It was almost time for them to get out of the tub and it was my turn to help them. As I watched on in silence, I noticed that my two year old son seemed to be coughing a little as if he had swallowed something that didn't taste good. I entered and immediately could see what it was he had taken into his mouth. "Have you been eating soap?" I asked. I'll never forget his answer. He looked at me with those big round brown eyes and said "Nope!" As he spoke the word, a bubble formed in his mouth and broke free, floating away from his shiny wet face leaving him without an explanation. I couldn't help but laugh at his attempt to hide the truth from his father. However, the truth was all over his face, literally. In fact, it was dripping from his chin and floating around the room. His expression was timeless. As cute as this innocent scene might have been, lying is not cute. It is even less cute when we try it with our God. Likewise, the truth is usually all over our face.

You may be thinking that this is a no brainer. After all, how can we lie to God? Well, we can't and get by with it, but that doesn't keep us from trying. Oftentimes, we aren't exactly honest with God when we go to Him in prayer. We often withhold certain confessions. Likewise, we are also guilty of sugar coating our sinfulness from time to time. This spiritual dishonesty can be for several reasons. First, it may be due to the fact that we are simply ashamed of our sinfulness. This is not necessarily a bad thing. We should be offended by sin, both that of others and that of our own. However, withholding the truth of sin is not God's will for us. Second, it could be rebellion, plain and simple. We may think that if we don't speak it, God will not be forced to deal with it. Therefore, we are off the hook. This is of course not true. Both approaches to our sinfulness only lead to deeper feelings of guilt and shame. This is not God's desire. The Cross was God's way of freeing us from any burdensome feelings of guilt or shame. Herein is the reality of being honest with God. He already knows our innermost thoughts anyway. You are only lying to yourself by withholding the truth. Besides, there is nothing you might have done or thought that He has not already seen a million times. Nothing you do can shock God. Now I do not say that to make light of sin. On the contrary, our sinfulness should make us sick. This sin sickness should drive us to repentance. It is there that we find true liberation. Holding back the truth from God is futile and only serves to cause us more discomfort. There is a genuine relief that comes when we are honest with God. So don't hold back! Open up to one whose love is unconditional. God can handle the truth.

The Thin Place: Ask, Answer, Pray.

Have you ever held back the truth or lied in your conversations with God? What was the result?

Have you ever experienced the feeling of complete freedom that comes when we honestly confess sin?

Are there any unconfessed sins right now which you need to honestly share with God?

March 8
A Country Never Visited

From Above: I Corinthians 2:9-10; Philippians 3:17-21; Colossians 3:1-2

Focal Passage: *"No eye has seen, no ear has heard, no mind has conceived what God has prepared for those who love him"* –I Corinthians 2:9

Here Below:

C. S. Lewis once wrote in reference to the reality of Heaven of his "inconsolable longing...for news from a country we have never visited." In this statement he is referring to a longing that should exist in the heart of all that look forward to their eternal destination. In fact, I would say that this longing exists in the hearts of most, if not all; even those whom we might refer to as non-believers. We are designed to crave existence beyond our earthly residence. The proof is easily seen as we look at the various cultures around the world. The afterlife is part of every culture's belief system in one form or another. They are all very different. Some are even bizarre, to say the least. As with all places though, if we want an accurate description, we usually seek out someone that has been there and back. Likewise, with Heaven it is no different. If we want a true explanation, we need to seek someone that has been there. In other words, for an accurate description of Heaven, we need to seek Jesus' description in His word, the Bible.

The problem is that God gives us a very limited description of Heaven in the Bible. We read symbolically about walls of jasper and streets where gold is used as asphalt. We also know that there will be no tears there. As a whole though, we are left with more questions than answers. We are left with questions about relationships in Heaven, worship in Heaven and many others. Believe me, as a Pastor, I have heard them all. More than once I've been asked by a well meaning child (and adult) concerning the eternal destiny of their deceased pet! I don't think God left us with these questions to frustrate us. On the contrary, I believe He did it for our good. God always knows just what we need. It is no different with our understanding of Heaven. He gave us just enough to keep us looking and asking. He gave us just enough to wet our appetites for a place we have never seen. However, we are not left with doubt. Jesus Himself refers to Heaven many times. Therefore, we can know without a doubt that Heaven is a real place. We can also rest assured that it is a place where we will want to dwell, if for no other reason than Jesus will be there. Looking to Heaven gives us strength for earth. Therefore, God's withholding of answers on Heaven must be intentional. We are told in the above scripture that no mind has ever conceived what is in store for those who love Him. Wow! Historically there have been some pretty beautiful artistic and academic conceptions of Heaven. Well, according to scripture, those descriptions fall terribly short. Aren't you thankful that the real Heaven is beyond human description and understanding? What a love

God must have for us to prepare such a place! What a difference that reality should make for us now! Look forward to Heaven in your future, but live for Heaven today!

The Thin Place: Ask, Answer, Pray.

Have you ever doubted the existence of Heaven? Why?

How does a genuine belief in Heaven affect how you face both good and bad times in the present?

Do you ever catch yourself longing for Heaven? Do you ever share this longing with others?

March 9
The View from Straight Street

From Above: I Samuel 16:7; Acts 9:1-22; I Corinthians 2:16

Focal Passage: *"All those who heard him were astonished and asked, "Isn't he the man who raised havoc in Jerusalem among those who call on this name?"* –Acts 9:21

Here Below:

If he were living today, we would call him a terrorist. He was a man with a simple mission. His mission was to eradicate this new band of rebels that would later come to be known as Christians, using whatever means at his disposal. He hunted them down, turned them in and even participated in their murders. His name was Saul. We of course all know him best as the Apostle Paul. It was no wonder the early believers had a hard time accepting his teaching and preaching at first. In the above passage we see Christians questioning his credentials, as we all would. After all, this was the man that just a few days prior had been trying to destroy them! Yet what they couldn't see was that God was seeing him from a different perspective. God didn't see "Saul the Persecutor". Instead, God saw "Paul the Apostle to the Gentiles". Who could have guessed that the same man that held the jackets of those who were stoning Stephen would one day write the "great love chapter" of I Corinthians 13? Who could have guessed that this now blind man on Straight Street would one day stand before kings in defense of the gospel? Well, I can answer that for you. God did.

One of the great frustrations of human existence is our inability to see in others and in ourselves all that God sees. We often make erroneous assumptions about others and even about our own futures. We get frustrated when things don't go our way. What we fail to see is that God may have a plan that is beyond what we can see. His perspective is that of a holy, righteous, all-knowing, all-powerful and all-loving God. Rightfully so, this is a perspective we can never totally achieve. Nevertheless, we are to strive to have the mind of Christ. In other words, we are to try to see life from God's point of view. This means several things. First, we must view others as does God; which means recognizing that God may have a plan for the Saul's in your life. He may want to turn them into a Paul. At the very least, He loved them enough to die for them. In turn, we are to love them as well. Second, we must also try to view circumstances from His perspective. God has an uncanny ability to use even bad times for His own good. Take the above passage for example. This persecution of the church in the book of Acts was the reason the Christians scattered all over the world, carrying with them the Gospel message. God used it for His purposes. He can use your circumstances as well. Sometimes to see the big picture means changing seats. It may mean going to our own figurative Street Called Straight and taking another look at ourselves and others. You will be amazed by the view. And you may be surprised at what He sees...

The Thin Place: Ask, Answer, Pray.

Has God ever surprised you by using unlikely circumstances or people for His purposes?

Are you ever frustrated by the uncertainty of the future?

How does trusting in God change the way you should view the uncertainties of the human experience?

March 10
The "Meekling"

From Above: Psalm 25:1-10; Matthew 5:1-12
Focal Passage: *"The meek will He guide in judgment: and the meek will He teach His way."* –Psalm 25:9 (KJV)
Here Below:

"We are gonna miss him so much. He is so gentle and meek. Whenever he is around, we just get the feeling that everything is going to be all right..." These were the words spoken to me years ago by a friend from a sister church after inquiring about the resignation of her pastor. She described him as gentle and meek. These qualities were his strengths and they are at the heart of his success as a pastor. He had like so many others encountered some difficulties in the pastorate. He was able to overcome them, not with an iron fist of force, but with meekness and gentleness. As a result, his church flourished in a time when many would have crashed. I remember thinking to myself that day that I would like to have that said of me one day as well. It is a worthy goal for all of us and a quality expressed perfectly in the example of our Savior.

There are great misconceptions concerning the definition of meekness. Meekness is not to be confused with weakness. Now there are times when it is used in scripture to describe the poor. There are also times when it is used to describe those who are "down and out" in other ways as well. The NIV Bible often translates the word "meek" into the word "humble". However, I am going to take it one step further with my very own loose translation. It seems to imply a form of spiritual contentment. This contentment is not damaged by sticky circumstances, whether it is finances, health, or anything that might cause us to be discouraged. It instead implies a degree of trust that exists in knowing that God will take care of us, regardless of what the day looks like. It is understanding that it is God, not we, that should be in charge of our lives. This form of surrender to God's will leads to a peace and contentment that nothing else in the world can offer. This calm coolness that comes with meekness is not a sign of weakness. On the contrary, it shows a great degree of self control in the face of adversity. This self control is a sign of strength. It takes a stronger person to control our human instinct to retaliate, to express anger and to make our will known than it does to remain meek and gentle. No one would ever describe Jesus as being a weakling; yet, he was meek. In this meekness, He was strong enough to take upon Himself the sins of the world. Likewise, by exhibiting meekness, we are opening ourselves up to be used in a mighty way by God.

Put aside self today and surrender your will to God. Don't be a weakling! Be a "meekling" instead.

The Thin Place: Ask, Answer, Pray.

What circumstances have you encountered in which you found it difficult to remain meek and gentle?

What message does meekness send to those around you in everyday life?

How might an improved spirit of meekness better enable you to be used by God in your life?

March 11
God is Great...Like it or Not!

From Above: Job 38, 42:10-17

Focal Passage: *"Where were you when I laid the earth's foundation? Tell me, if you understand."*-Job 38:4

Here Below:

There was a dialogue I once witnessed in a movie in which a person was declaring their unbelief in God. After proclaiming their atheism, the other person responded with a statement that has far reaching implications. They basically said to the self proclaimed atheist that God's existence was not dependent upon their belief in Him. God was going to be Himself whether this person believed in His existence or not and whether he agreed with God or not. I am not sure if that is the best way to win over an atheist; nonetheless, it is true. It is pride that suggests otherwise. While God is worthy of our worship and praise and desires our worship and praise, He is not dependent upon it. Put simply, God can do as He pleases and doesn't owe man an explanation of His ways, just as He tells Job above. For chapters prior to this one, God listened to the back and forth dialogue between Job and his friends. All seemed to have advice to give Job. At the heart of it is the idea that God had been unfair to an otherwise just man. There were those who told him to curse God. There were those questioning God's actions, including Job. Let's not be too quick to judge him for that. After all, he had experienced a degree of grief the likes of which most of us will never face. He had questions as any of us probably would. Yet, after chapters and chapters of questions and advice, God decides to speak up. In what might seem sarcastic from anyone else, God speaks out of the midst of the storm. "Where were you...?" He says. Good question!

He is basically reminding Job of what he already knew. If God can handle the mechanics of creation on His own, He can handle our problems. While He loved Job, He owed him nothing. Please do not misunderstand. God was not being prideful or arrogant. He was stating fact. How many times do we question God's actions or inactions as if we somehow know better? How many times have we heard questions like "How could a loving God let such bad things happen to good people?" These are real questions; nevertheless, God's greatness is not lessened by our misfortune. Death, sickness and troubles come as a result of a fallen world, not because of God. Even in the extreme case of Job, God had a purpose, which included blessing Job beyond anything he had known. We may not get an explanation this side of Heaven for things that happen. That is ok. Trusting in God means accepting His greatness, regardless of circumstances. How? By recognizing that God's unlimited power goes hand in hand with His unlimited love!

While He owes us nothing, out of love He has given us explanation in His word. Everything He has done from creation to the cross and beyond is grounded in His love for us. God is God. We are His beloved children. That is enough explanation for me. How about you?

The Thin Place: Ask, Answer, Pray.

Have you ever questioned God? Be honest.

How easy is it to accept that God may answer those questions and He may not?

Why is understanding God's omnipotence important to the Christian life, specifically yours?

March 12
Now or Later

From Above: Ecclesiastes 9:1; Ecclesiastes 12; Hebrews 11:23-26

Focal Passage: *"So I reflected on all this and concluded that the righteous and the wise and what they do are in God's hands, but no man knows whether love or hate awaits him."*-Ecclesiastes 9:1

Here Below:

If one is not careful, it would be easy to come away from the above passage (along with most of Ecclesiastes) feeling as if nothing in life really matters. We might think that life is just a futile struggle for a short time and then we die. But we cannot stop reading Ecclesiastes until we get to the end of the book or else we miss the point. You see, in the above verse the writer comes to the conclusion that life is uncertain at best. After experiencing all that life has to offer, he realized that even a righteous person may find life to be complicated at times. Even if we live what we would consider a "good" life or a wise life, there is no guarantee of instant reward. We can't predict whether we will receive in turn love or hate, good or bad. Yet, in the end of his quest, the great Teacher of Ecclesiastes found that even in the midst of an uncertain reward, it is still to our gain to serve God faithfully.

What did He find that brought him to this conclusion? He recognized what many others before him had discovered.

Take Moses for example. In the great faith chapter of Hebrews, Moses is listed among the greatest heroes of faith. In so, he is keeping company with such heroes as Abraham, Isaac, Joseph and Jacob. We would all quickly agree with his placement in this roster and in verse 26 we see why. It teaches that Moses thought disgrace for the cause of Christ was better than any earthly reward. We are told that he kept looking forward to his reward. He wasn't expecting any great pat on the back in the here and now. After all, he was just being obedient. Why should he be rewarded for doing what he was told to do? Faith is about being obedient whether we receive recognition or not, all the while knowing that our reward will come at a later time. This is why Jesus tells us over and over in the gospels that we are to serve as to not be seen by men, but by God. Our reward is coming, in His time. Trusting the fact that God rewards those who faithfully follow Him and at the same time understanding that it may or may not be during our life time will change how well you handle the joys and the troubles of life.

We often become discouraged when a reward for righteous living is not immediate. If not viewed through eyes of faith, we can as a result become reluctant to put ourselves in that place of service again. If reward is your motivation for service, then you may find yourself disappointed. Service is to be done out of love and a holy reverence for God. The reward may come now and it may be later. He may wait until Heaven is your home to reward you. It is God's choice. But God is true to His word; He will reward the faithful. Our drive should be like that of Moses. We need to trust in the reward ahead and stop worrying about receiving it now. Don't worry about the trophy until you have first completed the race.

The Thin Place: Ask, Answer, Pray.

How willing are you to do acts of service that will probably go unnoticed by others?

Have you ever felt as if your faithfulness had gone unnoticed by God?

What rewards have you received for faithfulness and how do you think they will compare to Heaven?

March 13
The Errand Boy

<u>**From Above**</u>: I Samuel 17; Mark 9:35; Colossians 3:17

Focal Passage: *Sitting down, Jesus called the Twelve and said, "If anyone wants to be first, he must be the very last, and the servant of all."*-Mark 9:35

<u>**Here Below**</u>:

I once heard a man share his testimony of when he first came to faith in Christ. For years the church bus had come to his house every Sunday to pick up his children for church, which he gratefully welcomed. It wasn't until years later that he personally accepted the Lord unto salvation. After his conversion, he was so overwhelmed with a sense of making up for all the years of ignoring God that he desperately sought any way in which he might serve God. The only way he could find to serve the Lord at first was by volunteering to wash that same church bus that had come to his house for all those years. He said "I would have licked that bus clean if that is what it took to show God how grateful I was for saving me." It wasn't until a while later, after years of serving God in ways such as this, that God finally called him to preach. I think he understood what Jesus was talking about in the above passage. There is no job too small if it is being done for the Lord.

Perhaps every young boy's favorite Bible story is that of a young shepherd boy slaying the great giant Goliath. We all dream of being that mighty warrior rushing the field ahead of all and saving the day. Yet, what we often forget as we read this story is that David didn't go there that day to pick a fight. He didn't go there to slay a giant or to try to impress his king. He was carrying a bread and cheese sandwich to his brothers. He was their errand boy. He, unlike his brothers, was not able to spend day after day in the midst of this adventure. He had to tend his father's sheep while the rest of them had all the fun. This wasn't the only time this happened to David. Do you remember when Samuel was going to anoint him as king? Even his own father didn't think about including him in the lineup of kingly candidates with his brothers. He was in the fields with the sheep, faithfully carrying out his duties. Yet, in both situations God chose the errand boy. Why? Perhaps it was due to David's servant spirit. After all, he was a man after God's own heart. Was Jesus not the "Suffering Servant" of men?

The lesson here for each of us is that service unto the Lord is great, regardless of how mundane or inglorious it may seem. Our willingness is more important to God than our abilities, strengths and social status. So whether it is washing the church bus, mopping floors, cutting grass, changing diapers or whatever else may come along, do it for the Lord. Your work will not go unnoticed by the one that matters the most. There are no small jobs when it comes to our big God. Who knows where that seemingly insignificant task may lead when done for the Lord? Will you be God's errand boy?

The Thin Place: Ask, Answer, Pray.

Has there ever been a time when you felt as if your act of service was insignificant?

What are some of the less glamorous acts of service in your home, church and community?

What would happen if these acts went undone? What new ways can you serve in this manner?

March 14
The View from the Top

From Above: Psalm 46; 2 Timothy 1:7

Focal Passage: *"For God hath not given us the spirit of fear; but of power, and of love, and of a sound mind."*-2 Timothy 1:7

<u>Here Below</u>:

Along the back of my former yard were countless Chinaberry trees. These trees really aren't good for much of anything. They make a mess in your yard with those sticky berries that they shed. Not only that, but they don't really grow big enough to even be used as a shade tree. They are not very attractive and basically do nothing to ascetically improve the landscape. However, they do have one redeeming quality. Their bark is fairly smooth and their limbs grow in such a way as to make a good climbing tree. So with the ease of which you can climb one along with the arsenal they provide with those berries, these trees make a natural playground for the children. Climbing a tree such as these can be an adventure for the children or for the childlike. More than once however, I have been delivered a desperate message from one of my kids that one of the others had climbed too high and couldn't get back down. I then had to go to the rescue and get them down. I am not too critical of this mistake though. After all, what kid hasn't dreamt of the view from the highest limb only to reach it and find the trip back down was too treacherous? As I consider those trees and my children, I often wonder what it is that drives them to climb higher than what is safe. Is it a longing to see the world from the top or could it be that they know that if they climb too high that their father is there to rescue them? Is that the key to their courage? I think it is.

Countless times in scripture, Jesus begins His encounter with individuals by saying these words, "Fear Not!" Time and again we are told to fear not, to trust in God and to call upon Him in our times of need. It is a reoccurring theme throughout the word of God. It is almost as if God wants us to reach for that highest limb. Too often we fail to reach our spiritual potential due to fear. Yet, we are told that as children of God, we do not have a spirit of fear, but of power. In other words, God is ultimately going to be there to help us down when we climb too high. The problem with succumbing to our fear is that we never see the view from the top of the tree. We miss out on the blessing of reaching farther than we can on our own strength and we miss the blessing of having God steady us when our spiritual knees begin to tremble. Now I am not talking about foolishly going where we should not go. I am referring to the refusal to settle for the easy path or the easy climb. God desires for us to reach! He wants to perform amazing acts in each of our lives. For that to happen we must be willing to climb higher. Are you reaching for the highest limb or are you content with the ones in reach? Nothing is beyond the reach of our God. Have faith in Him and climb with the courage that comes in knowing your Father is there to catch you if you fall. The view from the top is worth it...

The Thin Place: Ask, Answer, Pray.

Have you ever failed to reach your fullest potential due to the fact that you didn't try?

If so, what kept you from reaching higher and further?

Is there anything that God couldn't do with your life if it was fully surrendered to Him?

March 15
Keep the Change

From Above: I Samuel 10:1-10; Ephesians 2:13-22; 2 Corinthians 5:17

Focal Passage: *"As Saul turned to leave Samuel, God changed Saul's heart, and all these signs were fulfilled that day."*-I Samuel 10:9

Here Below:

In the story above from I Samuel, we see the anointing of King Saul. In it we also see an interesting little phrase that we might easily overlook. It says that "God changed Saul's heart". After experiencing three different verifications of God's purpose in his life, Saul's heart was changed. This is an important passage because it shows us once again that God is, has been and will always be in the business of changing hearts and lives. While this passage does not have the same implications as the New Testament passages concerning rebirth, it does show us what is important to God. God desires change to take place in the heart of His children. In fact, we are told that we are renewed day by day (2 Corinthians 4:16). In other words, we exist in a constant state of change, or more appropriately, a constant state of growth.

The problem we encounter is that we often do not like what change suggests. It suggests letting go of things with which we are comfortable. For God to change our heart means changing our wants and desires and adopting instead His wants and desires. This can sometimes be frightening. We do not like surrendering our will in exchange for that of someone else, even if it is God's. It requires trusting in something we cannot see. It requires faith.

As we read on in the life of Saul, we see that he had a difficult time with the change God was bringing in his life. Eventually, he let his own will supersede that of God and it brought about his downfall. You see, God, kind as He is, will only change our heart to the degree that we are willing to allow. He will never force His change upon us. We must desire it. Likewise, it doesn't happen all of a sudden. In fact, it takes a lifetime to develop fully the desire for more of Christ in our lives. This is why it is a daily task. Each day we are to start fresh in our surrendering of will. Each day we are to start over with our letting go of self. Each day we are to welcome His change. While it is a change we allow, it is also a change only God can bring into completion. Remember, it is God's business to change. Our job is to simply follow and trust in Him.

The Thin Place: Ask, Answer, Pray.
Would you say that you welcome change or are you resistant to change?
How exactly is the Christian life a life of change? Do we ever stop changing as a Christian?
What changes do you think God desires for your life right now?

March 16
Crossing the Line

From Above: Jude 1-25

Focal Passage: *"To him who is able to keep you from falling and to present you before his glorious presence without fault and with great joy--"*-Jude 24

Here Below:

I have heard it said before concerning a fear of heights, "It is not the fall I am afraid of...It is the sudden stop at the end!" How many of us can relate to that statement? We all have our phobias to some degree. These phobias can turn a grown man into a frightened child. Some may seem silly to us, but to the person with the phobia, it is a serious matter. Likewise, there is one phobia that can be spiritually overwhelming and crippling. It is a fear that I have encountered among many a sincere Christian in times of trial and personal disappointment in their own lives. It is the fear that one might have crossed the line and committed some particular sin or committed enough sin that they fear that they have lost their salvation. We might say that this fear of crossing the line is the fear of "falling from grace."

I do not wish to make light of this fear. After all, I have met many who have struggled with this concern; but I do not necessarily think of this apprehension as a bad thing. This struggle implies a concern for their own spiritual well-being. This is the first step toward victory over those besetting sins we struggle with from day to day. However, I do believe that scripture assures us that this fear is ungrounded.

The book of Jude, thought to have been written by the half brother of Jesus, gives us reason for assurance. He opens the letter in verse 1 and closes it in verse 24-25 with a reminder to us that we are "kept" by Jesus. In other words, Jesus is strong enough to keep us saved. The erroneous premise many begin with when expressing worry over their eternal security is that something they have done <u>is able</u> to cause the loss of their salvation. This is wrong for a very simple reason. Nothing we have done resulted in our salvation. We did not save ourselves. It is foolish to think then that I am capable of undoing my salvation. I cannot undo what only God was strong enough to do in the first place. It was Jesus' sacrifice that saved me. Now, Jude addresses the fact that this assurance is not a license to sin. On the contrary, it should be a motivation for grateful living, expressed by a desire for righteousness. It is also an encouragement to know that nothing and no one, including myself and my enemies, can take from me what only God could give. His grip is too strong. I can face a battlefield or a hospital bed knowing that my eternity is secure. I don't have to fear the sudden stop at the end! Whatever happens, I am in the grip of God. With this security comes freedom and strength. Trust in the grip of God.

The Thin Place: Ask, Answer, Pray.

Has there ever been a time when you thought you might have lost your salvation?

Are there any sins that you feel are not covered by the sacrifice of Jesus?

What difference does your eternal security make in your everyday approach to life?

March 17
Don't Make Him Laugh!

From Above: Psalm 37:1-13; Proverbs 3:31-35; James 4:4-7

Focal Passage: *"The wicked plot against the righteous and gnash their teeth at them; but the Lord laughs at the wicked, for he knows their day is coming."*-Psalm 37:12-13

Here Below:

Why is it that the bad boys always seem to get the girl? Why is it some cheats and frauds can get away with millions with only a slap on the wrist while the average Joe can't get a break on even the most minor offense? How is it that the evil in our day can figuratively get away with murder and go seemingly unpunished or even thrive while those trying to live a righteous life struggle just to stay afloat? These are questions I have been asked and have asked myself. I believe they are fair questions, though not easily answered. The more I study scripture, the more I see that these types of questions are as old as mankind itself. In Psalm 37, David addresses the issue in a song. This must have been for a reason. There must have been those crying out for justice in his day. This Psalm was meant to be a comfort to any who might be feeling as if God hadn't noticed the inequities of life.

In the above verse, we find our answer to these age old questions in an aspect of God's nature not often attributed to Him. It says that "the Lord laughs"! How about that? While we are fretting over the evil flourishing apparently unhindered, God is laughing at them. Now, let's be careful to not read this as some sort of indifference or apathy concerning evil. On the contrary, it is a reminder of just how serious God does view evil and sin. He is also not laughing at their actions. His Son went to the cross because of these actions. He is laughing at the fact that they and we tend to think that it has gone unnoticed. In a very real sense, He is laughing at our own self-assuredness. To think that we can do anything out of God's line of sight is laughable to Him. He knows their day is coming, as is ours! However, as we read about God laughing at humanity's overconfidence, we must remember that Jesus wept as he looked over a lost Jerusalem. You see, God's hatred of sin and His love for the sinner go hand in hand.

God is able to see our lives from an eternal perspective which we cannot yet see. He sees eighty years or so on this earth as a moment in eternity. Our short time here determines our eternity. A few "moments" of faith here and then we have forever in Heaven. That is one inequity I don't mind! Thank God for this imbalance! I would much rather receive His mercy and grace than His justice. So the next time you begin to think that it is unfair that the evil often prosper, remember that their day is coming and so is yours. In the meantime, we should concern ourselves with our own destiny and that of our loved ones and neighbors, all the while simply trusting that God knows what He is doing. After all, isn't that the definition of faith? Trust in the God who laughs.

The Thin Place: Ask, Answer, Pray.

Have you ever fretted over the prosperity of the ungodly in your life experiences?

Is it possible that God's patience is the reason for His withholding punishment? Or His love for sinners?

Has there ever been a time when God withheld punishment for your sins?

March 18
The Pleasing Priority

From Above: 2 Corinthians 5; Ephesians 5:8-10

Focal Passage: *"So we make it our goal to please him, whether we are at home in the body or away from it."*-2 Corinthians 5:9

Here Below:

How much of our time do we spend trying to meet the requirements of others, both perceived and actual? At work, we have bosses to satisfy and the customer is always right. In our relationships there are expectations with which we often struggle to meet. The problem with these scenarios is that sometimes the boss is impossible to satisfy, the customer is not always right and those with whom we have relationships can be unreasonable. Pleasing people can be a very taxing endeavor. In fact, I believe that much of the stress we encounter in our time is a result of overcompensating attempts to please others. This overwhelms us eventually, due to the fact that it can never be completely accomplished. It is impossible to please everyone all of the time.

Paul understood this fact all too well. Even the Apostle Paul had those whom could not be pleased with his words and actions. However, in the above passage, he reminds us of whom we are to strive to please. He tells us that pleasing God should take priority, even to the point of physical death. In times when others may not understand our choices or even like our choices, our first concern should always be pleasing our Lord. His opinion should matter more than even that of our closest confidants. If they truly know us and love us then they will understand. Sure, there are times when we must strive to please others, such as in a work or family situation; nonetheless, if pleasing others contradicts God's will, then it is time to reevaluate.

Is this easier said than done? Perhaps. Yet, with God's Holy Spirit help, we can reset our pleasing priority. In pleasing God first, we free ourselves of the burden of being stretched too far and too thin. Likewise, we are better equipped to handle criticism when it inevitably comes. Not to oversimplify the matter, but if God is pleased, the opinions of others don't seem so major. Yes, we are to give of our best in service to others; but we do this not to please them, but to please God. So smile as you face that impossible boss or that cranky customer. Remember that God will be pleased with your Christ-like attitude. Please Him first and the others will take care of themselves.

The Thin Place: Ask, Answer, Pray.

Do you ever get frustrated by trying to meet the expectations of others?

Do the expectations of others ever contradict what you know to be God's will for your life?

How different would your relationships be if your first priority was to live for the Lord and His purposes?

March 19
Get Back Up!

From Above: John 21:15-25; Acts 2
Focal Passage: *"Those who accepted his message were baptized, and about three thousand were added to their number that day."*-Acts 2:41

<u>Here Below</u>:

Probably the most beloved disciple is Peter. We love him because in him we see parts of ourselves. Peter was just a "good ol' boy" with which we can all relate. Even though Peter often suffered from "foot in mouth disease", no one would ever question his loyalty; that is, no one but himself. With all his greatness, probably the most oft remembered event from his life is the denial of Christ on the night of His arrest. It was a terrible night that Peter had thought he was prepared to face. Yet, as we all do from time to time, Peter stumbled when the circumstances turned sour. Can you imagine the heartache he must have felt as the rooster crowed that next morning? Here is the key to this story though. Jesus knew Peter would deny Him. He predicted it. He expected it. He also knew it when He gave Peter His name, which translated means "the Rock". He knew what Peter was capable of becoming. Even as Peter swore to never forsake Christ, Jesus knew He would. Yet, let's not forget that Peter did lob off a Roman Officer's ear in the defense of Jesus on the same night. He was no coward. He just had a moment of weakness as do we all. Nevertheless, this event must have been devastating for the fisherman we all love.

Yet, just days later we see this man, who had been afraid to admit to a servant girl in the courtyard that He even knew Jesus, preaching to crowds of thousands. In one day three thousand souls were added to the Kingdom. What made the difference? Where did this courage come from? Well, he had been restored by the resurrected Christ and filled with the Holy Spirit of God. On the beach that morning, Jesus very lovingly encouraged him to get back up again. Three times Peter denied. Three times Jesus questioned his loyalty. He did this not to shame Peter, but to assure him of His love. In this conversation, Jesus was letting Peter know that God still had a purpose for His life.

This story is so special because it is for every "good ol' boy or girl" out there that has ever stumbled and fell. Jesus came to save us, not to condemn us. He knew Peter. He knows you as well. He knows what you are capable of if you will only submit yourself to Him. He knows what He can do with your surrendered heart. He is never done with us because of a failure. He just wants us to get back up, knock off the dirt and go at it again. Let Jesus restore you today.

The Thin Place: Ask, Answer, Pray.

Has there ever been a time when you denied Christ with your words or actions?

How serious are your failures compared to that of Peter's?

Is there any reason why God wouldn't do the same for you as He did for Peter? Ask Him.

March 20
My Last Day on Earth!

From Above: Psalm 39:1-7; James 4:13-17

Focal Passage: "*Show me, O LORD, my life's end and the number of my days; let me know how fleeting is my life.*"-Psalm 39:4

Here Below:

I was once asked by a teacher to explain what I might do today if I knew that today would be my last day upon this earth. Now I ask you the same thing. What would you do? Would you spend the day eating your favorite foods and engaging in your favorite activities? Would you do something you've always wanted to do, but never had the chance? Would you go somewhere you've always wanted to go? Or would you spend it in the quiet of your home surrounded by those closest to you? Would you maybe spend it trying to right some wrongs? I guess there is no right or wrong answer to the question. Everyone would face that day differently. However, the unfortunate reality is that more times than not, we are not aware of it being our last day on earth until it is too late. We are not guaranteed a death bed exit with a lengthy preparation time. Yet, we are all guaranteed an exit. As far as we know, this day may truly be our last day upon this earth.

How then do we live, if the length of our lives is so uncertain? Well, to borrow from an overworked yet appropriate cliché, we live each day as if were the last. This means making sure there is nothing left undone in our lives. Spiritual procrastination can lead to regrets in that final moment. Throughout scripture there is an urgency to settle things quickly both with God and with others. We are implored to heal broken relationships as soon as possible. We are told that now is the time for our salvation (2 Corinthians 6:2). It is a reoccurring theme throughout scripture to make the most of each day. Take care of what really matters now so that when that day comes, you can face it with everything settled.

These words are not meant to depress us as we think about the fleeting nature of life. On the contrary, it is healthy to consider. It is meant to help us seek the abundant life right now, instead of putting it off until later. David understood the weight of regrets when he wrote this Psalm; yet, he also knew the solution. After singing of the brevity of life, he states that "My hope is in You" (Psalm 39:7). To live every day as if God were coming for us soon means to live a life that pleases Him. This lifestyle leaves us regret free. I hope that day is a long time away for both you and me. However, the question remains. What if today was your last day upon this earth? Are you ready?

The Thin Place: Ask, Answer, Pray.

Are there any words that need to be spoken to loved ones that you have been putting off?

Are there any unreached goals in your life that could still be attained?

Is there anything you would regret not doing if today were your last day? Be honest.

March 21
Louder than Words

From Above: Matthew 7:18-20; James 2:14-26

Focal Passage: *"As the body without the spirit is dead, so faith without deeds is dead."*-James 2:26

<u>Here Below</u>:

I heard someone once described as being "so heavenly minded that there were of no earthly good." Have you ever met anyone like that? They talk a good talk. They may even be able to quote chapter and verse from scripture. Yet, when it comes to living a life of faith, they offer very little. In fact, these types of "Christians" often get in the way of the gospel message. They can do more harm than good for the Kingdom. Many times I have encountered those who want nothing to do with Christianity due to an encounter with one of the many "hypocrites" within the church. Unfortunately, they may be true in many instances. Nevertheless, as I see it, there is always room for one more. The Christian life is about growing by God's grace. If we are honest about it, we can all be a little insincere from time to time. There is nevertheless a definite need for greater consistency between our message and our walk.

In fact, James addresses this in Chapter 2 of his letter to the church. The book of James is probably the most practical letter in the New Testament. He addresses the fact that our lives should match our speech. In the above passage, we see what is a controversial passage for many. Some struggle with it because they feel it paints a thin line between a grace based and a works based salvation. I think it teaches just the opposite. In no way does it claim that our salvation comes as result of works or deeds. Instead, it teaches that works come as a result of real faith. The deeds are the proof, not the means.

He goes on to teach that just like a body without a spirit is useless or dead, so is a faith without deeds. Our deeds are in one sense our spiritual pulse. If we can't detect that pulse, the faith must be dead. A dead body is not really good for much, is it? It only gets in the way. If not dealt with properly, it will eventually begin to smell, if you will pardon my illustration. So, our faith then is not measured by our knowledge of scripture or our ability to communicate that knowledge.

Put simply, it doesn't matter how spiritual you sound if your actions are saying something else. Our faith has a purpose and that purpose is best revealed by our actions. Looking the part is not enough. We must live the part if we are to be useful to the Lord.

The Thin Place: Ask, Answer, Pray.

How important do you feel it is for one's actions to match their speech?

Do you know anyone that talks spiritual only to live another way?

What would others say of your spiritual condition based upon what they see in your actions?

March 22

Oh, You Little Devil!

From Above: Ephesians 6:11-18; Hebrews 2:14-15

Focal Passage: *"Since the children have flesh and blood, he too shared in their humanity so that by his death he might destroy him who holds the power of death--that is, the devil--"*-Hebrews 2:14

Here Below:

Perhaps one of the most dangerous lies told in our day is that there is no real devil. He is real. We can know this without a doubt for several reasons. First and most important is because God's word says so. We are told of Jesus' encounter with him and given specific instruction on how to deal with him. Second, we can see his handy work everywhere we turn. One doesn't have to look very far to see lives wrecked by what can only be described as satanic influences. We see people committing acts so horrid that no other explanation seems adequate. Third, a Christian seeking to commit wholeheartedly to God has probably encountered him personally at one point in their lives.

Herein lies the danger of disbelief. The Bible is clear that we are at war against powers of darkness. To dismiss the Devil's existence is invite him to tamper with your life. He works with lies. It would be nice if real life was like the Hollywood versions of the Devil. We could easily recognize him is he came to us in a red suit with a pitchfork. We could also recognize him if he came wearing a black suit, with his hair slicked back and smoking a cigar like some sort of mafia hit man. He doesn't work like that! Instead he comes as an angel of light telling smooth sounding lies. These lies might be something as simple as the following. You don't need God. You are a good person without all that religious stuff! There is no hell. A loving God would never allow you to go to Hell! Life is short. Do what you want with your life. Your happiness is all that matters! Sound familiar? These lies sound good enough on the surface, but they lead to death and destruction. Unfortunately, these lies are the philosophy of many in our day.

Well, I am saved. What does this have to do with me? Well, it has everything to do with you. The Biblical warnings about Satan are usually written specifically to Christians. He is going to leave the non-believers alone. They are right where he wants them. The bottom line is this; Satan has lost you the moment you accept Jesus. However, by messing with your witness, he can still win others. This is why we must be on our guard. Never underestimate the enemy. On the same token however, do not fear him. As a Christian, you know intimately someone greater than Satan. That is why he flees when we resist (James 4:7). He is scared; not of you, but of He who lives within you. So, the next time he gives you trouble, claim the promises of God's word and remind him of to whom you belong. Take that you little devil!

The Thin Place: Ask, Answer, Pray.

How serious do you take the existence of Satan and his demonic influence?

Would you say that you have ever been under attack? How did you handle it?

In what ways could the enemy be influencing you now?

March 23
Free To Fall

<u>From Above</u>: Deuteronomy 30: 9-20; John 14:1-15

Focal Passage: "*See, I set before you today life and prosperity, death and destruction.*"-Deuteronomy 30:15

<u>Here Below</u>:

My all-time favorite movie would have to be *Braveheart*. William Wallace, played by Mel Gibson, was fighting for the independence of Scotland. In his final scene, we see him being tortured before a cheering crowd of English onlookers. In one final agonizing breath, he screams out a word that best describes what he and his companions had been fighting for all along. "Freedom!" he screams. This word would start a revolution that would ultimately lead to his nation's liberty. This word has led to many revolutions around the world, including our own American Revolution. It is something we all cherish and something we all too often take for granted until it is threatened. The concept of freedom has also been a subject of debate among Christians throughout the ages. I am not speaking of political freedom, though that is definitely a result of this doctrine. I am referring to the freedom to be and live however we may choose. There have been many theological disputes over the subject of the free will of mankind. While it is not a subject we can completely cover in one short devotion, it is one in which we can find great encouragement.

To say that man has freedom to choose right or wrong is not placing a limit on the sovereignty of God. On the contrary, it verifies the sovereignty of God. In His omnipotence, He chose to allow us freedom of choice. Think about that for a moment. Put yourself in His place. What if you could determine whether those around you loved you or not? What if you had the power to make others obey you? What if you, not them, could determine their destiny? Sounds good, huh? There is one problem with that kind of control though. You would never really know if they genuinely loved you or if they loved you only because they had no other choice. You see, God desired a genuine relationship with each of us. Therefore, He gave us the ability to choose, even though that meant we would from time to time hurt Him with our choices and perhaps even reject Him all together. Scripture is filled with a call to choose life. Jesus asks us to follow Him, implying their there is another choice. We have, as it says in the above scripture, the spiritual choice of life or death set before us. While we are asked to make the choices that are pleasing to God, He loves us enough to let us make a mess of our lives if we so choose. Admittedly, there have been times when I wish He had just stepped in and said I am taking over from here. Yet, out of love, He let me fall in order to see my need for His guidance. It is not that He doesn't want to be involved in our decisions. It is just that He wants <u>us</u> to want Him to be involved in our decisions. Thank you God for the freedom to make bad choices! Now help me to make good ones.

<u>The Thin Place</u>: Ask, Answer, Pray.

Do you find the concept of the free will of man an encouragement? Why?

Has there ever been a time when you chose to go in a direction different than God would have liked?

Does understanding God's choice to give you free will cause you to want to please Him more or less?

March 24
Great Lengths

<u>From Above</u>: Isaiah 30:18-19; 2 Peter 3:9, 15

Focal Passage: *"Yet the LORD longs to be gracious to you; he rises to show you compassion. For the LORD is a God of justice. Blessed are all who wait for him!"*-Isaiah 30:18

<u>Here Below</u>:

Out of love for us, God has given us each the prerogative of choice. With the cross, He has taken that choice and essentially divided mankind into two categories of people. There are those that accept His gift and those that reject it. While we thank God for the privilege of choice, we also need to remember that this free will choice came at a great cost to our Heavenly Father. It cost Him the life blood of Jesus Christ, His Son. That is the great length that God would go to see that we make the right choice, which is to accept the salvation offered us in Jesus. As we enjoy this freedom we have in Christ, we must never forget the lengths to which our Lord suffered so that we might choose life over death. Free will is free for us, but not to God. Yet, He was willing to endure it out of love for each of us. What a love!

Think about that for a moment. I have a wife and four children and I have many friends. As much as I love all of my friends, I do not believe that I could sacrifice even one of my four children to save the life of any or *all* of my friends, much less a friend that might not even appreciate it afterwards. Yet, that is exactly what God did for us! Why? Because He longs to show us grace and forgiveness. As God granted us free will, He knew there would be some that would choose to look away. However, His love was so intense that He would do whatever it takes to assure us a place in eternity with Him. It was not indifference that led God to give us free will. It was love. He longs to take care of us. He longs for a relationship with us.

I grow so weary of hearing those deists in our day that say that God created the world and is just sitting by and watching it spin. They say that God isn't interested in the affairs of men and that how we live really doesn't matter. It bothers me due to the fact that I know just how far God was willing to go just to be a part of our lives. To say that He doesn't care about me is to say that Jesus died for nothing. Not only does He care for me, He longs to be a part of my life, both in the big decisions and the little decisions. According to Isaiah, we are first and foremost on the mind of God. We are everything to Him. The great lengths God has gone to only validate the great worth He sees in each of us. I have many people who love me, but there is only one that has ever died in my place.

The Thin Place: Ask, Answer, Pray.

How should understanding God's extreme love effect our attitude toward righteous living and service?

What is the difference in serving God out of duty versus serving God out of gratitude?

Do you really feel as if God longs to be with you? Why or why not?

March 25
Rubbed the Wrong Way

<u>**From Above**</u>: Psalm 34:17; Psalm 55:17; Psalm 145:1-19

Focal Passage: *"Evening, and morning, and at noon, will I pray, and cry aloud: and he shall hear my voice."*-Psalm 55:17 (KJV)

<u>**Here Below**</u>:

Many people approach prayer as they might approach a magic lamp. If we just rub it the right way, then the genie will pop out and grant us our wishes. Once I was even given a "prayer cloth" and told that if I rubbed it between my fingers as I prayed, God would be more likely to answer as I wanted. While it did not help my prayer life, it did make a good polishing cloth for my car!

While there is nothing necessarily wrong with bringing our petitions to God in prayer, it is meant to be so much more than a wants or needs list. Prayer is not a means by which we can receive everything we want in life. Instead, think of prayer as communication. Now imagine that every time you communicate with your closest friend or spouse, that you begin or end that conversation with a list of things you want them to do for you. Better yet, what if they did that to you? Your relationship would suffer to say the least. Well, isn't that what we do with God at times? Prayer is more than just giving God a list of desires. In fact, our prayer life is a one on one conversation with the Creator of the Universe. It is a form of worship. It is also evidence of a submission to the will of God. Therefore, our hearts must be prepared as we approach God in prayer. Many times in scripture we see that a submissive spirit is a prerequisite to answered prayer. Righteous living and repentance open the door for God to answer. Spiritually preparing ourselves and persistently calling upon God recognizes our inability to manage things on our own strength. It is a recognition of God's power, ability, and desire to work in our lives. Likewise, to live a life of prayerlessness is in a very real sense boastful. By withholding our prayers we are saying that we believe we can handle it on our own. We are placing more faith in ourselves than in our almighty God.

The book of Psalms is basically a book of prayers. The Psalmist above shows us the importance of praying with humility throughout the entire course of a day. It is not something we do once and we are finished. Prayer is meant to be a daily and all day offering (I Thessalonians 5:17). It is a way of life. To maintain a spirit of prayer throughout the day increases the probability of an answer as well as increasing your joy. Constant communication with God leads to a constant peace. Keep in mind, prayer is more than just what we get from God. It is also what we can give to God. We give of ourselves and He in return pours Himself into our lives, filling us to the rim. So put away the magic lamp and the prayer cloth and instead *rub* away any unrepented sin or unforgiveness from your heart that might be hindering your prayer life. Polish your heart and trust in a God who longs to hear from you.

The Thin Place: Ask, Answer, Pray.

How much of your prayer time is spent requesting things from God compared to time praising God?

How often do you pray throughout the course of a normal day?

How easy is it for you to recognize answered prayers? Are there times when it is easier than others?

March 26
Who is that Grey Haired Man in the Mirror?

From Above: Psalm 73:26; 2 Corinthians 4:16-18

Focal Passage: *"Therefore we do not lose heart. Though outwardly we are wasting away, yet inwardly we are being renewed day by day."*-2 Corinthians 4:16

<u>Here Below</u>:

The other day as I was getting a haircut, the young lady cutting my hair made a comment that had significant impact on my ego. I told her that I wanted my hair cut pretty short this time. She replied "Yes, I've noticed that a lot of men want their hair short because it makes it more difficult to see the grey hairs..." Wow! So much for her tip! I couldn't help but laugh at her comment, because she was only being honest about what is becoming increasingly more evident as I gazed into that mirror. I am getting older and my body is beginning to openly rebel. What amazes me the most about aging though is how quickly it happens! I am not sure if it is the fact that I have reached that middle age period of life or if it is due to the fact that I have small children, but I am beginning to appreciate the fleeting nature of life. It seems as only yesterday I was graduating high school and had the whole world ahead of me. Now I find myself being condescended to by attractive young hair stylists! Yesterday, my kids were just infants. Today, I am unable to help them with their math homework. Oh well, such is the nature of life.

One thing I have noticed about this fleeting life phenomenon is this; the more we enjoy life, the quicker it seems to pass. Those days in which we are unhappy seem to drag on and on while the good times fly right by. In some ways this reality seems to be a little cruel. Yet, I do not believe it was intended to be taken that way. On the contrary, each day is one day closer to our eternal life. Those seemingly never-ending rainy days of life perhaps feel that way on purpose. Could it be that God is trying to help us see the importance of making the most of each day, whether good or bad? It is in those times when everything seems to stop moving for us that he could be giving us another chance to regroup and go at it again, this time with a better attitude. As a result, that day that we wish would go away could be transformed into a day that we wish would never end. You see, the child of God shouldn't fear the speeding nature of life. We should look at it as a reminder to us to make use of the time we are given. If we understand the inevitable reality of death, we can better live life in a way that is pleasing to God and filled with more lasting memories. Someone once said "We start dying the moment we are born." This is true. But it is when we understand that death is not our enemy that we can truly start living! So cheer up! We are beings created for eternity! Make the most of today, but remember that for the Christian, there are endless tomorrows ahead!

(Anyway... At least my hair is turning grey and not turning loose......yet!)

The Thin Place: Ask, Answer, Pray.

How quickly does your life seem to be progressing? Why do you think that is?

Is aging something you fear or is it something you welcome?

Would you say that you try to make the most of your time or that you use your time wastefully?

March 27
Oh Happy Day!

From Above: Psalm 4; 2 Peter 1:1-11

Focal Passage: *"You have filled my heart with greater joy than when their grain and new wine abound."*-Psalm 4:7

Here Below:

As a child, probably the most anticipated day of the year is our birthday. It is a day filled with singing, parties, gifts and quite honestly, loads of narcissistic fun. It is one day out of the year when we are permitted to be a little bit self-absorbed. After all, this day is all about us and most of us are ok with that. Besides, we all get that one day out of the year. For the child, this day seems to take an eternity to arrive, but then something happens one day without real warning. What used to be a day we longed for has turned into a day that we had rather do without. What was once the happiest day of the year can now sometimes be a day of difficult introspection or at least just another day. Instead of feeling happy, we just feel one year older. I don't believe it is because we necessarily feel unhappy about growing older. I think it has more to do with the fact that as we mature, what makes us happy in life changes. This is natural and I believe it to be spiritually healthy.

You see, the birthday for the child is all about what we receive. It's about the gifts, the songs in our honor, the parties and the overall attention we receive. It is a day of ego on overload. Yet, as we mature, we inevitably see that happiness is not about what we get out of life so much as what we put into it. Admittedly, some of us never outgrow this selfishness in life. Many look at life as one continuous birthday celebration, making everything about them. They expect everything to go their way, all their desires to be met and everyone singing their praises. When it doesn't happen, they then find disappointment in life and become unhappy with their circumstances. Nevertheless, as we grow spiritually, we find that true happiness and fulfillment isn't about being the center of attention and having our every fantasy fulfilled. It is not about having everything always go our way or always getting everything we want. It is about surrendering to one greater than ourselves and humbly following His lead. We are told time and time again in scripture to practice self control. Why? Because to repeatedly indulge our passions as if we somehow deserve it, eventually brings us to a point when it no longer satisfies. On the other hand, if we do practice self control and humility, we find joy and happiness in even the simplest pleasures in life. This doesn't mean we don't have those ecstatic moments of happiness in life. It means just the opposite. We have them more often. When you realign your heart to seeking happiness in the simpler things of life, the things that please God, they seem to come along more often. Self control leads to a happiness that nothing in the world can give. It is a lasting happiness. It is a joy unhindered by circumstances.

The Thin Place: Ask, Answer, Pray.

Looking back, at what times in your life were you the happiest? Why is that?

Likewise, at what point in your life were you the unhappiest? Why is that?

Has selfishness ever led to unhappiness in your life? How can this be avoided in the future?

March 28
In Plain View

From Above: Psalm 84:11-12; Luke 12:1-34

Focal Passage: *"Do not be afraid, little flock, for your Father has been pleased to give you the kingdom."*-Luke 12:32

Here Below:

I wonder how much of our time is spent in worry of what might or might not happen tomorrow? The uncertainties of tomorrow can, if left unchecked, cause us to fret to the point of ruining the day in which we now reside. Oh, how quickly we forget the promises found in the word of God that assure us that God has only the best intentions in mind for our tomorrows! Now does this mean that tomorrow is always going to be better than today? Well, I guess this is a matter of opinion. However, in one sense I believe tomorrow is always better; in that, tomorrow is still unwritten.

If we could ever wrap our mind around the fact that God is in our corner when it comes to facing tomorrow, it would definitely influence our attitudes toward the unknown. In the above scripture, Jesus reminds us that God is "pleased to give you the kingdom". Notice how he begins. "Do not be afraid..." He says. It is also good to read the entire passage to see exactly what Jesus is talking about. He is speaking on the subject of worry and the uncertain future. The verse immediately following it is instructions for the disciples to sell everything and give to the poor as they head out on their lifelong discipleship quest. Talk about an uncertain future! They were definitely looking at one. Yet, Jesus tells them to fear not. Why? Because the unseen future for them was sitting in plain view for Jesus. The same is true of our tomorrows.

It is not that there aren't some very frightening things in the future that we might not yet be able to see. It is just that God is greater than anything that might be there. Therefore, each new day is an opportunity to trust in Him. I have often told my children when they express fear of the dark, "There is nothing there in the dark that is not there in the daylight. You just can't see it." Well, there is nothing to fear about tomorrow. You just can't see it yet. But God can! And there is nothing there that He can't handle! So do not waste your time worrying over what hasn't even happened yet! Instead, trust in the one who sees our future in plain view.

The Thin Place: Ask, Answer, Pray.
What are some worries you feel concerning the future?
Have these worries ever preoccupied you to the point of missing the current day's joy?
What are some ways you can surrender tomorrow to the Lord today?

March 29
The Face on the Stone Floor

From Above: Hebrews 12:1-3; Philippians 2:5-11
Focal Passage: *"Let us fix our eyes on Jesus, the author and perfecter of our faith, who for the joy set before him endured the cross, scorning its shame, and sat down at the right hand of the throne of God."*-Hebrews 12:2
Here Below:

As we approach the celebration of Easter, let us reflect upon the personal nature of this holiday. It is perhaps the most intimate of all the days we celebrate on the Christian calendar. The Easter season forces us to consider exactly what has taken place on Calvary and why it has taken place. Perhaps one of the most perplexing of all scripture is that found in Hebrews 12:2. When we think of the terrible ordeal that Jesus had to endure as he walked path to the cross, the word "joy" is probably the furthest thing from our mind. Yet, there it is in black and white. Jesus considered it joy.

This point was driven home to me in extreme clarity a few years ago as I had the privilege of a trip to the Holy Land. Many of the sites we visited were thought by most archaeologists to be the place from scripture that they traditionally claimed it to be; while for others, there were a couple of different theories as to the exact location. However, for some, there was no doubt as to the accuracy of the location. There were a couple of sites in particular that we can know with absolute certainty that Jesus was there. One such site was the long steps leading to the courtyard of the High Priest Caiaphas. Another was called *The Place of the Stone Pavement*, referring to the place where Jesus had subsequently been flogged and beaten. This place still had the original stone floor that Jesus himself would have stood upon as He took a beating that was meant for you and me. As I touched those cold stones that day, knowing that my Savior had stood there bleeding for me, the harsh reality of that hard floor moved me beyond words. I had always understood the Cross, but for the first time it had become overwhelmingly personal. And to think He considered it joy, is almost more than a person can comprehend. Yet we know it is true. I don't believe this necessarily means that Jesus thought of the pain and suffering as joy, but it was the end result of what He was doing that brought Him joy. His death meant life for us. You see, it was you and I that he saw standing at the end of that long set of stairs. It was your face and mine that He saw etched on that stone floor. It was you and I that He saw at the summit of Calvary's Hill. To Jesus, the ends justified the means. He was doing this out of love for us. To Him it was worth it. Not only worth it, but it was a cause for joy. We should in turn consider living for Him a joy, no matter the difficulties we might face. Let this Easter season be a season of personal reflection for you.

The Thin Place: Ask, Answer, Pray.

Do you ever find yourself complaining about the difficulties of the Christian life?

Do you ever find yourself forgetting about the personal significance of the Cross?

How does understanding that the Cross was for "me" change the way we look at Christian living?

March 30
The God Who Can Clean House

From Above: Mark 11:15-19; Romans 8:29-39

Focal Passage: *"The chief priests and the teachers of the law heard this and began looking for a way to kill him, for they feared him, because the whole crowd was amazed at his teaching."*-Mark 11:18

Here Below:

What images come to mind when you think of Jesus? What was his physical appearance like? We often create for ourselves mental images of Jesus, based upon our own preconceptions. These mental pictures are often based upon scripture, but many times they are derived from less reliable sources such as books we have read or movies we have seen. Too often the modern media version of Christ is one of a mild mannered, meek and an almost weak and effeminate nature. While He was most certainly meek and humble, weakness is not a description accurately backed by scripture. The above account from the Gospel of Mark attests to His strength, both physical and spiritual.

Here we are, just one day after the triumphal entry into Jerusalem, and we see Jesus do something that we don't often consider consistent with His nature. With this and the other gospel accounts, we see Jesus walking into what was meant to be a solemn place of worship, making a makeshift whip out of leather cords and then kicking over benches and knocking down money changing tables. In Mark 11:16, it says the Jesus wouldn't allow anyone to even bring merchandise through. And notice, no one tried to stop Him! What a scene that must have been! This doesn't exactly paint a picture of someone I would want to arm wrestle! How about you? Well, while we may not often think of Him in this light, it is in complete agreement with His character. His determination and intestinal fortitude in the face of opposition, even to the point of laying down His own life, shows a strength grounded in love that is the exact opposite of weakness.

Likewise, His strength of spirit was always purposeful. He wasn't on a rant when He charged the money changers in the temple. He was restoring the proper use of God's temple. When He stood silent before His accusers, it wasn't stubborn pride, but resolve to save the lost. His driving purpose was always to change the hearts of men into one acceptable unto God. Only Jesus could do this. The same is still true today. Only Jesus can overturn the tables in our life that need to overturned. Only He is strong enough to restore our house to a house pleasing to Him. Only Jesus can restore us to a right relationship with God. When we need to "clean house", how encouraging it is to know that we have someone as strong as Jesus running to our aid and fighting in our defense! Today, create a new image in your mind of Jesus, one of strength, courage and heroic love. Turn to a Savior who fears nothing!

__The Thin Place__: Ask, Answer, Pray.

What images come to mind when you think of Jesus? Why is that?

How should Jesus' strength of character encourage us as we live the disciple's life?

How can you be more like Jesus in this respect today?

March 31
Get Real!

<u>**From Above**</u>: Matthew 21:23-46; John 15:1-5

Focal Passage: *"Therefore I tell you that the kingdom of God will be taken away from you and given to a people who will produce its fruit."*-Matthew 21:43

<u>**Here Below**</u>:

Here we are just a few days away from the Cross and we see Jesus once again making the most of an opportunity. In the above passage of scripture, He is utilizing a teachable moment for the benefit of the Chief Priests and teachers of the law, and for us as well. With His arrest and betrayal looming ever before Him, He characteristically uses the moment to help others by teaching us the importance of being genuine through the use of parables. To teach this, at this critical time in His own life, shows us the importance of the subject matter. Not overly concerned with social etiquette, Jesus is addressing the religious hierarchy of His day right in the middle of the temple courts. In keeping with modern vernacular, Jesus is "schooling them in their own house." He is calling them out and revealing to them and to all their real spiritual condition. They were hypocrites. Sure, they looked the part. They were living right and doing all the right things, keeping the law. They were even well versed in the scriptures. Yet, Jesus points out very in a very straightforward manner that the tax collectors and prostitutes are closer to the Kingdom of God than they. This must have been like a slap in the face to these men. To put it simply, in spite of their so called "spiritual status", they had missed the point of the scriptures which they supposedly knew so well.

God's desire for all of us has always been authenticity. Every time Jesus confronts the religious leaders of His day, it was always the same story. They were leaning upon their own self-righteousness as opposed to that which can come only from God. The problem with self-righteousness is that it always falls short. We can fool ourselves, but we can't fool God. He can see past the outside and see us for our true selves. Inside, they were dirty and in need of rebirth. The same is true of each of us. Even those of us who have placed our faith in Jesus often get caught up in doing "religious things" such as going to church, serving and even studying scripture to the neglect of what God is most concerned about. We neglect confession, repentance, mercy, forgiveness and the like. What we are when no one is looking is more important to the Lord than what we appear to be when others are looking. Now this doesn't mean we do not ever mess up. On the contrary, it means being honest about it when we do. God is more pleased with a sincere and honest failure than with a successful hypocrite. So, listen to the words of our Savior. Examine your heart and get real with the Lord today.

The Thin Place: Ask, Answer, Pray.

How closely aligned are your outward actions and your inner self? Be honest.

What would others think of your spiritual life if they could see what only you and God can see?

Most importantly, is there anything hidden in your heart that needs to be addressed?

4

April

April 1
Call Me a Fool!

From Above: I Corinthians 1:17-31, 4;10; 2 Corinthians 5:10-17

Focal Passage: *"For the message of the cross is foolishness to those who are perishing, but to us who are being saved it is the power of God."*-I Corinthians 1:18

Here Below:

As we consider the Cross, one can't help but notice the irony of it all. Our Messiah, King and Savior did not free His people with feats of conquest on fields of glory. Neither did He accomplish His goal with social, political, or civil achievements. He instead gained victory by laying His life down and allowing Himself to be physically nailed to some dirty old wood. There were those in His day that simply did not understand what He was doing for them. They expected Him to be the hero charging in on His white horse to save the day. Instead, He came as a suffering servant. This baffled many then as it does today.

People are still missing the point of the Cross. It has always been this way and I suppose it will remain until He returns. In our day we often hear Christianity erroneously referred to as a crutch for the weak minded or ignorant. Well, this attitude should not surprise us.

Paul understood this dilemma. More than once in the two letters to the Corinthians, Paul refers to the cross as foolishness or to Christians as fools for Christ. He didn't mean this as an insult. On the contrary, I believe he considered it as a compliment. In fact, in 2 Corinthians 2, Paul says that if others consider him to be out of his mind, then he is out of his mind for Christ. He understood that there are always going to be those who can't grasp the message of the Cross. After all, the teachings and actions of Jesus are contrary to our sinful human nature and instincts. To save our lives, we must lose them (Matt. 16:25). We must love our enemies (Luke 6:27). Truths such as these go against our natural human tendencies. Those who have never experienced the freedom that comes in following Jesus in these respects, cannot truly know what He meant by them. But to those of us that have tasted of His salvation, we know the freeing nature of His words. To us, it is the power of God at work in our hearts and lives.

What does this mean for us? Well, it means that we shouldn't always expect those around us to understand our relationship with God and our desire to follow His will, and it also means we should be okay with that fact. The Christian life is not supposed to be reasonable. If it were, there would be no need for faith. The cross and resurrection are both about letting go of "common sense" and trusting in a God that is willing to leave Heaven to face the depths of Hell for you and I. Foolish? Perhaps. I guess it all depends upon your perspective. To me, being a saved fool is better than being a lost man of reason. Embrace the ironies of the Christian life. I thank you God that I can't always explain your ways! Thank you for being bigger than my intellect and reason and loving me in spite of my faults and rebellion! I consider it a privilege to be a fool for you. Embrace your inner fool today!

The Thin Place: Ask, Answer, Pray.

Has there ever been anyone that questioned your faith, considering it to be foolish or a waste of time?

How should we respond to those who consider Christianity foolish?

If your life does not cause others to question your motives, what does it say to the lost you encounter?

April 2
Pass the Cup

From Above: Mark 14:32-46; Romans 6

Focal Passage: *"Abba, Father," he said, "everything is possible for you. Take this cup from me. Yet not what I will, but what you will."*-Mark 14:36

Here Below:

In the Garden of Gethsemane, we see the incarnation illustrated in one of the most beautifully heart wrenching scenes in all of history. Here we see the human Jesus, with blood and tears running down His face, kneeling in solitary prayer, honestly admitting His desire to avoid the physical pain that is awaiting Him. However, at the same time we see the divine Jesus acknowledging that the will of the Father trumps any trepidation His human heart may be feeling. We see the will of God win out in this very personal struggle that Jesus has expressed within that prayer. Jesus knew what had to be done. In Luke's account of this beautiful scene, God sent an angel to comfort His Son in His time of need.

This verse is important to us for many reasons. First and foremost, it shows us the depth of God's love for each of us. Not only does Jesus' willingness to take whatever comes, but God the Father's willingness to allow it, shows us the strength of His love for His children.

Second, Jesus is illustrating what he had been teaching us all along. The will of God is to be our driving force in life. To please God is our purpose. Sometimes it is painless. In fact, it can be enjoyable. However, there are times when it comes with a price. More times than not, the things that cost us the most spiritually speaking, are the things that we ultimately cherish the most. It is in sacrifice that we receive the most. Again, this is one of the ironies of the Christian life. To truly find our lives, we must lose them (Matt. 10:39). Jesus didn't necessarily mean by this that we must physically lay down our lives, though that could be the case. He meant that we must sacrifice our will for the will of the Father. His Gethsemane prayer was about this surrender of will. He was honest enough to admit what he wanted to happen to God, yet faithful enough to follow His will anyway. This brings us to a very real question today. Are we willing to face whatever God wills or are we more apt to choose the easy way out? Remember the Garden when you face that decision. Remember his tears. Remember that He chose not to pass the cup, but to take it.

The Thin Place: Ask, Answer, Pray.

Has there ever been a time when you were called upon by God to sacrifice something of worth to you?

Did you make that sacrifice? If not, why? If so, in retrospect are you glad?

Why do you think we often forget that the Christian life is a life of sacrifice when it is so well illustrated in the cross?

April 3
The Wood

From Above: Isaiah 53; Mark 15:1-39

Focal Passage: *"But he was pierced for our transgressions, he was crushed for our iniquities; the punishment that brought us peace was upon him, and by his wounds we are healed."*-Isaiah 53

Here Below:

It was an ugly thing. It was supposed to be. It had the smell of death upon it. Riddled with nail holes, this piece of wood was stained with the blood of executed criminals. Its purpose was not simply to kill those who had the misfortune of being nailed to it, but to prolong their death in a way that was physically agonizing and emotionally humiliating. Death was meant to come only after hours and hours of having humanity's worst poured upon you. It was a device that would reveal the depth of horror which the human mind can conceive. It was repulsive. It was disgusting. It was sin in physical form. And upon it hung our Savior.

Likewise, it was a heavy thing. It was weighted down with every sin you and I ever committed. Within the grain of that wood was every lie I ever told, every lustful look I ever gave and every jealous thought I ever had. It was filled with knots of my envy, my greed, and my pride. It held within itself my shame. It held within its being my disgrace. And upon it hung my Savior.

It was also a beautiful thing. Within its design was the possibility of redemption. Within is structure was the emancipation of generations of lost souls among which I belong, struggling to find peace. Within its purpose was my freedom and salvation. It held the dreams of countless millions of broken hearts. In this epic moment in time, the children were once again reunited with their Father and the Father with His greatest love. On this gnarled, stained, stinking and at the same time beautiful piece of wood hung the hopes of the entire world. And upon this Cross hung our Savior.

The Thin Place: Ask, Answer, Pray.

Have you taken time today to reflect upon your role in the Crucifixion?
Have you taken time to thank God for the Cross of Christ?
Have you taken time today to repent of your sins? Do so now.

April 4
A Tomb With A View

From Above: Matthew 28; I Corinthians 15:1-20

Focal Passage: *"He is not here; he has risen, just as he said. Come and see the place where he lay. " —Matthew 28:6*

Here Below:

Let's put it in perspective this morning. Imagine if you will that you recently lost a loved one. Assuming that it was unexpected and perhaps tragic, you have been overcome with grief since the moment it happened. It has been a few days and you have decided to go to the grave to view the flowers and to straighten them up a little and to make sure the head stone is correct. You go with some reluctance, because the death of this friend or family member is still so fresh upon your mind and heart. The thought of going once again to the place where their body lies, leaves you feeling lost and empty inside. Yet, as you get closer to the grave, you begin to sense that something strange has happened. When you arrive at the cemetery, you find that the grave is wide open. Trembling with fear, you muster up the courage to look inside. It is empty! Where a dead body should be lying, you see only cloths, neatly folded in a familiar manner. Then turning, you see your loved one alive and well. What would you do?

What a life changing moment for all of us! Though we were not physically there, it nevertheless changed our lives that morning. In fact, it is safe to say that this empty hole in the ground changed the world. Life now had new meaning. What once was compared to a "vapor" that comes and in an instant is gone (James 4:14), now is seemingly endless. What once had no purpose, now has depth and value. A life that once might have been empty and void of joy is now filled. And all because the tomb was empty! The resurrection is the defining moment of all time. Without it, Christmas would have no meaning and the cross would be just another sad story. The Bible would be just another ancient writing from some obscure place in the world. There would be no church. Had Jesus' body been there that morning when those ladies arrived, the world would be unrecognizable. I venture to say that personally we would be as well. Imagine how differently we would view the milestones of life without the resurrection. Birth, death, and everything in between would be without hope. So, remember the resurrection the next time you feel empty. Let the emptiness of that tomb remind you of your great worth to God. And don't let the resurrection joy be temporary! The whole point of the empty tomb is that His gift of joy is meant to last forever in your heart.

Have you ever thought about why the stone was rolled away? Jesus didn't move that rock so that He could get out. Remember, He could walk through walls. It was moved so that we could see in.

The Thin Place: Ask, Answer, Pray.

Have you ever thought about how different your life might be with the resurrection of Christ?

How has the resurrection helped you in times of trial or loss?

How can we show our appreciation to God for the resurrection?

April 5
Resurrection Insurrection

From Above: Acts 1:13-26, 4:31-37

Focal Passage: *"With great power the apostles continued to testify to the resurrection of the Lord Jesus, and much grace was upon them all." –Acts 4:33*

Here Below:

Something happened. These men, that had for three years been followers of Jesus, had spent the last few days in virtual hiding. They had abandoned their Lord on the night of His arrest and had been in hiding ever since. Yet, in a matter of just a few weeks we would see these cowardly acting men turning the world upside down with the good news of Jesus. Peter would preach a message in which literally thousands would find salvation. What made the difference? What happened? What caused the revolution? Well, they had met the resurrected Jesus. They had dined with Him. They had fished with Him. Peter, whose heart must have been broken over the betrayal he had committed, had been restored on the beach that morning. And they had been filled with the Holy Spirit of God! Put simply, they had been themselves resurrected.

As they sought to replace Judas, one of the criteria for the new apostle was that he had to be a witness to the resurrected Christ. Throughout the book of Acts we see them preaching not just about

Jesus, but about His resurrection specifically. There was no compromise on this subject. Why? Well, they recognized that it is the heart of the Christian faith. Without it, nothing else really matters. Why is it then that we seldom discuss the resurrection except during the Easter season? After Easter, we rarely discuss it except in passing reference. Now we do reflect on the cross quite often, as well we should. But the fact remains that without the resurrection, the cross would be meaningless.

It wasn't until the disciples made the resurrection a reality in their lives that they were of any benefit to the Kingdom. When it became personal, their mission became personal, and it was then that they were filled with the Holy Spirit for the purpose of good works. The same is true for you and I today. Until we recognize the very intimate nature of the cross and the resurrection, we will be of little use to our King. In the resurrection, there is life, both literally and spiritually for us and others. Death was defeated on that third day, and it kept taking a licking in the days to come. This is still true today. Every time we proclaim His life, death gets a black eye. This is why we must be resurrection minded every day! In it there is power, freedom and life.

Let today and everyday be your Resurrection Day! You may be surprised what God can do with your resurrected heart.

The Thin Place: Ask, Answer, Pray.

Do you feel that your heart is in need of resurrection today? How so?

Is there any reason why God might not want to give you a fresh start today? Why or why not?

How can we demonstrate our belief in the resurrection of Jesus in our daily lives?

April 6
Emmaus Love

From Above: Luke 24:13-31; John 16:33

Focal Passage: *"Then their eyes were opened and they recognized him, and he disappeared from their sight." –Luke 24:31*

Here Below:

Their hopes were dashed. "We thought He was the Messiah" they said. They were leaving Jerusalem with their heads hanging low. Yet, something happened along the way that they did not expect. They met the resurrected Jesus. However, it was not the joy filled emotional encounter you might expect. On the contrary, the travelers that day were so enveloped in their grief that they did not even recognize the man with whom they spoke. It wasn't until their "eyes were opened" that they realized that Jesus had been with them the entire time.

Let's not be too quick to criticize them for their reaction. After all, how often do we do the same thing? Our human nature leads us to often focus on the trials and troubles of the moment to the detriment of all else. This is especially true when the unexpected happens. We allow our suffering to overwhelm us to the point of missing God at work in the midst of our crisis. Just like those pilgrims, we miss Jesus standing right in front of our face.

Perhaps, we do this because we fail to look at all circumstances as possible instruments of God. God can use both the good and bad things that happen to shape us and mold us. This kneading process is not always a pleasant experience; yet, in the end we are better for the kneading. This doesn't mean that God causes bad things necessarily to happen. In fact, it can be sometimes due to our actions or inactions. Nevertheless, God can still use them. The important thing is that we keep our eyes looking for the one who might be right in the middle of our circumstances. We must always remember that God is with us, even when we might not be able to see Him. He has promised to never leave us or forsake us (Hebrews 13:5). Remember that Emmaus Road love today. Open your eyes to His presence.

The Thin Place: Ask, Answer, Pray.

Looking back, can you see a time when God as at work and you didn't see Him?

How has that affected how you view trials and suffering?

Is it possible that God is working in your life right now in that same manner?

April 7
The Going Away Gift

From Above: Acts 1:1-11

Focal Passage: *"On one occasion, while he was eating with them, he gave them this command: "Do not leave Jerusalem, but wait for the gift my Father promised, which you have heard me speak about. For John baptized with water, but in a few days you will be baptized with the Holy Spirit." –Acts 1:4-5*

Here Below:

Jesus left with us the perfect going away present. Isn't it just like the Lord to "not" leave His children empty handed? Jesus was finished with this part of His earthly ministry. It was time to ascend to Heaven. He had made many appearances in His resurrected body, removing any doubts to its reality. He had performed more miracles. He had shared more truth. Now it was time to leave His children and His church to carry out the mission He began. He knew there would be tough times ahead; so, what does He do? He gives us the promise of the Comforter.

With Jesus, His disciples were limited to His presence in a physical form. Jesus, being a human, could only be in one place at a time. Now, we would no longer be limited to His presence in that manner. He understood that within the human heart is a longing for the presence of God. If you do not believe this, just look at the different beliefs around the world. People of every culture are searching for God. The problem is that many are looking in the wrong places. Jesus and the Holy Spirit are evidence that God desires for our search to lead to His presence in our everyday lives. This is the reason God promised us the presence of His Spirit. Now we would no longer be limited by space.

God could be with us anywhere and everywhere. He knew of the incomplete nature of the human soul. Without God, we are not whole. We were created for relationship with Him. The presence of His Holy Spirit in our lives is the perfect expression of His love and His desire to fulfill our greatest need.

The Spirit filled life is a life of completeness. In it, we find peace in times of trial, strength for times of testing, comfort in times of mourning and companionship during times of loneliness. How sad it is that more of us do not seek the guidance and comfort of the Holy Spirit more regularly. He is a gift to not be ignored.

The Thin Place: Ask, Answer, Pray.

In what wrong ways do we often seek to fill the longing for God's presence in our lives?

How is the Spirit filled life different from life apart from the presence of God?

Is there a need in your life for more of the Holy Spirit presence?

April 8
Up the Creek

From Above: 2 Kings 6:1-7; Jeremiah 32:27

Focal Passage: *"I am the LORD, the God of all mankind. Is anything too hard for me?" –Jeremiah 32:27*

Here Below:

In the first few verses of 2 Kings 6, we see one of scriptures' most interesting stories. At first glance it might leave one wondering as to why this story is even included in the Bible. Of course, there are no accidental inclusions within the word of God. If it is in there, then there must be a morsel of truth included for our benefit. Indeed, this is no exception. The story of the floating axe head is a story that should bring each of us great comfort.

Here we see a story of an unnamed man who accidently loses a tool while working. What man among us cannot relate to this story? How many times have I lost a hammer or a screwdriver? However, there is more to this than just losing an axe head. It was a borrowed axe head. This may not seem like a big deal to us. We can go to the local hardware store and buy another, right? Well, in Old Testament times, this was an expensive tool. Losing a borrowed tool meant that you would have to work off the value of the borrowed instrument. In other words, you lose the tool, you take its place. This man was looking at some hard labor in exchange for this simple accident that could have happened to anyone. But God was not going to let that happen.

This story teaches us two things. First, it teaches us that God cares for His children. He did not want to see this man, who by the way was working for God when the accident occurred, have to suffer for His mistake. Second, God is interested in every detail of our life. As we read this, our first impression is that it is no big deal. These kinds of things rarely are unless they are happening to you! We see a lost tool, but this man saw his future in jeopardy. He was literally "up the creek". This story confirms that God is interested in the everyday details of our lives, no matter how big or small we see them. Why is it then that we so often forget to turn to him with the little things? God is just as interested in the little things of life as He is the big things. Keep in mind, from God's perspective, they are all little things! So trust God in all aspects of your daily walk. Don't limit what God can do? You never know, you might just have your own axe head that God wants to float, a miracle to perform. But it will never happen until you first trust Him in the minor details of your life as well as the major. They both matter to Him.

The Thin Place: Ask, Answer, Pray.

Have you ever had a problem that you thought was too insignificant to take to God in prayer?

Has God ever surprised you with an answer to one of life's smaller crises?

What "smaller" needs do you need God's help with today?

April 9
The Thirst Quencher

From Above: Matthew 25:31-46; Mark 9:41;

Focal Passage: *"I tell you the truth, anyone who gives you a cup of water in my name because you belong to Christ will certainly not lose his reward."* –Mark 9:41

Here Below:

With four small children in my home, it is rare that I get the pleasure of enjoying a soft drink or glass of tea without having to share with one of those little sad eyed beggars. "Daddy, can I have a swallow?" they ask. For me, it is impossible to deny them a drink. After all, they always look so pitiful, and I know that there is nothing more refreshing than a cold drink at just the right moment of need. I usually cave in and share my drink as they share their germs.

Well, Jesus tells us in Mark 9 that there is reward for those who willingly share with those who thirst. Of course, He was not speaking solely of situations such as the one I just mentioned. There is also some significance to the language used in this passage and the question as to whom Jesus was referring. Nevertheless, the principle is the same, regardless of who is receiving the drink of water. God rewards a giving spirit. Even something as small and seemingly insignificant as giving someone a glass of cold water could bring peace and comfort to someone and could ultimately bring glory to God. This act brings even more of a blessing when it is performed without the expectation of ever being acknowledged. Our goal should be to quench another's thirst, not to receive a pat on the back for our good deed. This is the mark of a truly giving spirit.

Think of this cup of cold water a little more figuratively. Has there ever been a time when someone gave you just the right word of encouragement at just the right time? It may not have seemed like much to them and perhaps others, but to you it was the difference between a day of depression or discouragement and a day of joy and comfort. You never know when God might use those little insignificant acts and words to touch the heart of another. We do not know what another person may be feeling in that moment. Therefore we should always be ready to give of ourselves, great or small, to others. They will be blessed. You will be blessed. But most importantly, God will be pleased. Look for opportunities today to share a cup of cold water with a thirsty soul.

The Thin Place: Ask, Answer, Pray.

Think of a time when an act of kindness or word fitly spoken brought encouragement to you.

Has there ever been a time when you have done the same for someone else?

What opportunities might you have today to be an encouragement for someone?

April 10
Who Wants to Live Forever?

From Above: Deuteronomy 6:1-9; Proverbs 3:1-6

Focal Passage: "*My son, do not forget my teaching, but keep my commands in your heart, for they will prolong your life many years and bring you prosperity.*" *–Proverbs 3:1-2*

Here Below:

Who wants to live forever? This is a question that has been asked by many over the years and even put to music several different times. By asking this question, one is either decrying the futility of life, trying to rustle up some courage for the moment or else they are trying to provide reason for doing something unreasonable or unsafe. While the question may make for a cool rock and roll ballad, the statement itself is dishonest. We can sing it, we can ask it, we can even use it to support our politics and social ideology, but the reality is that we go to great lengths to prolong our lives. We spend countless dollars trying to appear young and to live longer. Psychologist deal with people daily who find themselves in an emotional crisis for no other reason than the fact the number of days remaining in their lives is shorter than the number of days behind them. We call it midlife crisis. Well, call it what it you will, but the fact remains that most of us do want to live forever.

This is not unusual, and it doesn't even have to be unhealthy. It could go back to the fact that we were created to spend eternity in fellowship with our creator. Therefore, there is this longing for life eternal in our hearts. This is a good thing. The problem comes when we try to achieve this goal by using methods that the world offers, methods that ultimately fail. This is not new. In fact, God responds to this longing countless times in scripture by giving us helpful instructions as to how to prolong our lives. It can usually be summed up by keeping God's commands and living for Him. Does this mean that we will live 100 years is we live a faithful Christian life? Not necessarily. Sometimes the good do die young. The fact remains that we live in a fallen world and sometimes tragedies do occur. However, the principle in these life affirming passages is sound. If we are living for the Lord and avoiding the trappings of sinful lifestyles, we are less likely to face the damaging results of living outside the will of God. Think about it. Sinfulness always leads to despair. Broken relationships and unrealized dreams and potential inevitably come as a result of sinfulness. Do the evil sometimes prosper? Yes. But ultimately it catches up to them. The result will be stress and heartache. These conditions will definitely shorten your life. This is not God's plan. Life is meant to be filled with joy and peace. It is in following God's recipe for long life that we find these qualities. It is in surrendering to Him that find a longer more satisfied life here and now and an eternal life to come. So yes, as a matter of fact, I do plan on living forever. How about you?

The Thin Place: Ask, Answer, Pray.

How well do you accept the fact that you are getting older? Any regrets?

What would you do differently if you could go back and do it all over again?

What can you differently now that might help you to realize more fully the abundant life God promised?

April 11
A Eunuch Experience

From Above: Acts 8:26-40; 2 Corinthians 6:1-2

Focal Passage: *"For he says, "In the time of my favor I heard you, and in the day of salvation I helped you." I tell you, now is the time of God's favor, now is the day of salvation." –2 Corinthians 6:2*

Here Below:

In Acts chapter 8, we see a man that decided to do today what might could have waited until tomorrow. The story of the Ethiopian eunuch is a heartwarming story of faith and commitment and in it we also see the urgency of the life of faith. After coming to the realization of his own sinfulness, this man decided that he need not wait until tomorrow to do what needed to be done right now. After placing his faith in the risen Savior, he sees water and basically asks "Why not now?" Of course, the meeting between Phillip and this man was obviously a divine appointment. The Lord uses it to convey the importance of living for God in the here and now.

Throughout scripture we are taught that today is the day. Jesus warns us about worrying about tomorrow. Likewise, He also warns us about planning too far ahead. Why does He do that? Well, it could be that He understands the nature of our existence more than anyone, being our Creator. Therefore, he emphasizes to us the urgency of making the most of the moment. This *carpe diem* attitude is more than just a catchy philosophy. It is an acknowledgment of the fact that this moment is all we really have. There is no guarantee of future opportunities. So, to put off a commitment to Christ to a later time is to gamble that commitment. In other words, it is not a commitment at all. We would not likely gamble that which has real value to us. Such is the life of faith. If our faith has meaning to us, we must exercise it daily.

The Ethiopian eunuch taught us something very important that day. If the Lord leads us to water, then jump in. Don't put off until tomorrow what may never come again. Seize the moments God gives you today.

The Thin Place: Ask, Answer, Pray.

Have you ever missed an opportunity due to procrastination?

Do you feel as if there is an opportunity before you right now to exercise your faith?

What can you do today to seize the moment God has given you?

April 12
Behind the Scenes

From Above: John 6:23-27; Colossians 3:17

Focal Passage: *"Do not work for food that spoils, but for food that endures to eternal life, which the Son of Man will give you. On him God the Father has placed his seal of approval."" –John 6:27*

Here Below:

I have learned as a Pastor that the greatest and most important workers in church life are those that do not care to be recognized for what they do. They are the ones that diligently do the things that most of us take for granted. I am referring to the things that we just assume will be taken care of and we never really give much thought as to how. Such workers care little for credit for their deeds and are also usually the ones most cheerful in their work. The cheerful worker is always the more fruitful worker. This principle is true in all areas of life, not just church work. When we take ourselves out of the work equation, the load is lifted, and the results become a joy rather than a point of stress. Perhaps this is what God intended all along.

Part of the abundant Christian life is recognizing that all things matter to God, but that God at the same time is more interested in our willingness to serve faithfully more so than the outcome of our service. Put simply, success is not always achieving the desired outcome. Success is found more accurately in faithfully working for the right reason and with the right attitude. This is why we are to do all things for the glory of God, not just those tasks we deem of greater value or those tasks for which we may receive recognition. All things are to be done for God's glory.

So, wherever you may be in life and whatever you may find your hands doing, do it as if it mattered to God, because it does.

The Thin Place: Ask, Answer, Pray.

Has there ever been a time when you worked for the Lord without the promise of recognition?

On the other hand, has there ever been a time when you were bothered by not being recognized?

What can you do for the Lord today?

April 13
The Space Cowboy

From Above: Philippians 1:1-11; Colossians 2:6-7

Focal Passage: *"Being confident of this, that he who began a good work in you will carry it on to completion until the day of Christ Jesus." –Philippians 1:6*

Here Below:

As a child, I couldn't decide whether I wanted to be a cowboy or an astronaut when I grew up. So, I just decided I would be both. How about you? Many young boys have such dreams. Likewise, little girls often dream of being ballerinas or princesses. These kinds of dreams are natural. However, as we get older, we begin to face the realities of life and very few of us find ourselves living those fantasies of childhood. Life becomes more serious as we age, and our dreams transform from the fantastical to the more practical. Even then we do not always follow through and we find ourselves disappointed. This disappointment can lead to complications in our personal lives, and it can also lead to lasting mistakes and regrets. We can avoid this by rethinking how we dream.

While there is nothing wrong with dreaming big, our dreams must fall in line with God's will for our lives. In fact, I would say that God wants us to dream bigger. It is His desire to give us the desire of our hearts. The problem rests in the fact that His will and the desire of our hearts do not always intermingle. Too often we set our minds on things that we desire for ourselves and miss the bigger picture God has in store for us. While our future plans may seem the perfect plan for us, they will only fall short if God is not in the midst of the planning. Life with God at the center never leaves a person feeling as if they have unrealized dreams. On the contrary, life with God always leaves you with more than you expected. Perhaps it is His will for you to be a cowboy or an astronaut or both. For me, it was something even more challenging, rewarding and dangerous. He made me a preacher, pastor, and a parent. For you, God's will could be equally exciting, if not more! Following God doesn't mean giving up your dreams. It means trusting your dreams to one whom can make them come true. Make God's will your will and you will never be disappointed.

__The Thin Place__: Ask, Answer, Pray.

How does your life look now compared to how you had once hoped it would look by now?

Are there any unrealized dreams in your heart?

How do these dreams fit into the will of God for your life?

April 14
Accept No Substitute

<u>**From Above**</u>: Matthew 5:13-16; John 15:1-5

Focal Passage: *"In the same way, let your light shine before men, that they may see your good deeds and praise your Father in heaven."* –Matthew 5:16

<u>**Here Below**</u>:

Recently having made an effort to eat healthier, I have realized one undeniable truth. Though the label may say "salt substitute", it is not a substitute for the real thing. It does not have the same flavoring quality as real salt. Salt is very unique and distinctive in its flavor and use. We are told by Jesus in the above scripture that salt without saltiness is good for nothing. Basically, it is sand! Likewise, He furthers this illustration by telling us that a light is meant to be seen. We do not light a lamp only to hide its illumination. Put simply, a light you cannot see is just as useless as a blown bulb. Neither can do what they are designed to do.

It is interesting to see that Jesus first gives us these words of instruction immediately following the Beatitudes. In other words, this principle is meant to be a part of the everyday attitude of the person of faith. Why? Because just like that salt substitute, Jesus knew that there is no substitute for the real thing when it comes to sharing our faith. He is expressing the urgency of integrity. To profess with our mouth one way of living and to live our lives in a different way is to negate the usefulness of our witness. We become that useless salt or that blown bulb. In fact, I would take it even a step further to say that an insincere life can even become harmful to the Gospel message, only resulting in others being pushed even further away from the truth. Therefore, it is vital that we maintain a life of genuine faith. When we exhibit the fruits of the spirit, the result is a drawing effect, not a pushing effect. All of God's creation is drawn to light. Likewise, we prefer our food to have flavor. Jesus was telling us that we are that flavor and light to the world. Live a life of authenticity today.

The Thin Place: Ask, Answer, Pray.

Has there ever been a time when your personal life got in the way of your witness? How so?

Is your life such that others can see the difference that comes with a life of faith?

What can you do differently today to be saltier and to shine brighter?

April 15
Trash Talking

From Above: Philippians 3:7-9; 2 Timothy 2:4-6

Focal Passage: *"What is more, I consider everything a loss compared to the surpassing greatness of knowing Christ Jesus my Lord, for whose sake I have lost all things. I consider them rubbish, that I may gain Christ"* –Philippians 3:8

Here Below:

Dung. In the King James Version, Paul is translated as saying that he "counts them as dung". The NIV uses the word "rubbish". Either way, you get the picture. I personally prefer the King James translation of the above verse. I think it is probably more of what Paul had in mind as he referred to the things he had lost as a result of placing his faith in Jesus Christ. Paul considered those things trash compared to what he had gained.

One of the misconceptions of the Christian life is that in order to live it successfully, we must give up everything we enjoy or value. This simply is not true. It is not that we must give them up. It is just that what we enjoy or value changes. Of course, the Christian life can at times be accurately viewed as a life of sacrifice; but what we gain far outweighs anything we might lose along the way. Most certainly there will be times of surrender as we grow in faith. There are things we cherish or behaviors that we indulge in that may very well conflict with the promotion of a life of faith. There is also the surrender of our own will in exchange for God's. Though not always easy, this surrender is normal and healthy. In fact, the things we give up may not even be bad in and of themselves. Sometimes they just don't fit into the plan that God has for us. This is why we must *try* to look at gains and losses through the eyes of Jesus.

Notice that Paul didn't say that the things he had lost *were* rubbish. He said that he *considers* them rubbish. You see, it wasn't the things he had lost that had changed as he came to faith. It was Paul himself that had changed. What was once important to him was as garbage now! The priorities of his heart had been changed by the Holy Spirit of God. Suddenly everything had been placed into one of two categories. There were the things that had eternal and lasting significance and then there was the other stuff, the leftovers, the rubbish, the dung. What mattered in the eyes of eternity was all that now mattered. The same is true for you and me. Compared to knowing Jesus, everything else is meaningless. Only our relationship with Him and what we do with that relationship lasts. That is all that matters. To grab hold of the life God has for us means we must let go of what we cannot keep anyway. It is time to throw out the trash.

The Thin Place: Ask, Answer, Pray.

Have you ever given up as lost anything to please God in your life? What was it?

Have you ever regretted anything you lost as an act of faith?

Is there something in your life right now of which God would want you to dispose?

April 16
Changing Lanes

From Above: 2 Corinthians 3:18; Galatians 6: 12-18

Focal Passage: *"Neither circumcision nor uncircumcision means any-thing; what counts is a new creation." –Galatians 6:15*

<u>Here Below</u>:

One day as I was traveling the perimeter of Atlanta, I found myself suddenly sitting still. The traffic to either side of me was hurdling by at breakneck speeds, yet I sat motionless. The car a few spots ahead of me had stalled and come to a complete stop right in the middle of this busy and dangerous point on the highway. Once I discovered that I wasn't going anywhere and that I would not be going anywhere as long as I stayed put, I decided to attempt a merge into another lane. Merging into this traffic from a standstill was not easy. Yet eventually, a good Samaritan slowed down enough to let me move into their lane. Finally, I was moving again. There is a truth to be learned from this simple and common everyday experience. Sometimes a change of lanes is required if we ever hope to move forward.

Change. That is a word that we hear often as of late, and it is usually not in the best context. Change is a word that frightens many of us. After all, we do not like leaving what we know as comfortable for the unknown. Unfortunately, that is what change is all about. It means moving forward into the unknown. Sometimes change is good, other times it is not so good. Sometimes it is needed, other times it is to be avoided. Nevertheless, change happens. However, I do not believe change is something we should fear as Christians. Isn't the Christian life all about change anyway? From the moment we accept Christ as our Lord and Savior, He begins a process of changing us into His image. We usually call this growth. Call it what you will, it is still change. You see, not every change is something to be dreaded. On the contrary, it can be to our benefit.

This brings me back to the above illustration and scripture. As a child of God, sometimes we must accept change to develop into what God would have us to be. The change I am referring to is an inside change. It is not enough to change our outward appearance or actions. Anyone can do that. More times than not, God desires a change of heart. We are as He says above "a new creation". Manipulating our outward circumstances to look the part doesn't matter at all if we have not allowed our hearts to grow and adapt to His likeness. We must grow. To stop changing is to stop growing. To stop growing is to die. So, if you find yourself sitting still spiritually, maybe it is time to change lanes.

<u>The Thin Place</u>: Ask, Answer, Pray.

What happens in life when we fail to change with the times?

Are there particular changes that you find difficult to accept? Why?

Can God use our willingness to change for His glory? Are you willing to accept God inspired changes?

April 17
Decisions...Decisions...

<u>From Above</u>: Deuteronomy 30:19; Proverbs 4:25-27

Focal Passage: *"Make level paths for your feet and take only ways that are firm." –Proverbs 4:26*

<u>Here Below</u>:

Free will is a gift that at times can seem like a mixed blessing. Please do not misunderstand me. I am grateful for the freedom to choose that God has given me, especially when it comes to matters of a spiritual nature. However, I am referring to the fact that having free will means that we are sometimes faced with the daunting task of deciding which of two uncertain roads to take. Sometimes the decision is as obvious as black and white, while at other times it is not so clear. It is in those not so black and white times that life would be simpler if God would just make the decision for us. Yet, in His wisdom, He has allowed us to choose.

Every day we face these moments of decision. From the moment we awaken each morning we choose how we are going to face our day. Many of the choices we make are insignificant for the most part. For example, choosing what we are going to wear, what we are going to eat for breakfast and other such trivial choices really have little lasting significance, but not all choices are this trivial. We face decisions every day that could affect our lives either positively or negatively from this point forward. The consequences of these choices can have lasting and eternal impact on our lives. Therefore we must make every effort to make the right choice.

Thankfully, we are not left solely to our own weak and often flawed judgment making process as we face these decisions. God thought enough of us and understood enough about us that He did not leave us to face these decisions solo. He has given us His Holy Spirit. Isn't it amazing that we have at our disposal the Spirit of the Creator of the Universe? If this is true, and it is, then why do we not consult Him more often when facing difficult options? Is it pride? Stubbornness? Or is it that we think we know better than God? Is that not what we are saying to God when we fail to consult Him on matters of lasting importance? Well, it is never too late to change that approach to decision making. Start today by asking God to fill you with His Spirit and to guide you in your choices. Just because He has given us free will doesn't mean that He wishes to be left out of our decisions. On the contrary, His desire is to guide us in the paths we should go. Do not deny God His desire to help you today! Let Him help you to choose wisely.

The Thin Place: Ask, Answer, Pray.

What are some poor choices you have made in your past?

What are some decisions you are facing or will be facing in your near future?

Have you prayed for guidance as you face this coming decision?

April 18
Get Over Yourself!

<u>From Above</u>: Matthew 22:35-39; I Corinthians 10: 32-32; 2 Timothy 3;

Focal Passage: *"For I am not seeking my own good but the good of many, so that they may be saved." –I Corinthians 10:33*

<u>Here Below</u>:

Probably the best word I can use to describe the times in which we live would have to be the word "selfish". Think about it. So much of our society is geared around getting what we want and looking out for number one. Millions of dollars are spent on trying to give ourselves pleasure and happiness in life, many times at the cost of others. However, this attitude should not surprise us. In 2 Timothy 3, we are told that this is exactly how things will be near the end of days. In this letter, Paul warns Timothy that people will be "lovers of themselves". Can you think of a better description of our time than that? It sounds accurate to me. Paul then goes on to give other explanatory words to describe the nature of man in those days. The expressive terms Paul uses are all based upon the selfishness of man. This is why it more important than ever that we daily strive to be selfless instead of selfish.

As we read Paul's words to Timothy, we need to be careful to not think of it as applying to just everyone else, but also to ourselves. If you can't see it for yourself, then it is a sure sign that it is probably for you! We need to take inventory of our own hearts. Selfishness is not a sin that is always blatantly obvious. It is a sin that can very well begin with some not so sinful attitudes. For example, we may pat ourselves on the back after a job well done and feel as if we deserve certain things out of life. And if we are not careful, we can start believing that we are more worthy of certain blessings than others, because maybe we work harder or are trying to live better. What might start out as a strong and healthy work ethic can turn into a selfish attitude if not handled properly. Likewise, seeing others gain success in life can lead us to want the same, no matter the cost. Or even worse, we can let the *sinful* actions of others produce bitterness in our own hearts to the point of the total neglect of all other people. Selfishness is a sneaky sin that usually starts small. It then grows and grows until it consumes you. How then do we overcome it?

Well, more than once Jesus gave us the cure for selfishness. Put others first. Put simply, the best way to get over yourself, your own problems, your own disappointments and even your own success and pride is to put others ahead of yourself. Sounds too simple, huh? Well, Jesus told us the two greatest commandments were to love God and then love others. Why? When your concern is primarily for the welfare of others, it is hard to feel sorry for yourself or to feel as if you deserve more out of life. This is not just some pie in the sky prescription for happy living. This is what Jesus knew to be the solution for our selfishness. If there were less selfishness in the world, think how much better and peaceful life would be. So let it start with you today. Let's begin by getting over ourselves!

The Thin Place: Ask, Answer, Pray.

What are some examples of selfish attitudes you have witnessed in the past?

Have you ever exhibited those attitudes yourself? When and how?

What can you do differently today to help prevent selfishness from creeping into your own heart?

April 19
Anger Mismanagement

From Above: Proverbs 16:32, 22:24-25; James 1: 19-20

Focal Passage: *"For man's anger does not bring about the righteous life that God desires."* –James 1:20

Here Below:

One day, at church of all places, someone approached me with a comment concerning one of my children. It was not a comment concerning their behavior or my parenting or anything such as that. It was instead an intensely personal, ugly and unwarranted racial insult that I believe was merely an attempt to ruffle my feathers and cause a scene. It almost had the desired effect. I was intensely angered. However, I did manage to spoil their fun. I did not lose my temper and cause a scene. I was somehow able to keep my cool. I then very softly and reverently with my best pastoral voice whispered to this person that I was going to forget that I was their pastor if they ever spoke to me like that again. Now did I handle it correctly? Probably not. But by standing firm, while at the same time not losing my cool that day, I believe I did make it easier for reconciliation to later take place. This person eventually apologized, and we now have a amicable relationship. Even though I was justifiably, and I feel righteously incensed, had I responded with anger, I might be telling a different story today. I only wish I could say that I have always responded with such restraint. Unbridled anger always leads to further complications. More personal witnesses and relationships have been ruined by how we handle our anger than probably anything else.

Understand, there are times when it is okay to be angry. In fact, there are times when we should be angry. Anger over certain injustices can lead us to make necessary changes. Anger in and of itself is not sinful. Jesus Himself was angry at times. It becomes sinful when we let it control us. Ultimately, we hurt no one but ourselves by letting our anger get the best of us. Nothing good ever comes with a runaway temper. Self-control on the other hand is a fruit of the Spirit.

Letting go of our anger is for our own benefit. This is why we are told to forgive those who have harmed us or caused us grief. We don't just forgive when the one that has wronged us asks us to forgive them. We forgive them even if they never ask us to forgive them. Remember all that turning the other cheek stuff? Jesus meant it! He wants us to do just that. By doing so, we are not only honoring God, but we are helping ourselves. While others may hurt us, only we can control how we respond to that hurt. Bitterness is a *self-inflicted* wound. Don't let those wounds go untreated, thus letting the real enemy win. And don't let the heat of the moment cause you further angst down the road. Instead, ask God for self-control. Respond with forgiveness. Don't manage your anger. Dispose of it.

The Thin Place: Ask, Answer, Pray.

When was the last time you were really angry? What happened?

Did you handle your anger in that situation in a way that was pleasing to God?

What steps can you take to respond to such situations in way that is more pleasing to God?

April 20
Something a Camel Once Taught Me

From Above: Proverbs 8: 10-21; Matthew 19:16-30

Focal Passage: *"With me are riches and honor, enduring wealth and prosperity."* –Proverbs 8:18

Here Below:

Hanging on my wall is a picture that has captured one of my favorite memories. It is a picture of me riding a camel with the skyline of Jerusalem in the background. It was taken during a tour of the Holy land a few years ago. Of course, what you cannot see in the picture was just how stubborn and difficult that camel had been acting. He was grunting and slobbering all over the place and wasn't cooperating with his master as I felt he should be. Nevertheless, I couldn't go to the Middle East and not go on a camel ride. So, I paid my fee and climbed aboard the filthy animal. All the while in my mind, I kept imagining this beast breaking free and running wildly through the streets of Jerusalem with me on its back screaming all the way, causing an international incident of some sort. Thankfully, that did not happen. It was a fun but anxious and highly uncomfortable experience. The worst part was getting the smell of camel out of my clothes and off my skin!

I think of that scene every time I read the above passage of scripture taken from Matthew 19. I believe there was more to the illustration of the camel going through the eye of a needle than just the animal's size. Everything I have ever seen of camels leads me to believe that they are stubborn and willful creatures with a mind all their own. Put simply, it is hard to lead a camel anywhere, much less through the eye of a needle. Jesus used this illustration to drive home a valid point. When we *stubbornly* hold on to the wealth of this world, it is impossible to grasp the wealth of the next. We must let go.

When Jesus conversed with this young man, He knew that he was a man of wealth and status. He also knew that this rich young ruler was a "good" man. He admitted to keeping the commandments. Yet, Jesus saw in his heart stubbornness. He was unwilling to let go of the one thing that stood between himself and the Lord. God is never satisfied with second place. This sad young man missed the eternal kingdom of God because of his love for wealth. For us, it may not be riches standing between us and the Lord. It may be something totally different. Nevertheless, the question remains. Would you be willing to give it up if that is what it took to follow Jesus? You see, Jesus was teaching us all that what makes us rich is not what we have or what positions we hold. In the end, all men are equal. Only what we do for the Lord has any lasting significance. It is not what we stubbornly hold on to, but what we willingly surrender that matters to God. The key to true wealth is found in surrender of self to God. Would you like to be rich today? Then let go of what you cannot keep anyway and take hold of what you can never lose.

<u>**The Thin Place**</u>: Ask, Answer, Pray.

Is there anything in your life that you could not surrender to the Lord if required?

Would you consider yourself a wealthy person, spiritually speaking?

Would you say you spend more time on things temporal or on things eternal?

April 21
Punch Bug!

<u>**From Above**</u>: Psalm 51:6; Proverbs 2:5-7

Focal Passage: *"Surely you desire truth in the inner parts; you teach me wisdom in the inmost place." –*Psalm 51:6

<u>**Here Below**</u>:

There was a game that I used to play as a child that perhaps you are familiar with as well. The first child to see a Volkswagen Beetle on the road would yell out "Punch Bug!" and then slug their friend on the arm, leaving him a throbbing bruise. Sounds fun, huh? Well, it was, I guess. I remember thinking to myself that one day I would like to have one of those strange little cars that had inspired this torturous game. That dream came true. One day I saw a 69 Volkswagen Beetle for sale. It was in pretty bad shape, but the body and frame looked to be pretty sound. I convinced myself that this would be a great restoration project to undertake, and I bought it. I reasoned that I could buy this classic car at this ridiculously low price, restore it and be the envy of all my friends. Who knows, I might even be able to resell it and turn a hefty profit! There was only one problem. I forgot that I knew nothing about Volkswagen engines. When I first started exploring this feat of German engineering, I realized just how ignorant I was on the subject. It was completely alien to me. For months I worked on this engine. I spent money on repairs and repair manuals and books. I researched the internet for self-help instructions. Yet, I was never able to restore the engine to road worthiness. In fact, I pushed that little silver Bug further than I ever was able to drive it. Finally, after months of laboring in vain and receiving my own share of cuts and bruises in the process, I sold it for less than what I had it in it, and I was glad to do so. "Punch Bug!" had taken on a whole new meaning for me! Even as I sold it, the new owner had to tow it away! The moral of this story is that true wisdom comes from knowing one's own limitations.

Too often we pride ourselves on our intelligence, only to find out the hard way that what we really know and what we think we know are not always the same. Thankfully there is a difference between intelligence and wisdom. Intelligence comes from studying and researching those things of interest to us. However, one can be an expert on a subject and still not have wisdom. Wisdom is being able to apply what we do know in a way that benefits ourselves and others. Wisdom is being able to make the right choices and avoid the wrong ones. Wisdom is being able to avoid things such as impulsively buying a broken-down VW Bug! Wisdom comes from knowing ourselves and our limits and tendencies.

Thankfully, wisdom is not something that we obtain from reading manuals or books. Wisdom comes from God. He gives wisdom and gives it liberally to all whom ask (James 1:5). It is found in His Word and in following His will. He desires wisdom for each of us. Notice the above Psalm. He desires truth and He teaches wisdom. It is not in human accomplishment, but it is a gift of God. Ask for it today!

The Thin Place: Ask, Answer, Pray.

Have you ever made any unwise choices in life? When?

What have you learned from these unwise choices you have made in your past?

What can you do differently to avoid the same mistake in the future?

April 22
Say When!

From Above: I Timothy 6:6-11; Hebrews 13:5-6

Focal Passage: *"But godliness with contentment is great gain."* –I Timothy 6:6

Here Below:

I have often wondered why our human nature makes it so difficult to be content with what we have when what we have is usually more than enough. We always seem to want just a little bit more than what we possess. This discontent is not limited to those of us who might be considered to have little either. Oftentimes those with the most are the ones that are the least content. It doesn't make sense; yet it is the truth. It must be part of the fallen human nature. It has little to do with our economic standing and everything to do with the condition of our heart.

God assures us in His Word that contentment with our circumstances and possessions is to be a real and practical part of the Christian life. Contentment is the precursor to peace. Spiritual and emotional restlessness is the ultimate outcome of having a discontented spirit. Nothing we gain will ever be enough if we can't at first be happy with what we have. There will always be something else we feel we must own or experience. It is a never-ending cycle of wanting and never quite reaching our goal. This leads to anxiety and feelings of inadequacy.

On the other hand, there is a true rest that comes from contentment. Some of the happiest and fulfilled people I have ever met had very little materially or even socially speaking. They looked at what they did have as real blessings. The difference between them and the discontented is that they know where to draw the line. They know when to say "when"! Oh, that we might all know that point in our life. Does this mean material wealth is wrong? Of course not. God has blessed us so that we might be a blessing to others and to His kingdom work. The key is found in being just as happy with less as with more. Recognize where your true blessings lie. Know when to say when!

The Thin Place: Ask, Answer, Pray.

Would you say that you are content with your life or that you feel like you need more?

What do you have now that really is more of a want than a need? Could you live without it?

Have you taken time today to thank God for the blessings of life that He has poured upon you?

April 23
The Ear Tingle

<u>From Above</u>: I Samuel 3

Focal Passage: *"The LORD came and stood there, calling as at the other times, "Samuel! Samuel!" Then Samuel said, "Speak, for your servant is listening.""* –I Samuel 3:10

<u>Here Below</u>:

I love the story of the calling of Samuel. He was still a boy and yet God had great plans for this young prophet. In the dark hours of the night, God began to speak to him. At first, Samuel thought he was hearing the voice of his master, Eli. It wouldn't be long before God revealed Himself to the boy and set his feet upon a path that would change the world.

In the above verse, we see a very important statement. Samuel says "Speak, for your servant is listening." You see, the content of that statement addresses the leading cause as to why so many complain that God doesn't answer their prayers. Could it be that He is answering, we just aren't listening? Wait a minute! Are you saying that God still speaks audibly to His children? Well, He can and He might; yet, more often than not He chooses to answer in other ways. The problem is not that He is not speaking to us or even that we do not pray. The problem is that we are often too busy and set on our desired answer to really hear His voice. What set Samuel apart was that he was truly listening for God. I love the promise God gives Him. He promises to do something that will set everyone's ears to tingling (vs. 11). You know what? I believe God still wants to do that. He wants us to open our hearts and ears to His words. He wants that kind of conversational relationship with His children. That has always been His desire. If we do that, He will lead us in the way that is best for us and will quite possibly set our ears to tingling for Him.

When you think about it, our prayers are often rude. We pray, asking for something usually, and then we say "Amen" and we are through. Imagine if someone called you and gave you a list of needs and before you could even speak, they hung up on you! Well, our prayers are often like that! God deserves better. So slow down and take time to listen. You might be surprised just how clearly God's voice can be to a heart that is truly listening. Let Samuel's statement be yours as well. Maybe God will give you an ear tingle today.

The Thin Place: Ask, Answer, Pray.

When was the last time you felt as if God was speaking to you?

Would you say that you listen for the voice of God in your life?

What can you do to help yourself be a better listener?

April 24
Up to Here!

From Above: Psalm 69:1-13

Focal Passage: *"But I pray to you, O LORD, in the time of your favor; in your great love, O God, answer me with your sure salvation."* –Psalm 69:13

Here Below:

One of things I love about King David is that as great of a king, warrior, and musician as he was, he was still abundantly human. By this I mean that he made the same mistakes as we daily do and some even worse. Yet, through it all he is known as a man after God's own heart. The above-mentioned Psalm gives us one more example of his humanity, and in so doing provides for us some wisdom for daily living.

In verse 13 we see that David knows from where his help and salvation derives. It comes from God. In a situation in which it seems the entire world is out to get him; David turns to God with this very open and honest prayer. However, did you notice verse 1? He cries out for God to save him, because he is up to his neck in trouble. He has waited, or so it seems, until he is almost over his head in trouble before this prayer song begins. He knew from where his help would come, but he waited until the last possible moment to cry out to God for help, or so the song implies. How often do we do the same thing?

All too often we wait until we are up to *here* in our troubles before we cry out to God. Why is that? Is it because we think we can handle it on our own? Is it pride? Or do we honestly look at God as more or less of a last resort? Granted, our prayer lives should be more than just requests and petitions. We need to include thanksgiving and praises as well. Not only that, but if you read on in this prayer you will see in verse 5 that part of it contained confession and repentance as well. Nevertheless, asking for help when needed should be a very real part of our prayers. Jesus taught us so. He prayed for help in His hour of need. You see, God should be the one we turn to first, not when all else has been tried and found lacking. The problem is that it sometimes takes us getting up to our necks in the troubled water to see our need for God's intervention. Don't wait until you are drowning to call out to God. Start your day by calling out to Him.

The Thin Place: Ask, Answer, Pray.

Do you tend to wait until your situation turns desperate to turn to God?

If so, why do you think that this happens?

What difference would coming to God first have made in this type of crisis situation?

April 25
WYSIWYG!

From Above: John 1:44-51 ; Hebrews 11:6

Focal Passage: *"When Jesus saw Nathanael approaching, he said of him, "Here is a true Israelite, in whom there is nothing false.""* –John 1:47

Here Below:

There is an old term used in computer programming called WYSI-WYG. It is an acronym for "What You See is What You Get". For example, it is often used when designing a website. If you are using a certain program that utilizes WYSIWYG design, then the finished site will look exactly as the design template in which you are working. There will be no hidden codes or formulas showing on the completed site. The finished product will look exactly as it does in design. Put simply, the outside will be identical to the inside. If only we could apply WYSIWYG design to our own lives! Maybe we can...

I love the above story. Recently doing a study of the life of Nathaniel has left me with the conclusion that like him or not, Nathaniel was honest. With him, what you see is what you get! When first approached by his friends and given an introduction to Jesus, Nathaniel responded by saying "Nazareth! Can anything good come from there?" Wow! What an insult. This insult revealed a social prejudice felt by him and many others in his day. Yet, when Jesus approaches, He pays Nathaniel with the above-mentioned compliment. It is almost as if Jesus was complimenting him on the fact that he was at least honest about his feelings toward Jesus, good or bad. It didn't end there. This transparency shown by Nathaniel opened the door for Jesus to reach him and teach him. Most importantly, it allowed Jesus to use him. Let's not be too critical of ol' Nate here. After all, just moments later he would declare Jesus to be a Rabbi and the Son of God. Here we see one of the first proclamations of Jesus' messiahship. While we know very little about him, we do know that Nathaniel went on to be one of Jesus' most faithful disciples, staying with Him and the others even following the resurrection.

If Jesus appreciated the honesty and integrity of Nathaniel, doesn't it only make sense that He feels the same about us? Perhaps Jesus would rather have an honest wrong answer than to have us try to impress Him with flowery words and fake living. God can do more with an honest wrong heart than with a deceitful wrong heart that may look the part of a faithful follower. Not only that, but God can more easily use that kind of honesty to reach others with His message of hope and grace. Just as with Nathaniel, God desires an open and honest relationship with you. Be honest with God today. Trust me, He can take it. In fact, He desires it.

The Thin Place: Ask, Answer, Pray.

Would you say that with your life what you see is what you get?

Do you appreciate that WYSIWYG quality in others? Why?

What can you do differently to help build that quality in yourself?

April 26
Sheepless Nights

From Above: Colossian 3

Focal Passage: *"Let the peace of Christ rule in your hearts, since as members of one body you were called to peace. And be thankful."* –Colossian 3:15

Here Below:

There is nothing more miserable than lying in a bed thinking of the busy day you have ahead of you and not being able to go to sleep. Maybe the events of the day behind you or the day to come are overwhelming and you just can't find the rest that you so want. You try counting sheep, warm milk or even reading (as I do) to help you sleep, but it still eludes you. There have even been times when I was so physically tired that I couldn't go to sleep! It is a torturous situation that can really wear on your physical self. Well, it is no surprise that oftentimes this physical exhaustion has more to do with our spiritual condition than our physical condition. Our spiritual restlessness can have devastating effects.

Worry is the enemy of all God's children. Why? Because it robs us of the joy that God intends for us. Even Jesus himself asked what we can add to our lives by worrying (Matthew 6:27). On the contrary, it takes away from the quality of life. Worry can also keep us from moving forward in our spiritual journey. It is like running with extra heavy ankle weights. It slows us down and ultimately wears us down. Yet, God's plan is for us to run with strength, endurance, and freedom. How then do we do that? Well, we must understand from where true peace of mind comes.

Notice the above verse and many others like it throughout scripture. Paul doesn't just say let peace rule in your hearts. He says to let the "peace of Christ rule in your hearts". It is not the peace of having your circumstances changed. It is not the peace of having everything go your way. It is a peace that comes only from knowing Jesus Christ and trusting in God's will to prevail. It is this peace that enabled Paul to sleep just fine in his prison cell even though his future was so uncertain. It is a peace that can likewise enable you and I to have a good night's sleep no matter what tomorrow may have in store. It is a peace that is stronger than circumstances. It comes when we totally surrender our lives to God. Notice what other advice the above verse gives us. It says to be thankful. So, are you tired of counting sheep? If you prefer a sheepless night over a sleepless night, try counting your blessings instead. God will honor that thought. It is his desire to give you sweet dreams. Seek His peace and you will find the rest you need.

The Thin Place: Ask, Answer, Pray.

Have you ever found yourself spiritually in need of rest? When?

What steps have you taken to find the peace you need in your life?

What changes you can make today that might better enable you to find deeper spiritual peace?

April 27
Impressed Yet?

From Above: Luke 16

Focal Passage: *"He said to them, "You are the ones who justify yourselves in the eyes of men, but God knows your hearts. What is highly valued among men is detestable in God's sight." –Luke 16:15*

<u>Here Below</u>:

One of the things that I find great comfort in is the fact that God has a totally different value system than men. Put simply, what is important to men may not always be important to the Lord. He is not easily impressed by men's social, political, or similar achievements. Please do not misunderstand. Achievement is not a bad thing. In fact, I believe God will honor our hard work and determination with blessings if we are careful to acknowledge His role in them. However, what I am saying is that God is more interested in our inner achievements than our outward appearance. Why? Because He knows that it is what is on the inside that makes us who and what we really are. Likewise, with God, we cannot manipulate our inner self for the sake of appearance as we can with our outward person. There are no political mind games with God. He knows the real you, like it or not.

The above scripture speaks very strongly as to how God values things. He says that what is of value to men, He finds detestable. Does this mean that what we think is important means nothing to God? Of course not. He is very interested in what interests us. He is however implying that the value system of the world is often in contrast to His. It also has to do with the order in which we place our priorities. All too often we treat others and ourselves according to the worldly system rather than how God would have us, basing our attitudes toward others on our earthly standards. We base decisions on this pattern of thinking as well. We even try to impress others (and God for that matter) with things that God finds unimpressive. This leaves us with a problem. Are we going to adopt God's values or keep some other form as our principle guide? And how do we change our values?

Well, the test for this is easy. What occupies the majority of your time, resources and thought life? This is what you value the most. Okay, how does this fit into what God's Word teaches as important? Once you answer these questions, you must then apply God's value system and act accordingly. It is not something that can happen instantly; in that, we can't change what's important to us overnight.

However, by spending time daily with God and His word, over time it will become easier and easier to recognize what is really important and to act accordingly. In time, you will find great value in the things of God. Start by taking an honest inventory of your heart. Who are you really trying to impress? Once you do this, you will find your life less anxious and your heart and mind will enjoy greater peace. Remember, God places His greatest value on you. Don't take that for granted!

The Thin Place: Ask, Answer, Pray.

What occupies the majority of your time, resources and thought life? Be honest.

What values do you have that are in agreement with the word of God?

What values do you have that are in disagreement with the word of God?

April 28
The Ultimate Cheat

From Above: Proverbs 14:32; Job 14:5; John 8:51

Focal Passage: *"Man's days are determined; you have decreed the number of his months and have set limits he cannot exceed."* –Job 14:5

Here Below:

It has been said that we can cheat at cards, cheat on our taxes and cheat on tests, but we cannot cheat death. Is this true? Well, it is for certain that we each have an appointment that we must all keep one day. The above passage from Job reminds us that our days are numbered and regardless of how hard we exercise or how healthy we eat, we cannot exceed the lifetime limit God has given us. As a bumper sticker I once saw reads, "Eat right, exercise and die anyway!" Well, I do appreciate the sarcasm of that bumper sticker philosophy, but its reasoning is flawed. One very important detail has not been taken into account. Death is not the end.

Many people read the above verse and find it disturbing. It reminds them of the futility that we sometimes feel concerning our lives and the uncertain nature of its length. However, I find the verse encouraging in many ways. It should serve as a reminder to us of the fact that God is involved in every detail of our lives. It is a reminder of the all-knowing and all-loving power of our God. Second, it should serve as an incentive for us to make the most of the time of which we are certain. That time is right now. I do not believe God included this in His word to cause us to fret or worry. On the contrary, I think He meant it to give our lives purpose. Third, it is a reminder that death is not necessarily something to fear or dread. We should view it as the ultimate victory. Why? Because through Jesus we can cheat death!

We can cheat death; in that, we have the ability to take away its power over us. More appropriately, I should say that Jesus has taken away its power over us. Not having the dark shadow of death hanging over our heads gives us a freedom and joy in life that nothing else can give. By living for God now, I rob death of its one ace in the hole. Don't get me wrong! This doesn't mean that we foolishly look forward to dying. Of course, we want to live a long time and experience life to the fullest. But we can only do that if we are able to focus on the moment without worrying that this might be the last one. The fact that my days are numbered is just further evidence that God is going to take care of me all the way. My eternity is set; therefore, my here and now can be abundantly lived. We can cheat death daily by living for eternity. It is the ultimate cheat.

<u>The Thin Place</u>: Ask, Answer, Pray.

Do you find comfort or frustration in the fact that your days are numbered?

How does facing our own mortality help us to experience life more fully?

How does your eternal destination effect the decisions you will be making today?

April 29
Lord of the Dance

<u>**From Above**</u>: 2 Samuel 6:12-23

Focal Passage: *"David, wearing a linen ephod, danced before the LORD with all his might,"* –2 Samuel 6:14

<u>**Here Below**</u>:

Remember your high school dances? The few that I went to were almost comical. As soon as a slow song would play, everyone would get up and hit the dance floor. But let the DJ play an upbeat dance song and everyone would head for the wall. It was as if we were all scared to really dance. When I think back on this phenomenon, I can't help but think of King David in the above story. Wouldn't it have been great to have been in the crowd that day? The Ark of the Covenant was passing by in an almost parade like fashion. Everyone had gathered for its arrival; for the arrival of the Ark was as the arrival of God Himself. It was truly a time of worship and celebration. Yet, we do not see King David standing reverently with his head bowed and eyes closed as the Ark passes. Instead, we see him, virtually naked, dancing up and down the streets in celebration. This should be significant to us for several reasons.

First, notice that David was not just dancing. He was "dancing before the Lord with all his might". Anyone can dance (or at least try). There is not necessarily anything spiritual about simply dancing. For David, this was more than just moving his body in time with the music. He was worshipping. In fact, he was giving it all he had. This is further evidence that there is more than one way to worship. The fact that he was dancing with all his might must have pleased God that day. Worship is more than just going through the motions. It must come from the heart.

Second, this story also shows us the importance of humility in worship. One thing you might not recognize until you dig deeper in this story is the significance of what David was wearing, or not wearing.

He was not wearing his royal robes as a king would normally be doing when coming into town in this fashion. Instead, He was nearly naked. It would seem as if he wasn't trying to draw attention to himself, but to God. He was laying himself bare before God and the world. This is truly part of worship.

Third, we recognize that a life of true worship may draw criticism from those who do not understand. David's wife was infuriated by the spectacle David was making of himself. On the other hand, David was only concerned with pleasing God. We should never let criticism from others hinder our own relationship with God. Worship is indeed a very personal and intimate experience; whether you are all alone in the privacy of your home or whether you are on the streets before a crowd of people. It is your time alone with God. Dance, sing, pray, shout, or sit reverently, but do it with all your might.

The Thin Place: Ask, Answer, Pray.

What forms of worship do you find the most comfortable and meaningful to you?

When you worship, do you often concern yourself with the opinion of others?

In all honesty, how do you think God views your worship demeanor?

April 30
All Worked Up

From Above: Psalm 118

Focal Passage: "*Shouts of joy and victory resound in the tents of the righteous: 'The LORD's right hand has done mighty things'*" –Psalm 118:15

Here Below:

To witness a genuine display of the human propensity to mismanage our emotions, one need only attend a child's softball, football, soccer or wrestling match. At one of my children's wrestling matches, I once saw a parent screaming at the top of their lungs at their child for losing a match. And I have seen otherwise gentle and nice parents in the stands ready to fight officials over a call with which they disagreed. Likewise, I have seen people that normally are quiet and reserved screaming and shouting for joy. I am constantly amazed at how we can get all worked up over things that really do not matter in the long run and show so little emotion over things that do. Of course, I understand that everyone has different priorities and interests; therefore, we respond in different ways. However, the fact remains that we seem to have no problem expressing emotions, good or bad, over certain temporal and spiritually neutral things, while we often fail to express the slightest emotion over things of lasting and spiritual significance.

The above Psalm is a reminder to us of the importance of emotion in the life of a spiritual person. We often shy away from the feeling aspect of the Christian life for fear of emotionalism. Granted, this can be a problem. However, emotions themselves are not bad, especially when it comes to spiritual matters. We have a reason to shout and sing. It is again, a form of worship. To withhold our natural emotions is not necessarily showing reverence to the Lord any more than expressing them is necessarily worshiping. On the contrary, shouting and singing is only noise if it isn't coming from your heart. When it is a heartfelt emotional expression, God is pleased with the noise we make. It must be like the relationship between a parent and child. I know for me; I find great pleasure in hearing my children laugh and play and sing. It shows me that they are happy and taken care of. I see it as a compliment to the parenting of my wife and me. God must see it the same way with His children. Besides, we have every reason in the world to get emotionally worked up. As a born-again child of God, I have been forgiven of every rotten thing I have ever done and will ever do. I have been given the keys to the Kingdom of God and promised an eternal home in Heaven. When we really slow down and think about all that God has done for us, it should cause us to either want to shout or cry. To consider what God has done and not feel emotional over it, causes me to question one's sincerity. Don't insult the Lord by holding back your emotions from Him. Go ahead and allow yourself to get a little worked up today when you think of Him.

The Thin Place: Ask, Answer, Pray.

Would you consider yourself an emotional person? How so?

What is the danger of being over emotional? How about unemotional?

What are some ways you can express your appreciation to the Lord today?

5

May

May 1
Skeeter and the Armadillo

From Above: I John 4:1-11; James 4:7

Focal Passage: *"You, dear children, are from God and have overcome them, because the one who is in you is greater than the one who is in the world."* –I John 4:4

Here Below:

One night, not long after having moved to a new town to serve in my very first pastorate, I saw something I had never seen before. Walking around in my back yard was a creature that I had never seen alive. I had seen them lying on the side of the road, but never had I seen one alive and well. It was an armadillo. I quickly called my wife out to join me in my observation of this strange and ugly part of God's creation. In the meantime, the armadillo ran under a storage building we had behind our house. Well, I decided I would let our little dog loose to scare the armadillo out from under the building where we could see it. It was one of the craziest scenes I have ever witnessed. Our dog named Skeeter, went after that poor animal with no holding back. Did I mention that Skeeter was a Chihuahua? This tiny little dog chased that poor animal in circles all over our yard and finally chased

206

him into the woods. The irony of it all is that if that armadillo had just turned around and saw what was chasing him and making all the noise, he would have realized that he was bigger, stronger, and fiercer than Skeet could ever hope to be. That armadillo, with his razor-sharp claws, could have very easily have had Mexican for dinner that night if he had just turned around! Yet, he did not turn around to face his enemy. Instead, he just ran defeated into hiding leaving Skeet snorting and kicking around as if he were an alpha male pit bull or something.

I tell this story to help us understand a very important truth. Oftentimes, we find ourselves frightened by the evil in the world. We fear the forces of evil that are very real and very much at work. Yet, scripture tells us very clearly that we have no reason to really *fear* the Devil or anything he can do. The Bible does warn us of the Devil's strategy and purpose so that we are prepared for his attacks. Yet, in so doing, God also tells us how to deal with Him. We resist him. We do this not by our own strength, but by the strength of He who lives within us. He is bigger, stronger, and fiercer than our enemy could ever hope to be.

Like Jesus, as He faced Satan in the wilderness, we defeat him with a knowledge of God's truth found in His word (Matt. 4). We resist him with the Truth of God and strength of the Holy Spirit, and he will scurry into the woods with his tail between his legs just as that armadillo did. Sound too simple? Well, don't take my word for it. The next time you feel that the forces of evil are messing with you, just try God's solution. See the enemy for what he is, a yapping little annoyance. Throw some scripture at him. Claim the promises in that scripture and resist. Do this and you will be victorious.

<u>The Thin Place</u>: Ask, Answer, Pray.

Have you encountered what you believe to be the forces of evil at work in your life?

How did you handle this encounter?

What are some promises in God's Word that are meaningful to you that might be a good defense?

May 2
Picture Perfect

<u>**From Above**</u>: Psalm 8

Focal Passage: *"When I consider your heavens, the work of your fingers, the moon and the stars, which you have set in place, what is man that you are mindful of him, the son of man that you care for him?"* –Psalm 8:3-4

<u>**Here Below**</u>:

This time of year always serves as a reminder of the beauty of creation and our role in it. The weather is warmer and we can spend more time outdoors, enabling us to better appreciate how everything is green and growing. We spend time planting and working in our gardens with the hopes of future beauty and harvest. Even with the things we dislike about spring and summer, such as the pollen and allergy season and all the work involved in maintaining a yard, it still gives evidence to the power of God in maintaining His yard, our universe. I love this time of year.

As we appreciate the beauty of God's natural universe, we must also remember that among all if it's beauty and wonder, we are God's most prized creation. Of all things created, we are the only thing created in His image. That is really saying something about God and how much He loves us. I have seen some really beautiful picture-perfect scenery in nature, as we all have. I have seen sunsets that would make you cry. I have seen starlit skies that will humble you beyond words. I have seen God's animals carrying out their life tasks with an almost miraculous instinct, bringing one to a sense of awe and wonder that nothing else can. We can see His beauty on a beach, mountain or in a cloud. Yet, with all that beauty available to God, we are still His most cherished creation. In fact, I would say that these other things I have listed were created for our benefit. They were meant to point us to the love of God. He could have given us a two-dimensional world of black and white. Instead, He gave us the rainbow. Why? Simple. He loves us.

Today, when you go outside and see a bird at play or feel a cool breeze gently blowing across your face, remember your Creator. More importantly, remember the love your Creator has for you. Thank Him today for the beauty of His world. Thank Him for His love.

The Thin Place: Ask, Answer, Pray.

Do you ever spend time appreciating the beauty of God's creation?

How do you see yourself in light of God's creation? Do you feel loved? Humbled? Big or little?

What part of God's creation do you feel best demonstrates His love for you personally?

May 3
Fight or Flight

From Above: John 17

Focal Passage: *"My prayer is not that you take them out of the world but that you protect them from the evil one."* –John 17:15

Here Below:

Within nature, there is thought to be a fight or flight instinct instilled into every living creature. In times of trouble, we either turn to fight or we take flight by running away. I guess this is especially true when it comes to human nature. When troubles arise in our life, both physical and spiritual, we often respond in the same way. We either get defensive or else we try to run away from our problems. This instinct is often reflected in prayer lives as well. Think about it for a moment. The last time you were in trouble, how did you pray? Did you ask God to help you stand firm or did you ask him to take it away?

In John 17, we see Jesus just prior to His arrest and crucifixion. It was during a time when most of us would have been in full blown fight or flight mode. Instead, Jesus was praying. As you read the chapter you can see exactly how Jesus was praying. He was praying for Himself, His immediate Disciples and for you and me, those who would later come to faith due to the testimony of the first disciples. Notice how He prays for His disciples. First, He acknowledges that times are going to be tough for them. By doing so, He was foretelling of the coming persecution they would have to endure. But notice what he says in the above verse. He is not praying that God would remove them from their situation. On the contrary, he is praying that God will basically give them victory over the "evil one" during their time of trouble. Why wouldn't Jesus just pray that God would get them out of the situation? Could it be because He knew that how they would respond to the coming trials was part of God's plan for them? Could it be that He knew that enduring the coming trials would enable them to become the men that God wanted them to be? Could it be that God the Father's will superseded even Jesus' personal desires? The answer must be yes.

The same must also be true for you and me today. Does this mean it is wrong to ask God to remove you from a bad situation? Of course not. That may very well be part of God's will. However, it does mean being content to stay in a situation even if it is not the preferred position. Instead of praying for the flight out of your situation, try praying for the strength to fight for Him in your situation. That is how Jesus prayed. Shouldn't we do the same?

<u>**The Thin Place**</u>: Ask, Answer, Pray.

When trouble arises in your life, is your first instinct to fight or to run away?

When do you think it is appropriate to run from troubles? When is it not?

Has there ever been a time when you stayed in the fight reluctantly only to ultimately achieve victory?

May 4
The Bull's Eye

<u>From Above</u>: Psalm 139

Focal Passage: *"All the days ordained for me were written in your book before one of them came to be."* –Psalm 139:16

<u>Here Below</u>:

I once met a man that shared with me of how he had spent his entire life avoiding a specific calling he had felt as a young adolescent. Now well past middle age, he felt as if he had missed the purpose that was to be his in life. He had instead chosen to chase some dreams that he felt might give his life a happiness that his "calling" might not give. Financially better off, he would still have given up everything to go back and work toward fulfilling the purpose that had once been his. He had aimed for a target that was never meant to be his, and he hit it. The result was a life of regret. This is not the way it is supposed to be.

Scripture teaches us that God has a plan for each of our lives. This plan exists in the mind of God long before we are even formed in the womb. If this is true, why do so many reach different stages in life only to feel as if they have missed the mark? Well, it has to do with the free will of man given to us by God. While God knows the plan He has for us, He still allows us to choose other paths if we so choose. The problem is that any path other than the one He would have us take is less than what is best for us. This is why we must seek the way that God would have us to go.

In Christian circles we hear many references to finding God's will for our lives. There are countless studies and sermons out there to help with this search. Why? Because there is nothing so vital in life as knowing that you are right on target. It brings a satisfaction that nothing else can bring. It also helps us to avoid the regrets of an off-purpose life. While I have met many like the above man that would trade everything for another chance to fulfill this purpose, I have yet to meet a person living that purpose that would rather be somewhere else in life. The best place to be in life is always at the center of God's will and intent. Set your sights on God's target and you will never be disappointed.

The Thin Place: Ask, Answer, Pray.

Do you have a clear understanding of God's purpose for your life?

How well do your personal goals and God's purposes align in your life?

Is it ever too late to start aiming for the target that God has given you in life? Why?

May 5
Couch Potato Christianity

From Above: James 4:17

Focal Passage: *"Anyone, then, who knows the good he ought to do and doesn't do it, sins."* –James 4:17

Here Below:

There is no such thing as a couch potato Christian. When it comes to a life of faith, we are to be mobile. One of the struggles of the modern body of Christ is the fact that we would often rather watch others carry out the task of discipleship while we sit back in comfort and watch. A statistic I once heard said that 5% of the people within the church carry out 95% of the work. Having been a pastor now for nearly 3 decades, I trust this statistic to be accurate. This apathy unfortunately not only affects our service to the Lord, but also our personal growth in the Lord. How so? Well, many times we pat ourselves on the back for the simple fact that we have avoided a particular sin in life. We think that by avoiding some of the more obvious sins that we are living the successful Christian life. We may even go so far as to thank God for the strength to resist certain temptations. Yet, in so doing we sometimes forget one very important fact. Sin is not always an action. Sometimes by not doing something we are committing a sin.

Go. Tell. Share. Preach. Love. Do. These are all commands that we are given time and time again throughout the entire Bible. Not one of these words involves sitting still and watching the world go by. Instead, they are about getting involved in the world, with the ultimate goal of changing it. This doesn't only apply to missionaries and preachers. This is for all whom have been changed themselves by the love of the Master. It can also be applied to how we face major decisions and even minor daily decisions. Every time we encounter a choice, we are given an opportunity to follow God or to follow something else, to go or to stay. It is an opportunity to do or not to do. For fear of failure, we often choose to sit and stay than to go and do.

However, one day we must all give account of our lives to God. Thankfully, by the blood sacrifice of Jesus Christ, my sins are forgiven, and the penalty is paid in full. Yet still there will be an accounting. I think at that moment the sins I will regret the most will be the sins of not doing what I knew in reality I should do. With this in mind, we should try our best to avoid the consequences of couch potato Christianity. It is time to get up and do what we know to do. Even if we fail, at least we have done something. I think God will honor our efforts. With God leading us, it is possible to fail and still be a success!

<u>**The Thin Place**</u>: Ask, Answer, Pray.

Would you consider yourself apathetic when it comes to living for the Lord?

Has there ever been a time when you failed to do something for God that you later regretted?

Is there something right now that God is leading you to do in which you have not yet responded?

May 6
Slow Leak

<u>**From Above**</u>: 2 Kings 12:2-3; Romans 6

Focal Passage: *"Joash did what was right in the eyes of the LORD all the years Jehoiada the priest instructed him. The high places, however, were not removed; the people continued to offer sacrifices and burn incense there."* –2 Kings 12:2-3

Here Below:

Some friends and I once determined to embark upon what for us would be an all-day adventure. We were going to tube approximately ten miles or so down the Etowah River in the North Georgia Mountains on a hot summer day. We had planned everything precisely, taking into account the time it would take us, where our pickup ride needed to be and how much food and water we needed to bring. However, one thing happened for which he had not accounted. My inner tube had a tiny pin sized hole that had not been previously detected. About thirty minutes into our trek, my tube began to shrink. The pressure of my weight and the water caused the tube to lose air rather quickly. I had not noticed it before, since it only started losing air pressure as it was being used. As tiny and insignificant as the hole might seem, it made my day miserable. Every thirty minutes or so, I had to pull over to the side of the river and reinflate my tube. This went on for nearly eight hours! Why did this happen? Because I did not check to see if the tube was 100% and in good condition. What would have been a two-minute repair turned into an all day ordeal. My day was ruined. Likewise, we must not leave any part of our spiritual life unchecked, regardless of how insignificant it might seem.

The above story of King Joash gives us a perfect example. Joash began his reign in Judah rather successfully. Everything looked good. He had taken great pains to destroy the idols and worship of false gods that had so permeated the land prior to his becoming king. He managed to restore worship of the true and living God. Yet, there was one thing he missed. He had one small leak that he failed to repair. He did not destroy the altars established in the high places of the mountains. They were out of sight and out of mind and seemed insignificant. However, it wasn't long until this oversight leaked throughout the entire kingdom and once again the nation was living in rebellion to God. This all happened because the king failed to fix a tiny insignificant leak when he had the opportunity. You see, God wants 100% of our lives. We can't walk the successful Christian walk if there is one part of our lives that we have left unchecked. One tiny leak in our lives can lead to a life of sinking deeper and deeper into sin. Sin spreads. It is like a disease. It cannot go unchecked. To live as we should means to look at even the parts of our lives that we think are out of sight and out of mind, those parts that no one else can see. God can see them, and he wants those parts as well. He wants all of us, not just part. When you give your all to Him, you will find the ride to be smoother and more enjoyable. So, take time today to check for leaks. Give Him everything today.

The Thin Place: Ask, Answer, Pray.

Would you say that God has 100% of your life or is there a part you are withholding?

What might happen if you let certain areas of your life go unchecked?

What changes can you make today that will help fix any leaks you might have in your spiritual life?

May 7
Boomerang Belief

From Above: Isaiah 55

Focal Passage: *"So is my word that goes out from my mouth: It will not return to me empty, but will accomplish what I desire and achieve the purpose for which I sent it."* –Isaiah 55:11

Here Below:

Have you ever tried to throw a boomerang? It is not as simple as it looks. It does come back. However, getting it to come back to the place that you want is another story. I guess like all things, it takes practice to get the boomerang to return to the precise place that you desire. Evidence of this fact can be seen as you look at the roof of my house. My kids received a toy boomerang as a gift, and it always seems to find a home on our roof. Nevertheless, it is faithful to return. We always know where to find it when we need it.

The above verse refers to the boomerang effect of the word of God. This verse is a reminder to us of the returning nature of God's Word in the life of the believer. It testifies to the fact that God's truth is never shared in vain. Even in those times when we may not see the desired result right away, a seed of truth has been planted that in due time will take root and grow into a harvest. This bears witness to the power of the word of God. It has a way of penetrating hearts that we might consider impenetrable.

However, I think that this verse goes beyond just the proclamation of God's Word. I think it is safe to apply this principle of boomerang belief to the application of His Word as well. When we apply the truth of God's word to our lives, it will return to us in the form of blessings, both spiritual and literal. Not only that, but it will in turn spill over into the lives of others, thus fulfilling its purpose. You know, God has a way of changing everything He touches. One cannot encounter the true and living God or His Word without being changed to some degree. His truth always comes back to us to work His desired effect in our hearts. Ultimately however, it is up to us to apply it. The boomerang will not return until we first give it a try. Will you do that today? If so, be ready. You never know where the blessings might land.

The Thin Place: Ask, Answer, Pray.

How influential is the word of God in your life?

Can you name some of the times in your life in which God has been faithful to His Word?

Is there any reason to believe that God will not do that again?

May 8
Missing the Point of the Day

From Above: Psalm 65; John 10:10

Focal Passage: "*The thief comes only to steal and kill and destroy; I have come that they may have life, and have it to the full.*" –John 10:10

<u>Here Below</u>:

As I get older, I am discovering that I find the most pleasure in the everyday unexpected aspects of life. Things I once took for granted are now the things I cherish the most. These unplanned moments of life are the flavor of life. For example, I find immense joy in sneaking up behind someone and poking them in the ribs and watching them jump. How about watching quietly from around the corner your three-year-old son singing and dancing when he thinks no one is around? How about wrestling with your preteen kids? Or your wife!? Is there anything more inspiring than catching the sunrise or sunset from your back patio at just that right moment? Even chores like washing your car or cutting your grass can become a pleasure when approached with the right attitude.

Life is filled with daily adventures and pleasures that cannot be scheduled; yet, all too often we do not take the time to appreciate them. One fault found in most of humanity is our tendency to fill our hours with activities of such a serious nature that we miss the more enjoyable moments that occur so regularly. Daily living is inundated with opportunity after opportunity to just stop and appreciate life itself. Why then do we so often miss the point?

After all, the Bible teaches us very clearly that God's intent for us is to truly experience the life abundant and full. These things we fill our lives with are not necessarily bad things. Work and responsibilities are a natural, good, and expected part of the experience. The mistake comes when we so pour ourselves into these actions that we miss the joys along the way. We work so hard to make life better for ourselves and our loved ones that life becomes less enjoyable in the process. Time is so valuable. In fact, it is our most precious commodity. We must not waste a moment of it. Yes, there will always be work to be done; but along the way there is some fun to be had as well. The Christian life is meant to be enjoyable. It is not always easy, but it is still meant to be enjoyable. Don't so busy yourself as to miss the real adventure each day brings. Look instead for a new opportunity today to live it to the full. Have some fun today!

The Thin Place: Ask, Answer, Pray.

Would you consider yourself a busy person? Why or why not?

Would you say that for the most part you enjoy life, or do you find life more of a struggle?

What changes can you make in your behaviors and actions that might increase your daily joy?

May 9
A Face Only a Mother Could Love

From Above: I John 4

Focal Passage: *"Dear friends, let us love one another, for love comes from God. Everyone who loves has been born of God and knows God. Whoever does not love does not know God, because God is love."* – I John 4:7-8

Here Below:

Let's be honest for a moment. All babies are cute in their own way. However, sometimes the pictures we are handed of newborn babies are best admired through the eyes of their mother. From this reality comes the expression that refers to having "a face only a mother could love." I don't say this to be funny or to be crude. On the contrary, it speaks to the beautiful love found between that of a mother and a child. When I consider the love of God, perhaps the closest thing on earth that I can equate with it is the love that a mother has for her child. It is unconditional. She thinks her children are the most beautiful children ever born and she will love them with all she is until the day that she dies. She is slow to find fault and quick to find reason for praise. A godly mother is a living testimony of God's grace, mercy, and love.

I do not believe this happens on accident. I think God instilled in the heart of women the capacity to love in such a way. Sure, a mother sometimes must be stern with her children. She must discipline them in such a way as to raise them in the nurture and admonition of God's Word and principles. Yet, through it all, her driving force is love for her children. This sounds familiar, doesn't it? It sounds an awful lot like the way God loves His children. Perhaps when God looked at Adam in the Garden of Eden, He saw more than just the need for a companion for Adam. Perhaps He saw the need for a living example of a love that was not based on stature or performance. Just as God's love is not fault finding, neither is a mother's. That is why there is such a special relationship between mother and child. When my children fall and scrape their knee, they do not cry for Dad. Only Mama can wipe away those tears. This is not an insult to me as a father. It is simply an acknowledgment of the difference between man and woman. We can all testify to this truth. We all have special women in our lives that fill that nurturing need that we each have from time to time. It is beautiful; in that, it points us to God. Take time today to show thankfulness and appreciation for the special women in your life.

The Thin Place: Ask, Answer, Pray.

What women have been the greatest influence in your life and why?

What qualities do these women possess that are of the most encouragement to you?

Will you take time today to show appreciation to the special women and mothers in your life?

May 10
Do it Yourself Destruction

From Above: Proverbs 16:18, 26:12; 2 Corinthians 10

Focal Passage: *"But, "Let him who boasts boast in the Lord." For it is not the one who commends himself who is approved, but the one whom the Lord commends."* – 2 Corinthians 10:17-18

<u>Here Below</u>:

Being a new father of only a couple of years, I decided to build something special for my kids. They needed a new toy box in which to keep their growing number of toys. So, I set out to build them one that would be the envy of all the other kids in the neighborhood. Of course, I had never done anything like this ever before, but I imagined that it could not be that difficult. I have a friend that was well experienced in carpentry that offered to help, but I wanted to be a do-it-yourself kind of man. My pride would not allow me to ask him for help or advice. Needless to say, the toy box looked more like a coffin when I was finished with it. In fact, my wife offered to use it as one for me in the process! Building this box had been a nightmare. I had built it extremely big for the little room in which it would belong. It was so crooked and so ugly that I was ashamed for anyone to see it. I had put it together in the boy's bedroom and when we moved from that house, I had to saw the ugly thing in half just to get it out the door. I then used half of it as a doghouse. It went from being a toy box, to a would-be coffin, to a doghouse and finally to a pile of broken debris. And all of this happened because I simply was too proud to admit I needed help.

Pride is perhaps at the root of most of the problems we face in life. We try to do everything ourselves and often want to take credit for anything good that happens. This attitude totally leaves God's work in our lives out of the picture. Not only that, but it also negates our need for God's grace. Consider the above scripture. If anyone had a reason to boast of their accomplishments, it was the Apostle Paul. Yet, with all his accomplishments, he still understood that if it were not for the grace of God, he would have been nothing. If he were going to brag, He could only honestly brag on God and what God what done in his life. If this is true of Paul, it must be true of us as well. Pride is still at the root of most sin and selfishness and pride still comes just before the fall. We all stand in need of God's help and God's grace. There is no shame in admitting the truth. Don't let pride turn your toy box into a doghouse. Acknowledge your need for God today and God will honor your honesty and humility.

The Thin Place: Ask, Answer, Pray.

Has there been a time in your life when pride caused you to stumble?

In what areas of your life do you struggle the most with the sin of pride most often?

How can you avoid becoming prideful in the future?

May 11
Tug of War

From Above: Ezekiel 18:21-23; I Timothy 1:13-16

Focal Passage: *"But if a wicked man turns away from all the sins he has committed and keeps all my decrees and does what is just and right, he will surely live; he will not die." –* Ezekiel 18:21

Here Below:

Years ago, I visited a museum of strange and unique exhibits that had one very disturbing attraction. It was a tunnel. This round tunnel had mirrors on the side and one panel at the end of the tunnel that was spinning. This spinning panel reflecting in the mirrors gave the entire tunnel the illusion of movement. As you entered this tunnel, you felt as if you were spiraling down a funnel to the tiny opening at the other end of the seemingly endless tunnel. In actuality, the tunnel was only 8 or 10 feet long. The mirrors and spinning effect gave it the optical illusion of great length and movement, making it nearly impossible to walk a straight line and even harder to find the center of that walkway. If you stopped as you walked those few feet, you felt as if you were being pulled to either side, when in reality you were standing still. It was one of the strangest sensations I have ever experienced.

I could not take this pull very long. I hurried quickly and carefully to the other end to find freedom from this unnatural draw.

One thing I have learned about human nature is our tendency to allow ourselves to be pulled. We allow sin to pull us. We allow temptation to pull us. We allow circumstances to pull us. Pull us where? We allow these and other things to pull us away from the center of God's will. We are in a constant spiritual tug of war. This is why we must understand the true nature of repentance.

Many view repentance as a onetime thing. When we sin and are convicted of that sin, we repent, and we move on. Well, I am not sure it happens just like that. Yes, to repent is to turn away from our sin, but it is not something that necessarily happens all at once. True repentance is more than just a solitary action. It is a lifestyle. A repentant lifestyle is something we must all fully embrace if we are ever to withstand the pulls of the world against our hearts and minds. If we do not maintain a *daily* spirit of repentance, we will find ourselves yet again being pulled to the side. This is our fallen human nature. Yes, repentance is turning away from a particular sin; but we must then turn to God for strength to avoid it in the future. To do otherwise is to open ourselves up for more and more of the dizzying effect of an unguarded heart and ultimately set the stage for another stumble. Just like in the above museum attraction, the best way to get to the end successfully is to look straight ahead. We must keep our eyes on the grace of God. We cannot allow the world to pull us away from what God intends. Look to Him and He will help you avoid the pull and reach the freedom that awaits you.

The Thin Place: Ask, Answer, Pray.

What do you think is the difference between repenting of sin and feeling sorry for our sin?

Is repentance a part of your daily life? If not, why?

How would you describe the feeling of freedom that comes with true repentance?

May 12
Diving Deep

<u>**From Above**</u>: Proverbs 20:5; Romans 7:22-23

Focal Passage: *"The purposes of a man's heart are deep waters, but a man of understanding draws them out."* – Proverbs 20:5

<u>**Here Below**</u>:

How well do you know yourself? I suppose that sounds like a silly question. Most of us would agree that we know ourselves better than anyone else could possibly know us. Yet, I wonder how honest we are when it comes to how well we truly know ourselves. It is not an easy thing to sit down and really look into the deep recesses of our hearts and minds. Often when we do this, if we are honest, we probably see some things we do not like. However, an honest self-evaluation is a necessary part of the Christian life.

The above Proverb describes the purposes of our heart as "deep waters". These purposes could be considered those things which cause us to do the things we do. They are our motivations. These are the things that make us tick! Our motivation may be success, money, fame, sex, friendship, happiness, revenge, or just about anything else the human heart can devise. As you can see, some of these motivations are good and others are not so good. If we can as the great Teacher of Proverbs suggests, draw them out and examine them for what they really are, then we can best make the changes that need to be made. Not all our purposes are in keeping with the word and will of God. Dealing with these purposes head on is the first step in reaching a place in our lives in which we are centered on the will of God. Again, as the writer suggests, we must dive deep sometimes to find these purposes.

We can however find comfort in the fact that God is already aware of the deep-water drives in our life. Not only is He aware of them, but He loves us despite the ones that should not be there. He also is willing and able to empower you to change your purposes to that which is healthy for you and pleasing to him. This question remains for us today. Are we willing to draw out the deep-water purposes of our lives? Are we willing to face our true selves? Are we willing to dive deep? Are you? Dive in. You will be glad you did.

<u>**The Thin Place**</u>: Ask, Answer, Pray.

What would you consider your main motivation in life?

Where exactly does God fit into your motivations?

What changes would a change of motivation bring to your life?

May 13

Life is not a Sitcom

<u>**From Above**</u>: Proverbs 24:11-12

Focal Passage: *"If you say, "But we knew nothing about this," does not he who weighs the heart perceive it? Does not he who guards your life know it? Will he not repay each person according to what he has done?"* – Proverbs 24:12

<u>**Here Below**</u>:

On one of the episodes of the once popular TV show *Seinfeld*, the character Elaine discovered that her current boyfriend was to her surprise a Christian. She did not come to this conclusion by his lifestyle or by his testimony, but by the fact that his car radio was set to the Christian radio stations. Being herself an agnostic, this bothered her. When she confronted him on his faith, she asked him if the fact that she was not a Christian was going to be a problem for him. He responded with a statement that I have never forgotten. He said to her very matter-of-factly, "It doesn't matter to me. I am not the one going to hell." This statement was meant for laughs, and I guess it was also a dig at evangelical Christians. However, I have found that there are many who actually have the attitude that this sitcom character expressed so bluntly. For whatever reason, most show little interest in the eternal destiny of others. Nevertheless, we must remember that real life is not a sitcom and souls are at stake.

The above Proverb is a very interesting passage of scripture. If you read the verse just prior to the one above (vs. 11) you will see a reference to rescuing those being led away to death. The writer then addresses in verse 12 an apathy towards those suffering that many in his day must have been showing in their lives. These verses could definitely be applied to our Christian witness as well. Basically, the writer tells us that not knowing is not a valid excuse. Put simply, it just doesn't cut it. Indifference to the physical and spiritual condition of others does not alleviate us of our responsibility to others. Jesus left us each with the responsibility of reaching the lost and dying with a message of hope, love, and grace. It is our responsibility to know how others are doing, especially when it comes to their spiritual condition. To do otherwise is counterproductive to the cause of Christ.

For us this means we must be intentional in our relationships with others. We must care for others and help others in their time of need. We must share the love of Christ with others, both in spoken word and in deed. We are responsible for the wellbeing of others and one day we must give an account. It is so easy to become apathetic in a world that seems to think that one's spiritual condition is a matter of privacy. Yet, God's word teaches us differently. There is no real indifference when it comes to our witness. To do nothing is to work against the gospel. Look for opportunities today to get involved in the spiritual wellbeing of those you encounter. God will honor your attempt. Let His Holy Spirit lead you to a heart in need today.

The Thin Place: Ask, Answer, Pray.

Are you aware of the spiritual condition of those closest to you?

How willing are you to get involved in reaching those closest to you with the love of Christ?

Will you ask God to reveal to you a person in your life that needs the love of Christ?

May 14
The Scenic Route

<u>**From Above**</u>: Philippians 1:21-26

Focal Passage: *"For to me, to live is Christ and to die is gain."* – Philippians 1:21

<u>**Here Below**</u>:

As anyone can attest, the best scenery is often found along the unexpected paths we take. For example, on a recent mountain vacation, my wife and I took a road that was not necessarily the closest or the quickest route to reach our destination. Yet, along the way we saw some of the most beautiful scenery that the Appalachian Mountains have to offer. The extra miles and gas were definitely worth the view along the scenic route. We witnessed some of God's most extraordinary handiwork that we might have otherwise missed had we taken the shortest and easiest path.

The Apostle Paul understood this concept. Like all of us, Paul struggled as to whether it would be better for him to take the short route or the scenic route. In Philippians 1, we get a sample of some deep introspection from the heart of Paul. For him, it was a question of life or death. As he examined his life and the inevitable end he was facing in his service to the Lord, he questioned whether or not it would be better to go on living or to gracefully accept death. Now, I do not believe Paul was contemplating ending his life in this passage. On the contrary, he was simply searching for an answer as to which would be better. He stated in the above verse that living the Christian life is good, but dying is even better. Dying in the Lord would mean receiving his eternal reward and spending eternity in the presence of God. He was torn between the two. Finally, Paul came to the conclusion that instead of the easy and quickest route, he would instead to take the scenic route and go on living for the Lord. He decided it is best to remain. While death might be the quickest and easiest way to get to our desired destination, we might miss the adventure and beauty that God has for us along the way.

This challenges us to remember that life along the way is meant to enjoyed and that each moment is precious. God's desire is for us to see His handiwork along the way. Yes, we always need to be mindful of the beauty that awaits us at our destination, but we must also be aware of the beauty in the here and now. Like Paul, we must look at life in the light of Jesus Christ. After all, we have all of eternity to enjoy heaven. The opportunities to live for Him this side of heaven are but a moment. We must try to see each day through the eyes of Jesus. Look for His signature and His purposes in each new day. Take the scenic route.

The Thin Place: Ask, Answer, Pray.

Have you ever pondered as Paul as to whether it is better to live or die?

Is it possible to worry about the future to the point of missing the joys of today?

How can you better enjoy and utilize the time that God has given you?

May 15
A Real Pain in the Neck

From Above: Acts 19:1-20

Focal Passage: *"[One day] the evil spirit answered them, "Jesus I know, and I know about Paul, but who are you?""* – Acts 19:15

Here Below:

It is all about who you know! This is an old saying that gets thrown around a great bit in politics and in the social and vocational arenas of life. Often it is true. Many times, a more qualified person gets overlooked and someone else gets promoted or someone else gets an ideal job for no other reason than they are related to someone or else they are friends with someone that has some clout. My wife was once denied a job she had been promised for nearly a year at last minute so that the niece of her boss might have the job. It is disheartening to say the least. Nevertheless, who we know can be important. Likewise, who knows us can be revealing as well.

Consider the above passage. In this account in the book of Acts, we see the seven sons of Sceva trying to drive out demons in the name of Jesus. Notice the response they get from the evil spirit. He recognized Jesus and Paul, but he didn't know these people. Now at first glance, we may think this is good. After all, who wants to be known by evil spirits, right? Well, I don't know, but consider this. Maybe he didn't know these men because he did not see these men as a threat to his evil agenda. He knew Jesus and Paul, but these poor guys were unknown and then they were basically run out of town by the demon. I feel like there are many Christians today whose lives are like that of the seven sons of Sceva. They live their lives in such a way as to not be a threat to anyone, not even the Devil. This is not what God intends for our lives.

Do not misunderstand. We should never take spiritual warfare lightly and we should never invite trouble in that respect. However, as Christians we are called to be different. In fact, I am going to take it a step further and say that we should live our lives in such a way as to be a complete and total pain in the Devil's neck. It is when we do this that we make a difference in the world. Is your life like that? Or are you content to sit back and not make waves in the spiritual world? If so, let me give you this warning today. If the Devil is leaving you alone, it could be that he has you right where he wants you. Remember, the Holy Spirit within you is more powerful than any demonic force we encounter. Don't let him scare you. Instead, determine today that you are going to be a threat to him!

The Thin Place: Ask, Answer, Pray.

What are your beliefs on the subject of spiritual warfare? Why?

Has there ever been a time when it seemed that the forces of evil were working against you?

What can you do to strengthen yourself for the fight against these forces in the future?

May 16
If Only...

<u>**From Above**</u>: Luke 16:19-31; Hebrews 3:7-19

Focal Passage: *"But encourage one another daily, as long as it is called Today, so that none of you may be hardened by sin's deceitfulness."* – Hebrews 3:13

<u>**Here Below**</u>:

If only I could start this day over again! Have you ever spoken these words? We all have. If only we could go back and start again knowing what we now know to be true. Unfortunately, real life does not happen that way. We get one shot to make the most of the day we are given. My favorite movie of all time, *Braveheart*, is filled with great quotes. In this movie, William Wallace of Scotland asks his men as they were facing what seemed to be hopeless defeat in battle a question that rings true for all of us. He asked them essentially that if they were to walk away to safety instead of fighting, would they one day look back on their lives from their deathbed and say to themselves that they would trade every day since this day and their last for one more chance to stand up for the freedom for which they were fighting. It was an inspiring speech that led to victory instead of defeat. Why? Regret is a powerful motivator. None of us want to look back on our lives with regret.

This is especially true of spiritual matters. In the above passage from Luke, we see the story of the rich man and Lazarus as told by Jesus. While there is much to be said of this parable, perhaps the most striking element to me is the regret that the rich man was experiencing. He was looking back on his life and wishing he could just go back and tell his family that Heaven and Hell are real. Unfortunately, for him it was too late. Likewise, every day we are given opportunities to live for God. God brings people and circumstances in and out of our lives every day that might stand in need of a word of truth or encouragement. Don't let that opportunity slip by. It may never come again.

The question for us is the same as the one posed to the warriors in the above movie. When that day comes and we are looking back on our lives from our deathbed, would we be willing to trade every day from this day and that one for one more chance to do something different today? Would you? Give this day to the Lord fully and completely and there will be no regrets tomorrow.

The Thin Place: Ask, Answer, Pray.

Do you have any regrets concerning missed spiritual opportunities?

Has God placed someone or something in your life right now that could be considered an opportunity?

How can you heighten your awareness of God given opportunities?

May 17
Beating the Bad Busy

From Above: Lamentations 3:21-26

Focal Passage: *"The LORD is good to those whose hope is in him, to the one who seeks him; it is good to wait quietly for the salvation of the LORD."* – Lamentations 3:25-26

Here Below:

In my study of scripture, I have noticed a very real pattern that has to be more than mere coincidence. There are many times in scripture when the reference to seeking and searching for God is mentioned and many times you can look at either the passages prior or following the passage and you will see another reference to being still or simply waiting on the Lord. It is almost as if God is saying to us that to search after God sometimes mean just being still and listening. At least, perhaps God is saying that He is already at work around us and to find

Him we might just need to stop what we are doing long enough to see what is already there.

I have found this to be true in my own personal walk. Life can be so overwhelmingly busy at times. It can be a bad busy or it can even be a good busy. The hectic nature of simply carrying out the day-to-day activities of work and family can rush us through a day without a real break. Yet, it has been those times when I purposefully stopped what I was doing and simply waited for God to speak to my heart that I was able to hear Him the clearest. Even in our searching and seeking after Him, we can become so captured by the urgency of it all that we miss what He might be saying.

Notice the above passage from Lamentations, perhaps the saddest book in the entire Bible. Here in the midst of all the pain and suffering, the writer interrupts the grief to share the truth and hope of the above passage. It is when we stop, seek, and wait that we see the goodness of God, even in the midst of trying times. Sometimes we just need to sit down and be quiet. Oh, how I love those times when I can find a quiet room or a quiet corner of my backyard and just sit and listen! This is why activities such as hiking, fishing and other forms of solitude can be so refreshing, even though they take up physical energy. Our minds are cleared of clutter and our hearts are refreshed. God knows our needs. It is when we can rid our hearts of distractions that He is best able to reach those points of need. So today, find yourself a quiet spot. Go for a hike. Go fishing. Or perhaps you can just find a quiet room somewhere. When you find your quiet place, wait upon the Lord. He wants to be with you today.

The Thin Place: Ask, Answer, Pray.

Would you say that your life is a busy life? Good or bad?

What does it take for you to find a quiet place and time alone with God?

What changes are you willing to make in order to insure a daily time alone with God?

May 18
Under the Fig Tree

<u>**From Above**</u>: John 1:43-51

Focal Passage: *"How do you know me?" Nathanael asked. Jesus answered, "I saw you while you were still under the fig tree before Philip called you." –* John 1:48

<u>**Here Below**</u>:

In the first chapter of the gospel of John, we meet a character that would become part of the original twelve disciples. His name is Nathaniel. Nathaniel is one of the disciples of which we know very little. In fact, the passage in John 1 is the only time we ever see a conversation with Nathaniel. We do know that he was present after the resurrection on the Sea of Galilee fishing with the other disciples (John 21). Other than this, we know very little about him. However, we can see from this passage, that while we know little of him, Jesus thought a lot of Nathaniel. He saw in him an honesty that would make him a great follower and preacher of the Good News. Jesus could see his heart and knew what kind of man he could become if would just surrender his heart to Him. Nathaniel questioned this familiarity and Jesus responded to his inquiry in the above verse by making the statement about the fig tree. This is significant. In Jewish Rabbinic literature of the era, the statement "under the fig tree" had a special meaning. It was a kind of intellectual slang phrase meaning to study or to meditate on spiritual matters. For Jesus to state that he saw Nathaniel "under the fig tree" could be taken literal, figurative or both, as I believe. Regardless of how we interpret it though, the implication is that Jesus saw Nathaniel while he was meditating and reflecting on the Lord, searching for a greater understanding of His ways.

This leads me to this question for us today. If Jesus literally walked into your life today, what would He find you doing? Would he find you searching for greater understanding? Would He find you faithfully serving Him? Would he find you loving others? Or would Jesus discover you in the midst of something that might be embarrassing? I am not talking about something necessarily immoral or sinful, even though that can definitely apply as well. But would Jesus find you faithful in even the little things of life? Many times we focus so much on what we consider "major" that we fail to follow the Lord's lead in the simpler things. Hopefully Jesus would find you "under the fig tree" in your own life. Hopefully he would find you searching, serving, and studying the principles and precepts of a Christlike life. Don't be caught by surprise. Live your life in every moment and in every way as if God could drop by any minute. After all, He is always with us. We are never out of his view. When we are consistently faithful, we place ourselves in a position to best be used by God. This was true for Nathaniel. It is true for you and me. Let Jesus find you under the fig tree today!

The Thin Place: Ask, Answer, Pray.

What importance do you place on mediation and reflection in your daily schedule and priorities?

Do you seek God's direction on all matters or on just those things you feel are most important?

Where would God find you spiritually speaking if He walked onto the scene today?

May 19
Forgive and Forget

From Above: Mark 11:25; Matthew 18:21-22

Focal Passage: *"And when you stand praying, if you hold anything against anyone, forgive him, so that your Father in heaven may forgive you your sins." – Mark 11:25*

Here Below:

Have you ever said, "I can forgive someone for what they have done, but I will not forget it." This sounds okay, doesn't it? After all, we remember it so that we will not be hurt again. This seems reasonable and even somewhat spiritual. However, the truth is that it rarely happens this way. Let's be honest. All too often what we really mean when we say this is that we are going to forgive them, but only to a certain point.

What do I mean by this? Well, think of someone right now from your past that has hurt you. What thoughts come to mind? Do you still resent that person? Are you harboring feelings of bitterness toward that person? Perhaps these feelings only come out when you run across them in public unexpectedly. You may feel that you have forgiven them, as long as they are not around. But then you see them and "Bamm!" There it is again. If you are honest, you realize that you really haven't forgiven them at all. You see, partially forgiving someone is not forgiving them at all. When it comes to forgiveness, it is all or nothing.

Now this doesn't always happen all at once. In fact, Jesus told us in the above passage that we are to forgive "seventy times seven". He understood our difficulty in letting go of the past. Nevertheless, if we wish to grow in our own lives we must let go. If we don't, we are putting our own relationship with God in jeopardy. He will help us to be forgiving just as we are forgiven. Notice also that in no passage of scripture concerning forgiveness does it ever imply that there is a justifiable unforgiveness. In other words, we forgive whether they deserve it or not.

Isn't that how God works as well? Just as we have been shown grace, we must show grace toward others. A little unchecked unforgiveness can grow like a cancer. It also has the same effect. Don't allow it to remain unchecked in your heart. God will give you the strength to let it go today.

The Thin Place: Ask, Answer, Pray.

Be honest. Are you harboring unforgiveness in your heart today?
If so, what steps can you take to be more forgiving?
Is it possible that you need to seek forgiveness from someone today?

May 20
A Belly Full

<u>**From Above**</u>: John 7:37-39

Focal Passage: *"He that believeth on me, as the scripture hath said, out of his belly shall flow rivers of living water."* – John 7:38 (KJV)

<u>**Here Below**</u>:

Several times I have had someone say to me after a particularly moving worship service or experience something like this, "I could definitely feel the Spirit moving today!" While most mean no harm by statements such as these, I do believe they are making the statement under a misguided assumption. The Holy Spirit of God is not a feeling, nor is His workings based upon our emotions. The Holy Spirit of God is God, just as much as God the Father and Jesus the Son. He doesn't come and go depending upon how we might feel at the moment. The Holy Spirit is given to us completely upon our acceptance of Jesus as Lord and Savior. It is not a question of receiving Him in degrees. It is also not a question of how much of Him we feel we have received. The better question might be, how much of ourselves have we given to the Holy Spirit?

In the above passage from the gospel of John, Jesus gives us the promise of the Holy Spirit. This passage is one of those rare passages in which the writer not only gives us the words of Christ, but interprets them for us (Vs. 39). We are promised that out of those who believe in Jesus shall flow rivers of living water. In other words, the Holy Spirit shall so fill our hearts that what others shall see is the overflow. Put simply, it is God's Spirit within us that enables us to work, do and love as we should. This strengthening is not based upon the power of God. His power is endless. On the contrary, it depends upon how much of ourselves we surrender to Him. So, if you want to be filled with the Holy Spirit, you must make room for Him in your heart. Throw out anything that might be taking up space that is meant for Him. When you allow the Holy Spirit to have more of you, you will see more of Him.

<u>The Thin Place</u>: Ask, Answer, Pray.

At what times in your life have you best been able to recognize the work of the Holy Spirit?

Why is it easier to recognize the Holy Spirit working at certain times than at others?

How does a better understanding of the working of the Holy Spirit of God strengthen us?

May 21
Where the Wind Blows

<u>From Above</u>: Leviticus 19:16; Proverbs 25:23

Focal Passage: "*As a north wind brings rain, so a sly tongue brings angry looks.*" – Proverbs 25:23

<u>Here Below</u>:

The deadliest weapon is not forged from steel or powered by fire. It is instead made of flesh and we each carry one. It is the tongue. With the tongue we have the ability to destroy the lives of others, or we have the ability to bring life to others. However, nothing good can ever come from gossip. Even in those rare instances when we *feel* we can justify it, our purposes are usually found to be negative in the honest light of day, and the result is always hurt and trouble.

The writer of the above Proverb understood the damaging nature of gossip. He compares it to a north wind that brings rain. Just as this wind brings the rainstorms, the gossiping tongue brings with it anger and harm. Where this wind blows, there will always be a storm of heartache. It is inevitable. The opposite must also be true. Just as sure as a sly tongue brings trouble, an encouraging word spoken must bring life and joy. Let's face it. We like to talk. Most humans enjoy communicating with those within our own circles. The question is not whether the wind will blow, but from which direction and what will be the result.

The damage caused by words misspoken is immeasurable. We can all remember a time from our own past when we were harmed by words misspoken or a gossiping tongue. It can damage relationships and reputations almost beyond repair. Notice, I said almost... There is no damage so great that God and a healthy dose of forgiveness cannot mend. Nevertheless, the easiest way to avoid the damage is to avoid the unhealthy wind coming from a gossiping tongue. Don't let yourself be influenced by words that should not have been spoken in the first place. Avoid gossip and you avoid the damaging effects. Take care to notice from which direction the wind blows.

<u>**The Thin Place**</u>: Ask, Answer, Pray.

Have you ever been the victim of a gossiping tongue? When?

Have you ever participated in gossiping conversation at the expense of another?

What changes can you make in your life to help you avoid the dangers of gossip?

May 22
Personal Appraisal

<u>**From Above**</u>: Job 22:21-27; Matthew 6:19-21

Focal Passage: *"And assign your nuggets to the dust, your gold of Ophir to the rocks in the ravines,*

then the Almighty will be your gold, the choicest silver for you." – Job 22:24-25

<u>**Here Below**</u>:

Just because something was more expensive at the time of purchase doesn't necessarily make it of greater value. There are certain things I possess that I would gladly choose to keep over some of the more expensive items I own if it came down to choosing between the two. Why? Because their value is based upon other factors with which no price can be assigned. For example, a gift given to me by my children is of greater value to me than a large flat screen television. Likewise, some relics from my childhood are of greater value to me than a new car. These things are irreplaceable. A new television can be bought. A new car can be purchased. After all, in time these things are obsolete anyway. One day that new car will be an old car. That new TV will become technologically outdated. But these other more cherished possessions only grow in value. Therefore, we must be careful to assign proper value to our belongings, both literal and spiritual.

Job was a man with whom there was no lack of personal possession. He had everything the world could offer. Yet, when his possessions were taken from him, he did not lose the one thing that mattered the most to him. He still had his relationship with God. You see, even with all his possessions, it was God that gave him strength when the troubles came. Job learned the hard way that our earthly belongings are only temporary. They come and go. However, God is with us through it all. His love is our greatest and most valuable possession. He is your gold and your silver. So, keep your greatest valuable in a place of utmost safety and priority. It's time to do a personal appraisal. What is your possession of greatest value?

The Thin Place: Ask, Answer, Pray.

What would you consider your most valuable possessions spiritually speaking?

Why do you consider this your most valuable possession?

Is there anything that you would give in exchange for this possession?

May 23
A Kidney Punch

From Above: Psalm 116

Focal Passage: "*Be at rest once more, O my soul, for the LORD has been good to you.*" – Psalm 116:7

<u>Here Below</u>:

Forgive me if what you are reading is excessively personal. A lesson was learned this week that warranted interjection into this series of daily devotions. Thank you for indulging me. It was a lesson I feel I must share. It is also a warning for the reader.

It had been an unusually busy two or three weeks in the pastorate. I have attended or had a part in three funerals, two weddings, several marriage and personal counseling sessions, and other regular pastoral duties. Then there were the regular pastoral duties such as visitation and sermon preparation, preparing for a four-day long series of revival services with guest musicians and a guest speaker. I also had several family related doctor appointments, a trip out of town to visit family, and all the while trying to be a dedicated married father of four. It was also perhaps the busiest time of the year as far as family is concerned; in that, the school year was drawing to a close. Put simply, I was rushing everywhere, trying to squeeze as much out of each day as possible. As a result, everything was getting half done. This was reflected in the physical and spiritual condition of my home. I was missing precious time with family and getting little to no genuine rest. When I wasn't involved in ministering, I was thinking about it. It was to be a week of revival; yet, for me it was becoming perhaps the most stressful week I have ever encountered in the ministry. Then it happened. God caught my attention. Dressed in my black suit, sermon in hand, on my way to preach a funeral, in a matter of a few minutes and without warning, I was blindsided and laid flat on my back by a kidney stone. At that moment everything stopped, and I suddenly found myself with nothing else to do but pray.

Unfortunately, sometimes God must get our attention. Sometimes it is pleasant. Sometimes it is not. For me, it took a kidney punch and a couple of days in the hospital to remind me of my need for *quality* time alone with God. In the solitude of pain and in the quietness of the hospital bed, I found myself to have been missing God. The sad thing is that in all my running, I had not noticed. Do not misunderstand, I don't think God gave me a kidney stone, but I do feel the timing is more than coincidental. Who knows how long I had been carrying the thing; yet it chose this precise moment to move! Even in doing good things, we can still miss the point. Don't wait for God to lay you down to get your attention. He wants time alone with you. Despite my pain, I left that hospital bed refreshed and more aware of my need of time alone with God than ever before. Don't wait for Him to take drastic measures. Give yourself to Him today.

The Thin Place: Ask, Answer, Pray.

Would you say that you feel rested physically? How about spiritually?

Are you spending adequate time alone with God on a daily basis?

What habits can you change to assure you get the time with God that you need?

May 24
Explain Yourself!

From Above: I Peter 3:15-16

Focal Passage: *"But in your hearts set apart Christ as Lord. Always be prepared to give an answer to everyone who asks you to give the reason for the hope that you have. But do this with gentleness and respect,"* – I Peter 3:15

Here Below:

Have you ever been asked to explain yourself? Probably every child has been asked at one time or another by a parent to give the reason for why they do what they do. Likewise, adults are often faced with the same question. Sometimes the answer is easy to explain. Sometimes the answer is not so easy to provide. Depending upon the situation, we can even find ourselves in a place where we simply do not want to give the reasons for why we do what we do, good or bad.

However, when it comes to matters of faith, we do not have the option of keeping our reasons to ourselves. In fact, we are told by Peter in the above passage that we must always be ready to give the reason for our hope. We are to always be equipped and ready to explain our Christian motivations. We are not to lord these reasons over others, patting ourselves on the back for our good deeds. We are to do it in a Christ like manner, with gentleness and respect.

Think about that verse for a moment. It was written by Peter. It was written by the same man who denied even knowing Christ in the courtyard outside the home of the High Priest Caiaphas. It was the same man, but it was not the same Peter. He had grown in his faith and had come to realize the importance of expressing our faith to others. This doesn't necessarily mean standing on a street corner preaching, though that may also be the case. It does mean that in just our everyday conversations and relationships, we should be willing to let others know how important our faith is to us. It is not hard. In fact, for the Christian it should come as natural as bragging on children or family is to a parent. It is the most important thing that has ever happened in our lives. Therefore, sharing it with others should be a privilege, not a chore. Are you ready to explain yourself today?

The Thin Place: Ask, Answer, Pray.

How would you respond today if someone asked you to explain your faith to them?

Do you feel that you are adequately equipped to explain your faith?

How can you better equip yourself for these type occasions?

May 25
The Light at the End of the Tunnel

From Above: Romans 3:22-26; I Timothy 1

Focal Passage: *"This is a faithful saying, and worthy of all acceptation, that Christ Jesus came into the world to save sinners; of whom I am chief."* – I Timothy 1:15

<u>Here Below</u>:

On yet another would be outdoor adventure, I once made a discovery that reminded me of the crippling power of fear. As I was tubing down another North Georgia river with some friends, we came to a spot that we had long been looking forward too. There was a place in the river that forked. One fork went around the small mountain and the other went straight through it in a very narrow cave that had been bored straight through the ground during a mining period in years past. The tunnel was just big enough for an inner tube and its passenger. The water moved rapidly through this dark thin tunnel. From the mouth of this cave, the light at the other end seemed no bigger than a small coin. Once you neared the center of the cave, it became so dark that you could not see your own hand in front of your face. It was at that middle point in my adventure that I made my mistake. I turned on my flashlight. The ceiling of the cave was just a foot above my head, and it was covered with bats! I was paralyzed, being pulled helplessly through the remainder of the cave afraid to breath and afraid to speak for fear that I might startle the thousands of bats hanging just inches from my face. Those few seconds it took to reach the light at the end of the tunnel seemed to take an eternity. If only I had not known about the bats. You see, the problem with this is that the bats were there whether I saw them or not. Not seeing them or ignoring them did not change the fact that they were real. Turning off my flashlight did not make them go away. It also did not change the fact that I had a real problem.

Many times, we treat our troubled spiritual condition in the same manner. We pretend it is not there or we simply ignore it hoping it will fix itself. This doesn't change anything. We all have a common problem, and it is a problem that we cannot ignore, regardless of how difficult it may be to face. Understanding this is the first step in salvation and an important part of the daily Christian life. Paul understood this in the above passage. He understood his spiritual condition. He was a sinner. Yes, he was a sinner saved by grace, but he was still a sinner. We cannot ignore our own sinfulness. Yes, it is not always pleasant. Nevertheless, we cannot ignore the sins hanging over our head. We instead need to turn the light on, face them and repent. Then God will shower us with his grace, His light at the end of the tunnel. Facing the reality of our sins is not something we do just once when we first come to salvation. It is a daily exercise. This helps us face the doubts of tomorrow with confidence and peace. Don't ignore your sin. Face it head on. Trust in God and He will bring you through it.

The Thin Place: Ask, Answer, Pray.

Are you guilty of sometimes ignoring your spiritual condition? Why?

How does it make you feel to finally confess and repent of sins that you have ignored?

Are there any unrepented sins in your heart today?

May 26
Garden Variety Humility

From Above: 2 Peter 1:10-21

Focal Passage: *"For prophecy never had its origin in the will of man, but men spoke from God as they were carried along by the Holy Spirit."* – 2 Peter 1:21

Here Below:

My little backyard garden last year was somewhat impressive. I had some of the prettiest tomato and pepper plants that I have ever had in any of my annual attempts to garden. Likewise, they generated some of the best and most plenteous produce that I have ever grown. Yet, as beautiful as they were and as easy as it is to become prideful over such things, it doesn't change the fact that I had very little to do with the actual outcome. I bought the plants, but God brought them into being. I dug the holes in which to plant them, but God made the soil. I fertilized them, but God created the needed nutrients. I watered them, but God provided the rain and the water that filled my well. The reality is that I was more or less an observer in the entire process. However, I did enjoy the outcome! It is somewhat humbling when you think about it. How much of what we do would be nothing without the work of God in the details?

I think Peter understood this concept in the above passage. In 2 Peter, the fisherman had been reminding the readers of the simple truths of the Gospel. He had been retelling them the great stories from the life of Jesus. It probably would have been easy for Peter to lose perspective with all the attention he must have been receiving. After all, he was Peter. He had literally been with Jesus and had witnessed these events in person from His life. What for many were only stories of something they would dream of; they were a reality for Peter. He was there. In one sense, Peter had become a real celebrity in Christian circles in his day. Yet, as he was teaching and preaching and writing this great letter, we see that Peter was quick to remind them that these were not just stories, but these things really happened. Likewise, he was no hero. It was God that had worked all the miracles. The men involved in these stories and telling these stories were mere men being carried along by the Spirit of God. Just like those tomato plants, Peter would have been nothing without the power of God working in the background. While the above passage is a real testimony to the accuracy and authority of scripture, it also implies much more. It is a reminder to us that God is constantly working in and around the heart that is surrendered to him. It is a reminder to us to be careful to not take credit for something that in reality only God could accomplish. Just like Peter, we need to give credit where credit is due. This humility is the foundation upon which God is able to perform His greatest works in our lives. It is this ground in which God can produce the greatest fruit. Remember that it is He that gives us life and success.

The Thin Place: Ask, Answer, Pray.

What are some of the successes from your life in which you pride yourself?

Can you see how God was working to bring about those successes?

Have you given the appropriate amount of praise and acknowledgment to God for His work in your life?

May 27
What Giants?

<u>**From Above**</u>: Numbers 13:27-14:9

Focal Passage: *"Then Caleb silenced the people before Moses and said, 'We should go up and take possession of the land, for we can certainly do it.'"* – Numbers 13:30

<u>**Here Below**</u>:

In the above Old Testament story, we see a man of unique vision. Caleb was a man that did not see as other people were seeing. Instead of seeing the impossible, he saw the possible. Instead of seeing the giants in the land, he saw the fruit of the land. It was a time when everyone was insisting that the situation was bleak. The popular pressure was so intense that the others wished that they were still slaves in Egypt. All they could see was the bad that might happen. Instead of seeing the bad in the situation, Caleb saw the good. Oh, that more of us were more like Caleb!

How many times do we do the same as the Israelites in this story? When some challenge comes our way, we often only see what cannot be done. When troubles come our way, we often only see how bad it is and how worse it may yet become. Should this be the attitude of a child of faith? After all, we have promise after promise in the word of God that reassures us that God will never let us down. God reminds us over and over again that He will never leave us. Yet, when things don't go our way, we begin to dread tomorrow, and dream of days gone by. God's desire for us is to see Him at work in our troubled times and to see Him at work in our tomorrows.

Do this. The next time you face a challenge, ask yourself how God might use it to build you up and to bring glory and honor to himself. You see, to Caleb this was the perfect opportunity to show the world just how strong was his God. "We can certainly do it!" he said. Was he bragging on himself and his military might? No. They were outnumbered and outgunned. He knew this. He was bragging on the power of God to have victory in what seemed like a hopeless situation. Look for opportunities for God to work. Sickness can be an opportunity for God to do a miracle. A loss of income can be an opportunity for God to show you how He can provide. A family crisis may be an opportunity for God to change a heart. I could go on and on with a list of these opportunities. The point is this; when we are at our weakest, God does His best work. Try to have the same attitude as Caleb. See the world as God would have you too. See challenges as opportunities for God to work.

The Thin Place: Ask, Answer, Pray.

What are some giants you may be facing in your life?

Do you feel that God is capable of getting your though these situations?

Have you trusted God completely to help you find victory in these situations? If not, why?

May 28
We Don't Get What We Deserve!

From Above: Job 11:1-6; Psalm 103:17

Focal Passage: *"Oh, how I wish that God would speak, that he would open his lips against you and disclose to you the secrets of wisdom, for true wisdom has two sides. Know this: God has even forgotten some of your sin."* – Job 11:5-6

Here Below:

There is an old joke that I have often told that contains a pertinent Biblical truth. It is about a man that was one day sharing a recent photograph of himself with his friend. As he was showing it, he began to apologize for the picture. He said, "This picture really doesn't do me justice." As his friend looked at the image, he responded by saying. "Brother, you don't want justice. What you need is mercy!" Ouch! That was not exactly the response for which he had hoped. Nevertheless, it is a very true statement.

When it comes to our spiritual lives, we should be very thankful for the fact that even though God is a just God, he is also full of mercy and compassion. Instead of exercising justice and giving us what we deserve, He made a way for us to obtain mercy through His Son Jesus Christ. The Bible is clear on what we in our sinfulness deserve. Yet, God loved us enough to compassionately look past our sins and short-comings. That is, He looks past them if they are covered by the sacrificial blood of Jesus. As I consider my own weaknesses, I can't but help acknowledge what an amazing love He must have for me and for all of us.

Likewise, we are to love others just as he has loved us (Ephesians 5:1-2). Too often, we are guilty of being less forgiving when it comes to our relationships with others. When we are hurt, we feel as if we deserve to see justice carried out. However, many times we are guilty of confusing justice with revenge. This is why it is better to just do as Jesus taught and to simply forgive those who have hurt us. Don't get me wrong. There is a place for justice in our world and God does often deliver. But when it comes to matters of the heart, mercy always trumps justice. So, the next time someone wounds your spirit, try mercy instead of justice and see what happens next. I think you will be pleasantly surprised at the sense of freedom it brings. Most of all, take time to thank God today for not giving you what you deserve!

The Thin Place: Ask, Answer, Pray.

What are some examples from your own life of times when God has shown you mercy?

How would your life be different if God had instead exercised His justice?

How can you be more merciful toward others in your life?

May 29
A Bad Day Fishing

<u>**From Above**</u>: Genesis 45

Focal Passage: *"And now, do not be distressed and do not be angry with yourselves for selling me here, because it was to save lives that God sent me ahead of you."* – Genesis 45:5

<u>**Here Below**</u>:

There is a bumper sticker philosophy that goes something like this, "A Bad Day Fishing is Better Than a Good Day Working". I recently found this saying to be particularly true. It was a day that my children had long been anticipating. We were going to go fishing. Anyone with small children knows that fishing with young kids is anything but a relaxing day at the lake. For nearly six hours I constantly baited hooks, untangled lines, and repaired damaged reels and very rarely was I even able to put a hook of my own in the water. To make matters even worse, we only caught two small fish, too small to even bring home. Yet, as trying as it was, I would not exchange that day for anything in the world. The joy of watching my daughter catching her first fish is irreplaceable. Also, the joy of watching my two oldest sons fret over the fact that their little sister caught the only fish that any of the kids were able to catch was worth all the anxiety of the tangled and broken lines. What could have been a day of stress was instead a day of precious family memories that will last forever, a day that was very much needed. You see it all depends upon how we look at the situation in which we find ourselves. It all depends upon our attitude and our willingness to look for the good in any situation.

Perhaps the greatest story of all time in which this principle of maintaining a proper attitude is shown is that of Joseph in the book of Genesis. Here was a man that had been sold into slavery by his jealous siblings. He was separated from his family for years and imprisoned. Yet in chapter 45, we see him finally receive his opportunity to exact revenge on them and instead he offers forgiveness. Why? Because he could see that God was making something good out of all the bad things that had happened to him. He could see that though his past might have looked dreadful, God had used it for good. He had the proper attitude. It was a positive and God acknowledging attitude and it was this attitude that enabled God to use Joseph.

While a bad day fishing hardly equates to being sold into slavery, it was still an opportunity for God to give me something I desperately needed. He knew I needed that time with my children, and they needed it with me. To many it might have looked like a waste of time. To me it was priceless. I wouldn't change a thing about that day! Would Joseph have changed anything about his situation? I doubt it. God used his bad experience to make something good occur. He can do the same with you. It does however depend upon your attitude and your willingness to look for God at work, even when the fish are not biting. Are you willing to do that today?

The Thin Place: Ask, Answer, Pray.

Do you find it easy or difficult to look for the positive in every situation?

Do you find it easy or difficult to look for the hand of God at work in every situation?

What changes do you feel you need to make with your overall attitude?

May 30
The Pervading Word

From Above: Revelation 1:1-6

Focal Passage: *"Blessed is the one who reads the words of this prophecy, and blessed are those who hear it and take to heart what is written in it, because the time is near."* – Revelation 1:3

Here Below:

On the island of Patmos, John the Revelator wrote the above words for all to examine. In this passage, John instructs us to basically take the word of God seriously. He refers to the hearer of God's word as blessed. However, notice how he does not end with just hearing the word. He reminds us that we must take it to heart as well. The word must pervade our hearts. Is it possible to do otherwise? Yes, it is.

I once knew a young man that was gifted in his ability to memorize scripture. He was the envy of all like me that struggle with the memorization of scripture. He could quote chapter and verse by request. He was truly amazing. However, his lifestyle gave extreme evidence to the fact that while he knew the words, he was slow or resistant to applying them. He had not taken the words he was quoting to heart. We are to take the words of the Lord to heart. While John was specifically referring to the revelation that he received on the Isle of Patmos, this principle could definitely be applied to any or all parts of the word of God. It must become more than just words or else we have missed the point.

Why is the word of God so important for the child of God? Well, John gives us the reason. He tells us in this verse that we must take it to heart because the time is near. There is a definite sense of urgency in his words. He understood perhaps more than anyone else that we could very well be standing before God at any given moment. This leaves us with the necessity of making sure our heart and motives are in the right place. How do we know if they are in the right place? We do it by measuring them according to God's standard found in His Word. There is no other accurate standard by which to measure. Do not be satisfied with just reading the word. Let the word read you as well.

__The Thin Place__: Ask, Answer, Pray.

How does the word of God influence your decision-making process?

How often do you recall the word of God when facing tough choices?

Would you say that there is room for a deeper commitment to the word of God in your life?

May 31
Check Out Time is at 11

<u>**From Above**</u>: 2 Corinthians 10: 1-5; I John 2:14-17

Focal Passage: *"The world and its desires pass away, but the man who does the will of God lives forever."* – I John 2:17

<u>**Here Below**</u>:

On a recent trip out of town, I stayed one night in one of the nicest hotels in which I have ever had the privilege of staying. However, as I entered the room, I did see some things that I would like to have changed. I didn't like the art hanging on the wall. It was somewhat bland for my taste. Likewise, the furniture and carpet was not really to my taste either. As nice as it was, I felt as if I would like to change these things. So, I decided to go down to the local furniture store and buy some new furniture to furnish my room. I also checked into having some new carpet installed in the room, and I finished it off by purchasing some new artwork to decorate the walls. Now the room was perfect, and I was happy. Sounds ridiculous, huh? Well, it, is. Of course, this didn't really happen. It would be foolish to spend all this money and effort on a room that I would only be using for a short overnight stay. It would cost more than it would ever be worth. Yet, many of us do something even more ridiculous than this every day of our lives.

While there is nothing necessarily wrong with making the most of our lives in the time we are given on this earth, we do often invest an inappropriate amount of time and resources on something that will soon pass away. Just like the absurd futility of redecorating a hotel room, we spend our entire lives concerning ourselves with the things of this world only to finally see that our lives here are but a short overnight stay in the scope of eternity. Yet, we tend to neglect things of a spiritual nature, things that really make a difference in eternity.

When you think about it, it simply doesn't make sense to live this way. Worldliness is as silly as redecorating that hotel room when we know that we will soon be checking out.

When we check into that hotel room, very few of us concern ourselves with the decorations or the color of the carpet. Why? Because we know that we are only visitors and that this is not our home. In the same manner, we need to only concern ourselves with our real home. We are only visitors here and the home we have waiting for us far outclasses any home we could create for ourselves here. Instead of investing all your assets into a temporary dwelling, put them into a home that will last forever. Eternity is not something that begins when we die. Eternal life begins now. Live your life as such and you will find your room to be just right, no matter how it might be decorated.

<u>The Thin Place</u>: Ask, Answer, Pray.

How easy is it for you to get caught up in the world and its desires?

Why do we often have difficulties looking at things from a more eternal perspective?

What is the result of a worldly lifestyle versus a lifestyle of a more spiritual nature?

6

June

June 1
Worm Medicine

<u>From Above</u>: Jonah 4

Focal Passage: *"But at dawn the next day God provided a worm, which chewed the vine so that it withered." –* Jonah 4:11

<u>Here Below</u>:

The above chapter of scripture is taken from one of the most famous of all Old Testament stories. It is of course the story of Jonah. We are all familiar with this great story. However, there is one character in the story that you have probably never considered. In fact, if you are not careful, you might read this story and never even recognize the role this character plays in the great scheme of things. Nevertheless, God uses this character to get the attention of the story's protagonist in a very unique and unforgettable manner. I am not referring to the great fish of Jonah's story. Instead, I am referring to the worm of 4:11. God uses a worm to teach Jonah. There are many things we can learn from this worm.

Here is an instance when a man, with all of his flaws, finds himself at odds with the will of God. Things are happening that he doesn't understand and quite honestly, he doesn't like what he is seeing. He feels that God should have handled the situation differently. Now think about this for a moment. He is very honest with God in this chapter and tells him that he is angry with God's reaction to the people of Nineveh. It is really quite arrogant when you think of it. He honestly thought he knew more about how this should have been handled than God. In a sense, Jonah was saying that he was morally superior to God himself. You would think that the whole fish incident would have taught him differently! However, in response God uses a little worm to remind Jonah of his place in this world. God used this tiny part of creation to gently remind Jonah that there is nothing that He can't do and that His ways are ultimately the best. If God can use a worm to carry out His will, then He can use Jonah. Likewise, if God can control even our physical comfort, he must surely know what is spiritually best for His children.

However, there is more to this story than just God disciplining an arrogant child. This story is also a story of His love. When Jonah looked upon Nineveh, all he could see was their faults. God saw souls in need of a second chance. You see, this story is one of love, not only for Nineveh, but for Jonah as well. God could have struck Jonah down with leprosy for questioning His judgment and He would have been justified in doing so. Yet, out of love for Jonah, He instead in an almost playful manner sends a worm to take away His shade. It was just a little emotional slap on the wrist to shock Jonah into acknowledging God's wisdom and power and more importantly, His love. You see, whether it is big fish or a little worm, God's will is going to be accomplished. Don't wait for Him to send a worm to your life! Trust that God's wisdom, love, and way is always superior!

The Thin Place: Ask, Answer, Pray.

Has there been a time when you misunderstood God's will and perhaps even questioned His wisdom?

If so, how did that situation turn out for you? Was God's will ultimately what was best for you?

How can you remind yourself daily that God always has the best intent for His children?

June 2
Deep Sea Salvation

From Above: Micah 7:18-19; Ezekiel 18:21-22

Focal Passage: *"Who is a God like you, who pardons sin and forgives the transgression of the remnant of his inheritance? You do not stay angry forever but delight to show mercy. You will again have compassion on us; you will tread our sins underfoot and hurl all our iniquities into the depths of the sea."* – Micah 7:18-19

Here Below:

I love the ocean. Its beauty and seemingly never-ending expanse can bring even the proudest of hearts to a place of humility in its presence. Likewise, the music made by her rolling waves is a lullaby with which even the most angelic voice would have a difficult time competing. The ocean's beauty and mystery has inspired some of the greatest poetry, songs, and stories since the beginning of time. The ocean is by far one of God's greatest natural masterpieces. I always look forward to the summertime and those trips to the beach. However, as beautiful and majestic as it is, there is still a frightening aspect to it. There have been times when I was swimming or snorkeling and turned away from the shore to face the vast and boundless underwater expanse. It nearly takes my breath away when I do this. As the water seems to go on forever, the questions arise in my mind as to what may be out there in that infinite span. It makes one feel very small.

While we do not know exactly what may be out there, there is one thing that we do know. The Bible tells us that God has cast our repented sins into the depths of the sea. While this is of course figurative in nature, the point is clear. As God inspired the above passage, He understood just how deep our oceans can be. In fact, much of the underwater creation is still unreachable. God knew this when He inspired Micah to write the above passage. He was painting a picture of just how extreme God's forgiveness can be. In fact, Micah tells us that God delights in showing mercy to His children. Isn't it great to know that God has cast my repented sins to a place that man cannot reach? Unfortunately, we do try sometimes to reach those depths. We sometimes try to fish out our old sins and keep bearing the shame for something for which God has promised us complete forgiveness. Also, we often try to hold on to the sins of others as well. Thankfully, this is not what God means for us to do. That is the devil's trick. God on the other hand wants us to let Him cast those sins to the bottom of the sea. That is where my repented sins are and I would do well to remember that, as would you. Perhaps that is why the dark and unending underwater expanse is so frightening. Behind the misty dark curtain of the sea are sins that I never want to see again. Thank you God that I do not have to go there! Thank you God for your mercy! Thank you God for your forgiveness!

The Thin Place: Ask, Answer, Pray.

Have you ever found it difficult forgiving yourself for something that for which god has forgiven you?

What does God's word teach you about your confessed and repented sins?

If a holy and righteous God can forgive us, why do we have a problem forgiving ourselves?

June 3
Heart of the Matter

From Above: Ezekiel 36:25-27

Focal Passage: *"I will give you a new heart and put a new spirit in you; I will remove from you your heart of stone and give you a heart of flesh." –* Ezekiel 36:26

Here Below:

One can't help but feel somewhat helpless when viewing the daily news. Each day brings new qualms about the future. We see each day anew man's propensity for violence and strife. Likewise, we see man's tendency to sink further and further into moral decay. It is enough to cause even the most optimistic person to fret. As a parent, I often wonder what the world will be like when my children are adults. Yet, as we examine the troubled times in which we live, we must not forget that God is still in control and that He still has a purpose. Christ's delay in returning is evidence to the fact that God is not finished with man yet. He is still at work. What is God doing? Well, He is doing what He has always done. He is still in the business of changing hearts.

The above passage from Ezekiel testifies to the fact that God desires a change to take place within the heart of men. This was the case in the Garden of Eden, in the writings of the prophets and it was what Jesus taught. More so, it is still true today! God's purpose is to lead mankind to a life-changing encounter with Himself. Okay then, what does this mean for us? Well, it means the next time you turn on the news and feel as if the world is in a downward spiral, there is still hope. In fact, we can take it a step further and say that the times in which we live provides the perfect atmosphere for the truth of God to have the most impact. The time is ripe for God to do the most good. This reality should help us consider others in a new light as well. We need to perceive the ungodly of our day as people in which God would like nothing better than to change their heart of stone into a heart of flesh. In other words, He wants to see them experience His love in a way that will change their lives for all eternity. He wants them saved. Just like your heart has been changed, so can theirs. God can take even the hardest heart and turn it around. Never underestimate His ability to reach the lost. Think of the great men and women of the past that God used, people that most of us would have written off as products of an ungodly and deteriorating society. Such people include Paul the persecutor, Matthew the extortionist and Peter the denier. God used these men with all their faults to give us most of the New Testament, which we love and cherish. How? He changed their hearts, just as He still does today. Sure, the times we live in can be scary. However, the God we serve is still omnipotent and still wants the best for the world He created. We are still here because God sees in our world a great worth. Don't give up hope. Today more than ever we have grounds for a real hope, and it starts by remembering the change God has wrought in our own hearts and doing our part to help others experience it as well.

The Thin Place: Ask, Answer, Pray.

Do you ever feel overwhelmed by the moral and spiritual condition of today's world?

Are you guilty of "writing off" someone in your life in which you have felt was beyond reach?

How can you relate to that person differently so that the love of God might be seen by them?

June 4
The First Step

From Above: Deuteronomy 5:29

Focal Passage: *"Oh, that their hearts would be inclined to fear me and keep all my commands always, so that it might go well with them and their children forever!"* – Deuteronomy 5:29

Here Below:

As you study the Bible, particularly the Old Testament, you may see a pattern in the manner in which God deals with His children. He desires to lead them to places of great blessing and at the same time He expects of them to continue to follow His lead, even if it leads to a place of uncertainty. While it would probably be simpler for God to simply give us what we ask for, instead He reminds us of our own personal spiritual responsibilities. Do not get me wrong. When it comes to salvation, we are saved and kept by the complete and totally unmerited grace of God. It is not about what we do or how faithful we are in serving the Lord. Salvation is about His love for us. Nevertheless, as any good parent will do with their children, God does expect us to take some of the steps ourselves when it comes to our living for Him and enjoying the results. To reach the Promised Land, the children of Israel had to step out on faith and walk. We are asked to do the same as well.

The above verse from Deuteronomy expresses some of the frustration that God must sometimes feel when it comes to His relationship with His children. This "if only" type expression relates to us God's desire for things to go well with us. He wants us to have a life that is good and filled with joy and satisfaction. However, this verse also shows us that this will only happen when we have a healthy fear of God and a love for His precepts. Again, like a responsible parent, God is not going to just drop the blessing in our lap. He often wants us to take the responsibility of the first step. He desire is for us to have the desires of our hearts, but he wants us to desire Him even more. Notice also that there is a key word in this verse that is deeply significant. The word is "always". You see, we are often inclined to complain to the Lord when things do not go our way. On the other hand, God wants us to love and fear Him and keep His commandments always, despite the good or bad circumstances. This attitude requires trust and action on our part. Put simply, it requires us to take the first step of faith. Whether it be something as great as bringing a nation into the promised land or something as simple as providing the best wine at a wedding feast (John 2), we do have to be willing to take the first step of faith by having and expressing a trusting faith in God. This happens when our hearts are daily prepared to receive both the instructions and the blessings of God. Are you willing to do what it takes to provide the proper soil for God's promises to grow? Are you willing to take the first step?

The Thin Place: Ask, Answer, Pray.

Have you ever questioned the way in which God answered your prayers?

Looking back, can you see that you might have had some responsibility in the outcome of those prayers?

How can you better recognize your own spiritual responsibilities?

June 5
The Little Sins

From Above: Psalm 69:5; I John 3:1-11; Hebrews 8:12

Focal Passage: *"Everyone who sins breaks the law; in fact, sin is lawlessness. But you know that he appeared so that he might take away our sins. And in him is no sin."* – I John 3:4-5

Here Below:

Recently I broke a toe. This is the second time I have broken the same toe, just on opposite feet. Most would consider it not that serious; in that, it is my little toe or as some call it, my pinky toe. However, I have discovered in my life that the measure of seriousness when it comes to medical conditions is based upon whether or not it is you that has the medical condition! It may be only my pinky toe, but it hurts. All I can really do is tape it up and let it heal. Nevertheless, just because it is small doesn't mean that it will go unnoticed. With every limping step I take I am reminded of the fact that it is broken. Along with the pain is the embarrassment of it all. The last time this happened I had to preach a sermon wearing a pair of flip-flops since I couldn't wear my shoe on that foot. It may just be the pinky toe, but it upset my life for a few weeks.

I tell this story because it reminds me of the way we often look at sin. We like to classify sin as being big or little sins, serious or not so serious sins. I do not believe this is Biblical. Nowhere in scripture do we see sin classified in this manner. On the contrary, we see all sin condemned. Even those sins of the heart, that no one but ourselves may ever realize, are equated with murder and adultery by Jesus Christ Himself (Matthew 5). So you see, with God there are no little sins.

Sure, the consequences of our sin often vary in degrees of seriousness, but sin itself still has the same eternal effect. Sin separates us from God and unrepented sin hinders our relationship with God, ...even the "little" ones. To trivialize a sin is to trivialize what Jesus accomplished for us on the cross of Calvary. It was for our sin, that He died on the cross. It wasn't just for our big sins, but for all our sins.

If you are dealing with what you have considered as a little harmless sin, then you must seek God's mercy and forgiveness today. Don't ignore it, thinking it will simply go away. God will not allow that. Sooner or later, you will have to deal with it. Isn't it better to deal with it according to God's mercy and forgiveness? Just like that broken pinky toe, your sin cannot be ignored for long. Little or not, you will have to deal with the consequences. Also, like that broken pinky toe, a little sin has a way of crippling the whole body if not taken care of. Face your sin today and let God begin the healing process in your heart. His desire has always been to free us from the burden and shame of our sin. Do not take this forgiveness for granted. Seek his face today and you will find Him ready and willing to forgive you of any sin, big or small.

The Thin Place: Ask, Answer, Pray.

Have you ever been guilty of trivializing sins that you considered to be not so serious? Which ones?

Have you ever failed to repent of a sin because you felt as if it was not serious?

Do you have any unrepented sins in your heart right now for which you need to seek God's forgiveness?

June 6
Whoa, Whoa, Whoa...Feelings

From Above: Proverbs 16:32; Galatians 5:16-26

Focal Passage: *"Better a patient man than a warrior, a man who controls his temper than one who takes a city."* – Proverbs 16:32

<u>Here Below</u>:

Would you consider yourself an emotional person? Are you easily upset? While emotions in and of themselves are not necessarily right or wrong, they do have the ability to influence us in many ways. There is probably not one of us that has not at one time or another lost our temper, or as I often put it, popped our cork. It happens to the best of us. Likewise, there is also probably not one of us that has not at one time or another given in to something that otherwise we might have rejected simply because our "feelings" led us to surrender. Have you ever purchased something you later regretted simply because it felt like the thing to do at the time? You see, our emotions can unfortunately control us, and they can also be manipulated by others, thus giving them improper control over us. Emotions, as good as they might sometimes seem simply cannot be trusted. They are fickle. They change with every situation we encounter. This is why we must follow the teachings of scripture which instructs us to not be controlled by our emotions, but instead to control them.

It is only natural to have strong feelings concerning those things that are important to us. However, the regret and damage that comes from words misspoken or impulse decision making due to runaway emotions is tremendous. If only I had not said that! If only I had stepped back and counted to five before I reacted the way I did! These are statements we do not want to say of ourselves. How then do we avoid these "if only" statements? Well, it is not easy, but it is definitely possible. Some of the fruits of the Spirit include patience, gentleness and self-control. The ability to control our feelings is a gift from God. It is by His power that we can do this. However, as with all things spiritual, we do still have some responsibility in the matter. We must strive to have self-control. It doesn't just fall in our laps. We must seek it and work toward that goal. In other words, it may mean that you need to stop and count to ten before you react. It might also mean that you need to intentionally put off making major decisions for a time until you have enough distance from your emotions to make a rational decision. If you take these steps, God will honor your effort. The main thing is to let God have control of your emotions. While feelings can't always be trusted, He can.

The Thin Place: Ask, Answer, Pray.

Have you ever allowed yourself to be led by your feelings only later to regret it?

Are there times when you know that your feelings are leading you in the wrong direction?

What are some practical ways in which you can better control your emotions?

June 7
1 Out of Every 10 Lepers Agree

From Above: Luke 17:11-19

Focal Passage: *"Jesus asked, "Were not all ten cleansed? Where are the other nine?"* – Luke 17:17

Here Below:

The above passage of scripture is one of the most revealing passages of scripture concerning the tendency of mankind to quickly forget the reasons we have for expressing gratitude to God. Here was ten people healed of a terrible disease. Not only was this disease physically painful and repulsive, but it was socially crippling as well. To have leprosy was to be an outcast of the worst kind. In Biblical times, to have leprosy was looked upon as punishment for your sins. This was the justification used to show complete and total apathy toward the pain and suffering of the lepers. It was a miserable existence. Yet, here were ten people healed of this terrible affliction and only one of them comes back to Jesus to thank Him. Jesus had literally given these people their lives back, but only one out of ten returned to express their gratitude.

Notice however the strange order of events that takes place in this story. In verse 19, Jesus tells him to rise and go and that his faith had healed him. Wait a minute! Wasn't he already healed when he came back to Jesus? Physically, yes! However, the healing I think Jesus was referring to had more to do with the spiritual damage this man had endured with his condition. He was healed physically, but it wasn't until he turned to Jesus that he was truly healed. The beauty of this is in the fact that it is all centered on his gratitude to Jesus. This leaves us with a real challenge. How grateful are we to God for giving us our lives? Every day is filled with reasons to express gratitude to God for His blessings. Each day is a new opportunity to sing His praises. Regardless of the hardships we may face, we still have reason to be thankful.

If you had been among those ten, would you have gone back to Jesus? Sure, we would want to go to our family and friends and share our joy. But isn't it only proper to first thank the one who made it possible? Today, strive to be more like the one than like the other nine. Thank the one who has blessed you beyond measure. Give thanks to God today!

The Thin Place: Ask, Answer, Pray.

How easy is it for you to forget from where your blessings come?

What are some things right now for which you can thank God?

What can you do differently in the future to better express your thankfulness to God?

June 8
He Took My Bullet

From Above: John 15:13; I John 3:1-3

Focal Passage: *"Behold, what manner of love the Father hath bestowed upon us, that we should be called the sons of God: therefore the world knoweth us not, because it knew him not."* – I John 3:1 (KJV)

<u>Here Below</u>:

You are in a crowded auditorium. There are hundreds of people all around you. Some of them are strangers and also among them are some of the people most dear to you. Among them are your children, or grandchildren, or spouse and close friends. Suddenly a door swings open and in runs a masked gunman. He stands in the middle of this crowd waving his gun for all to see. He then turns to you, looks at your son standing by your side and says "I am going to shoot everyone in this room, <u>or</u> I am going to shoot your child! It is up to you!" What would it be? As a parent I can tell you that I am not sure how I would answer. As much as I might love everyone else, I do not think I could sacrifice my own son to save anyone else's life. I would hope that I could offer myself, but I am pretty sure that I couldn't let my son die so that others might live. As terrible as that sounds, it is the truth. However, as we think about his extreme illustration, we need to recognize that this is exactly what God did with His son Jesus Christ! What kind of love is that? That is the love God has shown for you and me.

There is no greater expression of love in the history of mankind that the one found on the cross of Calvary. God turned his face from the ugliness of the cross out of love for me! It is almost more than I can grasp. Yet, it is true. Do you truly understand how much God loves you today? Better yet, does your life reflect that you understand how much God loves you today? Many times, I have encountered people who ask questions like "Why did God let this happen to me?" or "If God is love, how come this terrible thing happened?" I understand those questions, but at the same time, when we ask those type questions it is almost as if we have forgotten what he has already done for us.

Let's go back to that auditorium for a moment. If someone allowed their child to be shot so that we might go free, we wouldn't go back to that person later and complain that they didn't do more for us. On the contrary, we would forever be in their debt. Yet, we do that with

God quite often. So next time you start feeling sorry for yourself and are tempted to complain about it, just remember that God already allowed His Son to take a bullet meant for you! I don't know about you, but no one else ever allowed their son to die in my place before! Therefore, my life needs to reflect that appreciation. What a love! What a God!

The Thin Place: Ask, Answer, Pray.

Have you ever questioned God's love for you when troubles arose in your life?

How often do you verbally express appreciation for the cross of Jesus Christ?

Does your overall lifestyle reflect appreciation for the cross of Jesus Christ?

June 9
American Idol

From Above: Acts 17:18-34

Focal Passage: *"God did this so that men would seek him and perhaps reach out for him and find him, though he is not far from each one of us.."* – Acts 17:27

Here Below:

In a time when humanity is supposed to have evolved past the point of idol worship such as that found in ancient times, we still find that humanity is predisposed to find earthly things to worship. While most do not have an Asherah pole or some other form of pagan altar set up in their back yard, one still doesn't have to look very far to see that there is rampant idol worship in our day. It is no coincidence that the most popular TV show in recent years bears a name which reveals that simple truth. We used to call them celebrities or stars. Now they are idols. Fame, fortune, youth, talent and other more worldly endeavors have taken the place of Baal and Asherah. However, as innocent or even good as these things might appear to be, they still serve the same purpose of those ancient idols of the past. They take a place in our lives that is meant only to be occupied by God. In a sense, that is the definition of idol worship.

You may be thinking to yourself as you read these words, that as true as they might be, they simply do not apply to you. I hope that is true. But idol worship can be even more benign than celebrity worship. It can be something as simple as a relationship, a career or even a hobby. If there is anything in your life that is more important to you than your relationship with the Lord, then you are at least in danger of idol worship. I would venture to say that it is something we have all done to one small degree or another. After all, the above passage from the days of the early church reinforces the fact that we are indeed inclined to worship idols. In fact, they took it so far as to create one so that no one or no thing would be left out. I wonder if we are so different today. Are we? Perhaps as a society we are still inclined to worship idols. But for us as individuals, the decision is still ours. Are we going to let anything take the place in our lives that belongs only to God? If we do, we are setting ourselves up for heartache in the future. These other things, as pleasant as they might seem, only lead to an emptiness that cannot be filled. This is why we must turn away from the unknown gods of idol worship and instead turn to the one true and living God. While people may have changed since the book of Acts, there is one thing that still remains true. God is not willing to take a second chair to anything in our lives. He wants first chair and nothing else will do. It is not pride, but it is because He knows what is best for you and He wants the best for you. Let Him be first in your life today.

<u>The Thin Place</u>: Ask, Answer, Pray.

What are some things you see in your everyday life that are idols for others?

What are some things in your life that could easily become personal idols? How can you keep that from happening?

June 10
Homesick and Happy

<u>**From Above**</u>: Philippians 3:17-20

Focal Passage: *"But our citizenship is in heaven. And we eagerly await a Savior from there, the Lord Jesus Christ,"* – Philippians 3:20

<u>**Here Below**</u>:

One of the major ironies of the human experience is the amount of time we spend preparing for and caring for such a short amount of our lives and we neglect the most important and longest lasting part. I, of course, am speaking of our eternal lives. Think about it for a moment. If we are truly blessed with a long life, we may get 70, 80, 90 or 100 years on this earth. Yet, compared to eternity, those 70, 80, 90 or 100 years are but an instant. Likewise, most of us spend the first half of our lives saving and working so that we can retire and live the last of our days in relative comfort and ease. Sure, we need to plan for the future. We have that responsibility. However, many foolishly invest everything into that endeavor while totally neglecting their spiritual lives and totally ignoring eternity.

I am assuming that if you are reading this devotion, then you have a general understanding of eternity. However, the question remains for all of us as to how important eternity really is to us. If your eternity is secured, have you taken the time to share your thoughts with others that you love? After all, eternity is a long time to spend away from those you love. How often do you share your faith and how often do you reflect on Heaven for yourself? If you are going to spend forever there, shouldn't it be something you think about quite often? You wouldn't go on a two-week trip without planning for it and thinking about your itinerary. Yet, many don't give eternity a second thought. It simply doesn't make sense.

Our belief in eternal life is truly a dividing point among humans. If we do not believe in eternal life, then nothing we do here matters anyway. That is a sad way to face life and it is not the way God intended. God's desire is for our lives to have meaning. That is what eternity does for us. It gives our short existence on this earth meaning and purpose. As a pastor officiating over countless funerals, I can promise you that believing in Jesus Christ and the eternal life He provides does make a huge difference in how we face both life and death. In fact, I would say that it is everything. But it is not something we need to put off thinking about until we are facing it. For the child of God, it should be a point of daily reflection. We may live here, but our citizenship is Heaven. It may make you a little homesick, but it is a homesickness that will make you more than a little happy! How homesick are you today?

The Thin Place: Ask, Answer, Pray.

How often do you think about Heaven and eternity?

What difference has a belief in eternal life made in your life?

How certain are you of the eternal destination of those closest to you?

June 11
Spiritual Spelunker

From Above: Psalm 142

Focal Passage: *"When my spirit grows faint within me, it is you who know my way."* – Psalm 142:3

Here Below:

The above Psalm of David is referred to as a maskil. A maskil is a contemplative piece of literature that is thought to contain insight and wisdom. It is wisdom that has come from a period of isolation and meditation. This passage is just that. The above words of David compose a prayer. This prayer song was written while he was hiding for his life in a cave. Knowing that gives the words special meaning. It is a very honest prayer that contains cries, pleas, complaints and acknowledgements of God's special power and strength. It has it all. David recognizes that though his situation is bleak, and his spirits are down, God knows his way. In other words, God knows what David needs to do. Indeed, He did.

In this passage we see the necessity and the liberating nature of being completely honest and open with God. It was in that period of being alone in that cave with God that David's faith was strengthened. In that place of isolation, all pretense was gone. It was unnecessary. God had brought him to a place where honest was all David could be. There was no one to impress and no one else to worry about. It took hiding in a cave to find it, but David found it. Sometimes it takes just that for growth to take place. Too often we are so busy trying to manipulate our circumstances that we do not take the time to wait and listen for God's direction. Sometimes His desire is for us to simply wait. Unfortunately, it sometimes takes us getting to our own spiritual cave to find that alone time God desires to have with us. The cries and pleas of our hearts might be best alleviated by simply stopping and listening. It is in those moments of earthly isolation that we are in the best position to hear from Heaven. Perhaps today you need to find a cave of your own in which to dwell. Perhaps today it is time to go on a spiritual spelunking expedition. Explore God's will for your life. Find that place in your own existence and listen to the God who desires to be with you more than anything.

The Thin Place: Ask, Answer, Pray.

How hard is it for you to find time alone to meditate and spend time with the Lord?

Has God ever led you to a place of isolation for your own spiritual well-being?

What schedule changes could you make that would enable you to have more time alone with God?

June 12
Hello Friend

<u>From Above</u>: James 1:17-21

Focal Passage: *"My dear brothers, take note of this: Everyone should be quick to listen, slow to speak and slow to become angry, for man's anger does not bring about the righteous life that God desires."* – James 1:19-20

<u>Here Below</u>:

How are you doing today? This is a statement that we say multiple times a day. Yet, how often do we really stop and listen for a response? It has become such an expected part of polite conversation that it has almost lost all meaning. Sometimes we say it so quickly in passing that we do not even give others a chance to respond. I know I am guilty of doing this at times. It is a reflection of the misguided busy nature that our lives often take in today's culture. We become too busy to care. It has also come to my realization that there are those out there who are just waiting for someone to ask them how they are doing. They are desperately seeking someone to show some interest in their lives. Perhaps they are missing the depth of a close personal relationship themselves or perhaps they are going through a hard time and just need someone to care. The world is filled with such people and sometimes they are right under our nose. The sad reality is that listening is slowly becoming a lost practice, and as a result relationships are becoming less than what God intends. After all, one sided relationships rarely last. We must take time to listen to others and spend less time speaking of ourselves.

We are given some great advice in the above passage of scripture. In fact, as scripture it is more than just advice, it is instruction. While it primarily appeals to how we deal with anger, it also says much more. Being quick to listen and slow to speak is essential to the Christian life. As children of God, we are to be His ambassadors to the world. If we are His representatives, then we must treat others as He would. In fact, we must love others as He does. This means putting them first. Practically speaking, this might mean stopping and truly listening to the story of how they are actually doing today. It is a simple gesture, but one that can have eternal consequences. You never know what someone might be facing behind their smiles. I have seen the above question, as simple and innocent as it is, bring an individual to tears, freeing them from the bondage of their problem with the realization that they are not alone. Isolation in a world filled with people is crippling to the spirit. We were not created for this. We were created for relationships. By listening to others, we make friends and most importantly, we keep them. So, the next time you pass by someone and ask them how they are doing, stop and listen for their response. It might just be that God has arranged this encounter for the sole purpose of you serving as an encourager for someone who truly needs it. Don't miss that chance. Do not miss an opportunity to be Christ's ambassador today.

The Thin Place: Ask, Answer, Pray.

Has there ever been a time in your life when you just needed someone to listen to you?

What individuals in your life do you feel you can turn to with the assurance that they will listen to you?

Who are some individuals that you encounter regularly to which you could strive to be a better listener?

June 13
A *Carpe Diem* Day

From Above: I Corinthians 9:18-27

Focal Passage: *"Do you not know that in a race all the runners run, but only one gets the prize? Run in such a way as to get the prize."* – I Corinthians 9:24

Here Below:

Years ago, a movie was released that quickly became one of my favorites. It is called *Dead Poets Society*. It was a movie about a teacher that inspired his students to strive and to achieve. This critically acclaimed movie brought at the time a mostly unknown Latin phrase into the everyday vernacular. *Carpe Diem!* Seize the day! This expression became the catch phrase for all of us inspired to make the most of every moment given to us. Seizing the moment is an appealing concept and a concept that I believe is Biblical as one can see in the above passage of scripture. Paul inspires us in the above words to seize the moments that God has given us. The analogy he uses is that of a race. In this race, this race of life, all run, but only one runs in such a way as to win the prize. I do not believe the Apostle is writing about us having a competitive spirit in this letter. However, he is acknowledging that only those who give it their all will ever reach their full potential. While this principle could be applied to many things of life, it is especially true in spiritual matters. We must make the most of the time we are given.

Through social media, I have been reunited with friends from decades ago. Yes, I said decades. I have been able to speak with friends with whom I went to elementary school. As we reminisce over old times, it seems as if they were just yesterday. I remember my parents saying things like that years ago and thinking to myself that they must be exaggerating. They were not. It really does seem as if not too long ago I was a student at Flowery Branch Elementary School. Time goes by so quickly. This realization has caused me to question my stewardship of the time God has given me. Sure, as I look back, I see many accomplishments, but there are also some missed opportunities for service. That is what Paul is acknowledging in this Corinthian letter. Time is like a race. It speeds along. For that reason, we must run in such a way as to win. In other words, we must take advantage of every opportunity we find to increase our effectiveness. We see these opportunities every day. Do we seize them, or do we let them slip on by? Sometimes we are so busy with the running of the race that we miss the opportunities God gives us to improve our speed! Time is too precious to miss these moments. Seize them! Let this day be your *Carpe Diem* day!

The Thin Place: Ask, Answer, Pray.

Would you consider yourself a good steward of your time? Why or why not?

Have there been missed opportunities for service to God in your past? When?

What changes can you make in your life to help you better seize the moment in front of you?

June 14
Together and Separate

From Above: 2 Corinthians 6:13-18

Focal Passage: *"Do not be yoked together with unbelievers. For what do righteousness and wickedness have in common? Or what fellowship can light have with darkness?"* – 2 Corinthians 6:14

Here Below:

The above passage of scripture is one of those passages that we sometimes have a difficult time accepting. It can be a bitter pill to swallow, depending upon our circumstances. Nevertheless, it is there and we must accept it and apply it to our lives. I think we find it a difficult passage because it requires of us to examine our relationships and the place that they fill in our lives. Many times this verse is used to counsel someone in a dating relationship or marriage. Yet, it applies to all relationships. Put simply, we are not to be committed to a relationship with an unbeliever. Wow! This sounds a little harsh. What about all the verses about loving your neighbor and treating others as yourself? How does this fit together? Well, it most definitely does fit together and without any contradiction.

You see, many of us take this verse too far and interpret it to mean that we are not to have anything to do with the lost. This is not the message Paul is conveying. On the contrary, he spent most of his time ministering to Gentiles, following the example of Jesus. Instead, what he is saying in this verse is that we must not go in the same direction as unbelievers. He uses this illustration to paint a picture of two oxen yoked together. The direction one goes must also be the direction the other goes. They are joined at the neck. There is no going separate ways. Likewise, we are not to allow the lost in our lives to lead us in a direction that we do not want to go. Instead, we are to be the one leading them to Jesus Christ. We are to be the influence. The problem lies in the fact that is so much easier to lead someone in the wrong direction than it is in the right direction. We must keep our relationships in the proper perspective. Again, Paul is not telling us to not befriend the lost. We are just not supposed to live in such a way as to join ourselves with their lifestyle. We are to maintain that spiritual distinction with the unbelievers until that point when they accept the Lord and become part of the bigger family that we as Christians inhabit. We are to be in the world, but not of the world.

So do not struggle with this verse. It is not telling us to rid ourselves of lost friends. If anything, it is telling us to love them even more. It is a deeper love that has the spiritual welfare of their friends at heart. We must love them with the love of Christ and keep that goal as the focus of our relationship. Do this and God will reach the heart of your lost friend. Love them in this manner and light will overcome the darkness.

The Thin Place: Ask, Answer, Pray.

Have you ever been unequally yoked together with an unbeliever?

What was the outcome of that relationship in your spiritual life?

Is there someone in your life right now in which you could better share the love of Christ?

June 15
Worship in the Woodshed

From Above: Proverbs 3:12; Job 5:17-18

Focal Passage: *""Blessed is the man whom God corrects; so do not despise the discipline of the Almighty.*

For he wounds, but he also binds up; he injures, but his hands also heal."
– Job 5:17-18

<u>**Here Below**</u>:

I used to think my parents were liars. There is no way that spanking your child could hurt yourself more than it does the one on the receiving end of that form of discipline. However, as I became a parent myself, I realized that there is great truth and wisdom in that proclamation. It is not easy to discipline your child, whatever method you might use. Yet, to neglect discipline is in my opinion a form of abuse. By the neglect of proper and Godly discipline, you are not preparing them for a life that is filled with boundaries. It is these boundaries that keep society in check. There are also certain boundaries that keep our own heart in check as well. Unfortunately, we have all found ourselves outside of those God given boundaries at one time or another. For this reason, as a good parent, God must sometimes take His children to the "woodshed" for a little discipline of their own.

Notice the above verse taken from the book of Job. According to this verse, the man that has been disciplined by God is a man that is blessed. We don't often think of discipline as a blessing, but that is exactly what it is. After all, a child that has been properly disciplined is a child that has someone in their life that loves them enough to try to lead them to make appropriate decisions. The same is true of our Heavenly Father. If God has taken the time to discipline us, it is because He loves us enough to care about how we live. However, we must be careful to not always put the credit on God when we feel we are being disciplined. Sometimes things that happen are the natural consequence of our mistakes. But even then, God allows us to face the consequences so that we might learn from our mistakes. Even that is an expression of His love. Does God enjoy it? I think not. Like us, it probably hurts Him worse than it does ourselves. But He does want the best for each of us and so He does what is sometimes necessary.

So, the next time you find yourself in God's "woodshed", don't complain. Instead, take note of what brought you there and repent. And most importantly, take time to thank God for caring enough to bring you there. You can worship Him, even in the "woodshed".

The Thin Place: Ask, Answer, Pray.

Can you recall times in your life when you feel that you had been disciplined by God?

What was the outcome of that discipline in your spiritual life?

Have you taken the time to thank God for caring that much about your life?

June 16
The Last Word

From Above: Psalm 37: 37; Isaiah 32:17; Matthew 5:9

Focal Passage: *"The fruit of righteousness will be peace; the effect of righteousness will be quietness and confidence forever."* – Isaiah 32:17

Here Below:

Many of us place great importance on getting the last word. As children, our arguments often included long bouts of going back and forth with one another saying things like "did too...did not", all the while hoping to get in the last word or the last insult. While our vocabulary may improve the older we get, our tactics often stay the same. Sometimes we go to great lengths to get that final stab in before we leave an argument. Granted, there are times we must take a stand on certain issues and times that we should try to make our view on an issue known. However, there is a fine line between needing to win an argument and wanting to win an argument. Unfortunately, it is a line I have crossed many times, as have most of us. This must win attitude is not the attitude we see exemplified in Christ.

As you study the life of Christ, you will see that even in those times when He was right, which happened to be every time, He still did not insist upon being seen as being right. Put simply, He did not have to win the argument. In fact, as Christ stood before Pilate, He didn't even try to defend Himself. This humility paved the way for others to see Him for who and what He really is. Jesus is the Prince of Peace. He told us in the Beatitudes that peacemakers are blessed; therefore, keeping the peace is a necessary part of the Christian life. The hard part for us to swallow is that keeping the peace sometimes means not insisting upon winning the argument. Sometimes it means walking away without getting in the last word. Oftentimes, that is the best way to win. Jesus didn't put up a fight and we would all agree that He won. The same can be true of us as well. If we insist upon being always acknowledged as right, we open the door for anger and for our tempers and that of others to flare. This is dangerous. Why? It is risky because we are not always right; and if we are in the right, the truth will eventually prevail whether we are acknowledged or not. So, we must decide if our winning the argument is worth the cost of a broken relationship or a damaged witness? The truth is that to yield a victory in an argument is to pave the way for peace and reconciliation. That should be our goal rather that winning an argument. When you get into a battle of wills and win, what have you really won? But in creating an atmosphere of peace and restoration, you may win a soul. Does this mean we should never be forceful in our views or ever be angry? Of course not. Jesus did both of these things, but He did it without sinning. There may be times when we must do the same. Just be sure it is an argument that God is concerned with you winning. As the above verse attests, the fruit and effects of godly and righteous living are these: peace, quietness and confidence. Let peace be the last word you get in today and come out a real winner.

The Thin Place: Ask, Answer, Pray.

Do you often feel that you must get in the last word in an argument? If so, why is this important?

Have you ever felt righteously angered and felt as if you needed to be acknowledged? When?

How present is humility in your Christian witness and how does it affect how you deal with conflict?

June 17
Conquer by Continuing

<u>**From Above**</u>: Romans 12:12; 2 Thessalonians 1
Focal Passage: *"Be joyful in hope, patient in affliction, faithful in prayer."*
– Romans 12:12

<u>**Here Below**</u>:
The above verse of scripture, among other things, addresses the importance of perseverance in the life of the believer. All three commands given in this verse imply remaining constant in our spiritual fervor in spite of the circumstances we might find ourselves facing. It is our hope, patience and faithfulness that will ultimately see us through these obstacles. It is an intimidating task, but one in which the rewards make the struggle well worth the waiting.

All throughout scripture we see that God desires for us to wait. He never acts impulsively or impetuously in responding to our cries. His answer to our prayers almost always comes with a period of waiting and searching. Perhaps He chooses to act in this manner because He himself is not affected by time. Or perhaps God chooses to do it that way to build our faith. After all, if He acted instantly every time we called upon Him, our faith would serve no real purpose. God wants us to love Him and to serve Him, even when the answers we seek may not be forthcoming. Our timetable is different than that of His and we must trust that His timetable is the best.

So, what does this mean for us? It means that we must keep doing that which we know to be right and that we must be patient and faithful to Him regardless of the fight we may be up against in this world. We must persevere, for we know that there is a reward ahead that will one day make the waiting seem insignificant, whether the reward comes in this life or the next. This especially has deep implications to the manner in which we serve God. We must serve Him faithfully, even when the rewards of our work might not be forthcoming. The life of faith is oftentimes a series of small steps and small victories. We might not see the results right away, but then again we might. But whether we see them or not, we are to continue living in such a way as to please our Heavenly Father. Don't sweat the small problems and make it a point to cherish the small victories. Do this and in time the challenges will seem less daunting and the victories will seem greater and more frequent. Even the bigger challenges you face will be eventually worn down by your steadfastness. Those who win are those who keep going.

The Thin Place: Ask, Answer, Pray.

Do you ever get discouraged by a lack of immediate results in your spiritual life?

Is it possible that you fail to see the real results that are taking place due to impatience?

How might you apply the above verse in your life so that you can be more effective in your witness?

June 18
Satisfaction Guaranteed

From Above: Psalm 145

Focal Passage: *"You open your hand and satisfy the desires of every living thing."* – Psalm 145: 16

Here Below:

How many times have you made a purchase of a product with a label declaring that your satisfaction is guaranteed? Sometimes the label says you will get your money back, other times it just makes the promise of satisfaction with no recourse for complaints. Yet, with all the promises and slick talking promotions, we still walk away from many purchases with buyer's remorse. We are often not satisfied, but the hassle and inconvenience of taking a product back often outweighs our dissatisfaction, and we just accept a less than perfect product. Unfortunately, we often settle for less than ideal spiritual satisfaction as well.

Just like those infomercials and ads promising something that in reality there is no way to truly guarantee, the world offers a promise of satisfaction and fulfillment that it cannot keep. As you look at those with whom we would consider worldly and successful, such as the rich, powerful and the famous, one thing is common among almost all of them. Very rarely do you see a soul that is satisfied. If they have money, they want more. If they have fame, their relationships are often a complete wreck. If they have power, they often become corrupt. Put simply, what they have is never enough. The world cannot satisfy the soul of man. Why? Because we were not created to find satisfaction in those things! We were created to find true fulfillment only in God. This is why every culture in the world has some form of spiritual belief. Though many are misguided, they are looking for satisfaction in something other than what the world can offer.

As children of God, we are to find satisfaction in God alone. This explains the phenomenon of those we see daily whom have very little as far as the world offers, yet they are the happiest and most content people on the earth. This may seem over simplistic to you today, but I promise you that wholeness in life is something that can give you a peace and joy that cannot be found elsewhere. This wholeness adds flavor and strength to life, assisting us in dealing with the unforeseen aspects of everyday living. If in God we are satisfied, nothing else has any power over us. If you want satisfaction guaranteed today, turn to the one source that can honestly keep that guarantee. Taste and see that the Lord is good. You will not have buyer's remorse. You will instead be satisfied beyond expectation.

The Thin Place: Ask, Answer, Pray.

Do you feel as if your life is fulfilling? Are you satisfied with your life to-day?

What do you think could help your life to be more satisfying?

How do your desires in life relate to what God wants for you?

June 19
Be Careful What You Ask For

<u>**From Above**</u>: John 14:5-17

Focal Passage: "*And I will do whatever you ask in my name, so that the Son may bring glory to the Father.*" – Psalm 145: 16

<u>**Here Below**</u>:

On at least three different occasions in the gospel of John, we see the promise written in red that we need to only ask for anything in the name of Jesus and it will be answered accordingly (John 14, 15 and 16). There are many who would misinterpret this promise to mean that we can simply ask for anything our heart desires in the name of Jesus and we will receive it. When this doesn't happen, we hear that perhaps our faith wasn't strong enough. Well, this is a total misguided understanding of this scripture. In fact, if you look to John 14 in verse 12 and 15 you will see that there is more to this promise than meets the eye. In verse 12, we are told that if we love Jesus, then we will be doing what He is doing. In verse 15, following the promise, we are again told that if we love Him, we will obey Him. What does this mean? It means that if we are living for Him and keeping His commands, then we will not be asking for things outside the will of God. In that instance, we will get what we pray for.

As I consider this promise and the above conclusion, I find great comfort. I find it in the fact that God doesn't bend according to our will. If God had given me everything for which I had ever asked, my life would be in a pretty sorry state right now. Looking back, I can see times when God didn't give me what I asked for and it was for my own good. At the time I couldn't see it, but God had a better plan ahead. Likewise, I also find great comfort in the fact that if God leads me in a certain direction in life, I can depend on Him to hear and answer my prayers concerning this direction. If what I am doing is according to His will, then there is nothing that I can't accomplish. I am only limited by the power of God, with which there are no limits.

Notice however the above verse. God does this so that He may receive the glory. There is a fine line between asking for what God wants and asking for what we think God wants. We must be certain that it is His will we are seeking and not our own. It is for His recognition that we can ask with full assurance of our prayers coming to fruition. We must remember, it is in our weaknesses that God's power is best glorified. So be careful what you ask for, but do not hesitate to ask. God's answer will far surpass anything you could accomplish on your own. Don't settle for less than what God wants in your life.

The Thin Place: Ask, Answer, Pray.

Think of a time when you felt as if God didn't answer your prayer in the manner which you desired.

Now, think of a time when God surpassed your expectations concerning an answer to a prayer.

How was God faithful to you on both occasions?

June 20
No Easy Task

From Above: Ephesians 6:1-4

Focal Passage: *"Fathers, do not exasperate your children; instead, bring them up in the training and instruction of the Lord."* – Ephesians 6:4

Here Below:

As you see the subject matter of this writing, you may be thinking to yourself that this is not for you. You may not be a father and you may not have a father, but I would guess that somewhere down the line you have had a man in your life that had specific impact on your development. It may have been positive, or it could have been just the opposite. Nevertheless, it is important to realize that being a father in our day is no easy task to say the least and the men and boys in our lives need all the encouragement they can receive. So, if you are not a father or perhaps do not have a father to consider today, let this be a reminder to cherish those other special men in your life. Besides, regardless of our station in life or our background, we all have a Heavenly Father to look to daily.

The first few verses of the above chapter are really all about relationships. First, we see the relationship between child and parent with the responsibility of the child clearly defined. However, the above verse is one that reminds men of their roles in the family. Men are the ones given the responsibility to guide the family in the right direction. In fact, we are specifically warned about stirring up anger in the hearts of our children. I don't think this means we should do everything to avoid making our kids mad or that we should give them everything they want. It means just the opposite. We are to raise them in such a way as to give them no reason to resent their upbringing. How do we do that? We prepare them for life by following the rest of the directions in the verse. We give them godly and biblical instruction. It is a serious responsibility. A man must never take it lightly.

Likewise, if you are reading this today and are not a father yourself, then take this opportunity to pray for the men in your life. Pray that they would have the strength to stand against the pressures of modern society that are working to diminish the role of the father. Pray that they might be strong and men of integrity. As you read this, you may be thinking of a man in your life that has been all of this for you in the past. He may or may not still be with you. Regardless, take time today to thank God for that man and if possible, give that man some of your time today. Most importantly, pray that the men in your life would be a reflection of the Father of us all. Pray for fathers today.

The Thin Place: Ask, Answer, Pray.

What kind of relationship would you say that you have or had with your earthly father?

Does this ever effect your relationship with your heavenly father? If so, how?

What can you do to be an encouragement to the special men in your life?

June 21
Easy on the Eyes

From Above: Genesis 2

Focal Passage: *"Thus the heavens and the earth were completed in all their vast array."* – Genesis 2:1

Here Below:

The beauty of creation is perhaps the greatest proof of the wisdom and the love of God. While there are many in our day that do appreciate the beauty and complexity of creation, they are still missing the point as to why it is divine evidence. If we are not careful, the love of all things natural can fill an unnatural position in our list of personal priorities. In a sense, we can choose to worship the creation instead of the creator. Do not fret. This is not an attempt at an anti-conservation debate. On the contrary, if the Bible teaches us anything about conservation, it teaches us that we are given the responsibility of caring for God's creation. It was a task specifically given to mankind. Likewise, creation was a gift specifically given to mankind. However, just as we see it as a precious gift, we need to also see it as a reminder of what was most important to God. Creation was designed for us. Of all His creation, we are the prize.

In verse 9 of Genesis 2, we see that God created the trees. Some He made visually appealing and others He made to bear fruit for our sustenance. Have you really ever thought about that verse? What purpose did God have in creating visually appealing trees? Did He have to make them beautiful? No. In fact, none of creation had to be beautiful to carry out its purpose; that is, unless part of its purpose was to bring pleasure to God's most treasured creation, you and me. You see, the beauty we encounter every day is extra. It was a bonus part of the creation that was meant to serve as a reminder of our special place in God's list of priorities. We are number one. With this said, the next time you view a beautiful sunset, just remember that it didn't have to be that way. God designed it as such so that you would look to Him. The wonder of creation is a love note from our God. Yes, there are trees that are easy on the eyes, as Genesis 2:9 suggests. This is no accident. They were created that way on purpose. That being, when you find yourself awestruck by a beautiful landscape or a crystal-clear night sky, instead of feeling insignificant, let it remind you of your great significance in the heart of God. That beauty is an expression of God's love for you.

<u>The Thin Place</u>: Ask, Answer, Pray.

What are some of the most beautiful scenes in nature that you have ever encountered?

Have you ever felt insignificant when looking upon the wonders of creation?

Take time today to thank God for giving you the gift of beauty and wonder and love.

June 22
Debt Management

<u>From Above</u>: Matthew 18:23-35

Focal Passage: *"The servant's master took pity on him, canceled the debt and let him go."* – Matthew 18:27

<u>Here Below</u>:

One can rarely turn on the television or the radio without hearing an advertisement for some type of debt management program. These programs are designed to attract clients that are in over their head with debt, with the promise of finding financial freedom at last. The idea of being freed from debt is an idea that all of us find appealing. This is especially true when it comes to the debts we owe that are of a more spiritual matter. However, forgiving the debts of others should be equally appealing for the child of God.

The above parable of Jesus is one that hits very close to home for many of us. One thing I have learned as I experience more and more of humanity is that an unforgiving spirit is as crippling as any disease or deformity. It can completely bring spiritual health and growth to a halt. As hard as this might be for us to take, I believe an unforgiving spirit is also a symptom of a hypocritical heart. This seems to be the point Jesus is trying to make with this parable. He reminds us each that we, as His children, have been forgiven a tremendous debt. Out of love for us, He has forgiven every wrongdoing and every sin I have ever committed or will commit. Yet, when we are hurt by a brother or sister, we often find ourselves unwilling to forgive them. Why is it that we cannot forgive others as God has forgiven us? In a very real and very troubling sense, what we are saying by harboring unforgiveness is that our standards are higher than that of God's.

There is also another point to this parable. By offering forgiveness to others, even when they may not deserve it, we are in actuality freeing ourselves from the bitterness and heartache of holding someone's debts against them. By forgiving, not only are we following the example of Christ and helping the recipient find freedom, but we are helping ourselves as well. Forgiveness is the best form of spiritual debt management. In fact, if you truly desire spiritual growth and freedom, it is the only way to manage your spiritual debts. We are to seek forgiveness and offer forgiveness. Listen to the words of Jesus today. Look to Him for the model of forgiveness.

The Thin Place: Ask, Answer, Pray.

Do you find it difficult to forgive others when they hurt you? If so, why?

Do you find it difficult to seek forgiveness when you have hurt others? If so, why?

Has God ever forgiven you of something in which you really did not deserve forgiveness?

June 23
Good God

From Above: I Corinthians 11:32

Focal Passage: "*When we are judged by the Lord, we are being disciplined so that we will not be condemned with the world.*" – I Corinthians 11:32

Here Below:

We've all seen it. A child is pitching a temper tantrum in the grocery store. He is upset because he wanted some candy or toy and is now showing out, screaming, and yelling at the top of his lungs. The frustration for us often comes when we see the parent either ignore the child at the expense of our shopping experience or the parent simply gives in and buys the kid that for which he is crying. As we witness this drama, don't we in the back of our minds question the parenting skills of this parent? We think to ourselves as to just how this parent should discipline this child or perhaps we even wish for a few moments alone with the child ourselves! While our discipline method may or may not be correct in this situation, we do understand that a child needs discipline. When they do not receive it, it brings to question the love and competence of the parent.

If all of this is true, why is it we often question the parenting skills of our Heavenly Father? We've all heard questions such as "How can a good God allow this to happen?" or "How could a loving God allow such a thing to happen?" We often ask these "Why me?" type questions whenever we face situations that are difficult. Yet, many times the difficulties we face are a result of sin. Granted, sometimes things just happen at no real fault of our own or they may happen as a result of the sinfulness of others. Nevertheless, we must conclude that all the difficulties of life are in general a result of sin in a fallen world.

If there were no sin, there would be no trials. These trials are often the simple and natural results of life outside of the will of God. In such a situation, for God to ignore our sin would be no better than that parent ignoring their troublesome child in the grocery store. It is because of God's goodness that our sin cannot be ignored. If He loves us, He must discipline us. Granted, it is not always easy to take, but it is always for our welfare.

The next time you find yourself in one of those situations, instead of questioning God's parenting skills or goodness, look to your own heart. Ask yourself if the trials you are struggling with might be the natural consequences of bad choices or sinfulness. If so, then repent and seek God's forgiveness and guidance. The purpose of His discipline is to always restore His relationship with you. It is an act of love. Treat it as such. We have a good and loving Heavenly Father.

The Thin Place: Ask, Answer, Pray.

Think of a time in which you have felt the discipline of God. What was the result?

At the time, did you question God's love for you?

What would it say about God if He were to ignore our sin?

June 24
Breakable

From Above: Philippians 2:5-8

Focal Passage: "*Who, being in very nature God, did not consider equality with God something to be grasped, but made himself nothing, taking the very nature of a servant, being made in human likeness.*" – Philippians 2:6-7

Here Below:

In his song titled *Breakable*, the contemporary Christian artist Todd Agnew writes this line:

You are Glorious

Infinite and Wise
You are mighty
Holy there is none beside you
But to save me from by brokenness
You became breakable

In this chorus, Agnew acknowledges both the divinity and the humanity of Christ. Oftentimes we think only of the sacrifice of Christ being that which he endured upon the cross. While that is definitely a sacrifice, and the greatest of all sacrifices, it is still not the whole picture. The sacrifice of Christ began many years before the cross. When Christ humbled himself and took upon Himself the form of humanity, it was truly a sacrifice. He sacrificed the glories of Heaven for the opportunity of living among us and ultimately dying for us. By doing so, Jesus willingly took upon himself all the struggles that accompany residing on this earth. Among these struggles are the earthly pains of growing up. He underwent the weaknesses of childhood, the awkwardness of adolescence and the responsibility of adulthood. When Jesus took the form of man, He was inviting pain, sorrow, heartache, rejection, sickness and death. As the song says, to free us from our broken state, Jesus allowed himself to become breakable. The all mighty, omnipotent, omnipresent and omniscient Creator of the Universe allowed himself to be broken.

As amazing as this reality seems, it gets even better. He allowed all of this to happen out of love for you and me. Think about that. Most people will not give up their chair for you to have a seat anymore. Yet, Jesus gave up Heaven so that we might be with Him. Don't forget that Jesus did all of that for you! When you fully grasp this reality in your life, it gives everything a whole new meaning and importance. Don't take His sacrifice for granted. Live for Him today.

The Thin Place: Ask, Answer, Pray.

What significance does the humanity of Christ have for your life?
Are you guilty of sometimes forgetting the sacrifice of Jesus?
How can you better acknowledge the sacrifice of Christ in your life today?

June 25
Tears in a Bottle

<u>**From Above**</u>: Psalm 56:8 (KJV); John 11:17-36

Focal Passage: *"Thou tellest my wanderings: put thou my tears into thy bottle: are they not in thy book?" –Psalm 56:8 (KJV)*

<u>**Here Below**</u>:

Tears come easier for some than for others. For me, it has really never been an issue. I let go of the "big boys don't cry" philosophy years ago. Yet, I do sympathize with those who do have trouble expressing their emotions through the outlet of tears. It is unfortunate that so many struggle with this concept; in that, I have found the shedding of tears to be very therapeutic. I might also add that they are a very biblical response to the deep heartfelt emotions we experience, whether they are good or bad.

John 11:35 is perhaps one of the most powerful passages of scripture in the entire Bible, even though it is the shortest. Jesus wept. What a mystery this verse can be! The Son of God, God Incarnate, God in the flesh is...is crying. When faced with a very human problem, the death of a friend, Jesus wept. And He wept knowing the miracle that was about to take place. Why is that? Could it be that He was overcome with sorrow over what His friends were experiencing? I'll let you come to your own conclusion as to why Jesus was crying. The point is that He was. By the way, this is not the only account we have of Jesus crying. If it seemed fitting for God to cry in moments of emotional extreme, then are we so much better than He that we cannot show our emotions in the same manner? In fact, not only is a healthy response to some events in life, but this story reinforces the truth that our tears are special to God. He can relate to our tears. The above verse even goes so far as to let us know that God keeps a record of our tears. He puts them in a bottle or records them on a scroll. That is how important they are to Him. Our tears do not go unnoticed by God. So do not be afraid to shed tears. They are perhaps the most honest and open expression of our need for God that we can give. So let them flow as a prayer to God in both good times and bad.

The Thin Place: Ask. Answer. Pray.

Do you have trouble expressing emotions through tears?

When is the last time you shed tears?

How do you think God feels when we shed tears of joy and of sorrow?

June 26

Blowing our Stack

From Above: Proverbs 29:11; Ephesians 4:26-27

Focal Passage: *"A fool gives full vent to his anger, but a wise man keeps himself under control." –Proverbs 29:11*

Here Below:

How many times have you done or said something in anger only to regret it later? Unfortunately, most of us can attest to the sick feeling of regret over words spoken in a moment of anger. It is perhaps one of the most troubling feelings one can experience. Perhaps this is because we know that once the words are spoken, they cannot be taken back. Even if forgiveness is sought and given, the words have still done their damage. Words misspoken are as dangerous as a bullet misfired. They can hurt with tremendous effectiveness. For this reason, we must learn to keep our temper under control.

The above Proverb speaks of the fool giving full vent to his anger. This verse is not implying that anger is necessarily sinful. In fact, Ephesians 4:26 speaks of being angry and not sinning. We also know that Jesus was angered in more than one gospel account, and He was without sin. In other words, there are times when anger is the appropriate response to our situation. However, it is when we "give full vent" that it becomes sinful, and we become foolish. Why? Because when we let our anger determine our words and actions, we are likely to become the fools to which the writer of Proverbs is referring. It is then that we do and say things that are not really us. If we are to be angry and not sin, we must be the ones in control of our tongues and hands. Practically speaking, even if we are rightfully angered, but we blow our stack, then our argument has been lost and our credibility is in question. The best response is a slow and reasonable one, with a spirit of compassion and forgiveness. Approach your anger with this attitude and you will never be the fool of Proverbs 29:11. Don't let a mistake in the heat of the moment bring you any regret! Face your anger with the wisdom of God's word. Let it be a moment of testimony to a life surrendered to the Lordship of Jesus Christ.

The Thin Place: Ask. Answer. Pray.

When is the last time that you lost your temper and said things or did things that you regret?

Have you sought forgiveness from both God and the other parties involved?

How can you practically avoid this full vent of your anger in the future?

June 27
Cleaning Your Plate

From Above: Luke 6:43-45

Focal Passage: *"The good man brings good things out of the good stored up in his heart, and the evil man brings evil things out of the evil stored up in his heart. For out of the overflow of his heart his mouth speaks."* –Luke 6:45

Here Below:

The other night, my family and I were enjoying a meal at a favorite restaurant. We were sitting in their outside dining area enjoying the cool spring evening air. We were eating one of my favorites, barbecue ribs, when suddenly I heard a sound of disgust emanating from my daughter! While the rest of us were up to our elbows in barbecue sauce, she had noticed a gnat stuck in the sauce on her plate of ribs. Almost unnoticeable, he was in a futile struggle for freedom against the sticky prison of that delicious sauce. Even after I set him free for her, and disposed of the contaminated rib, my daughter did not want to eat any more. That tiny gnat, as harmless as it seemed, had spoiled her dinner. It only took one little gnat to spoil a whole plate of delicious ribs, which she normally loved. What a shame! I had to eat them for her.

Isn't that the way sin works in our lives? Just like that little gnat, one unrepented sin hidden in the dark places of our hearts can spoil everything. We may think to ourselves that it is insignificant and does not matter. After all, we've taken care of the big ones, right? What is that one insignificant area of my life going to harm? Well, Jesus teaches us in the above passage that sooner or later those things hidden within our hearts will eventually surface. For this reason, we must never store evil in our heart. We must dispose of it quickly. Through repentance, God has given us a way to dispose of that sin before it does any more damage than has already been done. So don't think you can store it away and take care of it another day. Take care of it right now, before it spoils everything. Repent of it now and turn to the Lord. Just as my daughter turned to me for help in the above story, turn to Jesus. He will clean your plate for you!

__The Thin Place__: Ask. Answer. Pray.

Do you have any hidden unrepented sins stored away in your heart?

Why have you kept this sin hidden instead of repenting of it?

Is there any good reason why you cannot repent of it now?

June 28
Well, Bless My Soul!

__From Above__: James 1:17-18

Focal Passage: *"Every good and perfect gift is from above, coming down from the Father of the heavenly lights, who does not change like shifting shadows." –James 1:17*

<u>Here Below</u>:

You didn't earn it. You don't deserve it. If you have been the recipient of a blessing lately, it is because you have a God that loves you. According to the above passage, every good and perfect gift comes from God. If that is the case, and it must be since it says so in such a clear manner, then we must be careful to give credit where credit is due. These blessings come in various forms. Some are obvious, while others may be of a more personal nature, with their true meaning being revealed to only the recipient. They may be complex, or they may be simple. Regardless of how they come or of what form they come in; they all have the same origin. They come from God. He is the giver of all good.

When we learn to fully appreciate this fact and see the blessings for what they are and from where they come, we are one step closer to living the life abundant. This is true even if our blessing takes on a form that others around us may not recognize. It is our personal and intimate recognition, appreciation and gratefulness for the blessings that brings the joy to life that God desires for us. This joy is one that surpasses happiness. Happiness is based on circumstances. Joy is not. Joy can be experienced despite circumstances. Joy sees the good in all things. Joy recognizes the blessing. Joy acknowledges the Father of the heavenly lights at work in our lives.

<u>The Thin Place</u>: Ask. Answer. Pray.

What is your most recent blessing?

Do you think there is a purpose behind that blessing?

Have you taken the time to thank God for that blessing?

June 29
Stay Focused

From Above: Psalm 77

Focal Passage: *"Then I thought, "To this I will appeal: the years of the right hand of the Most High. I will remember the deeds of the LORD; yes, I will remember your miracles of long ago. I will meditate on all your works and consider all your mighty deeds." –Psalm 77:10-12*

Here Below:

The 77th Psalm, a psalm of Asaph, is a song that we can all relate to from time to time. In it, the writer refers to a time in which he was in distress. Put simply, he was in trouble. Perhaps something was not going the way he had expected it or perhaps some unforeseen crisis had struck. In it we see the writer responding to his problems in a very human way. He was admittedly complaining (vs. 3). He seems to almost be feeling sorry for himself. He even goes so far as to basically ask God where He has been throughout the whole ordeal. However, in verse 10 the song takes on a different direction. Here we see the most effective remedy in the fight against feeling sorry for ourselves. Here we see him taking the focus off of himself and putting it on the Lord. In that verse, the writer goes from thinking about the difficulties he has faced to thinking of all the blessings he has received. From that change of focus we see this song of self-pity turn to a song of great faith and worship. We feel the change of attitude in the writer go from one of complaining to one of appreciation.

You see, in times when we feel as if the whole world is against us, we need to refocus. Instead of looking at only the bad things in our lives, consider the many blessings God showers on us daily. When we examine the blessings of God in comparison to the trials of life, suddenly the trials don't seem so bad. When an unforeseen blessing falls upon us, the former trials seem almost trivial. It is all about our focus. So, what are you looking at today? Are you staring at the difficulties of life or are you looking at the blessings of God? Where your gaze rests will make all the difference in the world as to how you feel and to how others see you. Look to God's goodness and you will have no reason to complain.

The Thin Place: Ask. Answer. Pray.

How easy it for you to be distracted by life's trials?

What are some blessings you have received from the Lord in the past?

How might God be working through your trials right now?

June 30
Waving the White Flag

From Above: Jeremiah 10:23-24

Focal Passage: *"I know, O LORD, that a man's life is not his own; it is not for man to direct his steps." –Jeremiah 10:23*

Here Below:

The concept of surrender is one that most of us struggle with to some degree. Surrender is difficult for most of us; in that, it goes against our most basic human nature. Everything within us seeks to hold on to what we have, both literal and spiritual. The thought of allowing someone else a controlling interest in our lives or to exercise their will over our own is disturbing at best. We feel as if we know best when it comes to our own life direction. The problem with this philosophy is that it simply is not true. There is one that knows better. God knows the best direction for our lives. Doesn't it only make sense to surrender our will to the one who truly knows best?

The problem we often have with surrendering our lives to the Lord is the false belief that it is ours to surrender in the first place. As Christians, our lives have been bought and paid for by Jesus Christ. So, in reality, when we refuse to let God into certain areas of our life, we are not really failing to surrender. We are stealing from God. As the above verse states, "a man's life is not his own." We are exercising authority over something that really does not belong to us. Whether it is your relationships, your finances, your work life, your home life, your school life or your church life, it all belongs to God. So, the best thing to do is to let He who knows best take control. Just wave the white flag of surrender and give it back to Him. He knows best how to care for it. When you look at it in this light, you will see that you are really not losing anything when you surrender to the Lord. Instead, you are gaining everything.

The Thin Place: Ask. Answer. Pray.

What areas of your life do you have the most difficulty surrendering to the Lord?

Why do you think that is?

What are some practical steps you can take today to help you surrender it to the Lord?

7

July

J uly 1
The Naked Dream

<u>**From Above**</u>: Revelation 3:14-22

Focal Passage: *"You say, 'I am rich; I have acquired wealth and do not need a thing.' But you do not realize that you are wretched, pitiful, poor, blind and naked." –Revelation 3:17*

<u>**Here Below**</u>:

We've all had it. We've all experienced the dream. We analyze it. We try to find meaning in it. Comedians even make jokes about it. Yet, it is a dream that is only funny after we awaken to realize that is only a dream. At the time it is frightening! You know what I am talking about. You may be dreaming you are at work, school or in some other public place and it is a normal day. There is only one problem. In your dream, as you are carrying out some daily normal activity, you look down to discover that you are not dressed. Perhaps you are not wearing your pants or maybe you are just in your underclothes. Or perhaps, you are wearing nothing at all. Yet, in the dream, as you are going to work, getting on a bus or shopping or whatever it may be, it seems totally normal that you have forgotten to get dressed. The humiliation of discovering your nakedness only too late usually sends us spiraling to a sudden wake from our sleep. Whew! Thank God it was only a dream! Yet, according to the above scripture, many of us are walking around just as we were in that dream, naked and unaware of our true condition.

John the Revelator shares with us from his vision some very practical applications. Notice Revelation 3:17. In this verse, we find that it is possible to be completely ignorant of our own true spiritual condition. We think we are fine. We place value in life according to the world's standards. We think we are rich. We've got it all together! Yet, God sees us in our supposed "wealth" as "wretched, pitiful, poor, blind and naked". Just like in the dream, we are naked and we do not even know it! How does this happen? Well, that is the way the prince of this world works. He lies to us about what is important, making the world's values seem to be something we should strive to attain. All the while he is distracting us from the truth. Don't buy the lie! Instead, look to God for meaning and value. It is His grace and merciful love and our capacity to please Him in return that gives life value. Let His Spirit and His Word keep your eyes open to the truth about yourself and your spiritual condition. Wake up! Don't get caught naked and blind to the truth!

The Thin Place: Ask, Answer, Pray.

What are some worldly values with which you struggle?

In what ways do these values sometimes take priority in your life?

What can you do differently in your approach to these values?

July 2
My Spiritual Avatar

From Above: 2 Corinthians 5:10; Ephesians 6:6-8

Focal Passage: *"For we must all appear before the judgment seat of Christ, that each one may receive what is due him for the things done while in the body, whether good or bad."* –2 Corinthians 5:10

<u>Here Below</u>:

Perhaps you are familiar with the term "avatar". It is a term that has gained new meaning with the modern advances in the computer technology, especially in the gaming realm and with the recent popular movies. There are many gamers and web surfers out there that have created for themselves a personal virtual avatar. This avatar is in one sense, their alter ego. It is their face, personality and representative in the tech universe. The anonymity of the internet allows for people to create in their avatar traits that they themselves do not necessarily have in the real world. As a result, people are able to live completely contrasting lives, even develop relationships with others, all behind the guise of their avatar. They get to be something they are not in real life. Unfortunately, they are also often able to hide and shirk responsibility for bad behaviors they exhibit in their virtual universe. They hide behind their virtual avatar. For example, a married man may flirt, or worse, behind the face of his avatar. Even more extreme sins and crimes are committed behind the costume of a virtual avatar. The avatar makes it possible to hide from the responsibilities of our actions. This is not new to the computer age. People having been living dual lives since the beginning of time. However, while we may be able to live a duality before others, we cannot hide our real selves from God.

We often try to compartmentalize our lives, living one way in one area of our lives and another way in others. We do this with the hopes that we can fool others and perhaps find acceptance. We behave as Christian with one set of friends and differently with another. We are living a lie. We are living behind a spiritual avatar, hoping that the real us will not be discovered. The problem with this is that sooner or later the real us will be discovered. According to scripture, we each have an appointment one day to stand before God and give account for our actions, good or bad. Unfortunately, we cannot send an avatar in our place to this appointment. We must take responsibility. The best way to make that appointment go smoothly then is to start taking responsibility now! Taking personal responsibility frees us from the burden of keeping up appearances. I can be the real me, without fear of discovery or penalty. Taking responsibility is the first step in repentance. This leads to forgiveness and freedom. Don't hide from that which gives you freedom. Embrace truth instead. Shed your avatar. Confess your sin. Find freedom.

The Thin Place: Ask, Answer, Pray.

Have you ever been guilty of living a dual life? How so?

What happens when we try to live contrasting lifestyles?

How has confession and repentance made you feel in your past?

July 3
Don't Forget To Take Your Meditation!

From Above: Psalm 77

Focal Passage: *"I will meditate on all your works and consider all your mighty deeds." –Psalm 77:12*

Here Below:

You are sick. You are not sure what the problem is, but the symptoms are overwhelming. You cannot sleep. You cannot eat. You cannot make yourself comfortable. You have feelings of anxiety and nervousness. Nothing seems to help. To say you are distressed is an understatement. The prospect of another sleepless and comfortless night furthers your seemingly unending depression. Well, you are not alone. We have all been there. In fact, this ailment is one that is common to all people at least one point in their lives. Asaph, the writer of Psalm 77, understood the anguish of this spiritual sickness. He was suffering with it. He also gives us the prescription. To find peace from this condition, we must take a regular dose of meditation! In this beautiful song, Asaph cries out in agony and then concludes that the answer can be found by reflecting upon his memory of God's redemptive works. In other words, he meditates on the goodness of God. In the midst of his distress, he can reflect upon the fact that God has always been faithful to His children. This heartfelt meditation can calm even the most troubled spirits. More so, you and I have access to something that Asaph most likely did not. We have the written word of God.

I love to read. I especially love to read something that speaks to me personally. Well, there is a book that is about me. Its pages are filled with kernels of truth from my own experiences. As I read it, I see myself, both good and bad. In it I can find the answers to my intimate needs. Though I find myself on every page of this writing, it is not a biography or autobiography. It is of course the word of God. In the word, I find evidence of God's love for me. I find myself loved. Of course, one cannot just read the Bible and expect to find peace. We must take it a step further. We must meditate on the word. Meditation, unlike simple reading, is where we seek to find ourselves within the word of God. Mediation is what transforms the Bible from an ancient book of history and proverbial wisdom to a love story, where I am one of the main characters. Meditation is medication for the troubled or sin sick spirit. It is also a preventative in times of health against the above mentioned ailment. So don't just read the word! Take your meditation!

The Thin Place: Ask, Answer, Pray.

How often do you truly meditate upon the word of God?

Do you find it easy to meditate? Why or why not?

How can you better provide for a proper atmosphere of meditation in your life?

July 4
The High Horse

From Above: Genesis 17:1-6; Psalm 95: 6; Acts 9:1-8

Focal Passage: "*Come, let us bow down in worship, let us kneel before the LORD our Maker;*

for he is our God and we are the people of his pasture, the flock under his care." –Psalm 95:6

<u>Here Below</u>:

Two people, separated by thousands of years. Each is considered to be a hero of the faith. Both men were of elevated social standing in their time. One man was named Abram. The other was Saul. Yet, as high in society as they might have been, we nevertheless find each of them in the above passages of scripture on the ground in positions of great humility. This humility was perhaps key to God's willingness to use them. However, there is a major difference between the two men. Abram was willingly prostrate in worship and awe of God. Saul on the other hand was knocked to the ground by a vision of God. They were both on the ground, but for different reasons. One was expressing humility; another was humbled against his will. Yet, God used them both. Their humility was a turning point in their lives. Saul, though an unwilling participant at first, quickly changed his way of thinking. From that point forward, he knew true humility. His letters in the New Testament are filled with expression of this humility. Both men walked away from that falling down experience changed. Abram was now Abraham. Saul was now Paul.

Too often we allow our pride to get in the way of our relationship with the Lord. There is no room for personal pride in this relationship. It is when we humble ourselves that God is best able to do something with our lives. Doesn't it only make sense to do this willingly, before God is forced to do something drastic in our lives as He did with Saul? I do not know about you, but I would rather step down off of my high horse willingly than to be knocked off of it. I would prefer to gladly fall on my face before God, than to be knocked flat on my back. Yet, we must remember that God's response to both our humility and our pride will always be a response of love. He loved Abram and He loved Saul. If not, he would not have intervened in their lives. He knew what they could be if only they humbled themselves before Him. He was right. The same is true of you! God knows what you can be if only you come to Him with a spirit of humility and willingness. Will you do it willingly or wait for God to do it for you?

The Thin Place: Ask, Answer, Pray.

With which of the two men in the above scenarios are you the most similar, Abram or Saul?

In what areas of your life do you struggle the most with pride?

How can you express humility more effectively in your spiritual life?

July 5
Grandma Wouldn't Lie!

From Above: Psalm 119:105-112

Focal Passage: *"Your statutes are my heritage forever; they are the joy of my heart. My heart is set on keeping your decrees to the very end." –Psalm 119:111-112*

Here Below:

There are some words written in my oldest copy of God's word that have been an encouragement to me for forty plus years now. They are not part of the scriptures themselves, though I feel that they very well might have been inspired by God. They have definitely been used of God. Of this, there is no question. The words were written by my grandmother. She and my grandfather gave me this Bible on my eighth Christmas upon this earth. They are scribbled in her handwriting at the bottom of the presentation page. The words read "May this book always be your guide." My grandmother was pretty smart. The influence of these words has lived long past her own mortal body. They remind me every so often of the importance of following the word of God in all that I do.

The heartfelt value of the word of God in our lives is a gift we should strive to leave with those whom we love and know. It is a gift that never gets old or outdated. It never becomes old fashioned. In fact, the longer we carry this gift, the more precious and true it becomes, as is hopefully evidenced by our lives. A love for the word and truth of God should be as much a part of who we are as the other personal interests in which we involve ourselves. Think about it. Would you rather be remembered one day as a person that was determined and driven in their work, hobbies or interests or as someone determined to live according to God's statutes? All of those other areas of life are great, but even they can be enriched with an application of God's precepts. It encompasses all of life. To ignore the guide God has left with us is to sell ourselves short. Likewise, failure to pass the love of His truth on to others is to sell our future generations short and ultimately to deny them the blessing of prospering from its guidance. If you don't believe me, then take my Grandmother's word for it! Grandma was a smart lady, and she would never lead you in the wrong direction. Let God's Word always be your guide!

The Thin Place: Ask, Answer, Pray.
Where does the word of God stand on your daily list of priorities?
How obvious to your friends and family is your love for the word of God?
How can you better pass the value of the word on to those with whom you love the most?

July 6
Oh, You Dogmatist!

From Above: Joshua 24:1-17

Focal Passage: *"But if serving the LORD seems undesirable to you, then choose for yourselves this day whom you will serve, whether the gods your forefathers served beyond the River, or the gods of the Amorites, in whose land you are living. But as for me and my household, we will serve the LORD.""* –*Joshua 24:15*

Here Below:

I was once called "dogmatic" in an online discussion forum after stating my belief on an issue that was clearly defined in scripture. It was after quoting the scripture, the words of Jesus Himself in this case, and explaining my opinion on the subject at hand, that I was referred to in this manner. I must admit that I had to go and look up the word "dogmatic" before I could respond. I found the following. *Dogmatic- asserting opinions in a doctrinaire or <u>arrogant</u> manner; opinionated.* Wow! I went back and tried to honestly find where I had been arrogant in my posts. I could not. I had simply stated what I believed to be the truth according to the word of God and had done it in a kind, non-accusatory and loving manner. I apologized for any offense they might have felt, but assured them that I meant what I said. I have often regretted that apology; in that, I feel as if I'd done nothing wrong. More than likely, this person was under personal conviction on the subject. The truth does often offend, as well it should. As Christians, we should try not to offend, but never to the point of compromising on the truth.

The life of faith sometimes requires us to take a stand. Nowhere in scripture are we taught to bend to the will of those who disagree with the teachings of the word, regardless of their offense. Instead, we are taught to take a stand in those instances. We are taught to choose which side we are going to serve and them to remain faithful to that conviction. There is no halfway faith. We must choose one way or the other. However, upon choosing the issues on which we will take a stand, we must be careful to not confuse personal opinion with spiritual conviction. God's truth is the banner under which we must stand, not personal opinion, as sincere as they might be. God's Word should be the deciding factor. My online friend was in reality the one struggling with arrogance by questioning the truth clearly written in God's Word and spoken by Jesus. I was simply agreeing with God. My opinion was that Jesus knew what He was talking about! If that makes me dogmatic, then perhaps I am. In some instances, I believe that is ok, perhaps even desired, if we are being dogmatic about the right things.

Just make sure you are the right kind of dogmatist. Let God's truth be your standard and you'll never go wrong!

The Thin Place: Ask, Answer, Pray.

Have you ever been in a situation in which you had to take a personal stand?

What were the results of that stand? Was anyone offended?

Is it possible to handle these type situations without causing offense and without compromise?

July 7
Swallowing a Camel

From Above: Matthew 7: 1-5, 23:23-39;

Focal Passage: *"You blind guides! You strain out a gnat but swallow a camel." –Matthew 23:24*

Here Below:

Those who would preach that there is never a time to confront sin or to offend have obviously never read Matthew 23. Jesus does not hold back for fear of offending. He even goes so far as to call the religious leaders blind guides and whitewashed tombs. Yet, we must be careful confronting sin in such instances, for it is a form of spiritual hypocrisy that Jesus is addressing in this hard hitting encounter. He accuses the leaders of "straining out a gnat and swallowing a camel". Jesus sure had a way of bringing His analogies to life, didn't He? Yet, look at appropriateness of this imagery! One would think swallowing a gnat would be easy. It is not. I once swallowed one while speaking at an outside funeral service. I coughed and gagged and thought I was going to choke to death until I was finally able to set the little guy free. That is the point Jesus is making. We sometimes get choked up over the little things while we swallow the bigger, more dangerous things with ease. Put simply, we focus on small more trivial matters of sin and righteousness and ignore the more pressing and more damaging sins.

For example, we may spend most of our time serving faithfully in various capacities at church; meanwhile, we may not regularly engage in true personal and intimate worship. We may be quick to judge others for their lack of commitment to the Lord; meanwhile, we ourselves do not pray on a regular basis. We may even pride ourselves on our wholesome lifestyle and demeanor; yet, in our hearts we commit adultery and even murder. This is swallowing the camel. This does not mean that these "little things" are not important. It just means that our own true spiritual condition and relationship with the Lord is of vital importance to the Lord. It is what God sees that matters the most! We must strive to look at ourselves from His perspective. Whether it is swallowing a camel or a plank in our eye, we must begin with being honest with God and ourselves if we desire to be spiritually more tomorrow than we are today. So spit out that camel and pull out that plank! Be real with God today!

The Thin Place: Ask, Answer, Pray.

Are there any "gnats" with which you struggle? Any spiritual overemphasis in your life?

Are there any "camels" in which you have tried to swallow? Any sin that's been ignored?

What can you change to fix these type situations that may exist in your heart?

July 8
Praying for the Button Pushers

From Above: Matthew 5:43-48

Focal Passage: *"But I tell you: Love your enemies and pray for those who persecute you,"* –Matthew 5:44

Here Below:

We all have them in our lives. It is not pleasant; nevertheless, it is true. We all have those people in our lives that know how to push our buttons. Perhaps it is simply their personality or perhaps it is an intentional attempt to stir us up. Whatever it may be, we admittedly have a hard time liking them, much less loving them. Yet, we are told by the Master Himself that we are to love our enemies and pray for those who persecute you. We must love and pray for those button pushers in our lives!

Jesus would never ask anything of us that is impossible. Of course, as with most things and this especially, it is possible if we look for help and guidance from the Holy Spirit of God. Loving our enemies does not mean accepting or ignoring their bad behavior. It does mean loving them in spite of it though. Perhaps the best way to do this is to try to look beyond the behavior and consider the possible reasoning behind it. Ungodly behavior could be a sign of spiritual immaturity or even a sign that they are lost. It could also just mean that they are having a bad day or in the midst of a difficult personal situation. There are an infinite number of reasons as to why they might be difficult toward you or others. In fact, we must also examine ourselves to make sure we are not part of the problem. We cannot always assume that we are not part of the problem.

Sounds confusing, huh? How can we know for sure the cause and how can we know for sure how to handle it? It is not difficult. It is quite simple actually. Regardless of reasoning behind the behavior of others, there is one solution that always works. Here it is: Love your enemies and pray for those who persecute you! If we can do that, the reason doesn't matter! If we truly love them and react to them accordingly, we can know that we are not the cause. Likewise, they will be forced to respond to our love accordingly. Besides, have you ever tried hating someone that you are praying for regularly? Praying for someone's well being makes it difficult to hate them. All the psychological analysis in the world can't accomplish what simple love can do. Be intentional with your love today. Love and pray for the button pushers in your life!

The Thin Place: Ask, Answer, Pray.

Who are the people in your life that you have the most difficulty loving? Why is it difficult to love these people?

Is it possible that you have not really tried to love them? Have you prayed for them?

July 9
So Sorry...

From Above: 2 Corinthians 7:1-11

Focal Passage: *"Godly sorrow brings repentance that leads to salvation and leaves no regret, but worldly sorrow brings death." –2 Corinthians 7:10*

Here Below:

There is a difference between godly sorrow and worldly sorrow. Worldly sorrow is feeling sorry over your sin; that is, sorry that you got caught in it. Godly sorrow on the other hand is feeling sorry over your sin and agreeing with God over the seriousness of it. Though acknowledging the sin as wrong in the mind, worldly sorrow still harbors hidden feelings of approval within the deepest chambers of the heart. Godly sorrow is disgusted by the sin and ultimately leads to true repentance, which is free from shame and regret. Worldly sorrow leads us back to a cycle of sin.

If there is a difference, how then do we achieve godly sorrow verses worldly sorrow so that we might reach a point of true repentance and the freedom that follows? Well, we must acknowledge the first word in that statement. It is "Godly" sorrow. In other words, it comes from God. This does not mean that the sorrow itself comes from God, so much as it means that the sorrow comes as a natural result of our agreement with God. It is the result of true conviction. It goes beyond a simple head knowledge of sin. It is the desire to never again hurt the Lord with our rebellion. When we reach that agreement with God over our sin, we are less likely to ever return to that particular sin. If we never truly find godly sorrow over it, then we have most likely not truly given it up in our hearts, even if we have in our actions. That is why regret remains with worldly sorrow. This is also why God desires godly sorrow. He wants us to be free from regret and shame. It is our heart for which God cares the most. So what do we do? We pray that God might produce godly sorrow in our hearts over our sin. Pray for his help to truly let go of your sin. It won't necessarily happen all at once, especially if it is a habitual sin. Nevertheless, He will answer your prayer. A life of no regret is there waiting. Pray for forgiveness. Pray for godly sorrow. Pray for life.

The Thin Place: Ask, Answer, Pray.

Is there a particular sin with which you struggle repeatedly? If so, what is it?

Do you agree that this sin is indeed against the will of God for your life?

Do you truly feel godly sorrow over this sin or is it more of a worldly sorrow?

July 10
My Jesus

From Above: 1 Corinthians 2:11-16

Focal Passage: *"For who among men knows the thoughts of a man except the man's spirit within him? In the same way no one knows the thoughts of God except the Spirit of God. We have not received the spirit of the world but the Spirit who is from God, that we may understand what God has freely given us." –1 Corinthians 2:11-12*

Here Below:

I have many differing images of Christ decorating my home and office. Among the many images is a Jesus cut into glass, a Jesus carved out of olive wood from Israel and an original acrylic painting of Jesus, as well as several crayon depictions made by my daughter in Sunday School. However, of all the images, my personal favorite (kid pictures notwithstanding) would have to be a Jesus formed out of pure white sand supposedly taken from the Gulf of Mexico, complete with iridescent glitter for an added accent. It of course has the features of the common Jesus illustrated in our day, as do all the images in my collection. He has long flowing thick hair, a neatly trimmed beard and typical Anglo facial features. I believe that the real Jesus probably looked nothing like our futile attempts at portrayal. However, I like the sand sculpture because it reminds me of how we often try to shape and mold Jesus in such a way as to fit our preconceived notions of Himself. Instead of letting Him show us His true face, we often try to make Him look like us, figuratively speaking. Instead, we should be trying to mold ourselves into His image!

How do we know the true image of Christ? Well, we immerse ourselves into His word. Simultaneously, we pray for the Holy Spirit of God to reveal the real Christ to us. In Christ, we have the image of God the Father. Through the Holy Spirit, we have further revelation as to the true nature of God. Within the Trinity, we get the full picture of the one true God. Granted, understanding the Trinity and the nature of God is not simple. Don't worry! Theologians and philosophers have devoted themselves to this endeavor millennia before you ever tried and are only as close as you and me at understanding it! They are only as close as the Holy Spirit takes them. In truth, what we must do if we want an accurate image of God is to simply put away our personal notions of Christ, shaped by our experiences, prejudices and nature, and let Him show us His true self. When we see Jesus in truth we also see His amazing love for us. Seeing the real Jesus as opposed to "my idea of Jesus" can be a radical change of perspective. However, it is one that will change your life and change it for the infinite better. Don't limit your vision of Christ! Ask God to reveal His true self to you today!

The Thin Place: Ask, Answer, Pray.

How different do you think Jesus is from our many modern thoughts concerning Him?

Why do you think we imagine Christ being very much like ourselves in appearance and actions?

What do you know of Christ that probably differs from your own personality and way of life?

July 11
Cruisin'

From Above: Zephaniah 1:12; Revelation 3:14-22

Focal Passage: *"At that time I will search Jerusalem with lamps and punish those who are complacent, who are like wine left on its dregs, who think, 'The LORD will do nothing, either good or bad."* – Zephaniah 1:12

Here Below:

One of the favorite pastimes of teenagers in the eighties, at least in my community, was to cruise the mall on a Saturday night. Droves of teens would envelop the mall and just drive in circles. We would circle that mall for hours with our windows down and our stereos blasting the crazy new wave music or the big hair band rock music that was so popular during that era. It was an evening of totally useless fun. The crowds that would go cruisin' at one particular mall were so large that it was very easy to get caught in the long river of cars and be forced to go along with the flow of traffic whether you wanted to or not. One wrong turn and you would find yourself in the middle of a long and slow moving traffic jam. For this reason, one had to drive with purpose and intent. Otherwise, your Saturday night would be spent trying to escape the relentless horde of freewheeling teenagers with driver's licenses. Anyone unaware of the cruisin' tradition might find themselves at the mercy of these young drivers, whose only goal for the evening was to circle the mall indefinitely.

Many of us treat our spiritual lives in much the same way. We just cruise through life, avoiding the pressure that comes with making the tough decisions that inevitably come. Then we find ourselves swept away with the current ebb and flow of the world, all the while allowing others to make important decisions for us. When it comes to decisions of spiritual importance, we cannot allow this to be. Along with the perks of having free will also comes the burden of making wise choices. This reality leaves you and I with a daily choice to make. It is not always an easy choice, but it is nonetheless simple in its application. We must choose to either follow the will of God or not. There is no middle lane in which to drive. We cannot simply be complacent Christians, allowing the world and its circumstances to choose our destination. Put simply, we cannot merely cruise through life. The life of a disciple is an intentional life. We exist in a world that naturally pulls us away from the path that God would have us to follow. Therefore, we have no choice but to strive to live a life pleasing to God. This explains the many allegories used in scripture describing the Christian life, including such symbols as running a race, fighting a fight, carrying a cross, etc... These all insinuate a deliberate intent. They do not just happen on their own. The truth is that God is going to work whether we do or not! Doesn't it only make sense that the child of God would choose to get on board with Him. I don't know about you, but I want to go in the direction that God is leading. So don't get caught in traffic. Be a defensive driver and follow God.

The Thin Place: Ask, Answer, Pray.

Would you consider yourself more spiritually complacent or more spiritually intentional in daily life?

Have you ever found yourself swept up in circumstances that you felt were beyond your control?

Looking back, had you made wiser choices earlier on, could the conditions possibly have been avoided?

July 12
No Laughing Matter

<u>**From Above**</u>: I Peter 2:21-25

Focal Passage: *"He himself bore our sins in his body on the tree, so that we might die to sins and live for righteousness; by his wounds you have been healed."* – I Peter 2:24

<u>**Here Below**</u>:

How often do we make light of that which led to the crucifixion of our Lord? Wow! You may be thinking that this question is somewhat harsh. Nevertheless, it is a good question. Too often we joke about the sinfulness of mankind as if it were something to dismiss as funny. One cannot turn on the television without seeing someone who has become rich and famous by making so called jokes about such sins as those we are warned about in the Ten Commandments. Now do not get me wrong. I am not trying to sound legalistic in this subject. On the contrary, I appreciate a good joke as much as anyone else. Humor is a gift from God and I believe that He has a sense of humor. However, the more we make light of sin, the more likely we are to become numb to its seriousness and danger. This numbness is not from God. From whom then must it be coming? Granted, not every bad thing that occurs comes from Satan. The "devil made me do it" excuse just doesn't apply every time. Many things that happen are the result of living in a fallen world and due to our own sinfulness. Yet, I cannot help but think there is nothing the devil would rather see happen than for God's people to dismiss the seriousness of sin. By doing this, the significance of the cross and our need for salvation is diminished. Of course, there are those in our day that would argue that we have evolved past the need to label things as sin or as right or wrong. They would say that sin is relative and depends upon the individual's beliefs. This relativism is dangerous and ultimately hazardous to humanity. After all, how smart are we really if we choose to ignore a deadly disease that is blaringly obvious in our lives? Not very! Well, to ignore or to dismiss as harmless the deadliest of all diseases, sin, we are even....shall we say, less smart. We must never make light of that which can keep us from eternal life.

Let's make it even a little more personal. It was for our sins that Jesus had to die on the cruel cross. Okay then, imagine yourself making a sacrifice for someone else and later hearing that person making jokes about that for which you sacrificed. You would be hurt and perhaps even angry. Yet, this scenario happens all the time. Do not joke about that which led to the death of Jesus. Instead, train your heart to desire the things of God and to despise that which God despises. Do this by spending more and more time in the word of God and in the carrying out of His will. The more time you spend with God, the less likely you are to find sin amusing. Likewise, the more time you spend with God, the deeper your love for Him and joy in Him will grow and the more you will be able to appreciate humor in a proper setting. Saturate your heart with the things of God today.

The Thin Place: Ask, Answer, Pray.

Have you ever been guilty of making light of the sinfulness of others?

Have you ever been guilty of making light of your own sinfulness? If so, when?

In light of His Word, how do you think the Lord feels concerning our attitude toward sin?

July 13
Get Serious!

From Above: I Peter 1:1-9

Focal Passage: *"Though you have not seen him, you love him; and even though you do not see him now, you believe in him and are filled with an inexpressible and glorious joy,"* – I Peter 1:8

Here Below:

In the King James Version, it is referred to as joy unspeakable. According to this verse, it is the natural result of faith in Jesus Christ. Peter is speaking to those, whom unlike himself have never seen Jesus in the flesh; yet, their faith led to a joy that words cannot express, even in the midst of intense persecution. Think about that for a moment. At a time when one would be expected to be down and depressed, they instead exhibited a joy that couldn't even be described with a human vocabulary. There is a lesson to be learned here. Christians are to be recognized for their joy. Unfortunately, all too often we are known for just the opposite. Is it possible that we confuse righteousness with seriousness? Perhaps we confuse piety with intensity? The result of this way of thinking is a never-ending struggle to perform and never quite meeting our own set standards. The result is a life of spiritual stress, instead of a life of joy, such as God intends.

Joy is not simply another word for happiness. It goes much deeper than that. Joy supersedes any circumstance in which we find ourselves, good or bad. However, happiness is a tell tale sign of joy in the life of a believer. I am always skeptical of those who profess to be born again and yet never smile or laugh. If for no other reason than our salvation, we have reason enough to be happy. This doesn't mean a believer should walk around with a silly grin on their face all the time. This could only be artificial; in that, there are times when it is difficult for even the strongest Christian to smile. Nevertheless, we still have reason to be happy. Expression of this happiness is not a sign of weak faith. On the contrary, it is evidence of a stronger faith. When our faith is strongest, we have the least reason to fret. It is when our hearts are truly dependent upon God that we can smile, knowing it is going to be ok. Just because someone may not seem to be taking a circumstances seriously doesn't mean they are weak. It could mean they are stronger, trusting in God to take care of it all. Take the recipients of Peter's above letter for example. God's desire is for us to live that kind of life of joy and leave the fretting to him. So take time today to laugh a little and smile a lot. God can use those moments to encourage others just as he can use your more serious moments. Don't forget that true joy is serious business for the child of God. Be known for your smile rather than your wrinkled brow. Let joy be a driving force in your life today.

The Thin Place: Ask, Answer, Pray.

Would you say that others see a person of joy when they look at you? Why or why not?

Do you find it difficult or easy to express your joy? How so?

What can you differently to better express the joy you have in Jesus Christ?

July 14
What Lion?

From Above: Judges 14:1-9; Matthew 6:1-4

Focal Passage: *"The Spirit of the LORD came upon him in power so that he tore the lion apart with his bare hands as he might have torn a young goat. But he told neither his father nor his mother what he had done." –Judges 14:6*

Here Below:

While Samson obviously had his faults, he also possessed some admirable qualities. Among those found in this passage is his modesty. In fact, we might be able to say that in the above story Samson was exhibiting *extreme* modesty. He had just killed a lion with his bare hands and the Bible tells us that he did not even tell his parents, those closest to him. Most of us would probably run and tell everyone what we had done. For goodness sake, when we shoot a helpless deer from fifty yards away with a high powered rifle from hiding, we tell everyone, we take pictures and have it mounted and hang it on our wall for the world to see. Yet, Samson killed a ferocious lion with his own hands and told no one. One difference might have been that He had done this act after having been overcome with the Holy Spirit of God. For him, this act was done by God and for God's purposes. In that respect, it must have been for Samson a very private matter. There is definitely something to be learned from his example.

Modesty is something that is in danger of becoming extinct in our day. With the internet and all the social networking programs available, there is hardly anything that is not made public of our private lives anymore. People share things with complete strangers in this manner that would have one day have been a matter of extreme privacy and even shame. Our lives have become open books. While this can be dangerous, I guess in some respects this can be okay too; in that, it is harder to be fake to those who know everything about you. However, when it comes to personal spiritual matters between ourselves and the Lord, we have a Biblical mandate to be modest and to handle ourselves with humility. Jesus repeatedly throughout the gospel accounts warns us about promoting ourselves to others. As children of God, our lives should not point people to ourselves, but to God. Our lives are to be a reflection of Jesus Christ. A bragging attitude is the exact opposite of what we see in Christ. Instead, when it comes to our successes and strengths, it is best to let God do the bragging. If we are going to boast, then let's boast about the one thing worthy of our boasting, that is our relationship with the Lord. For us, it should be enough to know that God is pleased with our actions. Modesty is another way of giving God the glory for our successes.

<u>**The Thin Place**</u>: Ask, Answer, Pray.

Would you consider yourself a modest person? How so?

Think of a time in which you kept a time of spiritual success to yourself. Did God bless your modesty?

What improvements can you make in the future to help your life exhibit more modesty?

July 15
Answer Me This...

From Above: Mark 9:14-32

Focal Passage: *"'If you can'?" said Jesus. "Everything is possible for him who believes." Immediately the boy's father exclaimed, "I do believe; help me overcome my unbelief!" –Mark 9:23-24*

Here Below:

As a pastor, I am often asked some very strange questions. Among some of these unique questions I have been asked are the following. Will we see our beloved pets in Heaven? Will we eat food in Heaven? Why aren't the dinosaurs mentioned in the Bible? Or are they? What kind of fruit did Adam and Eve taste? Were there insects on Noah's ark? Did God create Satan? If so, why? This list of questions could go on and on. Please do not misunderstand. I am not making light of these questions. On the contrary, I take them very seriously. However, I am convinced that there are some questions that can never be answered this side of Heaven. Yet, I do recognize that these questions can be more than just trivial curiosity. For many they are expressions of doubt and doubt is nothing to dismiss. Doubt can lead one to stumble in their faith and ultimately lead to discouragement and a falling away from spiritual growth and progress. For this reason, we must learn to see doubt in another light.

In the above passage of scripture, we see a very exceptional statement. We see a statement of belief from the father of this demon possessed boy and in the same breath we also see him ask Jesus for help with his unbelief. Which is it? Does he believe or not? Well, if this passage tells us anything, it is that it is possible to have faith and yet not fully understand everything. After all, that is what faith is, is it not? It is possible to have faith in Jesus Christ and not understand everything there is to know about Him. We do not have to intellectually grasp the fullness of God to love Him and trust in Him. In fact, it is a good thing that our God cannot be fully explained. It is further evidence of His greatness. Besides, while the above questions may make for interesting conversation, the fact that we may not be able to answer them doesn't change the things that are really important. God has given us the answers to what matters most. In this miraculous story, Jesus healed the boy in spite of the unbelief of his father and others. God has given us enough to trust Him with our very souls. So don't be discouraged by unanswered questions and doubts! Look at these doubts and questions as proof of God's greatness. Instead of being discouraged, just dig deeper and learn as much as you can and just trust that God will answer the rest in His own way and in His own time. In the meantime, trust in the truth in which we have been given answers and be careful not to miss the beauty of what we can explain because of what we can't. Have faith in a big God.

The Thin Place: Ask, Answer, Pray.

What are some questions or doubts concerning God that you would like addressed?

Do any of these concerns change anything that you do know to be true of Him?

Is it possible that God has withheld an answer so that you might trust Him more?

July 16
Follow the Leader

From Above: I Corinthians 1:12-24

Focal Passage: *"What I mean is this: One of you says, "I follow Paul"; another, "I follow Apollos"; another, "I follow Cephas "; still another, "I follow Christ." –I Corinthians 1:12*

Here Below:

In the above passage, Paul addresses the tendency of humanity to follow men to the detriment of following God. This phenomenon can occur even when the men being followed are godly in their leadership. The above verse testifies to this fact. Paul, Apollos and Cephas or Peter were all leaders in which God was using to carry out His purposes. They were all leaders with strength and integrity. Yet, Paul understood the divisions that had arisen within the church as people were picking favorites and labeling themselves accordingly. He also recognized the need to remind the church to stay focused. Paul, and the other preachers had obviously never intended for this to happen. It was Jesus that was being preached and it was Jesus that they wanted to promote. This reminder is for us today as well.

We should not be too critical of the early church in this matter. It is very easy to get caught up in following a charismatic leader, especially if the leader is one of spiritual integrity. Many of us find ourselves following a favorite preacher, writer or theologian. This can be okay as long as we keep it in perspective. We should utilize all the resources available to us in the study of God. However, as we hear and study the thoughts of others on matters of spiritual importance, we must remember that we are disciples of Jesus first. In fact, we must be careful to accept the teaching of others only in relation to the truth found in the word of God. Put simply, we must be careful to recognize the difference between the opinions and interpretations of men and the word of God. There is only one gospel and we must follow it alone. This is especially true if a person's leadership is focused primarily on themselves. If it doesn't point to Jesus Christ, then we should not follow their lead. Jesus is to be our center of attention.

This principle not only applies to leadership, but it also applies to how we present ourselves on a personal level. Our lives should serve as a road sign directing others to Jesus Christ. Our actions and words should reflect the difference Christ has made in our lives. It is not our purpose to convince others to see things as we do, but to instead see life as Jesus does.

The Thin Place: Ask, Answer, Pray.

Name some spiritual influences from your own life in which you trust. Why?

Has there ever been a time when leaders in your life have left you disappointed? When?

How can one prevent being led in the wrong direction? How familiar are you with God's truth?

July 17
Where Have All The Cowboys Gone?

<u>From Above</u>: Psalm 32

Focal Passage: *"Blessed is the man whose sin the LORD does not count against him and in whose spirit is no deceit." –Psalm 32:2*

<u>Here Below</u>:

A few years ago there was a song that hit the airwaves by singer Paula Cole titled *"Where Have All the Cowboys Gone?"*. In this song, the writer bemoaned the loss in our day of integrity, strength and romance found in the archetypal cowboy of years long gone. This stereotype can easily be seen when observing the old movie westerns of American culture. A recent western movie marathon revealed a day long parade of men that most of us wanted to be as little boys and that most little girls wanted to marry one day. They were strong and handsome and could be counted on to fight for what was right. They were always portrayed as men willing to stand firm and face the enemy. Likewise, the cowboys of these movie fantasies were men of extreme integrity. With them, what you see is what you would get. In fact, in the older sometimes mythological type westerns, the bad guys wore black and the good guys always wore white, again revealing their intent to all. They were honest and strong, men to be admired. The problem is that these men were just actors.

Many of us are no different than these pretend cowboys. We try to portray one persona with our outward actions and words, while all the while we are something different within our hearts. Here is the catch, God knows the real you. In the above verse we see the importance of integrity. David, the writer of this Psalm, as you well know, should understand the importance of integrity of heart. In this song,

David extols the virtue of seeking God's forgiveness, but understands that it only comes when we are completely honest with God and are not whitewashing some sin in our own spirit. "In whose spirit is no deceit" is a statement that reminds us that we can lie to ourselves, but we cannot lie to God. We can put on the white cowboy hat and ride our white horse, but God sees the true us. This reality should not cause us to fear. On the contrary, it is reason for hope. After all, God sees the real me and yet He still loves me. His all seeing and knowing presence is not meant to be reason to fear, but reason for comfort and joy. It should inspire us to be men and women of integrity, both with others, ourselves and especially in our relationship with God. Integrity with God implies that we seek His forgiveness only when we really mean it. To do otherwise is only to be putting on an act, an act that He can see through anyway. Real repentance and forgiveness takes place when we decide to change what we do not like and what God would have us change. God is not nearly as impressed by our ability to act as he is with our willingness to be real. Even if the real you is less than what it should be, God wants you to be honest with Him. It is then that He is able to work His change and mold you into the person He desires. It is then that you and He can ride off into the sunset together knowing that good has triumphed.

The Thin Place: Ask, Answer, Pray.

Do you ever find it difficult to be honest with God about certain sinfulness? If so, why?

Does it help you to know that God already knows everything about you anyway?

What are the benefits of honesty with God versus withholding ourselves from God?

July 18
Fat and Flourishing

From Above: Psalm 92:12-14; John 15:1-5

Focal Passage: *"They will still bear fruit in old age, they will stay fresh and green," –Psalm 92:14*

Here Below:

In the King James Version of the above passage, it says "they will be fat and flourishing" instead of "fresh and green". I like both translations. While both are essentially saying the same thing, the KJV leaves a more lasting impression. The psalmist refers to the righteous as fat and flourishing. It is important to read the whole song to fully grasp his meaning. In it we see the lives of the righteous in contrast with the wicked. In it we see an age old question addressed. Why do the wicked get away with so much? Well, the answer is that they do not get away with it. Eventually there will be a reckoning. In the meantime, it is our job to simply live for God and strive for righteous living. Put simply, we are to bear fruit. While the wicked's evil deeds will eventually catch up with them, the righteous will still be bearing fruit in their old age. If ever this message was needed, it is today.

We live in a day when the wicked do seem to be getting away with murder. Yet, for the Christian, nothing has changed. We still serve the same God, a God who loves all and who desires salvation for all. This passage and others like it serve as a reminder to us that we shouldn't really expect the lost in our day to fully grasp what we are about as Christians until they first accept Jesus by faith as their Savior. It is then that the Holy Spirit is able to reveal to them the truth. Our task then is to simply bear fruit. In a time of spiritual drought and famine, we are to be fat and flourishing. Easier said than done, right? Well, look at it like this. Has there ever been a time in our lives when the harvest was so plenteous? Has there ever been a time riper for revival? Has there ever been a time when the gospel message was more needed? Has there ever been a time when people more desperately needed to see what true faith is all about? Not in my lifetime. This doesn't mean it will always be a welcome message. Nevertheless, it is a vital one. If faith is about bearing fruit in a lost world, then this is the perfect time to be a Christian. So don't lose heart. When the world seems to be going in the wrong direction, just follow the one who is not; that is, follow the example of Christ. Don't focus on the works of the evil and lost. Instead focus on bearing fruit. Focus on becoming fat and flourishing.

The Thin Place: Ask, Answer, Pray.

Do you ever get discouraged when you consider the spiritual condition of the world today?

In your opinion, is the world any darker today than it was before Christ was born? Why or why not?

How can we better see the spiritual condition of the world today as an opportunity for growth?

July 19
I Always Feel Like Somebody's Watching Me

From Above: I Timothy 4

Focal Passage: *" Watch your life and doctrine closely. Persevere in them, because if you do, you will save both yourself and your hearers. " –I Timothy 4:16*

Here Below:

Perhaps you remember the hit song from the 80's that shared the same title as this devotion? Its haunting melody and chorus had us looking over our shoulder whenever we were alone, always looking for that person watching us. Well, how true that song has turned out to be! I was taught this lesson a few years ago by one of my children. My oldest son was around 4 or 5 at the time. I had been complaining to my wife about some pastoral issues and was expressing my dread of a deacon's meeting that was coming in a few hours. Little did I know of the little eyes watching me at the time. My son Christian, then asked me a life changing question. He asked "Why are you going to that meeting?" I said "Because I have to. It's my job." He then asked again and again and with each explanation he would respond with "Why?". This went on for several minutes and I finally responded by saying that I was a preacher and went to these meetings because I loved Jesus. This seemed to satisfy him. He responded with "Well, if you love Jesus, I want to love Jesus too." Wow! Out of the mouths of babes... In that one statement, this child had reminded the importance of setting the right example, due to the fact that he was watching me even when I might not realize it. My negative attitude was not what he needed to see. He was watching me to see how he should feel, in this case how he should feel towards church. This principle not only applies to children watching us, but to all who might be looking.

In the above passage, Paul tells his young pastor friend Timothy to set an example for others. He also warns him to basically watch himself carefully. For us, this reminds us that our words and attitudes are to be such that we would lead others closer to the Lord, not further away. Put simply, we are witnesses whether we want to be or not. We are either witnesses to the life changing power of knowing Jesus or we are not. Either way, we are witnessing. So be mindful of the fact that you are being watched. Examine your own heart and test whether you are a proper witness. Do you feel like somebody's watching you? Well, that is because there probably is someone watching you. Let them see Jesus in you.

__The Thin Place__: Ask, Answer, Pray.
Think of people in your life to which you are a regular witness?
What kind of witness are you to these people? How so?
What can you do to improve your witness?

July 20
The "Ologies"

__From Above__: Ephesians 1:17-23

Focal Passage: *"I keep asking that the God of our Lord Jesus Christ, the glorious Father, may give you the Spirit of wisdom and revelation, so that you may know him better." –Ephesians 1:17*

<u>Here Below</u>:

Theology. Soteriology. Eschatology. Ecclesiology. Christology. Axiology. Patriology. Pneumatology. Angelology. Ontology. Typology. Etc... These words and many others like them make up the list of "ologies" used in the study of matters of faith. While each word is particular in its area of intellectual and spiritual interest, they together form the overall study of God and His infinite attributes in relation to man. They are each worthy of a lifetime of attention. However, to look at them listed in this technical fashion is a bit overwhelming to even the most studious of Christians. Let's face it. God is an overwhelming subject to study, as well He should be. Thankfully, our faith is not based on what we know so much as it is on who we know! However, we do not need to be expert theologians to have a growing knowledge of the Lord. In fact, I would go so far as to say that an intellectual grasp of these studies will only leave you weary if you do not first have a corresponding relationship with the Lord. You cannot begin to understand Him until at first you know Him! This may seem like a play on words, but it is the difference between a head knowledge and a heart knowledge, between simple intellect and simple faith. Some of the most spiritually keen minds I have ever encountered could probably not define one of the words listed above; yet, they live them out every day in their walk of faith. Knowledge and intellect are worthy endeavors, but only faith can save us and empower us to live a life pleasing to the Lord.

The reality of God's greatness and our limited understanding does not relieve us from the obligation to learn as much as we can about our Lord. Study is meant to be a natural part of the Christian life, done not out of duty, but out of love and devotion. In the above verse, Paul tells the Ephesian church that he is praying that they might receive wisdom and revelation. But notice the reason for this prayer. He is praying in this manner so that they might now God better. In other words, he is telling us that we should try to get to know better. To know someone better, we spend time with them. The same is true of getting to know God. Relationship is the best educator. Search and study the scriptures all you can, but let the Holy Spirit do the teaching. Do you want to know God better? Then get to know His Son and His Word. Spend regular time with God and He will reveal something new of Himself to you every day. Thankfully, we have all eternity to get to know Him! Let your studies begin fresh each day!

The Thin Place: Ask, Answer, Pray.

How deep is your intellectual grasp of theological issues?

How important is a deeper understanding of theological issues to you?

How can you improve your spiritual study habits?

July 21
The God of the Underdog

From Above: I Samuel 16

Focal Passage: *" But the LORD said to Samuel, "Do not consider his appearance or his height, for I have rejected him. The LORD does not look at the things man looks at. Man looks at the outward appearance, but the LORD looks at the heart." " –I Samuel 16:7*

Here Below:

How many of you reading this have ever felt the sting of being the last one chosen? As a somewhat small and clumsy child, I can remember more than once being the last one picked to be on a team in kickball at Flowery Branch Elementary. It was so embarrassing being the last boy standing, to say nothing of what it does to young boy's self image. Perhaps this is why I love the story of David so much. The above chapter in David's life is one that has given many a shy and dismayed heart encouragement. In this passage we see the ultimate underdog being chosen first. Understand this about David; even his own father did not consider him to be a candidate for what was happening. He had left David completely out of the lineup. Yet, David was the reason it was happening. God saw something in David that even his own family could not see. He saw his heart.

This passage teaches us two things really. First, it teaches us that God's perspective is radically different than our own. He sees people for what they really are and what they can become. Yet, we all too often judge others by their outward appearance and accomplishments. God looks deeper. God is not impressed by our looks or our achievements. He does however seem to be impressed by a heart that is surrendered to him. This brings me to the second point we can glean from this story; that is, God sees the real you. While David's brothers looked the part, God knew David was better suited to be the king He desired. We cannot fool God. There is no looking the part with God. Either you are real before God or you are not. Because He looks beyond our outward appearance, it is impossible for us to portray anything other than what we truly are. This can be a little scary. It is somewhat disarming to think that we have no secrets from God. It can also be comforting. You see, God knew David and still chose him. God must have known about the sin David would eventually commit with Bathsheba, a sin for which David would one day become infamous. Yet, God still picked David first. The same is true for us. God sees the real you and loves you in spite of your faults. God would rather you be spiritually honest with Him than try to impress Him with exaggerated credentials. Be real with God and He will be real with you. With God there are no underdogs.

The Thin Place: Ask, Answer, Pray.

Have you ever considered yourself to be an underdog?

Do you find it comforting to know that God sees the real you? Why or why not?

How can we find freedom in knowing that God isn't impressed by outward appearances?

July 22
The Keeper of the Money Bag

<u>From Above</u>: John 12:1-8; Malachi 6:3-10

Focal Passage: *"He did not say this because he cared about the poor but because he was a thief; as keeper of the money bag, he used to help himself to what was put into it." –John 12:6*

<u>Here Below</u>:

There is a very interesting and telling verse hidden away in the story of Jesus' anointing at Bethany. In the above verse, we see further evidence of Judas' deception. In this verse we see that not only did Judas betray Jesus with His arrest, but Judas had been dipping his hand into the disciple's treasury all along. Judas must have been very cunning to convince the others to let him be the keeper of the money bag, but he did not fool Jesus. The Lord rebukes Judas for his comment about the helping the poor. At first glance, His response can be a little difficult to interpret. Regardless of how we might explain it, one reason must have been that Jesus knew Judas was not sincere. The verse above implies that Judas was interested in the money for himself, money that had been set aside for God's use. Judas was usurping something that ultimately belonged to God.

It is easy to criticize Judas for this fault. After all, this is Judas Iscariot to which we are referring. Yet, as with most matters, we must also turn the lens through which we look with judgment upon ourselves. While we may not be dipping our hands into the offering plate, we can still be guilty of stealing from God. One way we can do this is by not sacrificially giving to Him as we should. We can also do this by not using our time as we should and by not using out talents as we should. These gifts and many others are often given to us to be used for God's purposes and glory. To use them to promote ourselves or our own personal agenda is like spending God's money on ourselves, and is in a very real sense robbery from God. On the other hand, when we spend these assets on the Lord and His work, we see an investment from which we are sure to profit. To rob God is to ultimately deny ourselves a blessing. It is self destructive and the gains we think we have obtained by doing so never truly satisfy. When God has given us so much, why do we want to take from Him what can only be His to use anyway? Give your all to God and you will never have unmet needs. Let God be the keeper of your money bag.

The Thin Place: Ask, Answer, Pray.

How do you think stewardship applies to less tangible things such as time and talents?

Do you consider yourself to be a faithful steward? Why or why not?

How could you improve your stewardship?

July 23
Working for Weeds

From Above: Matthew 9:35-38

Focal Passage: *"Then he said to his disciples, "The harvest is plentiful but the workers are few. Ask the Lord of the harvest, therefore, to send out workers into his harvest field."" –Matthew 9:37-38*

Here Below:

I once had a beautiful tomato garden. It was my first attempt at gardening since I had been married and had established a home. My wife and I were excited about the prospect of raising our very own vegetables. I guess in a sense it made us feel all grown up. Though our garden was small, we were very proud. I administered painstaking care to see that it was properly watered and fertilized. I took time to pull weeds on a daily basis and to protect it from any pests that might cause damage. My work paid off. I had managed to raise some of the most beautiful tomato plants I had ever seen. They were strong and green and had grown taller than any tomato plants that I had ever seen. Yet, there was only one problem. As beautiful as the tomato plants had grown, they did not produce one single tomato. A tomato plant that produces no fruit is useless. As beautiful as they appeared, I had basically worked this hard to produce overgrown weeds.

The lesson of this story is one that has come to be very important to me. I had not been a failure in my gardening venture. The reality is that sometimes, regardless of our hard work, we simply do not see the fruit right away nor are we promised that we will ever see it. In fact, Jesus teaches us in the above passage that our job is to simply work in the harvest field. It is God that delivers the harvest. This is important, because we often misinterpret results as evidence of success or failure. God does not equate results with success. On the contrary, He seems to view our success in regards to our willingness and our faithfulness in following Him. Even in those instances when it seems outwardly that we have been beaten or failed, it could be that we are in reality successful; in that, we have remained true to God's purposes through it all. This command Jesus gives us in the above passage is also a reminder for us remember our place in life. I don't know about you, but I am thankful that my job is to simply remain true to the Lord and leave the harvest to Him. This takes the pressure out of success and puts the joy back in serving. Trust in the Lord of the harvest today. Just be true to God and leave the results to Him.

<u>**The Thin Place**</u>: Ask, Answer, Pray.
By what standards do you judge successes and failures in your life?
As a whole, would you say that you are a success? Why or why not?
What have you learned from the failures you have experienced in life?

July 24
A Case of the "If Only's"

<u>**From Above**</u>: Habakkuk 3

Focal Passage: *"LORD, I have heard of your fame; I stand in awe of your deeds, O LORD. Renew them in our day, in our time make them known; in wrath remember mercy. "–Habakkuk 3:2*

<u>Here Below</u>:

What a prayer this prophet has prayed! In it, he acknowledges the many deeds of the past that the Lord has accomplished. He then calls upon the Lord to renew them and make them known in his day. As sometimes happens, if not usually, the children of God have once again slipped into a period of forgetfulness. They had forgotten the past promises and blessings of God. Habakkuk understood the need for remembrance. In this prayer, He asks God to remind the people of the delivering acts of years gone by and to repeat them in his generation. With the last phrase of the above verse, he also acknowledges very honestly how this must sometimes make God feel. It must frustrate the Lord to have us forget all that He has done when He has already done so much. Habakkuk recognizes this when asks God in His wrath to remember His mercy. Thankfully He often does just that.

The truth is that we are a forgetful people. God has given us His written word so that we might not forget His provisions as the intended recipients of the above prophecy had obviously done. Yet, we still fail to remember. Just let a crisis arise in our life and our attitudes cry out "Oh Me! Whatever will I do?" or "Where is God in all of this?" We think to ourselves, "If only God would do this..." or "If only God could do that..." We get down in our circumstances and we get a case of the "if only's". If only this or if only that... If only... Well, God is not an "if only" kind of God. God is a "trust in me" kind of God. The better "if only" attitude might be as follows. If only we could remember how God has brought us through similar, if not worse, crises many times before. If only we could remember how He has delivered us in the past, while we are still facing the storm of today. If only we could understand that what He has done in the past, He wants to do today! The next time you find yourself with a bad case of the "if only's", the key to recovery is simple. Just remember. Remember what God has already done for you. Why should this time be any different than before? He did not forsake you then. He will not forsake you now.

The Thin Place: Ask, Answer, Pray.

What are some struggles you are facing right now or feel that you might face in the future?

What are some similar struggles from your past in which God was there for you?

Is there any reason why God should not respond in like manner in the new situations?

July 25
Finger Pointing Faith

From Above: I Corinthians 10:12-13; Philippians 1:6; Matthew 7:1-5

Focal Passage: *"So, if you think you are standing firm, be careful that you don't fall! No temptation has seized you except what is common to man. And God is faithful; he will not let you be tempted beyond what you can bear. But when you are tempted, he will also provide a way out so that you can stand up under it. "–I Corinthians 10:12-13*

Here Below:

Many of us have a finger pointing faith. What do I mean by this? Well, this is an improper form of faith whose creed is simply "Not Me!" It is the belief that I could never be caught in the same sin as so and so. It is a dangerous belief and one that will almost without exception lead to a sense of failure. Why? Because try as we might, none of us are above temptation. Sooner or later, we might face a temptation in which we do stumble. We must never say that we would never do what we have seen others do! Likewise, we should never look down on others for giving in to something that perhaps is not a real temptation for ourselves. Nor should we blame others for our own missteps! We are all tempted, just by different things. However, the result is always the same. So to point our spiritual fingers at others for their failures is a mistake. We must begin with ourselves, all the while remembering our own spiritual vulnerability. Paul understood this. In the above passage, the great apostle states that it is just in that instance when we think we are standing firm, that we must be the most careful. There is nothing that we will face that other and maybe even stronger people before us haven't already faced and failed. Think about it. Those heroes of the faith such as Paul, Peter, David, Moses and Abraham could all attest to this truth. They all failed in some specific sense. Yet, they all persevered and became heroes of the faith. It was when they owned up to their own sin that God was able to use them. Their usefulness in God's Kingdom work had nothing to do with the successes or failures of others. It was their own attitude that enabled them to be God's tools. We must be honest with God and honest with ourselves.

Thankfully, in the above passage, Paul didn't just leave us with the reality of our own sinfulness and the inevitability of temptation. He then gives us the reminder of our way out. With every temptation comes an escape. I think this applies to before and after we respond, even if our response is one of giving in to the temptation. God's grace and mercy trumps any temptation we may face. It can strengthen us when are up against them and strengthen us when we fail. God understands our weakness. He loves us anyway and He wants to lift us up when we fall. So instead of pointing fingers, why not fold your hands in prayer. Pray for strength for others and pray for the same for yourself. God will honor that prayer. Do this and you are never a failure in His eyes. Turn to Him today.

<u>The Thin Place</u>: Ask, Answer, Pray.

Do find it easier to see the failures in the lives of others than in your own? If so, why?

Have you ever been guilty of passing the blame with your own shortcomings?

When you are completely honest with God concerning your own sin, how is His response different?

July 26
Cherishing the Training Wheels

<u>**From Above**</u>: Psalm 118; Matthew 6:33-34

Focal Passage: *"This is the day the LORD has made; let us rejoice and be glad in it. "–Psalm 118:24*

<u>**Here Below**</u>:

A recent birthday brought about some serious introspection in my heart. Remarkably, it wasn't my own birthday that brought about the deep thinking, but it was that of my four year old son. As I watched him riding his first big boy bicycle, I could not help but bemoan the fleeting nature of life. I was always told that the older we get the faster time seems to pass. I guess this especially becomes true when children enter the picture. It seems as if it were just yesterday that he was a baby. Likewise, I know that it will only seem an instant before I will be taking those training wheels off of that new bicycle. In fact, he has already requested that I do so, even though he is far from being ready to ride without them. After only a matter of a few hours, there was already a skinned knee. Yet, time will eventually force me to take the training wheels away and then nervously watch as he clumsily ambles his way down our driveway. Then one day, that big boy bicycle will be a car and he will be driving away to begin his own life and family. This inevitable reality is one of mixed emotions to say the least.

The preferred end result of this kind of thinking is echoed in the above Psalm. The writer tells us to rejoice in this day. This day is God's and we should appreciate it while it is here. Be glad for the time we now enjoy. All too often we allow our thoughts of the future to consume our minds and we are unable to enjoy the time we now have. This is not what God desires for us. He wants us to live the life abundant and that means to enjoy the blessings of this day. In fact, Jesus reinforced this thought when He told us to stop worrying about tomorrow. This is the day that we should be striving to enjoy. Instead of fretting over the passing of time, we should instead do our best to make this moment one to remember. This means appreciating the training wheels while they are there. It means letting those special to us be the center of our universe while we are able to do so. Take time today to show gratitude for the moment. Equally important, take time today to thank God for the fact that while time passes quickly, His love remains constant.

The Thin Place: Ask, Answer, Pray.

Do you ever struggle with the fleeting nature of time? If so, how?

Would you say that spend too much time worrying about the future?

Would you say that you generally try to make the most of the day you have been given?

July 27
From Wrestling to Resting

From Above: Genesis 32:21-32

Focal Passage: *"So Jacob was left alone, and a man wrestled with him till daybreak. "–Genesis 32:24*

Here Below:

The above story is one of the most interesting in all of scripture. It is also one of great significance; in that, in this story Jacob becomes known as Israel and a nation is given its name. One fact of this story that is especially interesting is when it occurred. This wrestling match occurred through the dark hours of the night. Jacob was awake in the middle of the night and literally wrestling with God, as he would soon realize in verse 30. Jacob was no stranger to struggle. He had struggled with his brother Esau and with Laban. He definitely understood the struggle that sometimes occurs in life. This time the struggle however was with the Lord. Can you relate? Have you ever been awake in the wee hours of the night in a struggle with the Lord? For some reason, that is when they often seem to come.

I think this story teaches us something very important about this kind of restlessness. Ultimately our struggles can be defined by whether we are going to do things our way or God's way. Just as with Jacob, our struggles ultimately are between ourselves and the Lord. Notice too that Jacob was holding his own physically with this strange man in this story; that is, until the Lord decided to remind him of his place. Sure, Jacob seemed to be doing alright in the wrestling match, but it only took a touch on his hip to cripple him for the rest of his life. Put simply, Jacob's control over his situation that night was only an illusion. That hip crippling touch was a reminder to Jacob and to you and me that God may allow us to think we are in control, but in the end, God was always the one defining the conditions of the situation. Likewise, by giving him a crippled hip, Jacob was left with a daily reminder of God's strength and purpose as well as his love. His love? Yes. Sometimes the scars we receive are meant to remind us later that God brought us through the crisis. God loved Jacob enough to teach Him this lasting lesson. Jacob understood this. He gave the place a name that would remind him of this fact. So the next time you find yourself in a wrestling match of wills with the Lord, just remember that His will is always for our welfare. His ultimate will is always one of love and security in our hearts, a security that strengthens us for the road ahead. The more you trust in him, the more you will find the struggles fewer and farther between. Follow His will to a night of spiritual rest and peace.

The Thin Place: Ask, Answer, Pray.

Have you ever felt as if you were wrestling with the Lord? If so, when and what was the outcome?

How has God used your struggles to strengthen you and help you grow in your faith?

Have you ever taken time to thank God for the lessons He has given you in life?

July 28
Slip and Slide Salvation

<u>**From Above**</u>: Jude 17-25

Focal Passage: *"To him who is able to keep you from falling and to present you before his glorious presence without fault and with great joy--to the only God our Savior be glory, majesty, power and authority, through Jesus Christ our Lord, before all ages, now and forevermore! Amen. "–Jude 24-25*

<u>**Here Below**</u>:

One day while still in college, I was returning from chapel services to my dorm room. Having responsibilities in chapel that day, I was later than most leaving and was virtually all alone as I headed back to crash in my dormitory. It had rained earlier that morning and the grass was soaking wet. Of course, my dorm was at the bottom of a huge hill and as you can guess by now, my slippery dress shoes combined with the wet grass led to disaster. I slipped and fell. I must have slid fifteen feet or further down the hill before I was able to clinch a handful of grass to help slow my descent. I quickly jumped up, looking about, hoping beyond hope that no one saw me fall. There was no one in sight and I quickly started toward my dorm in order to change before anyone saw the mud covering my clothes. But as I passed by the girl's dormitory nearby, I heard it. I looked up to see that there was a roomful of girls leaning out of their window giggling at me. They had seen the whole terrible ordeal. I had fallen and my fall had not gone unnoticed by others as I had hoped. It soon became a topic of hot discussion all across the college campus that day.

One thing we must endeavor to learn is that we as humans are predisposed to stumbling. Even the strongest of our kind will from time to time trip and fall. I, of course, am not referring to physically stumbling so much as I am referring to the inevitable spiritual stumbles we all inevitably face. As in the above story, we hope that no one sees our stumble; yet, rest assured it is seen by God if by no one else. However, this is not cause for dismay. It is instead cause for great relief. One key to living a healthy Christian life is grasping the fact that though we are saved, we are not perfect. God knows that and so should we. In fact, the above verse tells us who it is that is able to keep us from falling. It is not ourselves. It is Jesus Christ. In other words, while we should do our best to avoid temptation and sin, we should not feel defeated when we do trip and fall, spiritually speaking. It is for these stumbles that Jesus died. We have not been beaten. In Jesus, we have victory. Jude tells us that it is with great joy that Jesus presents us without fault. Being without fault is a result of what He has done, not us. He alone is able to do that. He has washed the mud off of us with His blood. So for us this means one thing. When we fall, repent. In laymen's terms, when we fall, get back up, knock off the dirt and try to avoid the slip next time. With God's help, you can. So don't beat yourself up! Accept His gift of grace. He offers it with great joy!

The Thin Place: Ask, Answer, Pray.

Do you ever have a hard time forgiving yourself for your shortcomings? How so?

Do you believe that God will forgive you for anything?

What does the above verse say to you specifically today?

July 29
Tolle Lege

From Above: Deuteronomy 6:1-9

Focal Passage: *"These commandments that I give you today are to be upon your hearts. Impress them on your children. Talk about them when you sit at home and when you walk along the road, when you lie down and when you get up. "–Deuteronomy 6:6-7*

Here Below:

Considered the greatest by many of the early Church fathers, Augustine had a very unique conversion experience. He is considered by many to be one of the greatest intellectual and spiritual minds that ever existed; yet, it was after hearing the simple words to a children's song that Augustine came to faith in Jesus Christ. At the time, he was intellectually struggling with the Gospel message and personally struggling with a very immoral and sinful lifestyle. Then one day while outside, he heard a child neighbor singing a song that contained the Latin phrase *Tolle Lege* repeatedly in the refrain. This phrase is best translated into English as "pick up and read". As he heard these words he saw a book containing scripture from the book of Romans. He did as the song suggests, feeling as if it were the voice of God calling him to do so. After having read a particular passage, Augustine trusted in Jesus for his salvation and the rest is history. This happened all because he picked up and read the word.

So many of the questions we have on spiritual matters could be answered if we would just follow the command found in that Latin phrase. Likewise, many of the misconceptions we have on spiritual matters could be clarified if we would do the same. God has not left us with unanswerable questions. Sure, sometimes the answers may be harder to find and sometimes we may not find the answer we want. Nevertheless, the answers are there. God understands our need for answers. This is why He has given us a hard copy of His word. In His Word, He acknowledges our need by instructing us to familiarize ourselves with His word. He even goes so far in Deuteronomy to instruct us to wear it on our heads and wrists and to post it on our doorpost, as our Jewish brothers and sisters still do to this day. While I am not sure if He meant it literally or not, the principle is still sound. We are to have God's Word in a prominent place in our lives, a place both literally and figuratively where we can get to it. In other words, we are to be in God's Word regularly and in such a way as to become familiar and comfortable with it, much as we might if it were a piece of clothing. As we familiarize our self with it, we must also be careful to remember that it is the literal Word of God. Remember this the next time you have questions and pick up your Bible. In your hands you have access to the actual mind and heart of God. Just as with Augustine, it can change your life. So pick up and read. *Tolle Lege!*

The Thin Place: Ask, Answer, Pray.

How has God used His word to speak to you in the past?

What scripture verses or passages would you say that are the most meaningful to you right now?

How familiar would you say that you are with the written Word of God?

July 30
Car Wash Christianity

From Above: Acts 3:19-20; Titus 3:5-6

Focal Passage: *"He saved us, not because of righteous things we had done, but because of his mercy. He saved us through the washing of rebirth and renewal by the Holy Spirit, whom he poured out on us generously through Jesus Christ our Savior,"* –Titus 3:5-6

Here Below:

The other day I washed my car. You know what happened the next day. It was what seems to happen almost every time I wash my car. It rained. Within hours of my labor, my shiny clean car was freckled with rain water spots and there was a light mud sprayed around all of my wheels. What was once clean, was now not so clean. In one sense, this seems to be a metaphor for life. Just when we think we have our lives cleaned up, it won't be long until we find ourselves dirty again, in need of another wash. Thankfully, it doesn't end there. We can be clean again. In fact, God's desire is to do the washing for us. Just like cleaning that car is ultimately futile, so is trying to keep spiritually clean on our own strength. If it were possible, there would be no need for the cross of Christ nor His grace and forgiveness. However, when God washes us clean, we are clean forever. Though we may stumble and get dirty again, our dirt will not penetrate or stain. God has made us forever clean.

However, we still have the responsibility of repenting and starting fresh in our walk with the Lord daily. Yet, we must never forget that God welcomes the new start. Everything about Him points to His desire to see us new and reborn. Even the facts of His creation testify to this part of his nature. He designed the universe as to have light and darkness, dividing our lives in to day and night. Each day is an opportunity to start fresh, to start clean. You see, it is not so much about our ability to start fresh or to remain clean as it His nature to do it for us. That is the message of the Bible. That is the message of Jesus. That is the message of the Christian faith. So repent of and learn from your mistakes and do your best to live for Him; but trust in Him to do the cleaning.

The Thin Place: Ask. Answer. Pray.

Do you ever feel dirty and in need of a spiritual wash?

How do you deal with those feelings? Do you turn to God with a repentant spirit?

Do you believe it is God's desire for you to feel spiritually clean?

July 31
Joy Along the Journey

From Above: Philippians 1:1-14

Focal Passage: *"Being confident of this, that he who began a good work in you will carry it on to completion until the day of Christ Jesus." –Philippians 1:6*

Here Below:

I once saw a bumper sticker that read "It's the journey, not the destination." This sticker was affixed on the back of a motorcycle. It was obvious that the owner appreciated the joy and free spirit associated with motorcycle travel. As true as this might be for that traveler, I do not believe this philosophy applies to matters of spiritual importance. How so? Well, first I do not wish to imply that the journey of Christian living is not filled with joy and excitement. On the contrary, it can be filled with great joy. However, we are never promised this. In fact, as you read the above verse and all of Philippians for that matter, you will see that Paul's letter is filled with expressions of joy in the journey. However, it is also good to note that the letter was written from prison. I think what must have kept Paul's spirits high during this ordeal was his belief that the destination made the journey worth the ride, no matter how difficult.

Well, you may think this is easier said than done. You are right. However, it is not impossible. Perhaps the best way to maintain a spirit of joy along the journey is to look forward instead of looking back. We must learn from our past, but we must not live in it. We must grow as a result of our hardships, instead of letting them stifle us. Most importantly, we must always remember that our journey will end at the feet of Jesus. At that point, any struggles we've experienced along the way will only seem trivial in comparison. So, do not get sidetracked by troubles along the journey. Keep your eyes on the destination and you can know the joy that Paul knew.

<u>**The Thin Place**</u>: Ask. Answer. Pray.

What positive lessons have you learned from your past? Negative?

Do you ever allow difficulties from the past determine your actions in the present? How so?

Would you say that you tend to look ahead more or look behind more along your journey?

8

August

August 1
Seeing it Through

From Above: I Thessalonians 1:1-5

Focal Passage: *"We continually remember before our God and Father your work produced by faith, your labor prompted by love, and your endurance inspired by hope in our Lord Jesus Christ. " –I Thessalonians 1:3*

Here Below:

Have you ever stood before a job and felt as if there was no way it could ever be completed? When working for such a big God, sometimes our tasks can seem a bit overwhelming, as well they should. All too often we settle for less than what we could accomplish simply because we fail to trust in Him for strength and power to see it to the end. Perhaps one reason this happens is our failure to do things with the proper motive. In the above passage, we are reminded of our preferred threefold motivation to see the work of the Lord to completion. They are faith, love, and hope. Our work is produced by faith. We do it out of commitment to God. Our work is also prompted by love. We do it out of affection for and a desire to please the Lord. Finally, our finishing the task is inspired by hope in Jesus. In other words, our enduring to the end of even the most difficult task is accomplished with the understanding that we press on with confidence in our Lord and Savior. If our motive is right, then the task is not so overwhelming.

I think it is fair to say that this passage not only applies to laboring for the Lord faithfully with acts of service, but the principle could also apply to serving Him with simple acts of obedience in the more personal aspects of our lives as well. If there is some attitude in your life that you feel God desires for you to have or not to have, to take on or to give up, and you feel as if it is just too big, then I have some good news for you. You can't do it! At least, you can't do it alone. The good news in this is that God never intended for you to try to do it alone! His will for each of us has always included being strengthened by His presence and the work of the Holy Spirit in our hearts. Those natural feelings of inadequacy that we sometimes feel do not have to be negative in nature. Instead, they should serve to drive us closer to God. They are just simple reminders of our need for more of the Lord in our lives. Remember, for God there is no task too big. Trust in Him to get the job done.

The Thin Place: Ask, Answer, Pray.

Do you ever feel overwhelmed in your commitment to the Lord?

How do you normally handle feelings of inadequacy when facing the tasks ahead?

How can you better handle these feelings?

August 2
Standing In It

From Above: Romans 5:1-2; Romans 12:1-3

Focal Passage: *"Therefore, since we have been justified through faith, we have peace with God through our Lord Jesus Christ, through whom we have gained access by faith into this grace in which we now stand. And we rejoice in the hope of the glory of God. " –Romans 5:1-2*

Here Below:

Let suppose for a moment that you have stolen my car. I have caught you in the act of stealing my car. You have no excuse. You felt like you needed it or wanted it and you tried to steal it. You are guilty. You are a thief. Now let's suppose for a minute that I called the police to report your attempted theft. After all, I would be in my rights to call them. You had admittedly committed a crime and were now going to face the consequences of your crime. That would be justice. Okay, now let's suppose that I do not call the police. Instead, I say to you "Forget it!" and tell you to just go away. I still have my car. There is no harm done. You would not be given the punishment you deserve. That would be mercy. Let's take this one step further. Instead of calling the police, I do something totally unexpected. Instead of just telling you to forget it and sending you away, I hand you the keys and give you my car. That would be grace. Not only have I pushed my rights aside and decided to spare you from what you deserve, I have given you something you do not deserve. I have shown you grace.

This is exactly what God has done for each of us that have trusted in Him. He has done more than just erased our debt or even forgiven us our debt. He has given us, the thieves, murderers and adulterers, the keys to His kingdom. We must always strive to remember this truth. It is by His grace we stand. The above passage reminds us of this simple, yet life changing truth. Understanding God's grace should serve to make the recipient of it gracious. If it is by His grace we stand, it is by His grace we should relate to others. None of us have any reason to boast. Were it not for grace, we would all be standing in deep trouble. So, the next time you are tempted to judge others for their sins, look at what you are standing in yourself. You are standing in grace. Thank God today for His grace and share it with others today.

The Thin Place: Ask, Answer, Pray.

Do you ever find yourself being judgmental of the sins of others? If so, how?

How should the concept of grace change the way you deal with others?

How can you show your appreciation for God's grace today?

August 3
Lord, It's Me Again...

<u>**From Above**</u>: I Timothy 1:12-17

Focal Passage: *"But for that very reason I was shown mercy so that in me, the worst of sinners, Christ Jesus might display his unlimited patience as an example for those who would believe on him and receive eternal life. "* –I Timothy 1:16

<u>**Here Below**</u>:

As a parent, I have learned that there is one necessary quality that we must possess if we desire spiritually healthy children. That quality is patience. Without patience, parenthood would be frustrating and ultimately a futile endeavor. Why? Because as children grow, they often learn by the mistakes they make. If we lose heart and act rashly over every mistake, we are sending the wrong message to the child and we could be interrupting the natural, yet sometimes painful process of growth that the incident could instead promote. Impatience takes the focus off of the mistake and puts it on the person. In essence, by exhibiting impatience, we are creating a works-based atmosphere within our relationships. Patience on the other hand sends to the child a different message. Patience says, "I am going to love you anyways, even when you mess up again and again and again!" Our relationship with our Heavenly Father is no different from this earthly child and parent relationship. Thankfully we serve a God of unlimited patience.

If you are like me, you sometimes wonder how God can be so patient with yourself. Oftentimes, my prayers seem to express the "It's me again" attitude and you wonder how many times God will hear the same plea for forgiveness. The mistake in that way of thinking is that we are equating God's limits of patience with that of our own. In the above passage, Paul described God's patience as unlimited when it comes to dealing with the sins of His children. If anyone should know of God's patience, it would have been Paul. Yet, Paul understood that his life was a perfect example of just how patient God can be with us. He recognized that God's unmatched love produced within Him an unmatched patience. Like a patient parent, God is going to support us in our attempts to get it right. He is willing to offer grace and forgiveness, if we are truly repentant and willing to honestly try again. He will wait for us if we trust in Him. So don't be afraid to approach God with an "It's me again" prayer. If it is heartfelt, God will hear it. In fact, He wants you to come to Him with those prayers. It is in those prayers that we grow.

The Thin Place: Ask, Answer, Pray.

Is there a particular struggle for which you keep going to the Lord seeking forgiveness?

Do you ever feel as if God may be tiring of the same old prayer for forgiveness? If so, why?

Do you believe God is able to help you overcome that habitual sin?

August 4
Jack is a Dull Boy

From Above: Ecclesiastes 5:12-20; John 10:10

Focal Passage: *" Moreover, when God gives any man wealth and possessions, and enables him to enjoy them, to accept his lot and be happy in his work--this is a gift of God. " –I Timothy 1:16*

Here Below:

Perhaps you remember the line from the old children's limerick which says, "All work and no play makes Jack a dull boy"? Well, I once met a man that lived that line. He was a distributor for a large soft drink company. In our conversation, he described working six days a week and anywhere from 16-20 hours a day often beginning at 3 or 4 in the morning. He admitted that he was growing weary and seemed to almost always be tired. I asked him as to the reason why he didn't search for a job with a more suitable work schedule. He replied by saying "I make too much money to work anywhere else." As he was justifying this self-destructive lifestyle, I couldn't help but think to myself of the obvious fallacy in his reasoning. He did have more money due to his job; yet he was never able to enjoy it, due to the fact that he was always working! Not only that, but he admitted that his family was suffering in his absence. There is a definite virtue in working hard and providing the best for your family. However, the best does not always mean the most. Sometimes we must simply stop what we are doing so that we might enjoy the life God has given us.

The Bible praises hard work. Of this there is no question. Yet, it also makes concessions for rest and relaxation. Even Jesus and the disciples would get away from time to time. Jesus would often head for the wilderness to get away from the crowds and the work that the crowds would provide (Luke 5:15-16). Was Jesus being selfish? Of course not! In fact, it was just the opposite. Being in human form (and also being Creator of that human form), Jesus understood our limits. He understood that His work, for lack of a better word, would be best accomplished if He was fully rested. The Bible doesn't tell us this, but I imagine that He and the twelve would probably from time to time just "chill out" for the sake of relaxation. How can I assume this? Because rest and leisure is a necessary part of the human experience! Our leisure time is not more important or less important than our work. It is equally important. In fact, after discussing the futility of overworking ourselves, the writer of Ecclesiastes states the fact that to be able to enjoy the fruits of our labor is a gift from God. This tells me that there must be a healthy balance between working and enjoying the fruits of our labors. When the balance becomes skewed, so do we. We either become overworked or we go lacking. Therefore, we must take our work seriously and our leisure seriously. We must guard our work ethic and our time off. We must guard our family time. We must make time for rest. It is a gift from God.

The Thin Place: Ask, Answer, Pray.

Would you say that you have a strong work ethic? How so?

How important do you view your leisure time?

How can your leisure time glorify God as well as your hard work?

August 5
It Looks Like Rain

<u>**From Above**</u>: Acts 3:19-20

Focal Passage: *"Repent, then, and turn to God, so that your sins may be wiped out, that times of refreshing may come from the Lord, and that he may send the Christ, who has been appointed for you--even Jesus. "* –Acts 3:19-20

<u>**Here Below**</u>:

When there is nothing else to talk about, there is always the weather. I wonder how much time we spend talking about the rain or the lack of it? It seems to occupy much of our conversational time together, especially in times of drought. Now do not get me wrong. The weather is serious business. Nothing can mess up your day more quickly than an unexpected thunderstorm or rain shower. Yet, there is one thing I have noticed about the weather. We can't change it! But it most certainly can change us. It is amazing to me just how quickly a little rain shower can refresh the dry earth. The grass in my yard had turned brown and would crunch under your feet when you walked upon it. Then it rained one evening. The next day the grass had perked up and was turning a bright and healthy green. Just like that. Overnight, a little rain had refreshed the parched life in my yard. It was now growing and vibrant. A little refreshing can make all the difference.

The same is true of our spiritual yards as well. Sometimes we find ourselves in a period of spiritual drought. We become dry and we seem to stop growing. It is then that we stand in need of a little refreshing shower. Well, the Creator of the rain stands ready to give us the refreshing we need. In the above passage we are taught that God desires to send us times of refreshing. He wants to perk us up and encourage our growth. Of course, there is a condition named in connection with His refreshing. It is repentance. To receive refreshment from God, we must first prepare the soil. We must come clean before God. It is only after a time of honest and open communication with God that He is willing to give us the refreshment we need. It is only after a time of heartfelt repentance that He can really work in our lives. It is not always an easy thing to do. Nevertheless, the refreshing period that follows repentance is always worth the toil that sometimes accompanies. So, with that said, how is the weather in your life right now? Could you use some rain right now?

The Thin Place: Ask, Answer, Pray.

Do you ever find true repentance difficult? If so, why?

What would you say the difference is between repentance and just feeling sorry?

What has been the result of repentance in your past?

August 6
Dealing with a Feeling

From Above: 2 Peter 1:16-21

Focal Passage: *" And we have the word of the prophets made more certain, and you will do well to pay attention to it, as to a light shining in a dark place, until the day dawns and the morning star rises in your hearts. "*
—2 Peter 1:19

Here Below:

Have you ever said, "I just don't feel like working today" or maybe "I just don't feel like bathing today"? Well, like it or not, sometimes we must do things that we may not *feel* like doing. In fact, one thing I have discovered, those times in which we do not feel like doing something is usually when we need to do it the most! For instance, in the above two examples, sooner or later we run out of money if we do not work and sooner or later your friends will demand you bathe! For our financial and social wellness, we must often do what we may not feel like doing. Likewise, the same can be said of maintaining our spiritual wellness.

Let's face it; there are days when we do not feel too spiritual. Sometimes there are things I would rather be doing than focusing on things of a spiritual nature such as praying, reading the Bible, worship, study and the like. This is normal. In fact, a healthy time of rest and relaxation is necessary. However, the more we stray from our spiritual discipline, the harder it is to get back into our routine. We must be careful to not make a habit of neglecting our spiritual condition. Peter understood this. In the above passage he points out that we cannot ignore the Lord, specifically His word, for very long. It is like trying to ignore a light in a dark room. We cannot ignore that light, no matter how hard we try. It is there and cannot be overlooked. Our eyes will be instinctively drawn to it. We should be the same with God's Word, both written and that whispered in our hearts and minds. This may mean taking the time to examine it even in times when we would rather be doing something else. It is in those times that we probably benefit the most from His word. Peter was giving us some good advice. He told us that we would do well to pay attention to it. Thankfully God's attention is not given based upon feelings, but upon His love for us. We should be same with Him. I have found that when I take the time to turn to God, regardless of how I feel, I usually find myself feeling better for it. Kind of ironic, huh? Well, turn to him today.

The Thin Place: Ask, Answer, Pray.

Are there ever times in your life when you do not feel too spiritual? When?
Why do you think these feeling sometimes occur?
What can you do to help avoid those times of spiritual complacency?

August 7
Mark Your Calendar

From Above: Acts 1:7; I Thessalonians 5:1-8

Focal Passage: *"Now, brothers, about times and dates we do not need to write to you, for you know very well that the day of the Lord will come like a thief in the night. "* –I Thessalonians 5:1-2

Here Below:

In the spring of 1990, I was given a pamphlet in a mall parking lot which stated that Jesus was going to return on a particular date in July of that same year. According to this pamphlet, with His return was going to be a time of destruction and basically the end of the world. Needless to say, that day has come and gone, and we are still here. Similarly, people everywhere held their breath fearing that the world was going end at midnight on New Year's Eve of the new millennium. Again, nothing happened. One question I always had about that particular date was whether it was going to happen at midnight of Eastern Standard Time or Central, Mountain or Pacific? Likewise, thanks to the Aztecs, everyone anticipated a date in 2012 when the world was supposed to end. Of course, the Aztecs didn't even see their own destruction. I guess that makes them a reliable prophetic source. The point of all of this is that it is further confirmation of the words of Christ in Acts 1. No human knows the dates which God Himself has ordained. People have been predicting the return of Christ for two thousand years and they have all been wrong. In fact, if we take the above scripture literally, if there is ever a date predicted, you can rest assured that it will not happen on that day; in that, no man knows when it will occur.

We shouldn't let the uncertain timing of His return frighten us or cause us great concern. It should instead be a source of extreme comfort. For the believer, it is not a "doomsday". It is a day of great anticipation and a day we want to see come. In relation, there must be a reason why God has not shared with us His schedule. Foremost among those reasons is His great love for you and me. First, the longer He waits, the more opportunities we have to accept Him as Lord and Savior. The longer He waits, the more that can be saved. Also, God understands human nature. He knows the human tendency to put things off until tomorrow. If we knew exactly when Jesus was going to return, we might just put off committing ourselves to Him until the absolute last minute. Likewise, not knowing should hopefully lead us to living as if it could be today. The New Testament disciples all thought it would be in their lifetime. You know what? It could be in ours. That's the point. When things may not be going well for you, just remember that this could be the day. Anticipation can help us push our way through the troubles of the day. The real question is not when He is going to return, but am I ready for His return? It seems as if God is more interested in today. Are you?

The Thin Place: Ask, Answer, Pray.

How often do you think of the return of Jesus Christ? Often or not so often?

How familiar are you with scripture concerning the second coming?

Do you eagerly look forward to His return?

August 8
Found Out

From Above: Numbers 32:23; Romans 6

Focal Passage: *"But if you fail to do this, you will be sinning against the LORD; and you may be sure that your sin will find you out."* *–Numbers 32:23*

Here Below:

In the above passage from Numbers, Moses relays a message from God to his people. In this message, God is affirming something that many would like to deny, or at least forget for a time. It is one word. That word is *consequences*. This passage is more than a warning that our sin is known to God or that it might come to light for others to see, though both of these can be considered true. It is a reminder that there is always going to be consequences to our sin. We may think that we have managed to get off free and clear, but even if only in our own heart, there will ultimately be consequences. Also, we must never forget that one consequence of our sins is the cross of Jesus.

I do not acknowledge this reality to discourage you. On the contrary, it is when we acknowledge our sin that we can be freed of it. Grace enables us to move forward, unimpeded by the weight of our sin. However, grace doesn't imply there will be no consequences. It simply means that we can find undeserved forgiveness for our sin. Grace however can lessen the effect of the consequences. How? Often the greatest consequence we struggle with is the damage caused within our own hearts and minds. It is possible to be disappointed in ourselves. We let ourselves down. We don't always meet our own standards or reach the spiritual potential that we feel we are capable of attaining. This can lead to regret and shame. Grace however, if understood and embraced, negates regret and shame. Of course, this all goes back to coming clean about our sin. We cannot sweep it under the rug. We must face it and deal with it. If we do not find it, it will find us. Sooner or later, we must all confront our sins. Why put off freedom? Face your sin today and beat it to the punch.

The Thin Place: Ask, Answer, Pray.

Do you believe that your sins will eventually catch up to you? If so, how?
Think of a personal example that proves this verse to be true.
Do you have any unrepented sins in your heart right now?

August 9
Shamey...Namey... Namey!

From Above: Romans 6:20-23; Isaiah 53:1-7

Focal Passage: *"What benefit did you reap at that time from the things you are now ashamed of? Those things result in death!"* –Romans 6:21

Here Below:

In the eighth grade, I had a teacher with a very unique teaching style. Perhaps eccentric might be the better word to describe her personality. Don't misunderstand. She was very effective in her passionate approach and I must say one of my most inspirational teachers, as well as one of my favorites. She was different in many ways. She was driving an electric vehicle decades before it was cool to go green. When her car was charging, she would drive a scooter to school. She was in her sixties at the time; so you can imagine the humor of this scene, especially to a middle-schooler. Likewise, she had several memorable expressions that were exclusive to her. One expression that we never wanted to hear in class was "Shamey...Namey...Namey!" If we ever found ourselves in trouble in class, she would say these words to us as she pointed to us with her index finger and scraped it with her other index finger. It was hard to keep a straight face when receiving this rebuke. With this expression, she had a way of making us laugh at our mistake and at the same time be ashamed of our actions.

While this approach may have been effective in a middle school classroom, the reality is that shame is not a laughing matter. In the book of Romans, often referred to as the gospel of grace, we see the damaging effects of sin and the ultimate consequence of a life of sin, its wages. Just a few verses prior to the famous 6:23 is verse 21, a verse that identifies the deceitful nature of sin. Paul asks of what benefit is sin? Sin always seems like the thing to do at the time. It usually seems harmless and promises a moment of pleasure or comfort and the reality is that it does sometime deliver on this promise. However, these supposed benefits are short lived. The end result is always shame and ultimately death. Shame is one of the heaviest burdens we can carry and one that we were never meant to carry. This is where this message of sin and its accompanying shame becomes the gospel of grace. Jesus on the cross has taken our shame upon himself. If you ever struggle with feelings of shame, know that it is unnecessary. As a born-again believer, your shame has been taken care of. This of course does not mean that we do not ever have feelings of regret. But God's desire is that we learn from our mistakes and let go of them. Only by doing this can we move forward in our spiritual growth. Don't let shame hinder that growth. Instead, let God free you from it.

The Thin Place: Ask, Answer, Pray.

Do you ever struggle with feelings of shame over past mistakes?

Have you truly repented of the sin that led to these feelings?

Do you believe today that God wishes to take away your shame if you would only ask?

August 10
Friends and Enemies

From Above: Exodus 33; Romans 5:10-11

Focal Passage: *"The LORD would speak to Moses face to face, as a man speaks with his friend." –Exodus 33:11*

Here Below:

In the above passage from the book of Exodus, we see one of the most heartwarming passages of the Old Testament. It demonstrates the very special relationship between Moses and the Heavenly Father. It doesn't fit the image of Moses that we often picture in our minds eye. We often think of Moses as some Charlton Heston type character standing on a mountaintop with stone tablets of law in hand and the wind blowing through his long white hair. As an alternative, in this verse we see God and Moses enjoying a more intimate type of relationship. We see them speaking to one another as friends. This idea of a friendship with God doesn't diminish His holiness as some suggest. Instead, it validates it. In His omnipotence, He has chosen fellowship with His creation. In fact, the Bible suggests that this was His purpose for creation all along.

Yet, something happens along the way. As we study scripture, we see that from Exodus to Romans, a change takes place. As God gives Moses the law, we then become increasingly aware of our inability to keep it without exception. We go from being friends with God to being described as enemies of God in Romans. However, notice what has not changed. Just as God was attempting to lead His children to fellowship with Himself with the law and Moses, He is doing the same in the New Testament with the cross of Jesus. What the law could not do, Jesus and grace did. With the cross, God reconciles us to himself, in the only way that is possible for us. This time reconciliation would be once and for all. So you see, God has always sought friendship with you and me. This has always been his desire. It is His desire today as well. This reality gives meaning to life. In fact, this relationship defines everything else we do or become. If we miss friendship with God, we miss everything. It was for this reason I was created. It was for this reason you were created. With that in mind, we must care for our relationship with God much as we would any other relationship. We do this by spending time with Him, trusting in Him, leaning on Him and making choices based upon our relationship with Him. All else should be relative to this relationship. By the way, isn't it wonderful to know that we have a friend that will never let us down?

The Thin Place: Ask, Answer, Pray.

Does the above reference to God and Moses as friends fit your way of thinking of God?

How does this concept of God as friend differ from the normal view of religion?

Do you ever consider yourself as a friend of God? If not, why?

August 11

No Doubt...Know Doubt...

From Above: John 20:24-29; Matthew 7:7-8

Focal Passage: *"So the other disciples told him, "We have seen the Lord!" But he said to them, "Unless I see the nail marks in his hands and put my finger where the nails were, and put my hand into his side, I will not believe it.'" –John 20:25*

<u>Here Below</u>:

Everyone knows old doubting Thomas. We are all familiar with the story above and of his need to see the wounds of Jesus himself, before he would believe in the resurrection. Yet, did you know that Thomas is only recorded as speaking three times in the gospels? One of three is the above scene by which he obtained his unfortunate nickname. However, the other two instances in which we see Thomas directly speaking tell a different story. They are found in John 11:16 and John 14:5. In each conversation we see Thomas making great proclamations of faith in Jesus and a desire to know Him even more. In fact, in John 11 we see Thomas ready to go to his death for Jesus if it is in keeping with the will of God! This doesn't sound like the man we often label as "Doubting Thomas"! It tells us of his great faith. I would take it even further and say that the above story of how he deals with doubt tells us something of his faith as well.

I don't think it was so much a fact that Thomas doubted in Jesus' promise to return or in His ability to be resurrected. I think it was more a fact that he wanted to see it for himself. After all, at this point, Thomas was the only one that had not had an encounter with the resurrected Christ. He wasn't content with merely taking the word of others. He wanted to see Jesus himself. Sure, faith means accepting what we cannot always see or explain. Nevertheless, there is still something to be said of the strength of personal experience in matters of faith. It is one thing to hear testimony of the power of God and the joy of personally knowing the Lord. It is another to experience it for yourself. Thomas wanted to taste and see for himself. Also, it is worth mentioning that Jesus willingly gave Thomas the proof he desired and immediately we see Thomas making yet another great proclamation of his faith in Jesus. "My Lord and my God!" he says. You see, it is not that our doubts are necessarily bad. It is when we allow our doubts to keep us from looking for the truth that they become bad. Oftentimes our doubts can lead us to the answers we need. We must always remain open to the discovery of God's truth. Do that and even your doubts can lead to a time of spiritual growth and greater faith! Do you have doubts? Then keep looking for the answer. God will reveal himself to all who truly seek.

The Thin Place: Ask. Answer. Pray.

Do you ever struggle with doubt concerning matters of faith?

Do you just let these doubts grow or do you intentionally seek the answers you need?

How has God relieved your doubts in the past?

August 12
Full Ambassador

From Above: 2 Corinthians 5:17-21

Focal Passage: "*We are therefore Christ's ambassadors, as though God were making his appeal through us. We implore you on Christ's behalf: Be reconciled to God.*" *—2 Corinthians 5:20*

Here Below:

An ambassador is basically defined as one given full authority to speak on behalf of someone else, usually of higher rank. Well, we are Christ's ambassadors! As Christians, this means we are given the responsibility of speaking on His behalf. We must understand that with the title of ambassador comes great responsibility. While we are to be imitators of Christ, we are also to be likeminded in our purpose and plans. Look at Paul's words above. His message is simple. Using his ambassadorial authority, Paul relays a simple message. Be reconciled to God. Part of our responsibilities as His ambassadors is to help reconcile others to God. Put simply, we are to do our best to help others 'get right" with God.

This is part of the Christian message that we often overlook. Many of us are content with making sure our own faith is secure, that we are "right with God". However, as ambassadors we are not speaking on our own behalf, but on the behalf of one greater than ourselves. We are speaking for Jesus. While He is concerned for our wellbeing, He is also concerned with the wellbeing of all. This task is a great privilege, as well as a great responsibility. It is not enough to simply look to our own spiritual condition. We must be concerned with the eternity of others. Having been reconciled ourselves, we should then look to the reconciliation of others. Don't misunderstand. While this may seem like a daunting task, it is one that should come naturally to the believer. After all, if our faith is genuine, it will be accompanied by a desire to see others come to faith, especially those with whom we are close. In that case, be the ambassador you are called to be. You may not always be a perfect representative. That is okay. Just do your best and trust in God for the results. Do this and your influence will be felt, and you will have more impact than you can imagine. Let his Holy Spirit guide you in these matters. The Holy Spirit will give you the words to say. You must simply be willing. So don't be shy with the truth. Speak up. After all, you have been given full ambassadorial status!

The Thin Place: Ask. Answer. Pray.

Do you find it easy to share your faith? Why or why not?

With whom do you find it most difficult to speak of your faith, strangers or those close to you?

How do you feel knowing that you are Christ's ambassador?

August 13
Faith and Cold French Fries

From Above: Philippians 2: 1-11

Focal Passage: *"Your attitude should be the same as that of Christ Jesus:"*
–Philippians 2:5

Here Below:

I wonder what Jesus would do if he were cut off in traffic? How would he react if the person in front of him in line at the local department store happened to have an item with no price tag? Or how would He respond if they messed up his order in a fast-food drive thru? Would He respond with abrasiveness, feeling justified in His response due to the carelessness of those involved in the scenario, resulting in His minor discomfort? Or would Jesus respond with kindness and compassion, understanding that there may be a million innocent reasons as to why this situation has occurred? We would be hard pressed to imagine Jesus blowing his top over something as trivial as the above events. It is hard to imagine Jesus giving a poor minimum wage making teenager a tongue lashing over the fact that his French fries are cold! Yet, how many times do we as Christians put our testimony in jeopardy over such silly scenarios? Too often, I am afraid. To make it even worse, we often act in such a manner with the attitude that it is okay, as if their mistake makes it okay for us to behave badly. We sometimes feel that perhaps the other person deserved it! Well, in such times we would do well to step back and check our attitude in light of that of Christ.

We are told multiple times in scripture that we are to be imitators of Jesus Christ. We are instructed above that we are to have the same attitude as Jesus. Paul even goes further to explain that attitude. Jesus was willing to surrender His deserved position in the universe for the wellbeing of others, even to the extent of the cross. It would definitely be a different world if we all had that same attitude! This is especially true of the church. This is one way in which we are called to be different. Our attitude is to be different than that of the rest of the world. When others might let the poor fast-food cashier "have it" for messing up their order, we are to be like Christ. Granted, this is sometimes easier said than done. Nonetheless, we are to have the same attitude as Christ. This doesn't just happen. We must daily seek the help of the Holy Spirit of God in this area. Our natural instinct is to be worldly. However, as new creations, we are indwelled by One stronger than our natural instincts. Look to him for guidance and strength. Don't let something trivial ruin your testimony. Instead, let your response be part of your testimony. Let is speak to the life changing power of faith in Jesus Christ.

The Thin Place: Ask. Answer. Pray.

What are some things that might cause you to react in a testimony damaging way?

Why do such things lead you to react in such a way? Why do they bother you so?

How can you purposefully try to react in a way that is more pleasing to God?

August 14
A Bug Moment

From Above: Psalm 34

Focal Passage: *"Whoever of you loves life and desires to see many good days, keep your tongue from evil and your lips from speaking lies." –Psalm 34:12-13*

Here Below:

In our family, we often have what we refer to as "bug moments". What is a "bug moment"? They often occur while we are in the car, and they also happen regularly late in the evening when the children are fighting sleep. A bug moment is one of those instances in which if our family's conversation was under surveillance by a stranger (if our home was bugged), they would probably think we have lost our mind, due to the silly nature of our conversations. These moments may include singing, strange animal noises made by my four-year-old, some really off the wall questions from our other kids and anything else you might imagine. It is a conversation that would probably mean nothing to an outsider, yet for a family they are fun moments, and they are special moments. Most families enjoy these times that are unique to their families and the personalities that make it up. Thankfully, these moments are usually private and are not under covert surveillance.

However, it would probably be good for us to consider all our moments as bug moments! I wonder how different our speech might be if we considered each word as one that could be overheard by others we had not intended to hear. What if those we deal with regularly in the workplace heard what we said about them when they are not around? What if our own friends and family did the same? Would they hear words of encouragement, or would they hear words of judgment? Would they hear words that give life or words that bring destruction? It is easy for us to speak of how we think things should be when those involved are not listening. Yet, we know that all too often these words have a way of getting back to those of which they are referring. This usually ends in hurt feelings. Besides, even if our home is not bugged, God hears our speech. Whether anyone else is listening or not, we should always refrain from words that tear down as opposed to lifting up. We should instead use the power of speech to build up others and to strengthen the Kingdom of God. Most of the conflicts and controversies that occur in this world begin with words carelessly spoken. How different things might be if we were more watchful with our words. Let's watch our words and consider every moment a "bug moment".

<u>The Thin Place</u>: Ask, Answer, Pray.

Have you ever been hurt by words thoughtlessly spoken? If so, when?

Have you ever caused hurt bywords thoughtlessly spoken?

How important is our speech when it comes to our relationship with others and God?

August 15

Days Like This

<u>From Above</u>: 2 Corinthians 9

Focal Passage: *"And God is able to make all grace abound to you, so that in all things at all times, having all that you need, you will abound in every good work." –2 Corinthians 9:8*

<u>Here Below</u>:

Have you ever had one of those days when everything you do seems to fail? Or a day when it seems everything takes twice as long as it should? Or else you must spend precious time redoing what you have already done? It could be something as simple as a flat tire or that your car won't start. It could also be something as exasperating as a computer crash. Whatever the reason, these types of days can discourage and frustrate to no end. Yet, how we deal with these times can be a testament to our faith.

We all have those days, but we each respond differently. Sometimes we get angry. Sometimes we get depressed. Sometimes we just give up and distance ourselves from the problem. Others of us may take the trials of the day with stride. Yet, the Bible seems to teach us that the best way to approach troublesome days is with grace. In the above passage, we see that God is able to shower us with grace in all times and in all things. This seems to imply that God can cover us with grace even in times when everything we touch seems to fall apart. In those times, we are assured that God will by His grace give us everything we need, for in Him we have all we need. This doesn't mean that everything will always go our way. On the contrary, it is instead a promise that God will be with us when life seems to get the best of us. By His grace we can "abound". This also reminds us of the necessity to include God in all that we do, whether it is a big task or a small one, He is interested is what we do. He cares about our successes and our failures. In either situation, God can be glorified by how we respond. Perhaps those frustrating days can remind us to step back, take a breath and seek the face of God. If we can do that, despite the outcome of the moment, we are not a failure. If our situation leads us closer to God, we are better for the experience.

<u>The Thin Place</u>: Ask, Answer, Pray.

How well do you deal with the frustration of a troublesome day?

Have you failed to let your circumstances, good or bad, lead you to deeper dependence on God?

How can you face these situations differently in the future?

August 16
Undeniable

<u>**From Above**</u>: Psalm 119:129-136; James 1:21-25

Focal Passage: *"The unfolding of your words gives light; it gives understanding to the simple."* –Psalm 119:130

<u>**Here Below**</u>:

You may try to deny it, as many in our day try to do. You may question its validity and authorship. You may even question its importance to modern man. However, none of these arguments against the word of God can be made with irrefutable clinical integrity. This attempted denial of God's truth has been going on for thousands of years and the word of God still perseveres. Nonetheless, let's push these more scientific arguments aside for a moment. There is one piece of evidence that disproves all the skeptical theories that are out there. How do you explain the lives that are changed from the reading of and application of biblical principles?

Too many lives have been positively affected, my own included, to deny the power of the Bible. God uses it to speak to us in ways that are miraculous and life changing. How many times have you opened the word and randomly read a verse, that turned out to be exactly what you needed to hear at that moment? How many times have you found yourself living in those pages written thousands of years ago? It happens to me all the time, as I am sure it does to you as well. That is the living nature of the word of God. It is not just some ancient writing or timeless piece of classical literature. It is the voice of God. I have read Homer's *Iliad*. I have read many of Shakespeare's plays. Yet, not one of these other pieces of literature changed my heart and life, as enjoyable as they might have been to read. Only God's Word can claim to have done that. Only the Bible speaks to me in my hour of need. How can that be explained away by the critics? It can't. So do not fail to recognize the resource you have in your hand. Bound in leather, written in ink on paper, you have the very heart and voice of God. Do not fail to turn to it when you are in need of answers. Its power is undeniable.

The Thin Place: Ask. Answer. Pray.

When is the last time God spoke to you from the pages of His Word?

How often does this happen?

How can you improve your Bible study, devotional and reading habits?

August 17
No Limits

From Above: Romans 2:1-6; I Timothy 1:15-16

Focal Passage: *"But for that very reason I was shown mercy so that in me, the worst of sinners, Christ Jesus might display his unlimited patience as an example for those who would believe on him and receive eternal life." –I Timothy 1:16*

Here Below:

I am not sure about you, but I am thankful that God's patience with his children is limitless! As any parent knows, patience is essential in order to maintain a healthy relationship with our children as they and we both stumble along the journey of life. It is a journey often filled with potholes, that despite our best intentions, we still seem to hit from time to time. In fact, sometimes we seem to go out of our way to hit them. Yet, God is patient with us, always willing to offer the sincere heart forgiveness and grace as we seek it. He does this primarily out of love for us. However, this is not the only reason God shows us patience.

According to Paul in the above verse, another reason is for the education of His children. He may be showing us unlimited patience as an example of how we should be as well. Paul considered himself the worst of the worst. It is hard for us to visualize Paul as the worst of sinners, because we primarily know him as the great apostle to the gentiles, responsible for the majority of our New Testament. Yet, Paul was not always that man. He was Saul, the persecutor, the terrorist. Yet, God forgave him and used him mightily, displaying for the world the unlimited nature of His patience. Put simply, if God could forgive someone guilty of sin as great as Paul's, then He must therefore be willing to forgive you and I as well. Paul's life reflected this. Before God's grace, Paul was a staunch legalist, ready to judge, try, condemn, and even execute those who broke the law. After God's grace, Paul was the man fighting against strict adherence to the law, breaking away from traditions, customs and rules He had followed his entire life. As a result, the word of God was spread beyond Jerusalem, which by the way includes you and me today! You see, Paul understood that part of the purpose of God's patience with our sins is that we may be patient with the sins of others. God's is unlimited. How is yours?

The Thin Place: Ask, Answer, Pray.

How patient are you with the sins of others?

Are there particular sins of others that you have an especially difficult time forgiving?

What if God related to you in your sin as you do with others? Does He?

August 18
More than Enough

From Above: I Kings 19:1-8; 2 Corinthians 12:9-10

Focal Passage: *"The angel of the LORD came back a second time and touched him and said, "Get up and eat, for the journey is too much for you.""*
—I Kings 19:7

<u>Here Below</u>:

We've all been there. We've all been to that place in life where we simply feel that enough is enough. Perhaps, like Elijah, you've been to that place where it seems the whole world is out to get you and there is nothing left to do but cry out to God asking Him to simply take your life. It is a moment in life when we feel that there is nothing ahead but heartache, and we feel as if it would be simpler to just "get it over with". It is a miserable and hopeless feeling. Yet, we do not need to despair. Even some of the greatest heroes of faith had those moments. Numbered along with Elijah in the above passage are numerous others such as Job, David, and Paul, all of whom reached a point in which they felt as if it would be better for life to just end. However, the Christian life is not a life of hopelessness.

This is one example of those times in which we should be thankful God doesn't answer our prayers in the manner we ask. For Elijah, this was not just a moment of self-pity. In essence, the world was actually out to get him. The evil queen Jezebel was seeking him out to execute him. Elijah had been faithful to God and as a result was now at the top of the evil queen's hit list. Hiding in the mountains, he felt as if there was no way he could ever be free of worry again. In this moment of weakness, he cries out to God for the ultimate deliverance. Out of love for His prophet, God provides Elijah with food and nourishment and rest, instead of the death he requested. God understands, as the above passage attests, that sometimes the journey is simply too much for us. It is okay to admit our feelings with God in this manner. He understands and desires to refresh our spirits. It is in those times when we especially need to lean upon the Lord, and it is in those moments that God is able to do His greatest work. When we are at our weakest, He is able to show us His strongest. When we feel we've had enough, God is more than enough.

<u>The Thin Place</u>: Ask, Answer, Pray.

Can you remember a time when you cried out to God as Elijah did in the above passage?

How did God respond to your prayer of desperation?
How can remembering these times help you in the here and now?

August 19
Something from Nothing

From Above: Genesis 1

Focal Passage: "*In the beginning God created the heaven and the earth. And the earth was without form, and void; and darkness was upon the face of the deep. And the Spirit of God moved upon the face of the waters.*" –Genesis 1:1-2 *(KJV)*

Here Below:

Regardless of your view of the beginnings of our universe, it all comes back to one undeniable truth. This truth is irrefutable, whether you ascribe to the Biblical account of creation or perhaps the "Big Bang" theory. Here is that truth. Everything we know to exist came from nothing. If your belief is that the universe is a result of atoms colliding in space and starting a chain reaction that resulted in what we see today, you are still left with the question as to the origin of those atoms. Every theory outside that of the Biblical explanation will lead you eventually to the conclusion that something had to come from nothing. Scientifically speaking, this is impossible. Therefore, the only conclusion we can *honestly* come to is that the substance of the universe was formed miraculously out of the nothingness. Hmmmm....It seems as if I have read that somewhere! The Bible teaches us that God created both the heavens and earth, light and dark and before that, there was a void (Gen. 1:2 KJV). This is more than just a lesson in creationism. This fact has far reaching implications that even reach into the deepest parts of our personal lives.

God has from the very beginning been in the business of making something out of nothing. In fact, was that not the message of Christ as well? He came to heal and mend the broken and despised. He spent most of His time with those that the world would consider as unworthy of a Rabbi's time, as nothing. Yet, those are the ones upon which Jesus seemed to focus His attention. Those people, including such characters as a prostitute and tax collectors (the thieves and thugs of His day) and even a terrorist (the Apostle Paul), would become the great heroes of the faith that we have come to love. In essence, Jesus took their lives and made something beautiful out of nothing. Whatever your lot may be in life today, God wants to make something special out of your life. If you think that you are beyond God's usefulness and that your life amounts to nothing, look up at the night sky or a beautiful sunset and remember that God made all of that out of nothing! If He can do that, He can take your life, as broken as it might seem, and make something beautiful out of it. Let the Creator do the creating and you will see the masterpiece your life can become.

The Thin Place: Ask, Answer, Pray.

Have you ever felt as if your life amounts to very little in the grand scheme of things?

What does the Bible teach about God's attitude toward humanity?

More specifically, what does the cross of Christ teach us about God's attitude toward your life?

August 20
Missing the Bus

From Above: Acts 4:1-4

Focal Passage: *"But many who heard the message believed, and the number of men grew to about five thousand."* –Acts 4:4

Here Below:

One day not too long ago, my seven-year-old daughter missed the afternoon bus at school. It seems as if she was talking to her friends and did not hear the announcement for her bus arrival. I received the call from her teacher requesting I come to school and pick up a very scared little girl. Perhaps her seven-year-old reasoning led her to fear that she might not get home or else she might have just been afraid of how mom and dad might respond. For whatever reason, missing the bus was an unpleasant experience for her. Having been there myself, I can definitely relate. However, one interesting thing about human nature and the God given gift of free will is that we sometimes choose to miss the bus!

We sometimes choose to not get on board. In the above passage, we see men so angered by the preaching of the apostles that they have them arrested. Yet, notice verse 4: "But many who heard the message believed." In other words, there were those who chose to ignore the message of the gospel and those who accepted it. There were those who got on board and those who decided to stay behind. This form of "missing the bus" is an unfortunate fact of life still today. While this reality is not necessarily an encouraging one, it does not really change anything for you and me. How so? Well, only God knows who is going to choose to miss this bus. Our responsibility is simply to invite others to get on board. If we do this and they choose to ignore the message, we have still done our job. A successful witness is not one that wins souls to the Lord. A successful witness is one that simply shares their faith. Understanding that should free us from the discouragement of witnessing to those who refuse to accept the Lord. Besides, the response is not always instant. Our words have a way of speaking years down the road. We may yet see them come to salvation. Nevertheless, this means we have an urgent message to share today. Don't let the bus pass by you or those whom you love! Here is the announcement, "He has arrived!" Share His love today!

The Thin Place: Ask, Answer, Pray.

What implications are there in relation to the free will we have been given?

How important is witnessing in the Christian life? Or, in your life specifically?

Is there someone important to you that has thus far chosen to reject Christ?

August 21
Déjà Who?

From Above: Romans 7

Focal Passage: *"I do not understand what I do. For what I want to do I do not do, but what I hate I do." –Romans 7:15*

Here Below:

Have you ever had one of the *déjà vu* moments? You feel as if you have lived this moment before in the course of your lifetime. It is hard to put your finger on it, but it just feels as if you have lived it already. We've all those rather eerie moments in time. Now think about it from another perspective. Have you ever had one of those moments when you think to yourself, "Haven't I already lived this *mistake* before?" You see in yourself a person that you thought had changed; yet, here you are, reliving the same old sins you thought you had conquered. Likewise, we have all had those moments that cause us to question ourselves and our spiritual condition. "I can't believe I did that again!" or "Who am I really?" are the questions we often struggle with when such instances occur. It can be discouraging. Yet, it does not have to be.

At first glance, you may not feel as if Romans 7 is an encouraging passage. After all, we see Paul dealing with one of these spiritual *déjà vu* moments. He is very honestly acknowledging that he often finds himself doing the things he knows better than to do. In this tongue twisting passage, we see and feel the desperation of Paul and we can relate. Despite his best intentions, he finds himself reliving old sins. Here I go again, doing what I know I shouldn't! The old me is showing his face once again! Well, I find this encouraging, not because of Paul's sin, but because of Paul's struggle. Even Paul struggled with his sin. This reminds me that there is not necessarily anything wrong with me when I struggle with old sins. It is as Paul says, "sin living within me". While salvation frees us from the weight of sin and the penalty of sin, we are however still sinners. I am not a failure in my spiritual life when I stumble. I am however in trouble when the struggle ceases to occur. When we become so accustomed to our "old sins" that we do not despise them, we are in danger of becoming hardened in our hearts. Thankfully, it doesn't end with the struggle. In the last two verses of the chapter, Paul recognizes from where his rescue from sin's cycle derives. It is found in Jesus. Yes, the struggle continues. But we continue with the knowledge that we have the victory in Jesus. Don't let your spiritual *déjà vu* moments tear you down. Instead, acknowledge your sin to God and let the moment press you toward a greater dependence upon Him; in which case you will be stronger and the sins weaker.

The Thin Place: Ask, Answer, Pray.

Do you ever find yourself reliving sins you thought conquered? How does it make you feel?

Do you believe salvation in Christ covers all your sin? Even the ones you fight the most?

Are there any sins that you need to confess today?

August 22
Jesus is for Losers

From Above: Matthew 10:39; John 12:25

Focal Passage: *"Whoever finds his life will lose it, and whoever loses his life for my sake will find it."* – Matthew 10:39

Here Below:

There was a contemporary/alternative Christian song released years ago (album *Squint* 1995) that stirred a bit of controversy upon release, mainly due to its title. It was titled "Jesus is for Losers". The singer, songwriter, and producer Steve Taylor, has a reputation of releasing songs with this type of shock value. Don't misunderstand. His songs were morally, spiritually and scripturally sound. They were also loads of fun. He was and is very gifted at expression of such Biblical truths as the ones expressed in the aforementioned song. There is a verse in it which reads:

I was groping, Groping around for some ladder to fame, I am ashamed...

If I was hoping, Hoping respect would make me some sturdy footstool, I am a fool

Bone weary every climb, Blindsided every time

Just as I am, I am weary and dry

Jesus is for losers, The self made need not apply

In this song, Taylor is only reiterating what Jesus taught many times. He taught that real life in Him only comes when we give up the idea that it can be found anywhere else or in anything else. To truly live, we must lose the world's idea of life. It isn't found in fame or fortune. It is not found in knowledge or abilities. It is not found in relationships. Real life is in Jesus. This teaching is not meant to discourage people from following Christ. On the contrary, it is meant to call genuine disciples. Jesus never sugarcoated what it means to be His disciple. Unfortunately, many of us have. Jesus was letting us know that He and His will has to be first in our lives if we are to become all that He intends for us to be. His will is to supersede our will. There is no room for the self-made man in the Christian life. We are to let Jesus do the making. This is what He means by losing our life. So, if by losing my life I truly find it, I guess being a loser is not all that bad. In fact, I want to be a loser. Are you willing to be a loser today?

The Thin Place: Ask, Answer, Pray.

Does the world view the Christian's dependence upon God as weakness or strength?

How is dependence upon God a sign of strength for the believer?

How does seeking God's will for your life make you stronger?

August 23
Waiting Tables

<u>**From Above**</u>: Acts 6:1-6

Focal Passage: *"So the Twelve gathered all the disciples together and said, "It would not be right for us to neglect the ministry of the word of God in order to wait on tables." – Acts 6:2*

<u>**Here Below**</u>:

The above passage of scripture is often overlooked by the average disciple of Christ; that is, unless we are considering the role of the deacon in the church. After all, in this passage we see the creation of the first deacons. It is definitely appropriate to consider this passage in view of their role and responsibility. In fact, this passage gives us a biblically correct understanding of the office of deacon. However, due to the specific nature of the passage, many of us fail to see the personal implications of the words, unless we are examining deaconship. This passage goes much deeper than just explaining the role of a deacon in the church. It is a reminder to us of the importance of balance in the Christian life.

The twelve disciples were becoming overwhelmed with their responsibilities. The number in the faith was increasing and they were very quickly becoming overworked. In serving the people, they were unable to devote themselves to study and preparation that was necessary, and they were beginning to overlook some due to the overwhelming number. So they delegated. Was there anything wrong with serving at the tables of the widows? Most certainly not! They were doing this out of love and service to the Lord. Yet, they were still human. They were limited as to their ability to serve everyone. This is further evidence that even the best of us can get our lives out of balance. Service is good. Study is good. Mediation is good. In fact, all of these things are necessary to the Christian. Yet, if either of them ever becomes overshadowed by the other, then we are headed for burnout.

This is not just a warning for career ministers or deacons. This need for balance is true for each of us. Oftentimes we pat ourselves on the back for our hard work and service and all the while our personal devotion and study falls by the wayside. It is possible to work so hard for the Lord that we actually neglect Him. We can wait on tables to the neglect of "waiting upon the Lord" (Isaiah 40:31 KJV). Do not forget for whom you are serving. Likewise, do not forget to put what you receive from study and devotion to work. Find the balance and you will find strength.

The Thin Place: Ask, Answer, Pray.

Do you ever find your spiritual life out of balance? If so, when?

Do you have a difficult time saying "no" to opportunities of service? If so, why?

Do you think it is possible to neglect God by overworking yourself for Him? How so?

August 24
Stretching the Truth

From Above: Zechariah 8:16-17; Colossians 3:9-10

Focal Passage: *"These are the things that ye shall do; speak ye every man the truth to his neighbor; execute the judgment of truth and peace in your gates: And let none of you imagine evil in your hearts against his neighbor; and love no false oath: for all these are things that I hate, saith the Lord." –* *Zechariah 8:16-17*

Here Below:

The most dangerous weapon available to the human arsenal is not the nuclear bomb. It is not found in chemical warfare or in terrorism. The most dangerous weapon available is the spoken word. More lives have been wrecked and more fights begun by the simple mishandling of the human language. The tongue can be an instrument that can bring great comfort and encouragement, but it can also be an instrument of great destruction. This is especially true when it comes to two things for which God seems to have a special dislike. In fact, in the above passage he says that he hates them. These two things are gossip and lying. The danger with these two sins is that once they occur there are no take backs. Once a lie has been spoken, even it is later proven to have been a lie, the damage is done, and a person's credibility has been forever tied to that lie. Its consequences are damaging and lasting in nature.

Much of the Bible is dedicated to the sin of lying and gossip. I would guess that there are more verses warning of these sins than any other. Why? Because they are so dangerous! Lies have led to split churches, broken homes and broken lives. God must have dedicated so much of His word to lying and gossip for a reason. It must have been due to our fallen human nature's propensity for this sin. Who among us has never lied? We all have. From the moment we start speaking as infants we start lying. This behavior unchecked can evolve from lying into something equally sinful, gossip. It may start off simple and seemingly harmless, but a lie spoken is never harmless. At the very least, it causes our integrity to be called to question. We can justify this behavior if we want, calling it a little white lie, an exaggeration or stretching the truth; but God calls it sin and according to His own words, He hates it. We must guard against our inclination to misuse our words. Put simply, if it does not uplift or edify others, it is best not said. Don't allow for the "no take back" situation in your life. Watch your words! Most importantly, honor God with your words.

__The Thin Place__: Ask, Answer, Pray.

Has your life ever been upset by the lies of others? If so, how did this make you feel?

Are you ever tempted to lie or gossip? When is this temptation the greatest?

Have you repented and sought God's forgiveness for the lies you have told?

August 25
Jesus Junior

<u>**From Above**</u>: Acts 11:25-26; Romans 8:29

Focal Passage: *"Then Barnabas went to Tarsus to look for Saul, and when he found him, he brought him to Antioch. So for a whole year Barnabas and Saul met with the church and taught great numbers of people. The disciples were called Christians first at Antioch." – Acts 11:25-26*

<u>**Here Below**</u>:

Have you ever noticed God's uncanny ability and predisposition to turn what was meant for evil into something good? We've seen these ironies in many formats. We've all witnessed tragedies transformed into spiritual triumphs. History is filled with such events. These spiritual ironies are further evidence of His omnipotence and unalterable will. In fact, the ultimate irony is that of the cross of Jesus. By His death on the cross, we are given life. While this is obviously the greatest of all ironies, it seems as if God does enjoy surprising us with unexpected outcomes even in some of the more ordinary events of life. We see a perfect example of God's sense of irony in the above story from the early church. In it, God takes a disrespectful nickname and turns it into a title of great esteem.

We see in Acts 11 the first time in which followers of Christ are referred to as Christians. However, the name "Christian" was more than likely meant as a name of ridicule and derision. It more literally meant "Little Christs". Basically, outsiders were referring to the believers in Antioch in this rude manner because they were different. They were behaving like Jesus. It was as if they were calling them "Jesus Junior" in mockery. This name was meant as an insult, but believers would soon be wearing it as a badge of honor. For the believer, there is no greater tribute than to be compared to the likeness of Christ. We only see this title a few times in scripture, and it was used to compliment those to whom it referred. More specifically, it was meant to honor God. What began as an insult is now the designation for the world's greatest faith.

Again, God's dramatic irony won over. Yet, it might have been a different story if those early believers were living is such a way as to dishonor the name they had been given. It was their differences from the rest of the world that won them this title and it was their faithfulness to Christ that enabled God to use it for good. You see, it is when we are the most faithful to God that He is most likely to display His penchant for the unexpected ironies of life. Be a "little Christ" today and tomorrow you can expect the unexpected!

The Thin Place: Ask, Answer, Pray.

Has there ever been a time in your life when God took something bad and used it for good?

Why do you think it is often after the fact that we see God at work in these type situations?

Would you say that your lifestyle would earn you the title "Little Christ"?

August 26
The Man in White

From Above: Matthew 25:35-36; Hebrews 13:1-3

Focal Passage: *"Do not forget to entertain strangers, for by so doing some people have entertained angels without knowing it." –Hebrews 13:2*

Here Below:

He was dressed in all white and standing just outside of the grocery store. His appearance seemed to glow in the hot afternoon sun. His face was gentle, and his deep dark eyes appeared somewhat sad. As the mysterious stranger approached the shoppers, they seemed to be unable to see him. However, this stranger in the glowing white was not an angel. He was a painter. His white attire was the uniform of a professional painter. In his broken English, he explained that he had come to our state on a painting job and had been accidentally left behind by his coworkers. His ride would not be back to get him until the next day, and it had been a while since he had eaten. He was asking for someone to give him some money so that he might buy some food. He was seeking help. Most just dismissed him with the words "not today" or else they ignored him all together. I agreed to buy him some food instead of just giving him cash and together we entered the store. He humbly picked out some sandwich foods and I purchased them for him. Along the way, I spoke with him a little of his faith and shared with him the truth of God's love. I then went back to shopping with my family. As we exited the store, I saw the man sitting on the sidewalk outside the store devouring the sandwiches I had bought him. I have always wondered about this stranger and how his life progressed.

I do not tell this story to boast about my own actions. On the contrary, for every stranger I have stopped to help in this manner, there have been a hundred I have passed by. I just hope that I do not find out one day that by doing so I missed an opportunity to show compassion toward one that God sent to me for help. We pass by many in our daily lives, both strangers and friends, which need just the right act of compassion and care that we can offer. Yet, all too often we fail to stop and offer our help. I am not talking of just giving money or buying food, though that might be the case. An act of compassion might be something as simple as just listening to the broken heart of a friend. Put simply, committing an act of kindness or compassion to anyone is a win-win situation. We win; in that, we may be serving the Lord or one of His angels. They win; in that, they have a need met and see the hands of Jesus at work. Don't miss the opportunities God may be sending your way. Don't just look away. By doing so, you may be looking away from the Lord. Instead, look at every opportunity to show compassion as an opportunity to serve God.

<u>The Thin Place</u>: Ask, Answer, Pray.

Think of a time when you helped someone in need? Why did you do it?

Have you ever failed to help someone that seemed to be in need? Why did you not help them?

Has there ever been a time when a stranger helped you in a time of need?

August 27
Wrong Place at the Wrong Time

<u>**From Above**</u>: I Chronicles 13; Proverbs 3:34

Focal Passage: *"The whole assembly agreed to do this, because it seemed right to all the people."* –I Chronicles 13:4

<u>**Here Below**</u>:

Occasionally, I like to tackle some of the more difficult passages of scripture. The above passage is one such passage. It is difficult; in that, we see our God, whom we know to be a loving and merciful God, strike down poor Uzzah for doing what seems to be a good thing. After all, he was simply trying to keep the Ark of the Covenant from being damaged in a fall. It seems at first glance to be out of character for God to react in the manner in which He did. However, a more intimate look will show that He was not out of character at all. You see, this story is more about David than Uzzah. This is one of those stories which we must read it in its full context.

As you read the whole story, you will notice something is missing. At the end of the previous chapter, David has just been recognized as king in Hebron. As new king, David wishes to bring the Ark along with him to the City of David. In deciding to make this move, David consults *almost* everyone. He consults his military commanders and all the people. He even invites everyone to come along and be a part of this ostentatious parade like display of his new position in the kingdom. However, what is missing in the story is that we never see him actually ask the Lord if it was His will that the ark be moved. We see him say in verse 2 that he wants to do this "if it is the will of God", but we never actually see him ask the Lord. The will of the people and the will of God are not always the same. God's response to Uzzah was perhaps His way of reminding them all exactly who was in charge. Put simply, Uzzah was in the wrong place at the wrong time, an innocent victim, not of God's wrath, but of David's pride. The large company of people and music and celebration was a tribute to King David and his leadership. It would seem as if God did not wish to share the spotlight with King David. David was not making a good start as king. After the Uzzah incident, the parade ended, plans changed and we see a less proud, more humble King David, at least for a little while.

There is a truth here for all of us. When we in our pride get ahead of God's plans in exchange for our own, we are in danger of falling. The scripture is filled with references to the dangers of pride. We must never fail to seek God's will before our own. In doing so, we may miss the greater blessing that God has in store for us. Don't allow yourself to be found in the wrong place at the wrong time as did David and Uzzah. Instead, find yourself in the center of God's will.

The Thin Place: Ask. Answer. Pray.

What lessons can you apply to your life from the above story?

How has God dealt with your pride in the past?

Do you truly seek to know God's will for your life before you make any important decisions?

August 28
Beautiful Feet

From Above: Isaiah 52:1-10

Focal Passage: *"How beautiful on the mountains are the feet of those who bring good news, who proclaim peace, who bring good tidings, who proclaim salvation, who say to Zion, "Your God reigns!""* –Isaiah 52:7

Here Below:

Of all the human body parts, perhaps the most unattractive would have to be our feet. They come in many different shapes, sizes and smells, none of which are very appealing. However, according to the above verse, there is a time when our feet are considered beautiful. Of course, Isaiah is using this figurative language to make a spiritual point. It is not so much the feet of the messenger that are beautiful as it is the message he brings. Often this verse is used in reference to ministers, missionaries, preachers, and teachers of the Bible. This is an appropriate interpretation. However, it is not limited to only those in the ministry. It in essence refers to all who share the good news. It is for all who witness. After all, in one respect, we are all ministers. We are all to have beautiful feet.

Our lives are to proclaim salvation and the Lordship of Jesus Christ. Sure, not all of us are as proficient as others in the oral proclamation of the gospel of Jesus Christ. Nonetheless, we have all been given the Great Commission. We have all been given the responsibility of witnessing and it is my belief that we have all been given the ability. There is more than one way to share good news. We can do it with our words, but we can also do it with our actions and our example. Put simply, there is more than one way to share the salvation of Christ. The key lies in whether or not our life proclaims the importance of the Lord versus the importance of self. If others see the difference Christ has made in your life when they look at you, then you are witnessing to His life changing ability. This does not relieve us of the responsibility of personal verbal evangelism, but it adds to its effectiveness. It is one thing to hear it, it is another to hear it and see it in action. Let the Holy Spirit guide you in your witnessing encounters. Let others see you live the gospel. Let them see your beautiful feet.

The Thin Place: Ask. Answer. Pray.

Do you feel as if you are an effective witness? Why or why not?
Are you comfortable speaking of your faith with others?
Do others see Jesus when they look at you?

August 29
The Dishonesty of Duality

From Above: Matthew 24:38-51; Galatians 2:12

Focal Passage: *"The master of that servant will come on a day when he does not expect him and at an hour he is not aware of. He will cut him to pieces and assign him a place with the hypocrites, where there will be weeping and gnashing of teeth." –Matthew 24:50-51*

<u>Here Below</u>:

In the above parable, we see some very strong words, to say the least. It is a warning against the danger of being caught living a double life. You see, the servant in the story is living a double life; in that, he is one way when he thinks his master is around and another when he thinks he is away and unaware. In his book, *God's Best for My Life*, Lloyd John Ogilvie refers to this behavior as "the dishonesty of duality." He, like Jesus in the above passage, warns us against this approach to life. Often, we are tempted to live one way in one setting or with one group of friends and another way in other settings or with other friends. Even the best of us struggle with this tendency. In fact, even the great Apostle Peter struggled with it. Read Galatians 2. We all have. Yet, the above passage shows us just how seriously Jesus takes hypocritical living. It is probably the number one stumbling block to the cause of Christ in our day. Perhaps this is one reason as to why we do not have a set date for the return of Christ. He wants to find us as we truly are and not how we think He wants to find us. Of course, we cannot fool God with the "dishonesty of duality." We cannot lie to Him. He knows the real you. There is no setting in which I can find myself in which God is not already there. To think I can fool God is truly irrational.

The problem with dual living is that sooner or later the two lives collide. When they collide, we are revealed as the hypocrites that we really are. However, this is a collision that can be avoided. It is simple actually. We must stop living a dual existence! The only person we are fooling is ourselves anyway. Sooner or later our friends will see the truth and we can rest assured God already knows it! So why wait for the inevitable! Instead, live in such a way that an unexpected visit from Jesus would not throw you off. Stop pretending to be something else to please people. Let pleasing God be your number one concern.

The Thin Place: Ask, Answer, Pray.

In what ways have you struggled with the "dishonesty of duality" with self and others?

In what ways have you ever compromised in the past in order to be accepted by others? Why?

What changes can you make that will assure you are not living a dual existence?

August 30
Stones of Remembrance

From Above: Genesis 12:7-8

Focal Passage: *"The LORD appeared to Abram and said, "To your off-spring I will give this land." So he built an altar there to the LORD, who had appeared to him. From there he went on toward the hills east of Bethel and pitched his tent, with Bethel on the west and Ai on the east. There he built an altar to the LORD and called on the name of the LORD." –Genesis 12:7-8*

Here Below:

Sitting prominently on my desk in my office are various stones. One of the stones was taken from the biblical city of Caesarea on the coast of the Mediterranean. It is a piece of stone and coral that composed the ancient Roman aqueduct which still stands in that place (despite the tourists taking little pieces of it home with them). Next to it is a stone that I bought from a merchant on the Sea of Galilee, which has a tiny fish scratched into its surface. Another stone came from the Garden Tomb in Jerusalem and another from the Dead Sea. I also have a stone taken from a stream in North Carolina where my wife and I once spent a romantic weekend in the mountains. I collected these stones and have displayed them in this manner to remind me of my trips and the significance of what happened in those somewhat sacred sites, as well as what happened to me spiritually on my pilgrimage. They are in a sense stones of remembrance.

In the Old Testament, we see many times when the children of God would build altars in particular places. These were not ornate or finely decorated as you might think. They were most likely just a pile of small stones left on the ground with no marker and no plaque. To the average passerby it would just be a pile of rocks. Yet, to the one that placed them there, it would be a place of great significance. When they would come across these stones, they would remember what God had done for them in that place. Oftentimes, God even instructed them to do so. Why? Because it is important to remember what God has done in our past. We need to set up these same types of altars of remembrance in our lives today. Granted, I am not talking about literally piling stones or even collecting them to display on your desk. Yet, figuratively speaking we do need to remind ourselves regularly of how God has spoken and dealt with us in the past. This helps us to see how He might wish to do it again. This might be in the form of a journal or a prominently displayed bible verse. Whatever form it might take, if it helps us to remember, God will honor it. We do not need to live in the past, but we do need to learn from it. Likewise, we especially need to remember the promises of the past, for they still hold true today.

The Thin Place: Ask, Answer, Pray.

What method do you use to help you remember special times from your past?

How has God used those methods to speak to you today?

What can you do differently to help you better remember God at work in your past?

August 31
The Fine Print

From Above: John 16:23-24; I John 5:14-15

Focal Passage: *"This is the confidence we have in approaching God: that if we ask anything according to his will, he hears us. And if we know that he hears us--whatever we ask--we know that we have what we asked of him." –I John 5:14-15*

Here Below:

One of the great things about modern times is that there is nothing we can't get if we want it bad enough. If we are looking for a particular item and we cannot find it in the local stores, all we need to do is to go online and we can find almost anything and usually at a good price. We place our order and within days or even hours it arrives at our door. Unfortunately, many have become too accustomed to getting what they want when they want it. We do not like to wait. Equally unfortunate is the fact that many approach their prayer life in much the same way. There are many promises in scripture that teach us that God is more than willing to answer our prayers. In fact, He is eager to answer them. Many mistake this to mean that God is ready and willing to give us whatever we ask for whenever we ask, whether it is material or spiritual in nature. The problem is that there is some fine print that we must consider in God's agreement to hear and answer the prayers of His children. The fine print can be seen in the above passage of scripture.

"If we ask anything according to His will" it reads. Many fail to grasp the significance of that little clause. That is unfortunate, because it is the difference between seeing your prayer answered and not. When things do not happen as we think they should or as quick, we can get discouraged and may even be tempted to give up on our prayer life. What we fail to easily see is that in reality, God's not answering in the manner we ask may be His way of explaining His will to us. Because He is holy and perfect, He cannot and will not answer our prayers in a way that is going to compromise His nature. This is true no matter how sincere our prayer may be. It is not because He does not love us or want to see us happy. On the contrary, it is because He knows that accomplishing His will in our lives is the one way to truly give us the

peace and contentment we desire. Put simply, He knows what is best for us. Once we can truly wrap our hearts around this truth and accept His will as best, then we notice our prayers begin to change. When His will becomes priority, you will notice that more prayers are answered as you ask. Why? Because you are praying according to His will! His will and your will are now closer to being the same. So don't fret over the fine print. Instead, seek to fulfill it and your prayers will be answered. Don't give up on prayer. Just keep praying until you see the answer He wants to give.

<u>**The Thin Place**</u>: Ask, Answer, Pray.

Have you ever become discouraged over unanswered prayers? If so, when?

Is it possible that it was answered, just not as you had expected?

How well do you understand God's will for your life?

9

September

S eptember 1
Direct Access

<u>**From Above**</u>: Romans 8:26-27; Ephesians 2:17-22

Focal Passage: *"For through him we both have access to the Father by one Spirit." –Ephesians 2:18*

<u>**Here Below**</u>:

Perhaps one of the most frustrating technological inventions of the times would have to be that of the automated voice menu. You know what I am talking about! You pick up the phone and place a call to quickly take care of some minor business detail or to speak with someone in particular and you get that monotone voice directing you to press one for this and press two for that. Oftentimes, after exhausting every option in an effort to get to the place you want, it will take you back to the main menu and you start all over again. Recently, it took me nearly half an hour just to speak with a living and breathing human being, only to have my business handled in about three minutes. It was so maddening. One could very easily damage their Christian witness with such a phone call! If only we could just go directly to the person we need to speak too without having to endure the never-ending menu of monotony.

Thankfully, we do not get an automated menu when trying to reach the Lord. We have direct access to God through the Holy Spirit. Because God the Father and God the Holy Spirit are one in the same, we who are indwelled by the Spirit have a direct extension to the Father. We get to forgo the menu and speak directly to the one to whom we seek. Not only that, but the fact that Christians are indwelled by the Holy Spirit of God, means that when we do seek contact with God through prayer, He already knows why we are calling. In fact, we are told that in those times when we do not really know how to pray, the Holy Spirit prays on our behalf with words beyond human expression. He knows why we are calling even before we call. Because God then knows the greatest need of our hearts, He also knows how best to meet those needs. Isn't it wonderful that God has given us a direct line to His heart? There is no being put on hold and no being taken back to the main menu to an endless loop of meaningless options. We can speak directly with God with full assurance that we have His undivided attention. Never take that privilege for granted.

The Thin Place: Ask, Answer, Pray.

Have you ever felt the need to pray, but just didn't have the words?

Do you feel that God understands the needs of your heart in times of silence such as those?

Do your prayers reflect that you believe that you have the very ear of God the Father?

September 2
Chameleon Christianity

From Above: Galatians 2:11-21; I Corinthians 9:22

Focal Passage: *"Before certain men came from James, he used to eat with the Gentiles. But when they arrived, he began to draw back and separate himself from the Gentiles because he was afraid of those who belonged to the circumcision group." –Galatians 2:12*

Here Below:

Peter. You've just got to love him. Why? Because in Peter we can usually see a little of our selves. Peter is the "everyman" of the Bible. If he isn't swallowing his own foot, he is tripping over his own shadow. He seemed to always get ahead of himself. Of course, this might be due to the fact that Peter was a man of great passion. He was also a man that Jesus thought enough of to name "The Rock". He was Jesus' right-hand man. Peter was a man of great importance to the Kingdom of God; yet, like all of us he made many mistakes. In the above passage we read Paul's account of a conflict that arose between these two great men of faith due to one of those mistakes. In this instance, Peter was accused of hypocrisy. Specifically, Peter was eating with the gentiles and seemed to be doing just fine until his Jewish brethren sent by James arrived in town. Then suddenly it was again inappropriate to eat as the gentiles were eating. You see, Peter was trying to be a "chameleon Christian". He was trying to live one way in front of one group of friends and another way in front of the other. He was trying to blend in with whatever crowd in which found himself. For so doing, he was rebuked by Paul and a rift was formed in their relationship.

That is eventually what happens with chameleon Christianity. Sooner or later, it catches up with us. The real you will eventually be seen and then you are left with the damaging reputation of a hypocrite. Paul believed that we can be honest and sincere while still being "all things to all people" (I Cor. 9:22). Insincerity is perhaps one of the greatest stumbling blocks to the Christian faith. If we live in such a way as to appear insincere, then our witness is weakened almost to the point of becoming useless. We must be true to our word. Chameleon Christianity is a weak Christianity and one that almost never leads others to faith. On the other hand, a life of integrity, even in the face of opposition, speaks volumes to the power of God to change and direct our lives. We must remain true, even when it hurts.

If we do, God will honor our efforts and down the road we will have fewer regrets. Be true to Him today.

The Thin Place: Ask, Answer, Pray.

Have you ever been guilty of being a "chameleon Christian"?

What was the outcome of that lifestyle?

When are you the most tempted to blend in with the crowd?

September 3
Bald is Beautiful

From Above: 2 Kings 2:15-22; Isaiah 52:7

Focal Passage: *"How beautiful on the mountains are the feet of those who bring good news, who proclaim peace, who bring good tidings, who proclaim salvation, who say to Zion, "Your God reigns!""* –Isaiah 52:7

Here Below:

In 2 Kings we see a story that at first glance could very easily be perceived as comical. Here we see the prophet Elisha mocked by an unruly group of youths. "Go on up, you baldhead!" they said. They were making fun of his bald head. As the great prophet Elijah's successor, it was important that he have the respect of the people to whom he was delivering God's message. Elisha curses the ill-mannered youth and 42 of them were mauled by two bears from out of the woods. Wow! What a story! It is one to which we can all relate. Who hasn't at one time wanted to call a curse down upon someone who has mocked us or ridiculed us? Yet, we must be careful to not misinterpret these actions. I do not believe that this curse was done as revenge to these smart mouth kids. It was not a malicious act. Instead, it is a story that teaches us the importance of showing proper respect for the word of God. Keep in mind, the Old Testament prophet was for lack of a better word, God's spokesman. Elisha's words were in essence the words of God. He had already proven himself to have taken Elijah's place and had earned respect from others. By insulting Elisha, these youth were making light of the word of God. This is something that God takes very seriously, as this story of the bald man and the bears attest.

Another one of God's spokesmen, Isaiah later teaches us that the feet of the one who brings the word of God is beautiful. He is not so much declaring the beauty of the messenger as he is describing the welcome that we should show the word of God into our hearts and lives. The word of God, whether spoken or written in the Bible, should be of such value to us as to inspire great respect and honor. For us today no longer living in the age of the prophets, we have the word of God given to us directly in written form. If not careful, we can very easily forget that the Bible we hold in our hands is the actual word of the living God. There is a reason it is usually produced with fine leather backing and gold or silver trim along the pages. It is not just another book. We are holding the very heart and will of God in our hands. We should respect it as such. And the best way to show our respect for the word of God is to apply it to our lives. So, pick up your Bible. Hold it. Feel it in your hands. Now live it. Within those pages is written God's will for your life. Within those pages is the word of God...and it is beautiful.

The Thin Place: Ask, Answer, Pray.

How much time do you spend daily in the word of God?

How important is the Bible to you when it comes to seeking God's will and purpose for your life?

Would you say that you have a healthy respect for the written Word of God?

September 4

I am an "Ignorant Ramus"

From Above: Proverbs 1

Focal Passage: *"The fear of the Lord is the beginning of knowledge: but fools despise wisdom and discipline." –Proverbs 1:7*

<u>Here Below</u>:

I had a professor once with a very unique sense of humor. One day in class, after having been asked a rather foolish question by one of my classmates concerning an upcoming test, this professor answered with a statement that I found hilarious at the time and have since used it myself. He said, "What are you people, a bunch of ignorant ramuses?" No, this is not a typing or spelling error. I have written it just as he said it. He was of course making a play on the word *ignoramus*. It may not be that funny in writing, but coming from him that day it was good stuff. Why? Because it was self-deprecating humor. In his insult, he was actually insulting himself and calling into question his own intelligence. The irony which made it even funnier is that he was perhaps the most intelligent person I have ever known, and one of the wisest. He had both a PhD and a ThD along with several other degrees. He taught both theology and philosophy classes and had written a couple of different books on complicated theological issues. However, whether intended or not, this joke of his does contain a spiritual truth that we would all do well to remember. Intelligence and wisdom are not the same thing.

What made the person in the above story wise was not his degrees, but his love for and devotion to the Lord. In fact, some of the wisest people I have ever met had no formal education. However, I think my esteemed professor did understand what Solomon taught in Proverbs 1. All the intelligence one can obtain in this world is useless if it does not begin with a healthy fear of the Lord. To pursue intelligence and to ignore the Creator of all that exists, is ignorance at its best, or I should say worst. Yet, many do just that. They will deny the evidence of God all around them and do it in the name of intellectual pursuit. It is not until we accept by faith the reality of God at work in our lives and all around us that we can truly understand the machinations of this universe. To do that, we must humble ourselves and know that there is a limit to what we can know on our own. The rest comes by faith and trusting in what resources we do have available, such as the

Bible and prayer. In so doing, we allow wisdom, not intelligence, to guide our lives. The result is better choices and fewer regrets. The pursuit of knowledge is good and a worthy and Biblical goal; but true wisdom begins in humility and trusting in God. So, how smart are you really? As for me, I am content in just being an "ignorant ramus".

The Thin Place: Ask, Answer, Pray.

Think of the wisest person you have ever known personally in your lifetime. Who is it?

What makes this person wise from your perspective?

Would you consider yourself an intelligent person? A wise person? How so?

September 5
Low Battery

From Above: Acts 3:19-20

Focal Passage: *"Repent, then, and turn to God, so that your sins may be wiped out, that times of refreshing may come from the Lord,"* –Acts 3:19

Here Below:

How often do you have spare moments? If your life is anything like mine, they do not come that often. I find my battery quite often in need of recharging. Yet, when they come, we need to be sure to make the most of the moment. We cannot waste the potential restful moments that come our way. Due to the busy nature of our lives, it would do us well to use those spare moments to recharge for what may be ahead. Granted, relaxation is not always a time of rest. For you, relaxation may be engaging in some sport or hobby that requires physical exertion. Though physically strenuous, activities such as biking, hiking or swimming are all relaxing to me. These type activities provide an escape from the everyday pressures of life, and I usually feel more energetic afterwards. I am sure there is a physiological reason for this. However, try as we might, there is still a spiritual aspect to true rest and relaxation. Whether it be by rest or play, in order to truly be recharged, we must first prepare our hearts.

Notice the passage above from the book of Acts. We are told by the Apostle Peter that times of refreshing come from God. That sounds wonderful, doesn't it? To rest in the presence of God is a worthy goal for all to seek. Yet, notice the prerequisite given to us by Peter. In the beginning of the verse, we see that we must first repent and turn to God in order to experience these times of refreshing. While this verse has much to say to the non-believer about salvation and repentance, the underlying principle is for all. In order to find true refreshing, we have to settle things with God. For the believer, this means we need to confess and repent of any sins of which we have yet to let go. You know this is true. There have been many nights when I couldn't sleep until I first dropped to my knees and settled things with God. Well, the good news is that God desires to give us rest. He wants us to be fully charged and ready to go. Will you be ready for the next spare moment that comes your way, or will it be wasted due to an unprepared heart? Don't let it slip away! Settle things with the Lord right now!

The Thin Place: Ask, Answer, Pray.

Would you say that moments of refreshing come as often as you would like in your life?

When was the last time you experienced a time of refreshing from the Lord?

What can you do differently in order to find more rest and relaxation?

September 6
The Temper Trap

From Above: Proverbs 22:24-25; 29:11; Galatians 5:22-26

Focal Passage: *"Do not make friends with a hot-tempered man, do not associate with one easily angered, or you may learn his ways and get yourself ensnared." –Proverbs 22:24-25*

<u>Here Below</u>:

Have you ever been trapped by your own words? Well, according to the wisest man that ever lived, it is a possibility. Notice Solomon's above proverb. It really addresses two issues. First, it has to do with wisely choosing our associations. It teaches that we shouldn't be around those that are hot tempered. But secondly and most importantly, it teaches us the danger of having a hot temper ourselves. After learning the ways of the hot-tempered man, we may get ourselves "ensnared" with our own actions and words. The hot temper is a trap. The problem with dealing with a situation with a hot temper is that with most things in life, the situation will soon pass. Yet, the words we have spoken in anger in that moment will last indefinitely.

There are those that seem to feel that passion over an issue makes one right and they use that passion to justify their anger and expression of anger. Some even boast about their hot temper as if it something of which to be proud. That is most definitely not the case. There are those that feel passionate about many things that are against the will of God. The same is true of a passionate anger. Just because we are angered does not guarantee that we are in the right. There is a righteous anger, but it is never expressed with a hot temper. A righteous anger is expressed after careful thought and consideration, not because our emotions ran away from us. Once we have allowed our temper to run wild, the words we have spoken cannot be taken back. The unfortunate part is that we often say things in those emotionally charged moments that we do not really mean. Yet, once spoken, we are forced to deal with the consequences; thus, we are trapped by our own misspoken words. All of this can be avoided by simply controlling our temper. Sometimes this may mean simply walking away. It may also mean conceding the last word to someone else. Personally, I would rather give someone else the last word than to get in the last word only to later regret ever saying it at all. Besides, is it possible to ever truly win an argument with a hot temper? All we are doing is damaging our witness and putting relationships at risk. Instead, pray for self-control. Self-control is the exact opposite of a hot temper and it is a fruit of the Holy Spirit. What does that say about the source of a hot temper?! You see, this is serious business. So don't let your temper trap you and don't let your emotions control the moment. Let the Holy Spirit steady you in those moments and you will avoid the temper trap.

The Thin Place: Ask, Answer, Pray.

Have you ever spoken words in the heat of the moment that you later regretted?

Have you ever had relationships damaged due to words misspoken in anger?

Do you feel that you have a hot temper? If so, how can it be changed?

September 7
10 Things to Do Before I Die

From Above: Romans 8:1-14

Focal Passage: *"Therefore, brothers, we have an obligation--but it is not to the sinful nature, to live according to it." –Romans 8:12*

Here Below:

I recently saw an article that was boasting 10 places that we must see before we die. I admit, with the exception of maybe one or two, I could care less about ever seeing any of them. Yet, to some this article must have had some appeal. After all, most of us have in our hearts a list of those things we would like to see or do before we die. Unfortunately, sometimes the things we hope to do are not always in keeping with God's desire for our lives. I have even had it said to me in the ministry concerning one's spiritual life, "Well preacher, there are a few more things I want to experience first and then I'll get things right with the Lord..." First of all, we may never have that chance to "get things right". Life is too uncertain and short. Second, how does one know that they will ever reach that point of desiring to "get things right"? Chances are that our list will only grow the older we get. Sadly, the truth is that it is not always the lost that have this attitude. Even those whom have trusted in the Lord sometimes hold on to things that they hope to experience in life, good and bad. Somehow, they have bought into the modern and humanistic idea that life is fuller having experienced more, even the things that we know are bad for us.

We even see this in the pulpit sometimes, don't we? We hear of sordid histories in the form of a testimony all the time. While I believe in these type of testimonies showing how the Lord has rescued one from their sin, there oftentimes seems to be an unjust amount of time spent on the sin. I've even had one Christian say to me that "I was saved as a child, so I don't have a testimony." What? Nothing is further from the truth. To come to the Lord early in life and stay faithful is a testimony of tremendous worth. Again, there is nothing wrong with a genuine testimony boasting of God's deliverance power, but it should not boast of sinfulness. Of that we should be ashamed. According to the above scripture, we have an obligation (or a debt as it says in KJV) to live according to the Spirit. Put simply, we do not owe our sinful nature anything, not even an explanation; but we do have an obligation to live according to the leading of the Holy Spirit. When we come to the Lord and are indwelled by His Holy Spirit, our eternal "to do list" should be filled with His desires, not our own. Sin should repulse us as our wants are exchanged for His. Surrendering your will for His is not loss. It is a gain that surpasses all others.

The Thin Place: Ask, Answer, Pray.

What are some things you would like to experience before you die?

Are all of these things in accordance with the will of God? Are any of them sinful in nature?

How do you think God feels concerning your to do list?

September 8
Closet Christianity

From Above: I Corinthians 9:14-19; I Peter 3:15

Focal Passage: *"Yet when I preach the gospel, I cannot boast, for I am compelled to preach. Woe to me if I do not preach the gospel!"* –I Corinthians 9: 16

Here Below:

Our faith is a very personal matter. Yet, we cannot confuse the personal nature of faith to mean that it is a private matter. It is very much a public matter; in that, we are to be ready to share with anyone who asks of the difference in our lives that comes as a result of knowing Jesus. This implies two things. First, it implies that our lives are different from others that are living without Christ. Second, it implies that we should not be ashamed of that fact knowing Jesus made that difference. It is after all, good news.

The Apostle Paul felt compelled to preach the gospel. In other words, he felt as if he had too. "Woe to me if I do not..." he exclaimed. Now, not all of us are called to preach and none of us are called to be Paul. Yet, our faith is not meant to be kept to ourselves. There is no such thing as closet Christianity. I cannot help but question the spiritual condition of those that would say that their faith is their own business. If our faith is genuine, it should be our desire to share it with everyone that matters to us. Sitting on this news without sharing it with even those we know personally makes one wonder if you really get what faith is all about. Again, this doesn't necessarily mean preaching to anyone. There is more than one way to share good news with someone. In fact, real faith should be evident and therefore an easy topic of discussion with those we love. Too often we allow fear of rejection or fear of mistakes to silence us concerning matters of faith. Fear of failure is understandable, though misguided. The only way to fail at witnessing is to not witness at all. We are compelled to share, not to get results. That is the job of the Holy Spirit. By our silence, we are fulfilling our fear of failure. The fear of making a mistake is also understandable, yet misguided. We do not have to be able to understand it completely and to explain it all theologically. All we need to do is explain what knowing God has done for us. And guess what, you alone are an expert on that. Besides, if the person you are sharing with is lost, how much more damage can you do to them by making a mistake than they are already facing without the Lord? Sharing your faith is a win-win situation no matter how you look at it. The only way to lose is to keep it to yourself. Woe to you if you keep it to yourself! Share His love today! It is easier than you might think!

The Thin Place: Ask, Answer, Pray.

How often do you speak of your faith with others?

Do you find it difficult to share your faith with others? Why or why not?

How often do you pray for opportunities to share your faith with those that matter most to you?

September 9
Spiritual Spam Filter

From Above: I John 4:1-6

Focal Passage: *"Dear friends, do not believe every spirit, but test the spirits to see whether they are from God, because many false prophets have gone out into the world." –I John 4:1*

Here Below:

At least once a week I receive one of those spam emails, usually from Africa, which states that someone I do not know has left me millions of dollars and all that is needed to receive a direct deposit of said funds is for me to release my bank account information. Sounds wonderful, doesn't

it? Of course, anyone should be able to see it for what it really is. It is a scam. What they are wanting is my account information to make a withdrawal, not a deposit. Yet, as transparent as this scam is, there is a reason why they send out thousands of these emails every day. Sooner or later, someone is going to believe it and send them their bank information. Someone in desperate need of financial help is going to fall for this lie and fall victim to further financial woes.

Well, the same is true of those who proclaim to have all the answers to our spiritual problems as well. We must be wary of those who claim to have found a new truth. There are those in our day, as well as in the Apostle John's day, who distort God's truth and proclaim it in a way that may sound good; yet, in the end it is still a distortion and a scam. We are warned against these false teachers all throughout the Bible. They will often mix in just enough truth as to sound convincing. Likewise, their teaching may even be positive in nature. In our day, they will often use affirmative words like tolerance and acceptance. In fact, it may even be that what they are teaching is true, but the problem is that they are simply not teaching the whole truth. While it may seem good, their cloaked motives however are anything but good. It is usually for personal gain of some kind. This truth then remains. We must beware, for it is possible for what seems to be good to be a manipulation of God's truth. This is why we must pray for discernment. We must pray that God will help us to see the lies for what they are and not be fooled by smooth talking trickery. The best way to see a lie as a lie, is to be familiar with the truth of God's word.

John also gives us a test. It is Jesus. If Jesus Christ is not acknowledged for whom He is, then it is not from God. Period. So, we do not have to fall victim to spiritual scams. We can trust in Jesus and His Holy Spirit to aid us. The bottom line is that we do not need a new truth. We need to trust in the Truth that has been there all along. Trust in the Way, Truth and the Life today.

The Thin Place: Ask, Answer, Pray.

Have you ever fallen victim to spiritual manipulation? If so, when?

What is the result of the false teachings that are out there today?

How can you strengthen yourself against the possibility of a spiritual scam?

September 10
They're Playing Our Song...

<u>**From Above**</u>: Psalm 63

Focal Passage: *"Because your love is better than life, my lips will glorify you. I will praise you as long as I live, and in your name I will lift up my hands." –Psalm 63:3-4*

<u>**Here Below**</u>:

Most couples have that special song that is considered "our song". Maybe it was first heard at a special moment early on in their relationship and then took on special meaning for them. To others this song may hold little meaning and may even seem silly. It doesn't necessarily have to fit some romantic mold to be a special song. It can be slow, fast, soft, hard and even goofy. Why? Because "our song" is a very personal and intimate possession. It doesn't have to speak to anyone else. It is uniquely ours. When we hear it playing, it brings to mind special thoughts of love and remembrance. Songs have a very distinct ability to refresh our memories in this way. This is not by accident. God created us in this manner. We are created in His image and His word seems to suggest that God loves music. In fact, the longest book in the Bible is basically a collection of love songs to the Lord.

In the book of Psalms, we have countless expressions of love, affection, adoration and praise for God. Within its pages, we find songs fitting for almost every situation that we encounter in life in which God can be seen and exalted. In other words, for every situation there is a love song to God that is fitting. Yet, appropriate as it is to claim these songs as our own and proclaim them in our personal and corporate worship, I wonder how often we fail to truly write our own songs? Don't get me wrong! I am not speaking of adding to or taking away from scripture and I do not even necessarily mean writing a song in the literal sense. I do however wish to imply that we should be taking the time to create our own expressions of praise and adoration to God, if only in our own hearts and prayers. Put simply, just as "our song" is an immensely personal thing, so should our worship of God be as well. Like that special song, our expressions of love to God should be of such a personal nature that they may not always have meaning to others. That is the type of intimate relationship God desires. Just as each of our lives and needs are unique, so should our worship be unique and special. God longs for these type of personal and sincere expressions; and guess what, He deserves them! There is nothing wrong with singing along to someone else's love song, but every now and then we should be singing our own heartfelt words. In fact, it should be daily. Just as His presence with us is continuous, so should be the praises of our lips. Let your heart sing of your love for God today. He longs to hear your song.

The Thin Place: Ask, Answer, Pray.

How often do you simply and truly praise God in your personal devotion times?

Why do you think we often fail to offer praise when we pray?

How can you specifically and intentionally set aside time for praise and adoration?

September 11
The Lord of 9/11

From Above: Psalm 27; John 15:13

Focal Passage: *"The LORD is my light and my salvation-- whom shall I fear? The LORD is the stronghold of my life-- of whom shall I be afraid? When evil men advance against me to devour my flesh, when my enemies and my foes attack me, they will stumble and fall." –Psalm 27:1*

Here Below:

It began as a day like any other. I was going about my normal routine on this day in 2001 when suddenly the world as we all knew it changed forever. Perhaps you can remember exactly what you were doing when you first heard the news that two airplanes had been flown into the World Trade Center in New York City and that one had crashed into the Pentagon in Washington. Those terrible live images coming from those scenes that were being fed to our televisions would be forever burned into our memories. For the moment, it seemed as if fear would be victorious. Yet, fear's victory was short lived. For even before the dust had settled, we began to hear stories of great heroes, of firemen, policemen, airline passengers and others that had stepped forward at the risk of their own lives to save others. On this day, when terror mistakenly thought it had won, one of the underlying principles of our faith was illustrated in a way that cannot be denied. The principle that shined forth that day is as follows: "*Greater love hath no man than this, that a man lay down his life for his friends.*" (John 15:13 KJV).

Even in the most desperate of times, we can see the hand of God at work if we truly look. As a result of our Christian nation being attacked, churches all across our nation were filled as they haven't been filled for years. People were looking to God for answers, some for the first time; which is exactly where they should have looked. It is when we trust in Him that we have victory over fear. In Psalm 27, we see David explaining this in a song. In verse 13, after singing of his enemies failed attempts to get to him, David acknowledges that he would have fainted (KJV) had it not been for his belief in God's goodness. He knew that God would not let evil triumph. This doesn't mean that evil doesn't sometimes get its way, as 9/11 proves. It simply means that God's grip is stronger than fear and terror and God's love is more powerful than any earthly force. Evil may have temporary influence, but God's touch is lasting and immovable. So, when you find yourself afraid of what may be ahead, as we all do occasionally, trust in the One that specializes in turning fear into faith and tragedy into triumph. Let Him do the same in your life today. God was there in 2001. He was strengthening heroes and comforting the wounded and scared. I believe He cried with us that day and I believe He has not forgotten the sacrifices; and neither should we. Remember that day and remember the Lord of 9/11.

The Thin Place: Ask, Answer, Pray.

Do you remember what you were doing when you first heard the news of 9/11/01?

How did your life change as a result of that day?

How do you deal with the uncertainty of life? Do you find it easy to trust in God?

September 12
A God's Eye View

From Above: Proverbs 30:1-5; Deuteronomy 31:6

Focal Passage: *"Who has gone up to heaven and come down? Who has gathered up the wind in the hollow of his hands? Who has wrapped up the waters in his cloak? Who has established all the ends of the earth? What is his name, and the name of his son? Tell me if you know!"* –Proverbs 30:4

Here Below:

The wise writer of Proverbs 30:1-5 recognized two life changing facts. First, God is all knowing. Second, he was not God. These two realities are of great value; in that, one of the greatest obstacles we face in this life is our inability to see things from God's perspective. If only we could, our tribulations would seem smaller and less signif-icant. Nonetheless, being human we cannot fully see the struggles as God sees them. This is where faith steps in. While I cannot see my trial from God's point of view, I can nevertheless stand confident in God's ability to see it. Not only that, but I can rest in His promises that tell me that He will never leave or forsake me (Deut. 31:6).

Unfortunately, when we are up to our necks in the water, we tend to forget who holds the water in place. This shortsightedness that we often exhibit when we are in trouble often leads us to make rash de-cisions based upon our emotions and our own limited knowledge. As a result, our problems often increase. It is when we wait and trust in God that we find the most relief and greatest comfort. This explains the repetition of such commands as to wait patiently throughout scripture. In essence, God is saying to us "If only you could see what I see..." If we could see them from His perspective, then maybe we would see that our problems aren't nearly as big as they seem from ours. Trust in the One who has perfect vision and the proper perspective.

The Thin Place: Ask, Answer, Pray.

Have you ever had a problem that turned out to be much less than it seemed at the time?

Do you think God understood that all along?

What does this say to us about worry and fear in the face of life's problems?

September 13
Panic Attack!

From Above: Exodus 14; Psalm 46:10

Focal Passage: *"The LORD will fight for you; you need only to be still.""* *–Exodus 14:14*

Here Below:

Do you ever find yourself in what I refer to as "panic mode"? Panic mode occurs when we find ourselves against a wall which seems insurmountable. It could be something as severe as an enemy attack or something as seemingly benign as an overwhelming to do list. These hair pulling moments occur for all of us from time to time. In those moments it seems as if nothing can possibly help us and we panic, only making the situation worse. When we allow ourselves to slip into panic mode, we often compound the problem by making poor choices based upon our feelings of the moment, which are usually exaggerated. In panic mode, wise decisions are rarely made.

We see a perfect example of this in the above account from Exodus. Here we see the Israelites just following their release from captivity. Pharaoh, regretting his decision to let them go, comes after them and they find themselves trapped between his massive army and the sea. They then slip into panic mode and suddenly they are criticizing Moses, their deliverer. Why couldn't you have just left us in Egypt? You see, they were panicking and suddenly slavery was preferable to freedom. After all they had already witnessed, they were ready to go back! I love the response given to them by the Lord. In verse 14, the Lord tells them to just be still. In other words, God was telling them to stop and count to ten before they did something rash that they would later regret. He reminded them that the fight was His. They were soon delivered once again, and Pharaoh was taken care of once and for all.

The same principle applies to each of us. When we find ourselves between an army and an ocean, instead of panicking, we need to just be still and let God work. Panic and worry only distorts the reality of the situation and leads to further unnecessary stress. The reality is that God is in control and God never has a panic attack. Sometimes we just need to walk away or simply sit still and let Him respond. Don't let panic mode moments determine the outcome of your life situations. Instead, stop where you are and let God do his thing, for lack of a better expression. Otherwise, you may miss out on having a front row seat to God's amazing work in your life. Don't panic your way out of a miracle! Just sit still and wait for God.

<u>The Thin Place</u>: Ask, Answer, Pray.

Have you ever panicked in the face of an overwhelming situation? If so, what was the outcome?

What is the usual outcome of panicking over life's overwhelming moments?

How has waiting for the Lord changed the outcome of these type situations in your life?

September 14
Mirror, Mirror...

<u>**From Above**</u>: Matthew 7:1-5

Focal Passage: *"Do not judge, or you too will be judged. For in the same way you judge others, you will be judged, and with the measure you use, it will be measured to you."* –Matthew 7:1-2

<u>**Here Below**</u>:

One sure sign of spiritual immaturity in an individual is an eagerness to point out the sins and shortcoming of others. Granted, there is a time when sin must recognized and confronted. We cannot ignore sin. Yet, we must also be very careful when pointing out the sins of others that we do not do it for the wrong reasons. It is to be done in love and for the welfare of the individual in question. Yet all too often it is not done for their benefit, but our own. Perhaps acknowledging the mistakes of others makes us feel better about our own. If we do find ourselves enjoying these type confrontations a little too much, then we need to examine our own hearts; in that, we are probably not where we ought to be spiritually. Our own hearts should be hurting with the individual, not feeling smug over their condition. After all, we are all under the same judgment.

Jesus warns us against judging others in the above passage. Now this passage is often taken out of context and many people misquote it by using only the first verse. We cannot overlook verse 2. It reminds us that we are going to be judged by the same standards by which we judge others. There is a fine difference between judging someone and confronting sin. Judgment is passing sentence on someone for their actions. Put simply, to shun someone or to treat someone in a different way due to their sin is judgment. The problem with this is the standard by which we use. Who determines what sin is worthy of judgment? Well, scripture seems to teach that any sin separates us from God. In other words, we all stand in need of judgment. This is why mercy and compassion are preferable to judgment. Jesus teaches us here that we had better take a long hard look at ourselves in our spiritual mirror before we judge someone else, to assure that we ourselves are not just as guilty. Unfortunately, our standards for others are often stricter than that which we place upon ourselves. What if God treated us when we stumble as we often treat others when they slip and fall? This is why we are not to compare ourselves to others. We are simply to love them. Only God is worthy to judge us for our sin. And guess what, He instead chose to give us grace. Let God's grace spill over into how you view others.

The Thin Place: Ask, Answer, Pray.

Do you feel that you are sometimes too critical of the mistakes of others? If so, how?

What causes us to be judgmental from time to time in our relationships with others?

What are some ways in which you can show more understanding with others when they stumble?

September 15
Purposeful Passion

From Above: I Kings 15:1-5

Focal Passage: *"For David had done what was right in the eyes of the LORD and had not failed to keep any of the LORD's commands all the days of his life--except in the case of Uriah the Hittite." –I Kings 15:5*

Here Below:

The exception clause at the end of the above passage sheds much light onto the life of one of the greatest heroes of faith the world has ever known, King David. Here we are looking back on the life of David posthumously and we see that he was truly a man that loved and served God faithfully. Yet, we also see that David was far from perfect. Of course, the story of Uriah was the story of Bathsheba. It was a story of adultery, treachery, and murder. It is a story that could compete with even the best movie dramas of our day. But even with this dark cloud in David's past, we still consider him "a man after God's own heart". We see this evidenced in the historical accounts of the rest of his life and in David's psalm writing. There is no questioning that David was passionate for the Lord. We see him dancing, singing and accomplishing great things all in the name of the Lord. Because of his repentant spirit and his overwhelming passion for the Lord, we know him as a hero of the faith, in spite of his many faults. Can the same be said of us? How passionate are you for the things of the Lord? Do you really long for the presence of God in your life? Do you really long to see His will accomplished? Do you really long to see and hear God daily? I believe David did and that is what set him apart.

We are quick to get passionate about other things aren't' we? We scream and yell for our favorite team. But it is as if we are often sitting on our hands in worship. This is so backwards from what it ought to be. Our passion for the Lord should be a driving force in our life, not a cause for shame. Yes, sometimes our passion for God is misconstrued by others, usually by those with no passion of their own. But in the end, God's perspective on our lives should be our primary concern, not that of others. When God looks at me, I want Him to see a passionate person. Think about it. Have you ever read of a great hero of the faith, ancient or modern, that was afraid to express themselves concerning their love for God? No. It is those that are passionate that God likes to use. This doesn't just apply to the world changing David's that exist. Passion may be all that is needed to change something smaller, maybe a relationship, family or a church. Like David, we don't have to be perfect for this to happen, just passionate.

<u>**The Thin Place**</u>: Ask, Answer, Pray.

Would you consider yourself a passionate person? Why or why not?

What things are the most passionate about in your life?

How can you become more passionate for the things of the Lord?

September 16
A Hoarding Heart

From Above: Luke 12:13-31

Focal Passage: *"Then he said to them, "Watch out! Be on your guard against all kinds of greed; a man's life does not consist in the abundance of his possessions.""* *–Luke 12:15*

Here Below:

I recently saw a television show that showcased different individuals suffering from what was referred to as the psychological disorder of hoarding. In each instance, the individual with the problem was being confronted by a family member or loved one along with a psychologist with a plan for recovery. The hoarders on this show had collected so many things over the years that there was barely room to even walk within their homes. Most were in danger of losing their homes for safety violations. One man had nowhere to sleep due to the accumulation of what most would consider junk. Another woman had spent her entire retirement, nearly $300,000 on stuff to fill her home and storage buildings. She had stacks of furniture, lamps, and knick-knacks, yet nowhere to eat or sleep. I am not a psychologist, nor do I wish to make light of their problem. The disorder diagnosis is legitimate in these cases. Yet, I can't help but notice that in each case the individual seemed to be looking for something missing in their lives and were filling their lives with things in hopes of finding the missing piece. Most of them had experienced some form of loss or crisis in their life and had responded with this behavior. They had a full house, but still had an empty heart. That is the problem with materialism. It leaves us wanting more.

While these hoarders are examples of extreme materialism, we can easily see how it might happen. In fact, if we are honest, most of us own way more materially than we actually need. We surround ourselves with things we like and want sometimes at the cost of what we really need. We place our confidence in things such as our wealth and property with the thought that increasing our belongings must therefore increase our security and happiness. Well, this is not true. It is a lie that has left many with enormous earthly assets and very few spiritual ones. The material life is a self-destructive way of life. We spend everything that is important in order to accumulate that which we cannot keep. We spend our time, our energy and even our families for the sake of stuff. Jesus warned us of this. He instead encourages us to spend our life on things that matter, things that last. To find real happiness, we must become content with less of this world and more of the next. He has given us the keys to His kingdom. That should be more than enough to satisfy. To experience the most of kingdom life, we must give up this one.

The Thin Place: Ask, Answer, Pray.

Would you say that your materialistic attitude is spiritually healthy or unhealthy?

Would you rather have more stuff or more of the Lord in your life?

Does your life truly reflect that want?

September 17
Clean

From Above: Matthew 27:1-26

Focal Passage: *"When Pilate saw that he was getting nowhere, but that instead an uproar was starting, he took water and washed his hands in front of the crowd. "I am innocent of this man's blood," he said. "It is your responsibility!""* –Matthew 27:24

Here Below:

All the scrubbing in the world would not clean his hands. Gallons of hand sanitizer would not remove the guilt of Jesus' blood upon his hands. In one very real sense, Pilate was responsible. He had the earthly authority to release Jesus. He knew that He had been wrongfully accused. Yet, he chose to do the politically expedient thing and give the people what they wanted, right or wrong. However, there are three things we must remember about this part of the story.

First, we must remember that Pilate wasn't really the one calling the shots. While he had the authority to release or keep Jesus, the real power belonged to someone else. Jesus allowed this whole scenario to take place and it was His choice to allow Pilate to hand Him over to be flogged and crucified. He could have stopped it, but didn't.

Second, we are just as guilty as we often accuse Pilate of being that day. It was for my sin that Jesus was allowing this terrible tragedy to be enacted. While I may not have played the role that Pilate played, I still had a part. It was my beating Jesus was about to take. It was my stripes He was about to wear.

This brings us to the third point of this story. If Pilate could not wash his guilt away on his own, can we? No. We are no different than Pilate. We cannot truly wash our guilt away. However, we know who can! We can be clean! As far as we know, Pilate never trusted in Jesus as his Savior. We can. And once we do that, we do not have to go through life wringing our hands in hopes of finding them clean. They are clean. They have been washed by the shed blood of Jesus Christ. Don't buy the lie of shame and guilt! As a believer, that has been taken care of. Jesus allowed the cross so that we might be free from the guilt and shame of our mistakes. He knew this when He arrived in that Bethlehem stable and later when He rode into Jerusalem on Palm Sunday. Our freedom from guilt and shame was all part of His plan. So put away the spiritual hand sanitizer and trust in the reality of the cross! You can live your life with clean hands!

The Thin Place: Ask. Answer. Pray.

Do you ever struggle with feelings of guilt and shame over past sins?

Have you truly repented of those sins?

Is there any reason to think that those sins aren't covered by the sacrifice of Jesus on the cross?

September 18
You Didn't Hear This From Me...

<u>**From Above**</u>: Proverbs 11:9,13; 17:9; 18:8; 20:19
Focal Passage: *"He who covers over an offense promotes love, but whoever repeats the matter separates close friends." –Proverbs 17:9*
<u>**Here Below**</u>:

Has anyone ever approached you with "You didn't hear this from me, but...."? If so, then my advice to you is to get away from that person! What they are really saying to you is "I am not supposed to tell you this, but I am going to anyway...and I want you to participate in my sin by covering for me and lying about where you heard it!" In other words, they are betraying a confidence and involving you in the matter. Furthermore, if they are doing this with news about someone else, then they will probably betray your confidence as well! In fact, let's not sugar coat it! It is gossip we are talking about here. It is gossip and it only causes pain and damages relationships. It is one of the most dangerous sins; in that, most of us do not give it much thought, even though it has the power to ruin lives. Never underestimate the destructive power of gossip.

The book of Proverbs testifies to this destructive power, as it is literally filled with warnings about the danger of gossip and God's dislike of it. The above verse is one such example. My own translation of this verse says that just because we know something "juicy" about someone, even if we know it to be true, does not give us the right to repeat it! To "cover over an offense" is the opposite of gossiping. I don't believe the writer of this verse is suggesting we lie. On the contrary, Proverbs is filled with warnings against that sin as well. Instead, it seems to simply imply that we don't always have to tell everything we know, especially if someone may be hurt. The ugly truth about gossip is that it really serves no purpose other than giving us a moment of perverse pleasure in the telling of it. As a result, people are always hurt. To withhold this kind of hurtful information is to promote love and to help keep relationships together. Again, for righteousness's sake there is a time to talk, and it is always time to tell the truth. However, gossip is talking out of turn and is never for the right reasons. It is selfish and destructive. Instead, when we hear something "juicy" we should be in prayer for those involved. Think of what a difference it might make in the lives of others if we prayed for them as much as we talk about them! Put simply, if you must talk about someone, then talk about them to the Lord! Pray for them instead!

The Thin Place: Ask. Answer. Pray.

Have you ever been the victim of vicious gossip? Have you ever been the one gossiping?

How did this gossip affect your relationships?

What are some practical steps you can take to assure that nothing like this ever happens again?

September 19
I'd Never Do That!

From Above: Luke 22:28-34

Focal Passage: *"But he replied, "Lord, I am ready to go with you to prison and to death." -Luke 22:33*

Here Below:

Jesus was preparing to go to the cross. The Last Supper had just been administered. Jesus had just warned the disciples of His betrayal and Peter "The Rock" had once again been warned of his own impending betrayal. In the above verse we see his response. We see in Peter the same response that we often have when confronted with the possibility of our own stumbling. Not me! I would never do that! Others may fall, but not me! I would go to prison or even death for you! We often say this when we see others stumble as well. We think to ourselves that we would never do what we have seen others do! Well, that is how Peter thought and we know how that turned out. If the one whom Jesus nicknamed "The Rock" could do this, then are we any less susceptible? Pride would have us to believe we are incapable of certain sins. The reality though is much different. If we ever think we are at a place where we cannot fall, then we are in danger of doing just that. Perhaps it was Peter's pride that led to his betrayal.

Thankfully though, the story did not end with Peter's failure. Even as Jesus warned him, He also prayed for him and believed that Peter would still be the rock that the others would look to in the future. He was right. In fact, even though Peter failed, he did do that which he told Jesus. He did eventually go to prison and death for Him. The problem was never Peter's heart and love for Jesus. The problem was his pride. It took this tough lesson to turn Peter into the man Jesus knew he could be. It took Peter understanding his own weakness for God to really work in his life. The same is true of each of us. When we realize our own weaknesses, we can more easily discover God's strength. It is then that we see the amazing power of God at work in our lives. Don't ever say "Not me!" Instead, look to God for strength.

The Thin Place: Ask. Answer. Pray.

Have you ever failed to live up to your own standards? How so?

How did God restore you in this situation?

What did you learn from the whole experience?

September 20

A Face Worth Loving

From Above: Psalm 27

Focal Passage: *"Though my father and mother forsake me, the LORD will receive me." –Psalm 27:10*

Here Below:

There is an old expression, an insult rather, that describes a person as having "a face only a mother could love". It is of course referring to someone as being less than attractive and the unconditional love that naturally comes from their mother, the one person we can trust to love us no matter what. However, there is one flaw in that insult. There are times when rejection comes from even those with whom we are the closest for any number of reasons. Unconditional love is not always the norm in life and rejection does take place.

Fear of rejection is one of the most prominent stumbling blocks out there. It can cause us to avoid new relationships and subsequently miss out on new blessings. To the other extreme, it can lead us to compromise on our values. We may do something out of character or act in a particular odd manner, or simply keep our real selves hidden, in order to hopefully avoid rejection by those whose opinions are important to us. This fear of being rejected will inevitably lead to a life of low self-worth and regret. Thankfully God doesn't behave as people often do!

We are promised in the above passage that even if our own parents reject us, God will not. He is letting us know here that His love is very much like the average parental love, but with a guarantee that goes even further. He will never forsake us or turn us away! You see, God's love is so much greater than any earthly love, even that of our parents. Unlike our other relationships, His affection is completely selfless. His love for us is not based on outward things such as our appearance or on selfish things such as what we can add to His life. You see, He doesn't need us. He is God. Instead, He just wants us. He loves us just because He can and because it is His nature to do so. What a promise! What meaning this fact gives our lives! So remember, whenever others reject you, God will not. You are special to Him. You have a face that your Heavenly Father will always love!

The Thin Place: Ask. Answer. Pray.

How important is being accepted by others to you?

How does it make you feel when you are rejected by others for any reason?

Does your life reflect the worth God has placed on your life?

September 21
Did He Just Call Me a Worm?

<u>**From Above**</u>: Job 25; Romans 3:21-26

Focal Passage: *"How then can a man be righteous before God? How can one born of woman be pure? If even the moon is not bright and the stars are not pure in his eyes, how much less man, who is but a maggot-- a son of man, who is only a worm!"" –Job 25:4-6*

<u>**Here Below**</u>:

Did he say what I think he said? Did Bildad the Shuhite just refer to you and I as worms? Yes, and maggots too! Wow! He sure didn't have a problem with expressing his thoughts. Yet, as we read Bildad's comments to Job about mankind, we do not need to be offended by this rather shocking comparison. Bildad was only expressing a fundamental truth about the life of faith. Basically, he was saying that apart from the Lord, we are not capable of much on our own. Compared to the righteousness of God, we are as repulsive as these lowly little creatures he mentions. I do not believe this was meant as an insult to mankind so much as it was a praise of God's holiness. Let's face it. Compared to God's perfect righteousness, Bildad was telling the truth. This ugly comparison was meant to drive home the wonder and beauty of justification.

Justification is a word that we hear quite often. Yet do we really appreciate its meaning? Justification is basically the process by which God, through the sacrifice of Jesus, has enabled us to stand before Him as if we had never sinned. By accepting the shed blood of Jesus, my sins are washed away, and I can now enjoy fellowship with a holy and righteous God. Bildad was simply expressing a need for a cleansing agent outside of ourselves that is strong enough to accomplish this washing away of our imperfections. Of course, justification doesn't mean that we become perfect. This is especially important to remember when I am struggling with my own sinfulness. It means that the penalty of our unrighteousness has been paid in full. Therefore, we can now appear to God as if we had never sinned in the first place. We can stand justified. Justification is our sin dept being paid in full by our Savior. Sanctification in turn is the process by which we become more like our Savior. None of this can happen until we fully acknowledge our need for a Savior that was willing to die in my place. In that respect, I am glad to admit that I am a worm. By admitting my "worminess" I can find freedom to become what God desires. You see, maggots and worms are both creatures that are living in a transitional form. They are changing. As a worm or caterpillar, we in time, from God's viewpoint, may become a butterfly. Or we can just wallow in our sin and possibly become fish bait. I choose to accept that I am a worm and allow God to transform me by His grace into His likeness. What about you?

The Thin Place: Ask, Answer, Pray.

How can pride in ourselves and accomplishments become a hindrance to our walk of faith?

What role does humility play in our justification and spiritual growth?

Does your life truly reflect an appreciation for the justification received in Jesus Christ?

September 22
Living for the Chase

From Above: I Timothy 6: 9-12

Focal Passage: *"But you, man of God, flee from all this, and pursue righteousness, godliness, faith, love, endurance and gentleness." –I Timothy 6:11*

Here Below:

Recently, I observed a debate over which could be considered the best car chase scene of all time in a movie. This type of trivia is always fascinating to me. One thing I learned from this debate was just how much we love the chase. Watching these cars run wildly through the crowded city streets dodging pedestrians and telephone poles keeps us at the edge of our seat. We desperately want the one in pursuit to catch his fleeing opponent and when they do we want to see them get away so that the excitement will continue. It is fun, as long as it is on the screen and not in front of you on the highway. Nevertheless, we love the chase. Unfortunately, many view real life in much the same way. Some spend their entire lives chasing after things they desperately think they need; yet, when they finally catch them, they realize that the object pursued was a disappointment. It may be that we are chasing after a certain career objective, financial success or some other tangible goal. While these can be worthy goals, they will ultimately leave us craving more of the chase instead. They simply do not fully satisfy. Why? Because they are temporal, and we were created for eternity.

We are warned about this in the above passage. We are told that instead of chasing after riches and the like, we are to flee from them. For some, we can certainly say that we have managed to flee from riches quite successfully our whole lives! Yet, one doesn't have to be rich to crave the things that money can buy. Instead, we are to pursue "righteousness, godliness, faith, love, endurance and gentleness". (vs. 11) This chase will leave us fully satisfied. Why? Because it is a chase that never ends! The more we pursue these qualities of life, the more opportunities we see to express them. Then the more we express them, the more we see our need for them and the more we love them. Then the chase continues. If we ever get to a point in life when we have stopped pursuing the things of God, we need to reevaluate our priorities. One sure sign that this may have occurred is an attitude of apathy. When we are chasing after the right things, we never grow weary of the chase. God will enable you and give you the strength you need for this chase. Look to Him and you will never grow tired of a righteous pursuit.

The Thin Place: Ask, Answer, Pray.

What are some tests we can use to measure what it is we are pursuing in our lives?

What does your time management say about what you are pursuing in your life?

How can you assure that your priorities are where they ought to be?

September 23
Giving It All Away

From Above: Exodus 25:1-8; Matthew 6:1-4; Acts 20:35

Focal Passage: *""Tell the Israelites to bring me an offering. You are to receive the offering for me from each man whose heart prompts him to give."* *–Exodus 25:2*

Here Below:

In one of the churches I pastored, there was a man of which I had to be very careful complimenting. One Sunday as he was leaving the church, I complimented him on the tie he was wearing. He took it off and gave it to me. More than once he tried to give me things or money in this manner. To try to deny his gift seemed to offend him, so I usually just graciously accepted. This was his way of expressing his affection. He was perhaps the most generous person I have ever met. He would literally give you the shirt off his back if he thought you needed it or wanted it. He also gave many private donations to those in need within our church. He was generous, but he was also humble in his giving. You could tell that his heart was in his giving. He was giving to the Lord. This is as God intends giving to be.

Giving has always been a matter of the heart. There are those that give out of obligation. They give their gifts to church or other charitable organizations out of a sense of obligation or as a tax write off. While we are taught to tithe and to give generously in the Bible, we are also taught to be genuine in our giving. We are to give out of a love for the Lord, not out of obligation. Let's face it, some can give their ten percent and never miss it. Likewise, some may give it and begrudge the fact that they have given money they might have used elsewhere, or they give expecting to get special treatment for their generosity. While giving is good, our gifts should come from a grateful heart determined to give God glory. I believe God can do more with a quarter that is given sacrificially than a million dollars given from an ungrateful heart. In the above passage, we see the building of the Ark of the Covenant. God did not demand all people to give to this endeavor. For His sanctuary, he wanted only those who heart prompted them to give. In other words, He wanted their hearts more than their money. It needed to be built upon love and grateful praise and worship. Those who followed their hearts at that time would receive blessings beyond imagination, they would receive the very presence of God in their midst. The same is true today. Except that today, His dwelling place is within our very hearts. The irony of all this is that a heart that is truly grateful is going to desire to give sacrificially to the Lord. In the end, that heart recognizes that what we give to the Lord, we never really lose. It is all His anyway. Give to the Lord today. Give of your money, time, talents and most importantly, give of yourself. You will never miss what you give to God.

The Thin Place: Ask, Answer, Pray.

Do you look at giving to the Lord as an obligation or as a privilege? How so?

Have you ever found yourself missing anything that you have given to the Lord?

How important do you feel sacrificial giving is to the Christian life?

September 24
The Great Escape

From Above: Mark 6:31-32

Focal Passage: *"Then, because so many people were coming and going that they did not even have a chance to eat, he said to them, "Come with me by yourselves to a quiet place and get some rest. So they went away by themselves in a boat to a solitary place." –Mark 6:31-32*

<u>Here Below</u>:

One of my favorite activities is to find a dark place and sit with a pair of headphones and listen to some of my favorite praise and worship music. With the headphones blocking out the external, I am able to break away from the noise of the world. In that place, I am able to escape, if only for a short while, from the hectic nature of the world around me and focus totally and fully upon my relationship with God. It is there that I have experienced some of the most worship filled moments in my life. We need this escape from time to time. Whether we use headphones, or just find a quiet place free from distractions, it is important that we try free ourselves from the noise of the world.

One of the reoccurring instances throughout the Gospel accounts of the life of Jesus was the need for Him and the disciples to escape the hustle and bustle of their ministry. More than once we see them going away intentionally for the purpose of having some alone time. This solitude is essential in the life of the believer. We must from time to time get away. It is during these times alone with God that we are the most apt to hear his voice. When we deny ourselves the noise of the world, we are making ourselves eligible for God's voice to penetrate our minds and heart. It is in those quiet moments that we are strengthened for the next clamorous moment that is inevitably coming. It is in these moments of silent stillness that we are refueled and equipped for the road ahead. These moments are more than just refreshers. They are one of the tools God uses to build us into the person that He sees us capable of being. The only way to be useful in the Kingdom of Heaven is to deliberately escape the kingdom of earth. If only for a short moment today, find a solitary place, sit still and be quiet. Let His still small voice drown out the distracting noise that flows from the stuff of life. Let this momentary escape be God's opportunity to speak. Make yourself available to His voice today.

<u>The Thin Place</u>: Ask, Answer, Pray.

How hard is it for you to experience moments alone with the Lord?

What do you do to create an atmosphere of solitude in your daily devotion times?

How can you improve in this area of your daily devotion time?

September 25
Out of Alignment

From Above: Psalm 15

Focal Passage: *"LORD, who may dwell in your sanctuary? Who may live on your holy hill? He whose walk is blameless and who does what is righteous, who speaks the truth from his heart" –Psalm 15:1-2*

Here Below:

Have you ever watched a movie or a TV show in which the soundtrack is just slightly out of alignment with the video? It is extremely frustrating. It doesn't have to be a great misalignment. It only has to be off a fraction of a second to totally ruin the presentation. The mouths of those on screen are moving, but they do not match the voices that we are hearing. It is very disconcerting. It can be an award winning movie, but if what you hear doesn't coincide with what you see, no one is going to take it seriously. The same is true of our own spiritual soundtracks. If the sounds others hear coming from our mouths aren't aligned with what they see in our actions, no one is going to take us seriously.

According to the above scripture and many others just like it, God desires honesty from His children. He desires that the walk of His child is "blameless" and that his voice "speaks truth from his heart". In other words, to be blameless, one's actions need to match one's words. Unfortunately, this doesn't always happen. Sometimes we speak in such a way as to make ourselves appear more spiritual, when in reality we are far from it. When we stray from the truth in this manner, it is usually to impress someone in our circle of acquaintances. Sure, sometimes we lie intentionally. More times than not we simply get caught up in telling our story and add to it to make it or ourselves seem more interesting to others. Unfortunately, it usually has the opposite effect. When the truth is ultimately revealed, as it always is, our image is damaged by our "misalignment". Our attempt to make an impression in this manner will only lead to making an opposite impression. Truth is always the way to go. Regardless of its weaknesses, God can use a heart that is sincere. One who speaks truth from his heart is of more use to the Lord than one that speaks flattery with the most eloquent of voices, regardless of public opinion. God's impression of us should be our first and driving concern. Otherwise, we are just one of those misaligned movies that nobody cares to see. Let your walk be blameless. Align your audio and video today.

The Thin Place: Ask, Answer, Pray.

How do you feel when the voices of others do not match their actions?

Has there ever been a time when your words didn't match your own actions?

What changes can you make to assure that your words and actions are in alignment?

September 26
Just Do It!

From Above: James 4

Focal Passage: *"Anyone, then, who knows the good he ought to do and doesn't do it, sins." –James 4:17*

Here Below:

I have to wonder sometimes how God feels about our prayers. I imagine some of them amuse Him and others probably frustrate Him. This is especially true in the case of those prayers in which we are seeking guidance or the strength to do right. While His nature probably prohibits any form of sarcasm, I would think that God sometimes just wants to say, "You already know what to do...Just do it already!" How often have we prayed for direction in a moral or spiritual matter when deep down we already know what we need to do? It happens quite often. As a pastor I encounter this quite regularly in counseling settings. More times than not, individuals know what needs to happen, they just haven't followed through. We have all been guilty of this. It is our flawed and sometimes weak human nature to seek confirmation from others on decisions that ultimately are very much our own. Fortunately, God has lovingly revealed to us much of what we need to know and do within His written Word. In the above verse, He has also warned us against putting off doing what we already know to be right.

Of course, it is just like the Lord to not leave us with a warning or rebuke without also giving us some encouragement. Along with a rather strong chapter of warnings against sinfulness and various colorful descriptions such as "adulterous people" and being an "enemy of God", God gives us a morsel of promise in verse 6. With all our faults, "He gives us more grace." Not doing what we know to be right is sin, but grace is available in those moments when we fail. There is one condition. According to verse 6, grace is given to those who exhibit humility. In other words, grace means acknowledging what we can't do on our own strength, accepting from God what we can't do on our strength and still striving to do our best anyway. In other words, grace means God would rather us mess up trying to do the right thing than to not try at all. So, if you know what to do, humbly do it and pray along the way. God's grace has you covered if you make a mistake.

<u>The Thin Place</u>: Ask, Answer, Pray.

Have you ever procrastinated doing the right thing? If so, when? What was the outcome?

Why do you think we often put off doing what we know to be right?

How does God often respond to our spiritual procrastination?

September 27

Passing the Test

<u>**From Above**</u>: 2 Timothy 3:1-7

Focal Passage: *"...always learning but never able to acknowledge the truth."* *–2 Timothy 3:7*

<u>**Here Below**</u>:

2 Timothy 3 always gives me goose bumps when I read it. It has this effect because of the specifically clear and chillingly familiar description it gives of the end of days and because it is a perfect description of the days in which we live. We live in a time in which we have more information available than in any other period of history. We have more biblical commentaries and theological writings available today than ever. We know more about God than any generation before us; yet, it seems we are farther away from God than ever. This all goes back to the fact that there is a fundamental difference between knowledge and wisdom. Many in our day are as the above verse states "always learning", yet they have still missed the point. The conclusion we must draw from this paradox is that the most pressing question is not how much we know about God, but how well we know God.

When it comes to our spiritual lives, the true test of wisdom is not how much knowledge we have accumulated, but how much we have applied. In other words, you can quote the Bible from cover to cover, but if you do not apply those wonderful words of life, it is all in vain. We must acknowledge the truth. We do this by openly living it. Some of the most spiritually mature people I have ever met have never had one day of theological training. Yet, their lives testify to their wisdom. Don't get me wrong. Biblical education is vital to spiritual growth. However, spiritual growth doesn't always accompany Biblical education. We must be intentional in our growth. We do that by putting it into practice. I don't think that God is nearly as concerned with whether we can define the intricacies of theology (the study of God) as much as He is concerned with our relationship with Him and with others. Remember, when Jesus walked the earth, He didn't choose the religious elite, the priests, or the scribes to compose His inner sanctum. He picked fishermen, tax collectors and other regular guys. Why? They were willing to learn and acknowledge the truth at the same time. You see, God is less interested in our resume than He is in our heart. This means we shouldn't fret over what we can't explain. Just trust in the Lord and the answers will come in His time. Give Him your heart first and then your head will follow. That is the definition of faith.

The Thin Place: Ask, Answer, Pray.

Do you agree that there is a difference between knowing about God and knowing God?

Do you feel your life expresses a link between understanding and application of God's Word?

How can you improve both your understanding and application?

September 28
Blurred Vision

From Above: Jeremiah 29:11-13

Focal Passage: *"For I know the plans I have for you," declares the LORD, "plans to prosper you and not to harm you, plans to give you hope and a future." –Jeremiah 29:11*

Here Below:

I was beginning to get a headache. All morning long I had been straining to read and my eyes were having trouble focusing. Everything appeared to be moving. It was very disconcerting. Finally, after enduring as much of this blurriness as I could, I took my contacts out and resorted to wearing my glasses. The next morning, I replaced my contacts only to find I was still having the same problem. I couldn't see. Then it occurred to me. My prescription was different for each eye. So, I took my contacts out and switched them around and guess what...I could see! If only our spiritual vision could be corrected so easily.

When it comes to seeing our true spiritual selves, our vision is blurred by our human condition. Oftentimes our vision can get blurred by circumstances, doubts, and fears. This is especially true when it comes to the future. We worry about what we cannot see. This happens when we forget that God can see what we cannot. He can see the future and He has 20/20 vision. Not only that, but when He sees our future, He sees the good that could occur if only we accept and follow His will. You see, we need to learn to view life as God does, through the eyes of eternity. Too many times the things that cause us grief are grounded in the here and now. If only we could learn to look past the here and now and see God's eternal plan for our life, many of our problems might be avoided. Likewise, our here and now problems would seem less dramatic. Think about it. Some of the stress points that caused us so much anxiety years ago can't even be named today. It is hard to see that when we are in the midst of that stress point. This is why we must trust our futures to God and do our best to see life through His eyes. When we find ourselves in a blurry moment, we need to change our prescription to fit God's vision. The more often we do that, the clearer our vision will be.

<u>The Thin Place</u>: Ask, Answer, Pray.

Do you ever worry about the future? Why or why not?

In your past, did you ever stress over things that are now inconsequential?

How do you think God sees your future?

September 29

Drill Here, Drill Now...

<u>From Above</u>: Isaiah 41:13

Focal Passage: *"For I am the LORD, your God, who takes hold of your right hand and says to you, Do not fear; I will help you.." –Isaiah 41:13*

<u>Here Below</u>:

We all have fears that plague us. What may cause great anxiety for one may not affect another in the slightest. Fear is very personal emotion. There is one place I fear more than any other. For you it may not mean anything. However, when I think of going there, it almost makes me nauseous. Nevertheless, I must from time to time go there. It causes my blood pressure to rise, my breathing to go shallow and my knuckles to turn white as I put a death grip upon the arms of that evil torture chamber chair in which I must sit. I am talking about going to the dentist. My fear is really irrational; in that, I have never really had a bad experience. It is the fear of what might happen that causes me to tremble. This fear was recently accelerated. As I was receiving some dental work, I could hear outside my room some remodeling construction taking place across the hall. There were drills grinding and saws screaming and comments from the workers such as "We are going to need to drill deeper..." and "Can you pass me that hammer?" It was like something from a sitcom. The hygienist attending to my dental work couldn't help but laugh. "Not exactly noises you want to hear at the dentist office, huh?" she chuckled as she worked the suction in my mouth. She understood my nervousness, for upon my last visit, she had offered to hold my hand as the dentist performed an extraction. I had laughed then and of course refused; though in the back of my mind, I was now tempted.

Well, God has given us the same promise of comfort. In the above verse, He promises to hold our hand in those moments of fear. He promises to help. Just as that literal hand holding gives us a sense of temporary security, God wishes to do the same for us eternally. When we are up against those truly fearful moments in life, we must take His hand and trust in Him. I will not go so far as to say that fear is the absence of faith, as some might say. After all, it is our human nature to fear and fear is not always sinful. Sometimes fear protects us from harm. It becomes a weakness when we let it cause us to stall or doubt.

The key to dealing with fear appropriately is to not be overcome by it. Instead, let your trust in God see you through it. Fear is not the enemy. The enemy is the enemy. So, take the hand of the One who has already won the victory.

The Thin Place: Ask, Answer, Pray.

What fears have you ever struggled with in your past?

How did God see you through those situations?

How does reflecting on these past fears help you deal with the fears of today?

September 30
You Stink!

From Above: Proverbs 27:6; Ecclesiastes 4:9-12

Focal Passage: *"Wounds from a friend can be trusted, but an enemy multiplies kisses." –Proverbs 27:6*

Here Below:

A pastor friend once told me to beware of those that try too hard to be my friend when I first arrive at a new place of ministry. He said, "Those same people to quickly sing your praises will be the same ones to eventually call for your resignation." Wow! I must say I didn't believe him at first. I must also add that it is not always the case. Nevertheless, it is sometimes unfortunately true. The underlying principle behind this advice is sound. We should beware of those that are too quick to flatter, especially when they do not yet know you that well. As the old saying goes, flattery will get you nowhere. The mark of a true friend is that they do not always tell you what you want to hear. As someone once said, a real friend will tell you that you stink while an enemy will hold their nose and tell you that you smell like a rose! Which would you rather have? Well, I would rather have a real friend. There is strength in friendship.

The Bible teaches us in Ecclesiastes that we are stronger when we have trusted friendships. This means we are stronger when we have true friends, and we are stronger when we are a true friend. Why? Well, friends help us to see life as it really is; therefore, we are better prepared for whatever may come. According to Proverbs 27:6, we can trust even the wounds caused by a friend; in that, a true friend has only our best interest in mind, even if to help us they are willing to inflict a wound. This leaves us with this mandate. When we find ourselves wounded by a friend, we need to ask why. Granted, not all wounds are for our own good. Sometimes friends let us down. However, sometimes we need to hear certain things that only a friend can say. We need to be sure that this is not what is taking place before we respond in a way that we might later regret. After all, it is not an easy thing to tell a friend something that they might not want to hear about themselves. In so doing, they are placing themselves in a position to be hurt as well. Take that into consideration the next time your friend says something you might not wish to hear. It takes courage to do what they have done. Not only that, but it might just be that you really do stink! They have most likely taken the risk of telling you the unpleasant truth out of love for you. So, appreciate your friend and be a good friend in return.

The Thin Place: Ask, Answer, Pray.

Who would you consider your best friend?

Are you able to share personal things with this friend, even unpleasant truths?

Are you able to receive constructive criticism from a friend without getting angry?

10

October

O ctober 1
The People Pleasing Paradox

<u>From Above</u>: Luke 6:26-31

Focal Passage: *"Woe to you when all men speak well of you, for that is how their fathers treated the false prophets." –Luke 6:26*

<u>Here Below</u>:

One truth that has taken me years to comprehend, and still not fully, has to do with the above verse. It is a truth that will totally change your life if you are able to wrap your mind and heart around it. That truth is this: If you are truly living the Christian life in this world, then you should expect that some people will not like it.

Notice the above verse. There is one word that changes the whole meaning of the verse. That word is "all". Jesus tells us that we should worry if *all* people are speaking well of us. In other words, if everybody is pleased with you, then one of two things is going on. One, somebody is lying to you; in that, there is no way you can do everything to please everybody without at least one person being turned off. Most likely, someone in this instance is flattering you with an ulterior motive behind their sweet words. Second, if all people are speaking well of you, then you might just be a people pleaser. The only way to have everyone

438

speak well of you is to try to please everyone, which is impossible unless you compromise in some way or another. Jesus reminds the reader that they used to speak well of the false prophets, which implies the kind of person that can receive the praise of all. They are false. People pleasing creates a paradox of sorts. You see, not everyone pleases God; therefore, it is impossible to be a successful people pleaser without displeasing God. Which is more important? We live in a fallen world, which naturally flows against the tide of God's will. We should expect the friction.

Understanding this principle is freeing to the believer. If we can ever get to a place in our lives where we are okay with the fact that there is no way to please everyone, then we are free to do what we know is right without reservation. Pleasing God should be our top priority. If others are pleased in the process, then that is a bonus. This doesn't mean that we ignore the feelings of others. It just means that we do not base our decisions on feelings, either our own or that of others. Instead, we seek God's will. So, if you ever find that everyone is speaking well of you, look out! You might just be in trouble.

<u>The Thin Place</u>: Ask, Answer, Pray.

Have you ever found yourself trying to please everyone?

If so, what was the outcome? How should you have handled it differently?

How can you avoid this people pleasing attitude in the future?

October 2

Caught in the Undertow

<u>From Above</u>: Hebrews 2:1

Focal Passage: *"We must pay more careful attention, therefore, to what we have heard, so that we do not drift away." –Hebrews 2:1*

<u>Here Below</u>:

Once, while on vacation on a beach in the Gulf of Mexico, I decided to enjoy one of my favorite beach activities. I love to find myself a float and paddle out just beyond the crowds and the breaking of the waves and just lay back, close my eyes and relax. When you close your eyes, it is as if you are all alone in the world when you are out there, even though the people and their sounds are within earshot. On this particular occasion, the warm gentle waves along with the sounds of the ocean had created a mesmerizing effect, and as a result I was about as relaxed as a person can get this side of sleep. I am not sure how long I had been out there when I finally decided to look up. However, I did not recognize the beach. The undertow had pulled me down the beach. Thankfully it had pulled me down the beach and not out to sea. My friends had been busy doing their own thing and had not noticed how far I had drifted. I was now nearly a half mile down the beach from where I started. It was a long walk back. The same can happen in our spiritual lives as well. If we are not careful, as we are warned in the above verse, we can find ourselves drifting. It usually happens when we are too relaxed and are not paying attention to what really matters. It can happen and we may not even see it.

Spiritual growth must be intentional. It does not just happen. In fact, our fallen human nature is inclined to drift away. We live in a world in which the current is always pulling us away from the things of the Lord. We must guard ourselves against this undertow. We do this by staying grounded in His word and never taking for granted that we have a tight grasp on our spiritual life. Notice the above verse. We must pay attention to what we have already heard. Do you see what the writer is suggesting? We have to never assume we have it all figured out. We need to continue to meditate on the things with which we are already familiar. There is always room for improvement and growth. Those with this humble attitude are more conscious of their true spiritual condition and are therefore less likely to drift away or backslide. Don't get caught in the undertow. Stay alert.

The Thin Place: Ask, Answer, Pray.
Have you ever found yourself backslidden or drifting away from God?
What led to this period of drift in your life?

How can you avoid this ever happening again?

October 3
Lemon Face

<u>From Above</u>: Exodus 34:29-35

Focal Passage: *"When Moses came down from Mount Sinai with the two tablets of the Testimony in his hands, he was not aware that his face was radiant because he had spoken with the LORD.*

30. When Aaron and all the Israelites saw Moses, his face was radiant, and they were afraid to come near him." –Exodus 34:29-30

<u>Here Below</u>:

Recently, my wife told me very matter of factly to stop scowling. Just as I was about to stand up and preach a sermon, she whispered these words of "encouragement to me". She said I looked as if I was mad at the world. The truth is that I wasn't mad at all. I simply was fighting a sinus headache. Yet, my face was sending the wrong message. Have you ever met someone that no matter their circumstances, they always look as if they have swallowed a lemon? We all have. Perhaps you, like me have even been that lemon face person. It happens. Let's face it. Sometimes life lends itself to a sour countenance. Nonetheless, we need to take notice of the message our face may be sending to others.

I love to read of the encounters of Moses and God in the book of Exodus. In this particular encounter, we see that Moses' appearance was altered by exposure to God's glory. I think this is more than the Charlton Heston type transformation that we see in the movies. It was more than just a glorious new head of blond hair and a tan. He was glowing. He had been in the presence of God and even his physical appearance testified to the fact. Well, while this is obviously different from anything you and I will ever experience, the principle is still there for us to consider. Shouldn't God's presence in our lives be evident to others? Shouldn't even our very own physical appearance testify to the difference God can make in our lives? I believe it should. As Christians, we have every reason in the world to be happy. Our faces should express that joy. Now this doesn't mean we should walk around with fake grins on our face all the time, nor does it mean that Christians don't have bad days. It simply means that our lives should express a joy unlike that of the world. I have seen from my perspective in the pulpit, many a face that looks as if they have no joy at all. I know it is not true of all. Yet, that is the message we often send. Awareness of this fact can mean the difference between being approachable or unapproachable. People are not interested in getting to know or becoming what the sour lemon face represents. People are attracted to joy. After all, with Jesus as our friend, we have no reason to scowl. Be happy and let your face share the message of that happiness. Don't be a lemon face believer.

The Thin Place: Ask, Answer, Pray.

What does your average countenance say about you personally? Is it good or bad?

What situation most often causes your countenance to fall?

What message does your face send those around you on a daily basis?

October 4
Walkabout

From Above: Psalm 119:41-48

Focal Passage: *"I will walk about in freedom, for I have sought out your precepts." –Psalm 119:45*

Here Below:

Meditation is more than memorization. It is more than just reflection. Meditation includes application as well. Meditation is taking what we read in God's Word and giving it feet. Psalm 119 is primarily about the importance of God's Word in the life of the believer. It is no coincidence that it is the longest book in the Bible. However, as important as meditation is in the life of a child of God, it is not meant to be burdensome. In fact, according to the above verse, it sets us free.

To walk about in freedom. Doesn't that sound appealing? To walk about in freedom, we must let God's Word walk through our heart. It is the study of scripture and its subsequent application that leads to this freedom. This happens; in that, the Bible is more than just a history book. It is a book about me. It is a book about you. When we read along its pages, what we are reading is God's account of His love for us and guidance in how we can have the life He desires for us. God is the protagonist and our relationship with Him is the theme. When you read it in that context, you cannot help but be changed by it. To live according to His precepts is to live a life free of the world's entanglements. The application of God's Word is liberating. Don't just read it! Don't just memorize it. Don't just study it. Let it soak in. Meditate and walk about in freedom.

The Thin Place: Ask, Answer, Pray.

Do you truly meditate on the word of God?

When you study the word of God, do you look for yourself in the passage?

What passage of scripture has God used lately to teach you something of yourself?

October 5
An Amazing Graze

From Above: Daniel 4:1-28

Focal Passage: *"You will be driven away from people and will live with the wild animals; you will eat grass like cattle and be drenched with the dew of heaven. Seven times will pass by for you until you acknowledge that the Most High is sovereign over the kingdoms of men and gives them to anyone he wishes." –Daniel 4:25*

Here Below:

In a very real sense, it is arrogance to believe that we can control our own destinies. This was a lesson old king Nebuchadnezzar would have to learn the hard way. He was fixing to be brought down to the level of an animal. The prophetic dream interpreted to him promised a future of living and grazing like a cow in the wilderness. He was going from highest position in the land to that equal to a hamburger! His pride and arrogance in the face of the Lord had brought him to this point. He was being reminded in a very unforgettable way that God was still the King, even over Nebuchadnezzar. It all happened just as the dream had predicted (Daniel 4:28).

We are no different than old king Neb. Occasionally we need reminding that God is still King. Hopefully we can acknowledge that in our lives before we find ourselves eating grass! Nevertheless, from time-to-time God does have to remind us. In fact, it often takes retrospection to see that God was in control in our lives even during those times which seemed out of control. Oftentimes, God chooses to mold us and move with a silent hand. He sometimes chooses to be our silent partner. But make no mistake, he is there, and he is more than a partner. He is the one calling the shots. The choices we make in life in regard to this reality determine the direction we will go. This is why seeking His will should always be our top priority. God is always moving. The real question for us is whether we want to move with Him or against Him. Make the choice before you find yourself grazing in the field of incorrect choices.

<u>**The Thin Place**</u>: Ask, Answer, Pray.

Have you ever failed to see God at work behind the scenes?

Looking back, can you see how God was instrumental in bringing you to where you are now?

How can you be more aware of God at work in the present?

October 6

A Constant State of Change

<u>From Above</u>: Romans 12:1-5

Focal Passage: *"Do not conform any longer to the pattern of this world, but be transformed by the renewing of your mind. Then you will be able to test and approve what God's will is--his good, pleasing and perfect will." –Romans 12:2*

<u>Here Below</u>:

My favorite part of the year includes the weeks or months in which we see the changing of the seasons. It is always refreshing when we start to see the weather cooling after a hot summer or the temperature rising after a cold winter. While each season has qualities we can appreciate, there is just something pleasant about the change. Unfortunately, we do not look at change in other aspects of life as pleasant. In fact, most of us are resistant to change. We can even take our dislike of change so far as to demonize change in almost any form. How often do you hear complaints about the ever-changing society in which we live? How often do we ourselves bemoan the ever-changing cultural climate? Granted, some of the changes we see are not changes for the better and are worthy of our complaints. However, not all change is bad either. In fact, growth is change.

Christians are oftentimes the world's worst when it comes to accepting change. There are churches all across our nation that are in trouble for no real reason other than they refuse to change their ways of reaching the ever-changing world around them. They equate changing to meet the needs of the world as changing to be like the world. As a result, they may lose their effectiveness. This is unfortunate; in that, the Christian faith is really based upon the concept of change. It starts when we are "born again" and then as we continue to "be transformed by the renewing of our mind". It is a never-ending process of change and it is a good change. In fact, as you study the above verse, you will see that this transformation is the key to our ability to test and know God's will for ourselves. In other words, we must remain open minded. This doesn't mean to compromise to the patterns of the world; but remaining open minded in the sense that God is constantly doing new things in an ever changing world. The very next verse in Romans 12 goes from the subject of change to the subject of pride. Paul warns us against thinking more of ourselves than we ought. Put these verses together and they warn us against thinking our usual way of approaching life is always the right way. It could be that God is leading us to change some things. In fact, you can count on it. God is all about changing us from what we are to what we could be, in His good, perfect, and pleasing will. Are you open to His change?

The Thin Place: Ask, Answer, Pray.

Would you say that you are more open or more resistant to change?

Why do you think we are often resistant to change?

How can we test whether a change is for the better or for the worse?

October 7
The First Step

From Above: Psalm 51

Focal Passage: *"Restore to me the joy of your salvation and grant me a willing spirit, to sustain me." –Psalm 51:12*

Here Below:

Psalm 51 is one of the most personal of all the psalms. It is a song of deep sorrow. It is a song of genuine grief over sin. David is crying out for forgiveness and restoration. In the above verse in particular, we see him asking for a restoration of joy. Along with this request is an interesting statement. He requests that God would "grant me a willing spirit." Different translations differentiate as to whether or not this is a prayer for willingness on the part of God or willingness on the part of David himself. From either perspective, this willing spirit is to be part of that joy which sustains David. David's sin is such that it has caused a heartfelt distance from his Lord. He wanted to get back to where he was supposed to be. Most likely, the proper interpretation of the verse would be that David was praying for his own heart condition. With that being true, the above statement implies that part of the journey back involved a certain amount of willingness on the part of David. As with all things, God desires us to take the first step back to Him.

When this verse refers to receiving God's forgiveness and restoration, it implies that there was at one time a healthy relationship in place that has since been damaged by sin. That is how sin works. In other words, sin on the part of a believer can distance us from God. We maintain our salvation, but our joy in the presence of God is damaged. To restore it, there must be willingness on our part. Are we willing to confess? Are we willing to repent? Are we willing to forgive others? Are we willing to forgive ourselves? Are we willing to make the necessary changes in our lives to show God that we wish to do what is necessary to find restoration? Are we willing to learn of God? God desires restoration, perhaps at any price. After all, the purpose behind the cross was one of restoration. Yet still, it is still up to us to accept his forgiveness. Free will requires our willingness. God is not going to force even His love upon us. His desire is for us to come to him willingly. This principle applies to all aspects of faith. So, this ultimately leaves us with this question. What are you willing to do to get right and stay right with the Lord? Are you willing to take the first step on the journey back to where you need to be?

<u>**The Thin Place**</u>: Ask, Answer, Pray.

How willing are you when it comes to following the will of God?

Have you ever struggled with willingness when it comes to matters of restoration?

What if being in right relationship with God means dealing with some difficult changes?

October 8
Caught in the Current

From Above: Isaiah 56:4-8

Focal Passage: *"The Sovereign LORD declares-- he who gathers the exiles of Israel: "I will gather still others to them besides those already gathered.""*
–Isaiah 56:8

Here Below:

One Christmas, I was given a gift that I have wanted my entire life. My wife bought me a saltwater aquarium. Being an aquarium enthusiast, I have always wanted to set up a saltwater aquarium, primarily due to the beautiful diversity of saltwater fish. Along with the beautiful brightly colored fish that are available, there are also striking anemones and sponges that are available to decorate this mini ecosystem. As I slowly added fish to my tank, I would find myself staring for lengthy periods of time at the bold diversity of it all. There are bright yellows, blues, purple and oranges making up the color scheme of my aquarium livestock. Yet, though the fish come in all shapes and colors, they live together in perfect unity. Even the sinister looking horseshoe crab gets along fine with the others. This tiny sample of God's creation has taught me much of God's point of view. He created the diversity. This God designed diversity not only exists in the ocean, but everywhere. Look around you today. We are as different from one another as those aquatic friends of mine. God had quite an imagination when He created mankind. We are all different. Granted, our differences often cause problems for us, but they do not have too. Just as my fish get along despite their differences, so can we. In fact, as you read Bible passages like the one above, you will see that God intends on calling people from all walks of life to a relationship with Him.

Too often we feel as if we must be exactly like others around us in order to find acceptance. We tend to gather with others that look and act like we do, much as those fish school together. Yet, in so doing we are in danger of losing our God given individuality. While there is not necessarily anything wrong with being with others with whom we have shared interests, it is good from time to time to stretch ourselves a little. The danger lies in the fact that we often get so accustomed to our own "schools" that we fail to see the value of others. We get swept up in the current of one particular way of thinking and we miss out on the blessings of God's diversity. Remember, God created the diversity, and He calls to us all. We need to celebrate His creativity. Don't get caught in the current! Don't let others determine your life course! Don't let the other fish cause you to miss the blessings of His diversity. Instead, let God confirm the beauty of it all.

The Thin Place: Ask, Answer, Pray.

Would you say that you enjoy the diversity of God's creation? How so?

How open are you to relationships with others that are different than you?

How does your individuality show to others? How are you different from those around you?

October 9
Nibbled to Death or Swallowed Whole?

From Above: 2 John 1

Focal Passage: *"Anyone who runs ahead and does not continue in the teaching of Christ does not have God; whoever continues in the teaching has both the Father and the Son." –2 John 1:9*

Here Below:

I was once asked this question. Is it better to be nibbled to death by minnows or swallowed whole by a shark? This rather humorous illustration could be applied to many of life's trials; yet, it is especially true when applied to the concept of compromise. It is my belief that a compromise on matters on spiritual significance is nothing more than allowing another little nibble to take place. While it may seem harmless enough, we forget that whether we are nibbled to death slowly or swallowed whole, in the end we are still just as dead! Compromise often has the same effect. We make a little compromise here and a little compromise there and before you know it, we are in critical spiritual condition, up to our neck in minnows, wondering how in the world we arrived at this place in our lives. I believe that most spiritual failures happen in this manner. They begin with a seemingly innocent and tiny compromise and ultimately lead to disaster. Remember that the end result is the same, regardless of the perceived size of our compromise.

For this reason, we must resist the temptation to compromise. Compromise is often looked at as a desired moral quality, exhibiting some sort of social enlightenment. We often applaud politicians and other political figures when they reach a compromise. Perhaps in some instances, it may be laudable. However, there is no room for compromise when it comes to matters of spiritual significance. I am not referring to matters of personal preference or manmade traditions. These things can cause great division. I am however referring to those things that contradict and work against the will and word of God. God's will is not always the easy way to go. Out tendency is to compromise and only go part of the way. Well, the above passage of scripture and others like it tell us what God thinks about compromise in this manner. Put simply, God is against it. In the end, it would be better to stand firm and fail than to compromise for the sake of simplicity. After all, we really do not fail when we are seeking to follow God. The world's measurement of success is not the same as God's. When we are obedient to him, we always win in His eyes. So, watch out for those minnows. Don't let them nibble away at God's plan for your life. Stand firm!

The Thin Place: Ask, Answer, Pray.

Think of an instance when you compromised on a spiritual matter only to later regret it.

What was the result of that compromise?

How might you have handled that situation different and others like it in the future?

October 10
Less is More

<u>**From Above**</u>: John 3:22-36
Focal Passage: *"He must become greater; I must become less." –John 3:30*
<u>**Here Below**</u>:

There is something to be learned from the above words first spoken by the "wildman" of the Judean wilderness. In this verse, John the Baptist was of course referring to his role in history in relation to the role of the one for whom he was preparing the way, Jesus. Yet, along with the prophetic implications of this verse is a principle of which you and I would do well to understand and to apply to our lives. For God's will to be accomplished in our lives, Jesus must become greater, and we must become less.

We live in a world that pushes the philosophy of human idealism. This form of humanism is the idea that we can do anything we set our minds to accomplish on our own strength, with a little hard work and determination. At first glance, this philosophy sounds very positive, and I guess in some instances it can be. However, this way of thinking makes it difficult for man to grasp the teachings of the Bible such as the one above. Nevertheless, it is there and it is true. The denial of self is a theme found throughout the scriptures. It cannot be ignored. The ultimate example of this principle is found in the actions of Jesus himself upon the Cross. Here we see Jesus deny his own divinity in order to accomplish the will of God. The irony of self-denial is that we in actuality do not lose anything by denying our self. Instead, we gain more of Jesus and his strength.

To deny our own will in exchange for the will of God only puts us in a stronger position to face whatever comes next in our lives. We are not weaker for denying ourselves. We are stronger. This was definitely true for John the Baptist. I would bet that you would have been hard pressed to find anyone who considered him weak! In fact, the king considered his strength a threat! The same applies to us. There may be others that may not understand our self-denial. They may not understand why you have chosen a certain path in your life or why you have chosen to not go a certain path. Nevertheless, it is God that searches our hearts and truly sees our motives. It is He that we should be striving to please. For this reason, we must allow ourselves to become less so that He can become greater. When we do this, God is better able to do something amazing with our lives. Less truly is more.

The Thin Place: Ask, Answer, Pray.

Has there ever been a time when you denied your own will in exchange for His?

What was the outcome of this self-denial?

If less of self is more of Him, how are you willing to deny yourself now and in the future?

October 11
A Man Apart

From Above: Nehemiah 7:2, Psalm 25:12-14

Focal Passage: *"I put in charge of Jerusalem my brother Hanani, along with Hananiah the commander of the citadel, because he was a man of integrity and feared God more than most men do." –Nehemiah 7:2*

Here Below:

He feared God more than most men do. He was a man set apart from the others. At least that is how Nehemiah saw him. What a compliment! His life was such that he stood out among men. It wasn't due to his intelligence, physical appearance, or charisma. It was his fear of the Lord that set him apart from other men; and that fear of the Lord made him the perfect man for the job of helping Nehemiah rebuild the walls of Jerusalem. The fear of God was his distinguishing mark.

The fear of God is the first step in finding our place in the kingdom of God. To fear the Lord is to acknowledge our need for His protection, guidance, strength and power. It is acknowledging our need for Him. Likewise, fearing God also means having a driving desire to please Him with our life. It implies seeking a level of closeness with God that goes beyond acquaintance and simple knowledge. This level of closeness is one that cares deeply for how we treat someone and how that same person sees us in light of our actions. To fear God is to crave an unblemished intimacy with Him. When we fear God, we are in the best position to be used by Him and in the best position to see Him at work in our lives. He desires it of us, not out of some human sense of pride, even though He would be right in feeling so. Instead, He desires us to fear Him in this sense because it brings us closer to Him. A right relationship with us is His greatest desire. It was for this reason that Jesus came. God wants intimacy with you.

So, with that said, how about you? Could the same be said of you as in the above verse? Do you have a healthy fear of the Lord? Are you seeking to please Him more than pleasing yourself or others? Are you truly seeking intimacy with God? Or are you going to be just one in the crowd? Let the fear of the Lord be your distinguishing mark.

The Thin Place: Ask, Answer, Pray.
What does the expression "the fear of the Lord" mean to you?
Would you say that you fear the Lord? Why or why not?
Would you say that others see in you a healthy fear of the Lord?

October 12
Good Grief

From Above: Lamentations 3:19-48

Focal Passage: *"For men are not cast off by the Lord forever. Though he brings grief, he will show compassion, so great is his unfailing love."* –Lamentations 3:31-32

Here Below:

The book of Lamentations is one of the saddest books in all of scripture. For this reason, it is often overlooked. It is probably safe to say that it has been a long time, if ever, since you have heard a sermon from the book of Lamentations. That is unfortunate. It *is* a sad book. It is a book of grief and crying out to God in a time of exile. The children of Israel had found themselves in captivity. They were taken from their homes and removed from their promised land. It was perhaps the most trying time in all of Israel's history. It was appropriate to grieve. However, as you read this book of laments, be sure to read it in its entirety. While there are many woes and mournful thoughts expressed within its pages, there are also some very beautiful praises and acknowledgements. In fact, chapter three has several references to God's unfailing love, His salvation, and His faithfulness. We are told to put our hope in Him.

You see, just as we often do, Israel had gotten herself into this mess. It hadn't just happened by chance or accident. They had systematically turned their backs on God, and as a result, they were reaping the negative consequences. The writer of Lamentations understands that and is crying out to God for restoration. All too often, instead of having the attitude of the writer of this great book, we play the blame game. Instead of lamenting our sinfulness, we lament our situation. It is not until we acknowledge our sin and repent that God is able to restore us. It is not until we acknowledge God's faithfulness, that we will be able to see it firsthand. We are reminded in this book that God does not take pleasure in seeing us in exile; nevertheless, that is what it sometimes takes for us to see our need. He doesn't want us to suffer. His desire is restoration. He longs to be in a right relationship with us. In order for that to happen, we sometimes need to lament. A godly lament is more than just regretting our mistake. It is striving to never go there again. We do this by repenting of our sin, leaning upon His grace, and trusting even deeper in the Lord. Our relationship with God must be the focus of our repentance. Put simply, a godly lament is a good form of grief. It leads to restoration.

<u>The Thin Place</u>: Ask, Answer, Pray.

Have you ever found yourself grieving over your circumstances?

What led to these circumstances?
How often do you feel real grief over your sinfulness?

October 13
Like Men Who Dreamed

From Above: Psalm 126; Matthew 19:26; Ephesians 3:20-21

Focal Passage: *"When the LORD brought back the captives to Zion, we were like men who dreamed." –Psalm 126:1*

Here Below:

Yesterday, we read the laments of a people in captivity. Today we see the results of their freedom. There is a distinct difference in the attitude. Psalm 126 is a song of ascents. It is a joyous celebration of praise to God for their return home. The writer exclaims that upon their return, they "were like men who dreamed." What a description! For years they had dreamed of freedom and now it was upon them. What seemed to be impossible was now a reality. As a result, their mouths were filled with smiles and laughter. You see, what we often forget is that we cannot "out dream" God. The problem for most of us is that we do not even try.

There are many reasons why we stifle our dreams. One might be the fear of disappointment. Second might be a lack of faith. Third and most likely is a simple misunderstanding of God's ways. God is not some rigid disciplinarian whose only desire is to keep us in our place. His will for our lives is not a box in which our lives must fit. On the contrary, scripture seems to teach us that we should dream and that we should dream big. The following of God's will is instead a key that opens up His limitless possibilities for our lives. He wants us to dream. Likewise, this psalm teaches us that there is a distinct dif-ference between those that dream and those that do not. Those that dream are happy. The dream of something better ahead and knowing that God is able to accomplish that dream brings a joy to the dreamer that circumstances cannot suppress. It is the difference between looking down and looking up. It may not always happen in our time frame, and it may not always happen as we think it should. Nevertheless, God does acknowledge our godly dreams, and as a result the dreamer is one up on those that do not. So, trust in the One that can make your dreams a reality.

The Thin Place: Ask, Answer, Pray.

What dreams do you have?

Has God ever let you down in the past? What does that say about your dreams?

Are there any self-made obstacles that might be standing in the way of your dreams?

October 14
God is a World Traveler

From Above: Jeremiah 23:23-24; Psalm 139:7-10

Focal Passage: *""Am I only a God nearby," declares the LORD, "and not a God far away?"* –Jeremiah 23:23

Here Below:

I had spent 13 hours cramped into a tiny seat in the middle chair of the middle aisle of the airplane. I quite possibly had the worst seat on the entire plane. My knees were aching from having not been extended for such a lengthy and miserable amount of time. By the time we arrived in Tel Aviv, I could hardly walk. This trip to Israel had taken me farther from home than I have ever traveled and most likely will ever travel again, and my body was reaping the consequences. However, I would not trade this trip for anything. It changed my life. Perhaps the most lasting morsel of truth I gleaned from this trip was not of a historical or geographical nature. It instead concerned the reality of the presence of God. In the back of my mind, I thought that going to the Holy Land would be a sort of spiritual pilgrimage for me. And it was.

However, as beautiful and moving as the biblical sites were to visit, I realized that I was no closer to God in Jerusalem than I was in Dublin, Georgia. Perhaps it would be better stated that I was just as close to God in Dublin, Georgia as I was on the streets of Jerusalem. You see, the presence of God in our lives has nothing to do with our *site*, but everything to do with our *sight*. Do we look for Him?

One reality that we would all do well to remember is that God is everywhere. I do not mean this in some new-agey mystical kind of way. This doesn't mean that God is in the trees and the rocks or the wind or any other similar sort of new age nonsense. However, it does mean that we cannot go so far away that God cannot come with us. I believe this to be literally true and spiritually true. We cannot move so far away from God spiritually that He is not aware of our circumstances. He may not like them, but He sees them. Not only that, but He wants you to see Him in them as well. The many verses in scripture telling us of God's inescapable presence are not meant to be taken solely as a warning about God seeing those things we think no one can see; but they are also meant to comfort us in knowing that God never loses sight of His children. I don't know about you, but I am glad that there is not a place in which God cannot find me. His presence gives me security. His presence gives me strength. This also means that I do not have to go on a pilgrimage to find God. He is with me all the time. So, the real question for us today is not whether or not He is there. The question is "Are you looking for Him?" Well, are you?

<u>The Thin Place</u>: Ask, Answer, Pray.

Have you ever felt as if you were too far away from God to experience His presence?

What circumstances can lead to this type of feeling?

How can you avoid this ever happening in your life?

October 15
Fool Me Once...

<u>From Above</u>: I Corinthians 10:1-13

Focal Passage: *"These things happened to them as examples and were written down as warnings for us, on whom the fulfillment of the ages has come." –I Corinthians 10:11*

<u>Here Below</u>:

There is an old saying that goes something like this, "Fool me once. Shame on you! Fool me twice. Shame on me!" There is definite truth in this saying. This aphorism is not so much addressing the importance of avoiding deception as it is addressing the importance of learning from our past mistake. We all make mistakes. Sometimes they are small. Sometimes they are not. Nevertheless, we would do well to take note and to learn from them. Making a mistake is one thing, repeating it something else. Spiritual growth requires that learn from our mistakes.

In the above passage of scripture, Paul is reminding the Corinthian church and us as well of the history of his people. He recounts the history of Israel immediately following the deliverance from slavery in Egypt. It is not a pretty picture he paints. It is one of spiritual shortcomings and failures. Yet, he also brings out a very good point about these stories. They were recorded. You might think that the writers of the Old Testament might not include the faults of the people in such detail. I don't mean lie about them, just not tell the whole truth. You would think they would rather pass a more positive account on through the ages. This historical revisionist type thinking so popular in our day is not God's way of thinking. He always deals in truth. However, the message of these stories is more than just an honest account. God inspired the writers to record these less than complimentary stories so that we might learn from their mistakes. Mistakes of the past are the best teachers we can find. This applies to both the mistakes of others and those of our own doing. God has given us the capacity to remember and to recall. Don't take that ability for granted. However, we must be careful to not confuse the concept of learning from past mistakes with dwelling on past mistakes. When it comes to our own mess ups, we must let go of them in the sense that forgiveness is available for all who seek. At the same time, we must remember them in order to not repeat them. If you can make this distinction, you can be both free from the past and make better choices in the future.

The Thin Place: Ask, Answer, Pray.

What are some lessons you have learned from past mistakes?

Have you ever failed to learn from past mistakes only to repeat them?

How has learning from the past helped you be stronger today?

October 16
Ex Nihilo

From Above: Romans 4:16-25

Focal Passage: *"As it is written: "I have made you a father of many nations." He is our father in the sight of God, in whom he believed--the God who gives life to the dead and calls things that are not as though they were."* –Romans 4:17

Here Below:

I must admit that I am not a very "handy" person. I am pretty good at maintaining things around the house, but when it comes to building things, I have never quite mastered it. I have made some pretty embarrassing attempts. Nevertheless, I am able to take some wood and build a box. I can also take some bricks and build a wall. But try as I might, I cannot make something out of nothing. The box starts with wood and the wall starts with brick. I can't just make a wall out of nothing. Yet, there is One that can. God spoke the world into existence "ex nihilo", which means out of nothing or from nothing. Only God can work "ex nihilo". This is one of the mysteries of God that defies our human understanding. We tend to think more concretely (pardon the pun). We tend to think of those things we can see or touch. It is hard for us to interpret God creating the world from nothing. Yet, that is the only explanation that fits. Even those that subscribe to the big bang theory of creation must agree that somewhere down the line the atoms they believe started this chain reaction had to come from somewhere. Of course, we know that God spoke the world into existence. It wasn't a big bang. It was His voice that started this big blue ball rolling upon which we live.

In fact, God specializes in exhibiting this type of creation all throughout history. In the above passage, Paul reminds us of this fact. He is referring to Abraham and the miracle birth of his son Isaac, right around his one hundredth birthday. You see, in that case and in many others, God was able to make something out of nothing. In these instances, it was literal. However, God also specializes in this "ex nihilo" creation in the figurative sense as well. He does this by making something out of what we may think is nothing. This is why we must never discount God's desire to make something out of our lives or the lives of those we might be tempted to right off. Likewise, we must never think that God can't use a particular situation to carry out his purpose and design. Trying to figure this out will drive us mad. Like creation, it goes beyond human comprehension. We must simply trust in God to do what He does best. So don't sweat over what you can't understand about God. Instead, learn as much as you can and trust Him for what you can't. After all, that is faith. Then just sit back and watch what He can do with nothing.

The Thin Place: Ask, Answer, Pray.

Do you ever marvel at God's ability to make something wonderful out of nothing?

Has God ever created something special in your life out of difficult circumstances?

Have you ever doubted God's ability to use a situation for good?

October 17
Excuse Me, But Your Faith is Showing...

From Above: Mark 7:24-37; 8:38

Focal Passage: *"Jesus left that place and went to the vicinity of Tyre. He entered a house and did not want anyone to know it; yet he could not keep his presence secret."* –Mark 7:24

Here Below:

If you ever want everyone to know something, just tell my seven year old daughter that it is a secret. She has never met a secret she couldn't tell. After telling her brother what his birthday present was hours before his party, I asked her why she couldn't keep it to herself. She responded, "I tried not to tell, but I just couldn't help myself." Such is the innocence and honesty of a child. If only we would stay that innocent and honest.

In the above story from Mark's gospel, we see Jesus trying to keep a secret. As He arrived in Tyre, He attempts to keep His presence a secret. Overwhelmed with the endless hordes of people following Him around, He must have needed a time of respite. Yet, He was unable to keep His secret as well. His presence was something that could not be kept a secret. Guess what? The same should be true for us as well! His presence in our lives cannot be kept secret. More specifically, our faith is not meant to be a secret.

Some would argue that our faith is a very personal thing, nobody's business but our own. Well, I don't believe the Bible teaches this. Our faith is personal; in that, it affects us on a personal level. Our salvation deals with *our* sin and *our* repentance. Yet, it is not personal; in that, we are not meant to keep the good news to ourselves. Hence, the title "good news." In fact, I would take this one step further by saying that genuine faith is impossible to keep a secret. If your faith is changing you into the likeness of Christ, then it should be evident to all those who know you. If your faith isn't showing, then maybe it is because it is not a life changing faith. There are some secrets that are meant to be kept. Your faith is not one of them! Like Jesus in Tyre, His presence should be obvious in our lives. And like my seven-year-old daughter, we shouldn't be able to keep to ourselves this great news that we have in our hearts. Like her, let it be said of us that we just couldn't help ourselves. Is your faith showing?

The Thin Place: Ask, Answer, Pray.

Do you think others in your life would be surprised to hear that you are a person of faith?

Why do you think we sometimes try to keep our faith to ourselves as if it is some secret?

How do you think God feels about this secretive type of faith?

October 18
The First Step

From Above: 2 Chronicles 7:14-15

Focal Passage: *"If my people, who are called by my name, will humble themselves and pray and seek my face and turn from their wicked ways, then will I hear from heaven and will forgive their sin and will heal their land. Now my eyes will be open and my ears attentive to the prayers offered in this place." –2 Chronicles 7:14-15*

Here Below:

Being the impatient people we are, we are often quick to question why our prayers are not answered sooner or at not answered in the manner in which we thought they should be. We often forget that we have a certain amount of responsibility when it comes to seeing our prayers answered. 2 Chronicles 7:14-15 is one of the most famous passages of scripture and one of the most quoted. It is especially applicable in matters of political or national prayer needs, and it is often quoted in such scenarios. However, the principle in this verse is first applicable to the individual heart. If we desire to see our prayers answered, the first step is that we must humble ourselves and seek God's face.

Practically speaking, this means that we may be the reason the answer to our prayer may seem slow in coming. Perhaps we have disregarded our role in the whole process. It could even be that God plans on using us as a means to bring the answer. How often do we pray that God might use us to solve our problems? Usually, we just pray to have them answered. You see, humility is recognizing our role in our situations and being willing to be used of God as a means of resolution, no matter what He requires of us. So, do not just pray for help. Pray that God might give you the courage to take steps in a direction that will bring the answer. Likewise, be open to discover the answer He wishes to bring, not just the answer you want. If they are not the same, you can rest assured God's answer is the best.

The Thin Place: Ask, Answer, Pray.

Do you any specific prayer needs right now in which the answer has been slow in coming?

Is it possible that the answer has come but in a way that you didn't expect?

Likewise, is it possible that God is waiting for you to take a step toward bringing the answer?

October 19
All Worked Up

From Above: Colossians 3

Focal Passage: *"Whatever you do, work at it with all your heart, as working for the Lord, not for men, since you know that you will receive an inheritance from the Lord as a reward. It is the Lord Christ you are serving.* " *–Colossians 3:23-24*

Here Below:

It is possible to work so hard at working that we forget for whom it is we work. This is especially true when it comes to our service to the Lord. Often, we find ourselves so engrossed in our service that it becomes more about ourselves than about the purpose or person that had first called us to service. Even in the most noble acts of service we can find our motives out of sync with this teaching. We are warned about this in the above verse. We are reminded here that in whatever we do, we need to remember that it is the Lord Christ we are serving, not men. We are even reminded by Jesus in the gospels that in those tiny acts of service to even "the least of these" we are in actuality serving Him.

Perhaps this phenomenon occurs because we are such a reward driven society. Success is often measure by the measurable outcome of our actions. This leads us to focus more on the job than on the One we serve. Christian service is the exact opposite of the rewards driven philosophy adopted by so many in our time. Christian service often means years of faithful service before we can see a measurable outcome. This does not mean we are not successful in our service. On the contrary, success is more a question of obedience than outcome. It is more about willingness than winning. So yes, we should strive to do our best when serving the Lord. However, we should not try to measure success by a standard which does not apply. Instead, our goal should simply be to please the One calling us to serve. That is good stewardship. That is being a faithful worker for the Lord.

The Thin Place: Ask, Answer, Pray.

Have you ever been so engrossed in your service to the Lord that you forgot His purpose in it?

Why do you think this is so easy to do?

How can you avoid this ever happening again in your service to God?

October 20
Dandelions and Wild Onions

<u>From Above</u>: Colossians 2:1-10

Focal Passage: "*I tell you this so that no one may deceive you by fine-sounding arguments.*" *–Colossians 2:4*

<u>Here Below</u>:

It is fall. Fall is my favorite season. It is my favorite for many reasons. Among those reasons are the cool air and the beautiful fall colors. Another reason is that fall marks the end of the grass cutting season. While I do not mind cutting grass, it can be a very time-consuming job. Yet, I recently noticed something about my yard. Though the grass has stopped growing, there are other things still going strong. Rising above the grass in my lawn are dandelions and wild onions. They continue to grow well past the end of grass season. These two weeds are really nothing alike. The wild onions are easy to identify. They look like onions you might find in your produce section of your local supermarket, only smaller. They also smell like an onion you might find in the supermarket, only stronger. The dandelions on the other hand can actually be pretty. They have pretty yellow blooms which are perfect for children to pick for their mothers. Yet, as pretty as they might be, do not be deceived. They are still weeds. They may not smell or look like the nuisance onion, but they are still weeds, which can ultimately ruin your lawn.

Many times, in scripture we are warned against being deceived. We are told to be cautious of those with slick tongues and smooth sounding arguments that contradict what God's word teaches as truth. Some of these spiritual frauds are like the wild onions, easy to recognize. Others are like those dandelions. They do not appear to be what they really are. Yet, they are still both weeds. In our day, there are many dandelion teachers trying to mess up our spiritual lawns and many are deceived by them. These include the voices out there that appeal to the emotional weaknesses we all share, while denying the truth of God. They teach a dangerous people pleasing version of the truth. It is a deception, and the number one tool used by the prince of deception.

Sometimes the real truth is not always pleasant. Yet, if it is indeed the truth, it is always for our best.

Personally, this means we must be able to tell the difference. To recognize the lies, we must be familiar enough with the truth to see them for what they are. In other words, we must know the word of God. Again, the lies are not always blatant heresies, but they are just as destructive. Don't fall victim to deception. Don't underestimate the weeds. Keep your lawn in check.

The Thin Place: Ask, Answer, Pray.

What are some anti-biblical lies being taught in our day that do appeal to our human nature?

Why do so many people fall victim to these lies?

Do you feel that you are comfortable enough with God's word to recognize the lies?

October 21
Digital Indifference

From Above: Revelation 3:13-22

Focal Passage: *"I know your deeds, that you are neither cold nor hot. I wish you were either one or the other! So, because you are lukewarm--neither hot nor cold--I am about to spit you out of my mouth." –Revelation 3:15-16*

Here Below:

While sitting in a doctor's office waiting room the other day, I noticed a very peculiar phenomenon. However, I must admit that I see am seeing it more and more often as the days pass. The room was filled almost to capacity, yet no one was speaking. Everyone in the room other than me had their heads down and their fingers flying as they were vigorously texting or surfing on their cell phones. Everybody! I was the only one looking up! It really makes me wonder how we managed to get by before these marvels of technology existed. Nevertheless, everyone was occupied with their phones to the point of being totally oblivious to what was going on around them. I honestly believe that I could have stood up and danced across the floor and I do not think anyone would have noticed! For example, no one seemed to notice the receptionist at the desk was singing and bobbing her head along with a James Brown song being played over the speakers. Another nurse in the hallway behind her was mocking her behind her back. Likewise, no one noticed the teenage girl that came in and sat among them wearing two different shoes, one work boot and one tennis shoe. She too was busily texting. There were these events and other remarkable happenings all around them, but no one could look up from their phone long enough to notice them. They were indifferent to their surroundings, and as a result they were missing some great fun.

Unfortunately, many of us approach our spiritual lives with the same sort of indifference. We get so wrapped up in the details of the day that we fail to see God given opportunities all around us for learning, sharing and ultimately growth. Also, we miss opportunities to be a blessing to someone who might need one standing right next to us. I wonder how many witnessing opportunities we miss due to our own indifference? This spiritual indifference is high upon God's list of things to avoid. The above passage tells us in a very direct way how God feels about lukewarm spirituality. Put simply, we need to look up every now and then and take notice of what God is doing. We cannot go through life with our spiritual eyes looking down. We cannot be indifferent to real life happening all around us. Look up and slow down and you may be surprised at the blessings that will come. Don't miss out on what God wants you to see!

<u>The Thin Place</u>: Ask, Answer, Pray.

What aspects of your life draw the most of your attention? How so?

Do you feel they require too much of your attention and possibly lead to spiritual indifference?

How can you better avoid this from happening in your life?

October 22
Because I Said So!

<u>**From Above**</u>: I Samuel 15: 22-23
Focal Passage: *"But Samuel replied: "Does the LORD delight in burnt offerings and sacrifices as much as in obeying the voice of the LORD? To obey is better than sacrifice, and to heed is better than the fat of rams." –I Samuel 15:22*

<u>**Here Below**</u>:

As a parent I have found myself doing things with my children that I swore I would never do when I was younger. For example, I remember one of my parents answering me with "Because I said so!" upon my questioning one of their commands. I remember thinking that this response was not exactly adequate. I wanted an explanation. Yet, to push the matter further would elicit an even more regrettable response, so I usually just let it go at that. Nevertheless, here I am years later telling my children the same thing. The difference is that now I can see that statement from the perspective of the parent instead of the child. As a parent, there are times when we just want our children to trust us and do what we say because we know what is best for them. In this instance, obedience to our command is an expression of trust. The same is true with our Heavenly Father.

In the above passage, the prophet Samuel reminds us that God is more pleased with an obedient heart than a great sacrificial offering. Keep in mind that this was first stated during the period of Old Testament history in which the old sacrificial system was still in place. Yet still God preferred obedience over sacrifice. Now this doesn't mean that there is anything wrong with sacrifice. On the contrary, a genuine sacrifice is pleasing to God as well. However, it is possible to fake a sacrifice in an attempt to appease God or perhaps hide our true inner spiritual condition. Nonetheless, God cannot be fooled. He sees our real intentions. He also knows a life that is lived in obedience to Him

is a greater testimony to our true heart condition than anything offered as a sacrifice. To obey God, even when it may not make perfect
sense according to our human reasoning, is perhaps the greatest form
of worship we can participate in. It is the ultimate expression of trust
in God and His ways. When we unconditionally trust and obey God,
we are acknowledging His power, strength and love and its impact in
our lives. Put simply, sometimes we need to do what God says just because He said so and leave it at that. Trust and obey!

The Thin Place: Ask, Answer, Pray.

Have you ever found it difficult to simply trust and obey God in your life?

If so, under what circumstances did you find yourself struggling with the choice to obey or not?

Have you ever found yourself disappointed after choosing to obey God? What does this teach us?

October 23
A Dead Dog at the Table

From Above: 2 Samuel 4:4; 2 Samuel 9

Focal Passage: *"And Mephibosheth lived in Jerusalem, because he always ate at the king's table, and he was crippled in both feet." –2 Samuel 9:13*

Here Below:

Hidden away in the books of Samuel is one of the greatest stories
of restoration and compassion in all of scripture. It is the story of a
boy named Mephibosheth. He was the son of Jonathan, David's best
friend who had died in battle with his father Saul. In those days, as
gruesome as it sounds, it was customary for the family of a previous
king to be killed upon the changing of family dynasties, such as in this
case. This was done to prevent the family from overthrowing the new
king and taking his kingdom away. Yet, David did not entirely keep
this custom, perhaps out of loyalty to his dead friend Jonathan. Instead, he placed Mephibosheth in a place of prominence in his king-

dom. He let him dine at the king's table and restored to him the lands that had once belonged to his father. Even Mephibosheth considered his life of no consequence. Upon meeting David, he referred to himself as a dead dog (9:8). Yet, David did not see him as a cripple or as a possible enemy or a dead dog. He saw the son of his friend. He saw one who was to be king had things turned out differently. Perhaps David had this type of special vision; in that, he was a man after God's own heart.

You see, the way we see people is not always the same way God sees people. Scripture is filled with such instances in which people were dismissed by the world's standards, yet God chose to use them. In fact, David is one such individual. He was just a shepherd boy when Samuel anointed him as the next King of Israel. He was the last of the family to be considered for that honor. You see, when God looks at us, he doesn't just see who we are. He sees who we might become if we allow Him to work in our lives. The greatest mistake we can make in life is to deny God the opportunity to mold us and make us into what we could be. We can never discount who we are or who others might become with the proper encouragement and guidance from the Lord. This concept should not only change how we live within our own hearts, but also how we treat others. Where we see a "dead dog", God may see someone worthy to sit at His table. Open your eyes to God's way of seeing things, both in yourself and in others.

The Thin Place: Ask, Answer, Pray.

Can you name an instance in which you were surprised by God's choice in using someone?

Why did it surprise you? Is it because you saw this person differently?

What does this say about how God might see you?

October 24
Half Empty

<u>From Above</u>: John 5:1-15

Focal Passage: *"When Jesus saw him lying there and learned that he had been in this condition for a long time, he asked him, "Do you want to get well?"." –John 5:6*

<u>Here Below</u>:

Do you want to get well? Why do you think it is that Jesus would ask this man such a question? After all, doesn't it only make sense that someone in the predicament that this man is in would want to be healed? Well, Jesus thought it necessary to ask. Perhaps Jesus understood our human tendency toward self-pity. Let's face it. Sometimes it almost seems as if some enjoy their misery. For them, the glass is always half empty and never half full. We often use our problems to gain attention from others or to justify our poor attitudes. As a result, we remain in a state of negativity and apathy. It is not good for us, and it is not good for our relationships to always focus on what is not going right in our life. It is definitely not a preferred quality found in a child of faith. The life in Christ should be one of joy and optimism. It is after all a life of hope.

Now this question doesn't mean that the man had no faith. In fact, he had been coming to this place for years to find healing. He simply needed reminding of where true healing comes. We sometimes get so accustomed to our situation that we fail to see God at work. In fact, we can become so complacent that we even stop looking. This man had been in this condition for 38 years; yet, Jesus still had to ask him if he really wanted to be healed. He had probably given up on ever being healed. Yet one thing this story teaches is to never underestimate God's ability to change our lives.

One approach I have discovered that helps me when I encounter problems in life is to imagine the future with the problem and without the problem. Then I must make the choice. Am I willing to do what it takes to move past the problem, and would the difference be worth it? Do not misunderstand. Just wishing a problem away doesn't make it happen. Not every problem is licked with positive thinking. Sometimes healing does not come as we might desire. Sometimes God chooses to change our attitude instead of changing our problem. Either way though, we are better off when we simply trust our problems to Him. However, God's ability to adjust our situation and our future often depends upon our willingness to adjust our attitude. I don't believe Jesus would have healed this man if deep down he didn't really want it. So, the real question comes back to this. Do we really want to be healed? Or are we happy with life as it is?

<u>The Thin Place</u>: Ask, Answer, Pray.

Have you ever met someone who seemed to enjoy their misery?

Why do you think this attitude occurs?

What does God's word teach about having a positive attitude?

October 25
Mathematics of the Mind

<u>From Above</u>: Matthew 6:24-34

Focal Passage: "*Who of you by worrying can add a single hour to his life ?*" *–Matthew 6:27*

<u>Here Below</u>:

My four-year-old son has a funny expression that he often utters with perfect comedic timing. Whenever he is asked a question that he does not know how to answer, he responds with the statement "Don't worry about it!" His innocent refusal to acknowledge his own inability to grasp the answer to the question always brings a laugh to our family. Perhaps this laughter explains his frequent use of the term. He likes to get a laugh. Nevertheless, his innocence on the matter of worry is educational. Wouldn't it be nice if we could all have that attitude concerning the things we can't explain in life? Regrettably, our tendency is often to worry about what we can't see or understand. Unfortunately, the irony of it all is that by worrying, we are actually adding to our problems. It solves nothing. In fact, if not dealt with properly, worry can actually lead to a downward spiral of self-destruction in our lives. For this reason, we must heed the above words of Christ. Jesus addressed the issue of worry in a manner that is about as straightforward as you can get. By worrying, we are not adding anything to our lives.

In recent years, psychologists have "discovered" the debilitating effects of stress and worry on the emotional and physical well-being of the human spirit. Well, Jesus warned us of this "discovery" two thousand years ago. If it doesn't add anything to our lives, the natural conclusion is that it takes away. It takes away time, energy and attention that might be better utilized elsewhere. Along with the emotional anguish it brings, it also brings physical maladies in the form of headaches, stomach-aches, and ulcers. And nothing about our situation changes, except that we are in a worse position to deal with it. By worrying we are taking away from the quality of life. Now this doesn't mean that we ignore problems we are facing. It just means that it is foolish to fret over things that we cannot change anyway. By doing so, we are subtracting from our lives. I don't know about you, but when it comes to the length and quality of my life, I would rather add than subtract! I was never very proficient in math, but this equation is fairly clear. Adding is better than subtracting. Life is too precious to waste by worrying. This is the math lesson Jesus was teaching and one we would all do well to learn.

__The Thin Place__: Ask, Answer, Pray.

What worries you the most in your life?

How do you typically deal with worrisome situations?

How might you better deal with it in a way conducive with the teachings of Christ above?

October 26
Not Always Black and White

<u>From Above</u>: I Corinthians 6: 11-14; Titus 3:8-9

Focal Passage: *"'Everything is permissible for me'--but not everything is beneficial. 'Everything is permissible for me'--but I will not be mastered by anything."* –I Corinthians 6:12

<u>Here Below</u>:

Christianity is not about "what we are not supposed to do" as so many seem to think in our day. Faith is not a matter of following a list of dos and don'ts, all of which are basically up for interpretation. It is about having a desire to live a life that is pleasing to God. However, this does mean that there are some things we should avoid in life, even though they may not all be sinful. This concept of self-denial is found all throughout the New Testament. Paul frequently addressed the issue. In the above passage, Paul addressed the philosophy of his day, which basically said that anything goes. Sound familiar? This idea that there is no right or wrong or that it is up to the individual to determine what is right or wrong for *them* permeates contemporary society as well. However, I feel Paul's answer still applies to those who follow that philosophy.

I believe there are some issues which are cut and dry, right and wrong. They are sinful in nature and go against the will of God. These are found clearly defined in scripture. They include such things as murder, adultery, idol worship, etc... Yet, the things we often struggle with the most are those in which scripture is not so clear about. These gray areas can often become a point of contention between believers with opposing views and are usually more a matter of personal preference than Biblical authority. Is it right for a Christian to ___________? You fill in the blank. You know what I am talking about. Feelings have been hurt, arguments have started, and churches have even split over such issues, which can at times be very trivial in nature. The best way to approach these divisive issues is to use Paul's approach. Whether or not we think it is permissible, is it beneficial? Is it profitable for everyone, as Paul writes to Titus? If it is not beneficial, then why waste our time engaging ourselves in it? Instead, we are taught in Titus 3 to focus on doing good. We are to devote ourselves to those things that we know can make a difference spiritually in the world around us. Put simply, there are things that simply do not deserve my attention, right or wrong, especially if my goal is above all else to live a life pleasing to God. Instead, I should devote myself to matters of greater importance. Likewise, if you don't know if something is profitable, it is most likely not. It is better to just avoid it and change your focus to what you know is beneficial. Oftentimes, it is not a matter of what I can and can't do so much as it is a matter of what I should do! Let God guide your choices, not the opinions of men.

The Thin Place: Ask, Answer, Pray.

What are some issues in your own life that might be considered a "gray area"?

How beneficial are these things in helping you accomplish God's will for your life?

How can you change your focus to those things that you know are beneficial?

October 27
As Good as Dead

From Above: Hebrews 11:1-13; I Corinthians 1:25-31

Focal Passage: *"And so from this one man, and he as good as dead, came descendants as numerous as the stars in the sky and as countless as the sand on the seashore." –Hebrews 11:12*

Here Below:

It is never too late for God to use you. To assume that your situation has moved you past a place of usefulness is to doubt the power of God. God is not limited by time, place, or circumstances. In the above chapter from Hebrews, we see a long list of people whom God chose to use in miraculous world changing ways. Abraham in particular became one of the greatest heroes of the faith and the father of a nation. Yet, he was described as being "as good as dead". Perhaps there is a lesson for us here. Maybe we are in a position to be best used by God when we come to that place in which we are no longer tempted to move forward on our own strength.

My understanding of history is simple. Those who have made the greatest spiritual impact on the world are those who understood their inability to do it on their own strength. This didn't come easy to Abraham, nor does it come easy to us. It took some major mistakes on his part to finally arrive at a place of total surrender to God. He did finally do so, and as a result he was able to see God's promise fulfilled. I do not think we are that different from Abraham in this respect. We may not be called to be the father of many nations; nevertheless, we are called to have a spiritual impact in this world. We are called to follow the example of Jesus and to live by His truth and word and to ultimately do our part in making disciples of all. This commission was for all of us. However, for our part to be accomplished, we must understand that it is by His strength alone that we will ever be victorious. For us, this means that to live a victorious life, we need to view life as if we are "as good as dead". This is not a negative view of life. On the contrary, this is the way to finding genuine fulfillment. It is a total trust in God. This takes the pressure off our own abilities and relies upon the strength of one with endless resources. This is another one of God's simple life changing ironies. Being "as good as dead" is the first step in finding real life. Don't think your dreams are out of reach! If God is in them, He will bring them to pass. Trust in one who gives life to even those "as good as dead".

<u>The Thin Place</u>: Ask, Answer, Pray.

Do you ever feel as if you are past the point of being useful in God's kingdom work?

What ideas often influence our personal evaluation of our own usefulness?

How do these ideas agree or disagree with the teaching of God's word?

October 28
Useless Fires

<u>**From Above**</u>: Malachi 1:6-14

Focal Passage: *"Oh, that one of you would shut the temple doors, so that you would not light useless fires on my altar! I am not pleased with you,"* says the LORD Almighty, *"and I will accept no offering from your hands."* *–Malachi 1:10*

<u>**Here Below**</u>:

There are many ways in which we try to fool others about our true identity. I am not referring to our name or physical identity. I am referring to that part of us that no one sees. It is that identity that remains hidden from others, even those closest to us. Not me, you may be thinking! I am the same everywhere I go! Well, I hope that is true. However, I would venture to say that most of us have some qualities that remain hidden. Usually, these qualities are not very flattering. I am certain that if it were possible for others to see and hear my thoughts, there are times when I would most assuredly be ashamed. Yet, with all of this said, we must remember that while we may be able to hide these traits from others, we cannot hide them from God.

In the above passage, we see the religious leaders of the day offering what God refers to as "useless" sacrifices. They were useless in that they were not sincere. From our perspective, they might have looked the part. But even then, it was a deceit. They were not offering God their best. They were giving him their leftovers. Their hearts were really not in it. To make it even worse, they were doing it primarily for show. They were building these useless fires in an attempt to deceive both God and others concerning their true spiritual state. It did not work then, and it does not work now. It is truly useless to try to deceive the Lord. For our worship to be acceptable to the Lord, it must come from within our true selves, not the person others see us as being. This may mean that we need to come clean and repent of some sin or sins before our worship has meaning. It is only after a true heartfelt conviction and repentance that we are able to "get real" with God. If you feel that your fires are useless today, then take this opportunity to stop and settle things with God. Repent and honestly seek His face and your fires will have meaning. He will welcome you with open arms. Don't light any more useless fires. Instead give your worship meaning today!

The Thin Place: Ask, Answer, Pray.

Are there inner traits within yourself that others do not see? Be honest.

Why do you keep these traits hidden?

How do you think God feels about these hidden traits?

October 29
Hard to Swallow

From Above: Ephesians 4:22-32

Focal Passage: *"Do not let any unwholesome talk come out of your mouths, but only what is helpful for building others up according to their needs, that it may benefit those who listen." –Ephesians 4:29*

Here Below:

I once had a lady compliment my preaching at the end of a church service. She said to me, "If you keep preaching like that, one day you will be a good preacher." Wow! What a compliment! I think. I tell myself that she meant well with her comment. She was a sweet lady and most likely she just had mixed up her words. I was not offended. In fact, I found it humorous. Nevertheless, under different circumstances I could have been offended. Words are powerful. With them we have the power to lift up and to tear down. I learned that day and on many others that the truth, good or bad, can sometimes be hard to swallow.

In the above passage we see two very significant verses. At first glance, it might seem that verses 25 and 29 are saying the same thing. This is not necessarily the case. Verse 25 teaches us the importance of speaking the truth. We are to be honest with our words. Verse 29 teaches us to only let wholesome and uplifting words come from our mouths. Now both of these verses are capable of standing alone. However, we must also view them together. When we view them together, we see that our words are always to be truthful, but not all truths necessarily need to be spoken. Don't misunderstand. I am not advocating lying. I just believe that these verses imply that sometimes we need to be careful in how we share the truth. Even the truth can be used to hurt or embarrass others. If we are not careful, we can even justify this mishandling of truth by telling ourselves that we are obligated to speak it. In cases such as this, perhaps we would be better to just stick to the truths that encourage and edify. Again, this doesn't mean we ignore those difficult truths that need to be confronted. We just need to use discernment and wisdom when delivering it. According to Paul in verse 29, our words should be delivered with the benefit of those who may be listening in mind. Sometimes the truth is hard to swallow. Sometimes it hurts. However, when it comes from the mouth of a child of God, it should be used to comfort and bring about healing. Let your words be those of Jesus.

The Thin Place: Ask, Answer, Pray.

Has anyone ever hurt you by mishandling the truth?

Have you ever been guilty of doing the same?

What measures can you take to assure that your words of truth are spoken in the right spirit?

October 30
Looking Out for Number One

From Above: Philippians 2:17-24

Focal Passage: *"For everyone looks out for his own interests, not those of Jesus Christ." –Philippians 2:21*

Here Below:

In Timothy, Paul had found a true friend. In fact, Paul states in verse 20 that he had no one else like him. There was something special about Timothy that Paul found of great value. What was it? It was the fact that he was selfless. He states in the above verse that Timothy was unlike most everyone else, who only seemed to have their own self interests in mind. Timothy had the concerns of Jesus first and foremost on his mind. This mindset is the exact opposite of selfishness.

Selflessness is still a defining quality when found. Human nature lends itself to selfishness. In contrast, when we see selfless acts being performed, it sets the individuals involved apart. It is also the most obvious trait found in our Savior. He was selfless to the point of surrendering the glories of heaven for a life of earthly struggles ultimately leading to a selfless death on the cross. His every action was one of selfless surrender. To deny self is to follow the example of Christ.

We live in a day when selfishness is often disguised as rights. We often demand our rights with a self-righteousness that we feel is warranted, sometimes at the cost of someone else's feelings. We want what we think we deserve and how dare anyone deny us our rights! Yet, the truth is that if we all really received what we deserve, we would be in a pitiful position. Thankfully, God doesn't give us what we deserve. He doesn't concern himself with our rights. Instead, He gives us grace. You see, the blessings of life are not rights, so much as they are gifts. Timothy understood this. He applied this principle to his relationships with others, putting them and the cause of Christ ahead of himself. For this reason, Paul found him to be a friend of great value, unlike any other. I would also be willing to bet that Timothy never felt slighted by putting others first. Instead, he had the honor of being called a friend like no other by the great Apostle Paul. By his selflessness, he achieved a position of great distinction and respect. Oh, that we all might be such a friend! Just think how different life would be if we all put the needs of others before our own! Is this dream of a selfless world just a pipe dream? Well, let's start with ourselves and see what a difference it makes.

The Thin Place: Ask, Answer, Pray.

Would you say that you honestly lean more toward selflessness or selfishness?

What are the negative effects of selfish behavior?

What are some changes you can make to become more selfless in your relationship with others?

October 31
Running Scared

From Above: James 4:1-10

Focal Passage: *"Submit yourselves, then, to God. Resist the devil, and he will flee from you." –James 4:7*

Here Below:

Today is a day when fear is first and foremost on our mind. Halloween brings about thoughts of ghosts and ghouls and it is a day when darkness seems to prevail. Don't misunderstand. I am not referring to the innocence of children dressing up and accumulating as much candy as possible through the American pastime of trick or treating. I'll leave that subject to your own convictions. However, Halloween does seem to focus on the darkness instead of the light. Yet, one thing we sometimes forget is that we have no reason to fear the darkness, or the devil hidden within the shadows. We do need to respect the devil's ability to influence, but we need not fear him. The bible's promises are clear on this subject. If we resist him, he will flee. He will not simply leave you alone. He will flee from you. You can send him running scared. How! James tells us how above.

We must be careful to read the entire verse. It is not simply a matter of resistance. It also involves submission. We must submit to God. A submission to God is the key to overcoming fear. Submission implies trust. By submitting to Him we are placing our trust, our welfare in His hands. With our life in His hands, we have little to fear.

With this is mind, we need not be afraid of the things we can't see. The things that go bump in the night are just noise intended to distract us from the security found in Christ. If we have anything to fear, it is life apart from Christ. He is the light that causes the darkness to flee. Like turning on a light will help dispel the fears of children at bedtime, so will looking toward the light of Christ dispel the fear of spiritual darkness. It is not our resistance that scares the devil to the point of fleeing. It is the power of Christ that sends him running with his tail between his legs. Look to Christ on this day of fear and you will find your fears relieved.

The Thin Place: Ask, Answer, Pray.

What fears do you struggle with personally? Why?

What results do these fears bring about in your life?

How can trusting in God help you to overcome these fears?

11

November

November 1
Outdone

From Above: Romans 12

Focal Passage: *"Be devoted to one another in brotherly love. Honor one another above yourselves." –Romans 12:10*

Here Below:

The above verse reads in the Holman Christian Standard translation as follows: "Show family affection toward one another with brotherly love. Outdo one another in showing honor." I like that translation, especially the last part of the verse. We are encouraged to outdo one another with our expressions of honor. How different would our lives be if everyone lived according to this principle? Think about it! If everyone was trying to "outdo" the next person with expressions of love and affection for that person, our lives would be complete. There would be no favoritism, no discrimination, no prejudice and no arguing when things don't go our way. Put simply, it would be heaven on earth!

Easier said than done, right? Well, maybe not. After all, I do not believe that God ever asks anything of us that is impossible; that is, nothing is impossible with His help of course. It was this type of selfless behavior that defined the early church. It was what made it different from the world around it. As a result, it grew exponentially. You see, this type of affection is fuel for growth, both on a personal level and on a corporate level. People are looking for these kinds of fulfilling relationships. More specifically, people need this kind of confirmation in their lives. I do. You do. We all do. God knows this better than we. This is why it is a reoccurring theme throughout scripture. In fact, Jesus taught us that is one of the top two most important commandments.

With this in mind, this is one instance in which competition can be very good for the Christian. Let's outdo one another in our genuine expressions of love. What you will find is that it is contagious. I know there have been times in my life when I have been outdone in this area. As a result, I wanted to do the same for someone else. So if we truly desire to see a world like the one described above in which there is no inequity in our relationships, it begins with our own individual heart. Determine today that you will not be outdone!

The Thin Place: Ask, Answer, Pray.

How has an expression of affection or brotherly love been a positive influence in your life?

How did you respond to that expression of honor?

How often do you intentionally show the same type of honor for someone else?

November 2

A Lesson Taught be Lepers

From Above: 2 Kings 7

Focal Passage: *"Then they said to each other, "We're not doing right. This is a day of good news and we are keeping it to ourselves." –2 Kings 7:9*

Here Below:

The above Old Testament story is one of great interest. It contains political intrigue, miracles and a message of faith. There are many spiritual truths in this story that could be studied today. In particular though, I want us to consider the four lepers mentioned first in verse 3. They are only side players in this story, yet they do something of great importance. They discover the abandoned enemy camp and then after a period of enjoying their discovery, they tell the king. They understood that good news of this nature needed to be shared. This small narrative is chock full of spiritual truths of which we can learn. Let's consider two of them.

First, notice it was *lepers* who discovered the blessing. It wasn't the king or his court. It was lepers, the outcast of the land that God brought to the blessing first. The prophet Elisha had prophesied that their famine was about to be interrupted with a blessing from God. However, the king's advisor told him that this was unlikely. It took lepers to reveal God's truth. The lesson here is that God can use anyone with a willing and open heart, regardless of our position in life.

Second, notice the attitude of the lepers. As lepers, they had every right to be angry with the world. They were the untouchables. Likewise, they were often called sinners and wrongfully blamed for their condition, which we now know is a physical disease contracted much like any other. Yet, leprosy was looked upon as their punishment. This perhaps justified people's desire to ignore these people in need. Yet, they did not simply keep the spoils of their find to themselves. They shared it with the others who were also starving. If only we all felt the same way about the great miracle that has happened in our life. They understood that it is wrong to keep life changing and life saving news to ourselves. They let everyone know. The same should be true of the change that has been wrought in our lives. God has blessed us with salvation and a joy that nothing else can match. Yet, many of us are content keeping this good news to ourselves. This is not why God has blessed us. The blessings we have are to be shared. It doesn't take a prophet or a king to do this. A leper is in a position to share it in a way that has greater impact. The same is true today. You have good news and you are surrounded by people who are starving for it! Don't keep it to yourself! Share God's blessing today!

The Thin Place: Ask, Answer, Pray.

Are you guilty of keeping God's blessing to yourself?

What do you think happens when we do not share the blessings with others?

How can you practically share the good news with someone this week?

November 3
Heart Disease

From Above: I John 3:21-22

Focal Passage: *"Dear friends, if our hearts do not condemn us, we have confidence before God and receive from him anything we ask, because we obey his commands and do what pleases him." –I John 3:21-22*

Here Below:

Are you ever guilty of doing what I sometimes do? Sometimes I get myself so worked up over a potential problem and allow my mind to run through every possible negative outcome to the point that I allow my imagination and emotions to chase my heart and mind into a state of worry and stress over something that hasn't even happened yet. As a result, this emotional frenzy can often cause us to neglect the greatest resource we have in preventing the problem from happening in the first place. That resource is prayer.

Looking back on situations such as these, I can't help but think of the above passage. It refers to our hearts condemning us. Many times I have allowed my heart to condemn me. This spiritual heart disease can condemn us to countless sleepless nights filled with unneeded and unwarranted stress. According to this passage, the solution to this heart condemnation is to have confidence in God, knowing that we receive *anything* we ask of Him in accordance to His will. Of course, we can't forget the final part of this passage either. God answers our prayers in this manner when we are living in obedience to His commands and living a life that is pleasing to Him. Many times when trouble hits we ask "Why?". I think maybe God is sometimes asking us "Why?". Why do we only turn to Him when we become desperate? Why don't we come to Him in prayer before the problems come? A lifestyle of prayer can prevent many of the probable trials we face. This means taking our needs to God before we run through every possible negative scenario in our minds. In fact, I believe we never even know about many of the potential problems we might have faced. A steady prayer life shields us from them. Still, the key factor here is whether or not we actually pray for those things that concern us. Like any loving father, God wants to hear from His children. Don't let your heart condemn you today. Let God handle your needs.

The Thin Place: Ask, Answer, Pray.

Have you ever worried over something for which you failed to include in your prayers?

Compare this experience to the times when you prayed instead of worrying?

How were the outcomes different?

November 4
Alone Time

From Above: Matthew 28:18-20

Focal Passage: "...*And surely I am with you always, to the very end of the age.*" *–Matthew 28:20b*

Here Below:

I once had an experience as a teenager that I will never forget. The youth group from my church had been in Atlanta attending a Christian concert. Upon leaving, there was some confusion, and to make a long story short, I was left in Atlanta. No one realized this fact until the different vehicles pulled up in our church parking lot an hour or so later, only to reveal that I was not there. Meanwhile, I was about 15 years old in downtown Atlanta around 11 pm. I must admit that it was a lonely feeling. Keep in mind, this was before cell phones! Nevertheless, I made it home safely. This truth can be drawn from this narrative. Sometimes people make mistakes. Sometimes we make mistakes. Sometimes we fail to do what we are supposed to do. The result can be that we are left feeling alone and facing an uncertain future. Here is what we must remember though. Feeling alone is not the same as being alone. I was never alone in that parking garage in Atlanta. God was with me.

God has given us multiple promises in His word that He will never leave us alone or forsake us. In fact, we often overlook this part of the Great Commission. Jesus is giving His final instructions and giving a final promise. Along with this command, He reminds us that He will be with us to the very end. He must have said this due to the fact that He understood human feelings. He understood that dark times might cause us to feel alone. He was reminding us again that feeling alone and being alone are not the same. He was giving us assurance that in those moments when we feel alone, He is still with us. In fact, it has been my experience that God may sometimes bring us to those places so that He might have some alone time with us! It is in those intimate times that we experience the most growth. When it comes down to just ourselves and God, we see our spiritual condition for what it really is. Then comes the growth. So when you feel alone, remember the difference between feelings and reality. God will never leave you alone. Instead, use those moments to spend quality time with the Lord.

<u>The Thin Place</u>: Ask, Answer, Pray.

Has there ever been a time in your life when you felt lonely?

How did you get to that point in your life?

Did God reveal Himself to you in those times? How so?

November 5
The Spiritual Spoiled Brat

__From Above__: Psalm 10; Romans 6:1-4

Focal Passage: *"Why does the wicked man revile God? Why does he say to himself, "He won't call me to account?""* –Psalm 10:13

__Here Below__:

Psalm 10 is a very revealing passage of scripture. It gives a perfect description of the mindset of many people in our time. It speaks of the attitude that there is no spiritual accountability for our actions and way of thinking. Many think they can live their lives without the inconvenience of consequences. The psalmist refers to the wicked man as one with doubts of God's sense of justice. Unfortunately, it is not always the wicked that have this belief. Many believers ignore what scripture has to say about this matter. Perhaps they take the concept of grace to the extreme. They see the fact that we are forgiven of all our sins to mean that we are not held responsible for them, as if God somehow doesn't notice or doesn't mind. Paul addressed this assumed license to sin in Romans 6. You see, it is an age old problem. It is also a very tempting way to look at life. After all, who wouldn't like to live life without consequences?

However, the truth of the matter is that consequences are inevitable. In fact, the psalmist recognizes in verse 14 that God is a witness to our actions and will inevitably render justice. The man that thinks otherwise is only fooling himself. This fact is important. We must remember that God will allow consequences to come. For the believer, this reality is not meant to bring about feelings of dread or fear to our heart and mind. On the contrary, as hard as they might be, consequences are further evidence of God's love. Huh? How can that be? Well think about it. In a healthy parent child relationship, a loving parent is not going to totally shield a child from the consequences of his negative actions. To do so would result in a child that feels they can do whatever they want. Put simply, a brat is created. Consequences on the other hand keep us in check. They remind us that we do have to be mindful of others and that our actions do matter. Well, our heavenly Father doesn't want us to become spiritual spoiled brats. He also knows that consequences today may prevent mistakes tomorrow. In the end, consequences promote growth. If we learn from them, we are better for it. So don't think for a moment that God will not hold you accountable. His love for you is too great to ignore your sin. So repent and trust in His love, mercy and grace.

The Thin Place: Ask, Answer, Pray.

Think of a time when you had to deal with the spiritual consequences of your negative actions.

What was the result of these consequences?

How did God speak to you through these consequences?

November 6
Soothing the Savage Breast

From Above: I Samuel 16:14-23; Psalm 33

Focal Passage: "*Whenever the spirit from God came upon Saul, David would take his harp and play. Then relief would come to Saul; he would feel better, and the evil spirit would leave him.*" –I Samuel 16:23

Here Below:

Saul was internally tormented. Perhaps it was guilt. Perhaps it was anger. Perhaps it was disappointment in his own mistakes, mistakes that had caused God to look to another for leadership in his earthly kingdom. Perhaps it was a literal demonic influence that had penetrated his heart. However we view this passage, this much is true. Saul was in anguish. Ironically, it would be the musical gift of his main rival, still unknown at the time, that would soothe the savage within. David's music would be the catalyst for calm in the heart of Saul. God's gift of music still has this effect. I recently purchased an album of a group that has literally taken the psalms and put them to music. These musical artists have tried to maintain the original intent of the scripture while adding their own creative flair to the music using a conglomeration of native and world instruments. The result is a worship experience that uplifts and calms the spirit. Sacred music has that effect. What makes it sacred? Sacred music glorifies God. It acknowledges God and His influence in our lives. Like prayer, it opens our heart to His voice both in corporate and private worship settings. Music enables us to push the distractions aside and listen to the life changing voice of God.

There is a reason as to why God inspired the writers with the Psalms. We often forget that the longest book of the bible is a hymn book. God must have done this to validate the importance of musical worship in the lives of His children. He created us in such a way as to gain strength from musical worship and meditation. As with Saul, it is also a soothing medicine for the troubled heart. This soothing quality is not dependent upon style or instrumentation. For some it is soft ethereal sound of the harp and for others it might be found with heavy roar of an electric guitar. Still for others it might be some of both. It is not the instrumentation, but the glorification of God that gives it this soothing quality. Never underestimate this valuable resource in those troubling times. God has given us this gift. Saul used it. David used it. Moses used it. Elijah used it. Mary used it. You can use it as well.

The Thin Place: Ask, Answer, Pray.

How important is music in your worship, both personal and corporate?
What styles of music do you find the most soothing?
How has God used music to speak to your heart in the past?

November 7
The Replacements

From Above: Romans 6:11-14

Focal Passage: "*Do not offer the parts of your body to sin, as instruments of wickedness, but rather offer yourselves to God, as those who have been brought from death to life; and offer the parts of your body to him as instruments of righteousness.*" –Romans 6:13

Here Below:

Many times, we interpret the above passage as referring to the bad habits for which we use our bodies. This can most certainly be a proper application. However, this passage is more than just an admonition to abstain from sinful sensual pleasures or from habits that harm our physical bodies. Probably most of us could give a hearty "Amen!" to that interpretation, even if we fail to live by it. But keep in mind, this passage is talking about more than just sexual immorality and substance abuse as some might interpret it. I think Paul is referring to any way in which we misuse our bodies. We might use our tongue to gossip or lie and our brain to scheme and plot. These are sins of the most damaging kind. Yet, Paul takes it one step further. Instead of merely focusing on the things we shouldn't do with our bodies, he tells us here as to how our bodies are to be properly used. They are to be looked upon as instruments of righteousness. In other words, they are the tools God uses to accomplish His will. Perhaps, the focusing on the positive use of these instruments is the key to overcoming the negative use.

Many people I encounter that are involved in unhealthy or unspiritual habits would be the first to tell you that they need to quit. I know it is wrong! I want to stop! I just can't help myself! There is much truth to these statements. The habits that are the hardest to shake are those that usually seemed the most innocent in the beginning. In fact, more often than not, we do not realize that it is a habit until it has already gained a certain amount of control in our lives. That is how bad habits work. But don't be dismayed. There is relief. The answer is found in the above passage. Offer yourselves to God. Put simply, *you* can't break the chain of habits that may be hindering your walk. But God can! Accept His forgiveness with a repentant heart and seek His Holy Spirit power. It is by His strength alone that you can whip the bad habits that plague your heart. Then make a conscious effort to use your body, both physical and mental, for the purposes of righteousness. Overcoming bad habits is not always an overnight accomplishment. Yet, when we form good habits to replace the bad, the bad begin to lose their hold. Good for bad. Holy Spirit power for self-help power. Following these replacements will aid you in your quest to overcome the bad habits of your life. Offer yourselves to God today.

The Thin Place: Ask, Answer, Pray.

Do you have any bad habits with which you are struggling?

What good habits can you start to replace these bad?

How do you pray when it comes to overcoming these habits?

November 8
The November In My Soul

From Above: Psalm 37:1-25

Focal Passage: "*The steps of a good man are ordered by the Lord: and he delighteth in his way.*

Though he fall, he shall not be utterly cast down: for the Lord upholdeth him with his hand." *–Psalm 37:23-24 (KJV)*

Here Below:

His name was Ishmael. He was the first person character in Herman Melville's classic literary masterpiece *Moby Dick*. In the early pages of this great novel, Ishmael refers to the time "...whenever it is a damp, drizzly November in my soul..." It is in those dark moments that this whaler felt the need to go to sea. It is in those shadowy and dreary mental moments that he felt the need to get away and start again. Can you relate to Ishmael's plight? We all have experienced our own "damp, drizzly Novembers". A more clinical term for this condition of the soul might be depression. We've all been there. The real question is not whether we ever get depressed, but how we free ourselves from it.

To free ourselves from depression, we must keep things in proper perspective. Notice the above psalm. In this passage we see an overwhelming list of things that would cause even those of the greatest faith to feel a little down and out. But there is a very important clause in the above verse that should change how we view this list of dark and drizzly depressing events. In the KJV it says "he shall not be utterly cast down". The NIV says "thought he stumble, he shall not fall". In other words, as bad as it might seem, God is not going to let you fall so far that He can't pull you out. Just as certain as we can all testify that life can cause depression, we can also testify that God has never let go of us. As the psalmist says, "...the Lord upholdeth him with his hand." The child of God has this assurance. We will ultimately experience victory, if we remain faithful to the Lord. Practically, what does this mean for those of us facing depression? It implies that we need to remember God's faithfulness when the world is trying to bring us down. Stop focusing on the world and its problems and focus on the Lord. Perhaps, we like Ishmael, need to get away for a little while. We need to get some fresh air and take a look at life with a renewed perspective. I have found that if I can step back and look elsewhere for a short while, that the problems tend to have less impact when I come back to them. This is not just pop psychology. It is Biblical. Jesus often left the crowds and went off alone for times of prayer and restoration. If this was necessary for Jesus, it is even more so for you and I. Let God have your damp, drizzly Novembers today!

<u>The Thin Place</u>: Ask, Answer, Pray.

When is the last time you would say that you were depressed?

Did you find freedom from that depression? How?

What role does your faith play in dealing with depression?

November 9
The Power of the Goofy Grin

<u>**From Above**</u>: Psalm 43, Ecclesiastes 8:1

Focal Passage: *"Who is like the wise man? Who knows the explanation of things? Wisdom brightens a man's face and changes its hard appearance."*
—Ecclesiastes 8:1

<u>**Here Below**</u>:

My youngest son has always been extraordinarily happy. From the time he was an infant, his most striking quality has always been his smile. Now at four years old, nothing much has changed. He smiles all the time. When he walks into a room, his cheerful countenance often draws the attention of all in the room. I know I am a biased father who unapologetically sees only the best in his kids, but I do not feel as if I am exaggerating when it comes to the power of this boy's goofy grin. When I have had a bad day, I can come home and without delay I am met with that little cheesy grin. Almost immediately I feel better and the worries of the day seem less. I pray he never loses that smile, for I have come to depend upon it.

Such is the influence of cheerfulness. It is contagious. It has the power to uplift even the most downcast soul. Why is it then that Christians can often be the most "un-cheerful" people we meet? Of all people, we have the most reason to be happy. As a pastor, I often see some of the unhappiest looking faces on a day when we should be our happiest! Now, don't misunderstand. I do not wish to make light of the struggles we sometimes face that might cause our face to appear downcast. But I do think that overall, Christians should be viewed as happy people. Why? Because we are loved by, cared for, protected by and paid for by a God that is all powerful and all loving and gives us a never-ending promise of life. Perhaps the reason my son is so happy is that he is too young to yet be emotionally affected by world. He knows he is loved and that his parents will look after him and that is all that matters to him. Well, shouldn't we be the same with our Heavenly Father? We have even more reason to be happy. After all, God forbid, I may let my son down one day; but, our Heavenly Father will never let us down. Likewise, our countenance, good or bad, is part of our testimony. If we walk around sad faced all the time, what message are we sending the world about our faith? So smile! You never know who might be watching and you never know who might be depending upon that smile. Let your face reflect the joy that God has placed in your heart.

The Thin Place: Ask, Answer, Pray.

Is there a person in your life whose cheerful countenance provides you with encouragement?

What impression do you think your countenance most often gives to those you encounter?

What changes can you make to improve your countenance?

November 10
Something a Pumpkin Taught Me

From Above: Job 32:1-10; James 1:5

Focal Passage: *"I thought, 'Age should speak; advanced years should teach wisdom.' But it is the spirit in a man, the breath of the Almighty, that gives him understanding." –Job 32:7-8*

Here Below:

It was a beautiful day and I had decided to do some yard work. Fall had come and there were leaves in the yard and other tasks that I had been putting off. One task that had really been nagging away at me was to dispose of the jack-o-lantern still sitting on our front porch left over from Halloween. For nearly a week I had looked at this pumpkin which now seemed so out of place. It was time to dispose of it and move on. However, as I went to pick it up I noticed something very peculiar. Its face had changed. It was a couple of weeks old now and age was taking its toll. The once sinister smile that my wife had carved into the pumpkin had morphed into something new. The pumpkin was drying out and the edges around the carvings were wrinkling and curling inwards. That once menacing smile now resembled a silly smile in need of dentures! That once grouchy looking jack-o-lantern now looked like a toothless and happy old man. I couldn't help but laugh at the spectacle. In the course of a couple of weeks, this jack-o-lantern had aged, wrinkled, lost his teeth and his grimace. Still, despite his condition, he still had a smile on his face! Symbolically, he seemed to be accepting the passing of time gracefully. I did not have the heart to throw him away. Days later, he still sat on my front porch.

If only we might accept the passing of time as gracefully and with a smile on our face! Instead, it so often seems as if we do everything we can to fight the passing of time. Do not misunderstand. A youthful attitude is very important. We just need to understand that our attitude has nothing to do with our age. Some of the youngest and most vibrant souls I have ever encountered were well advanced in years. You see, for the child of God, time passing should not be a curse so much as it is a blessing. Every day that passes, I am one day closer to seeing Jesus. Likewise, with every day that passes, I should be that much wiser in the ways of the Lord. Now wisdom doesn't automatically come with the passing of years. It comes when we ask of God. God desires to give us that wisdom which comes with time. With God given wisdom comes fewer past regrets, less worry for the future and happier today. It teaches us that time is not our enemy, it is our friend. As a child of God, we have all eternity. So don't fret the passing of time. Embrace it. Accept it gracefully. As with my pumpkin, let your smile speak of eternity.

The Thin Place: Ask, Answer, Pray.

Would you say that you accept the passing of time gracefully or do you fight it?

Why do you think we sometimes try to fight the passing of time instead of accepting it gracefully?

Would you say that you are wiser now than you were years ago? How so?

November 11
Living Backwards

<u>From Above</u>: Isaiah 58; Matthew 7:7-8

Focal Passage: *"The LORD will guide you always; he will satisfy your needs in a sun-scorched land and will strengthen your frame. You will be like a well-watered garden, like a spring whose waters never fail." –Isaiah 58:11*

<u>Here Below</u>:

Why me? How could a loving God allow this to happen to me? How many times do we hear this question? Too often, I am afraid. Ironically, it has been my experience that it is usually asked by those who have made little to no effort over the course of their lives to know the Lord. In many instances, worship, bible study and devotion to the things of God have been discarded from their lives. Then a crisis hits, and all of a sudden, they wish to blame God for not taking a more active role in the life in which they have denied Him access. I do not wish to sound critical. In fact, I think we've all done this to some small degree in our lives. I know there have been times when I chose my own will over God's and then questioned why things turned out the way they did. This backwards approach to life usually results in a pattern of stress and frustration and ultimately asking questions such as those above. It is when we strive to live centered on the will of God that we find the peace we seek and that God desires to give.

Speaking as one that has been both centered on God's will and at other times out of God's will, I can testify to the peaceful sense that comes with being right where God wants me to be. Of course, what we often forget is that being in the center of God's will doesn't mean that we are going to be free from trial. It could mean just the opposite. God's will might include tests of faith and endurance. We are never promised differently. However, if you know that you are where God wants you to be, even the trials will appear differently to you. They will appear less like problems and more like opportunities for God to work.

To find God's will for our lives, we must first do the things that God has already shared with us as being His will. His will is not some mystical secret. He has already given us 66 books that share with us many details of His will for our lives. Within the pages of the Bible is written God's will for you and me. That is the best starting place when seeking the will of God. Start living those words and the Holy Spirit will give you the rest. If you fail to do what He has already told you to do, then do not question when things don't go your way! Don't buy this backwards approach to life. Instead, trust in the One that would never lead you astray. Seek His will and you will not be disappointed.

The Thin Place: Ask, Answer, Pray.

Have you ever questioned God when things turned out different from your expectations?

If so, do you feel like you were living in the center of His will at the time?

Looking back, do you see a time when difficult circumstances might have been part of His will?

November 12
A Holy Love

From Above: Revelation 4

Focal Passage: *"Each of the four living creatures had six wings and was covered with eyes all around, even under his wings. Day and night they never stop saying: "Holy, holy, holy is the Lord God Almighty, who was, and is, and is to come.""* –Revelation 4:8

Here Below:

If I were to ask you to make a list of the attributes of God, it would probably be similar to the following: loving, merciful, compassionate, gracious, just, etc... Almost without exception, the first description associated with God is loving. That is ok. He is loving. We probably think of this first out of a sense of appreciation for the love He has shown us in sending Jesus to die for our sins. There is no greater love than this love. This much is definitely true. Likewise, all of the attributes in this list are appropriate. However, when it comes to truly describing God, we must not forget His holiness. In fact, His holiness is referenced more often than any other attribute in the scriptures. Yet, it is often further down on our list. I find this to be an interesting observation; in that, His holiness is what makes His love and compassion even greater. God's holiness is what makes the sacrifice of Jesus plausible. If He were not a holy God, then the sacrifice would have only a limited meaning. But thanks be to our God, He is holy!

Too often, we fail to acknowledge the Holiness of God as we should. Perhaps we so value the personal relationship we have with God that we are in danger of becoming too familiar. Do not misunderstand. The personal nature of our relationship with God is vital. It is for this reason Jesus died. God desires this relationship. Yet, it is God's holiness that makes this relationship so special. Therefore, while we can experience intimacy with God, we must never forget that He is still a Holy God. Moses knew Him intimately and he couldn't look Him in the face. The same is true of us. We can be intimate with God and still have a healthy fear and respect of His holiness. This is worship in its purest form. His holiness and His love go hand in hand.

I have often heard people joke about what they are going to say to God when they stand before Him in heaven one day. The reality however I suppose is going to be much different. I imagine that we will be so overwhelmed with His holiness that we will only be able to fall down on our faces in worship. We will not be able to ask silly questions! Thankfully, we do not have to wait until then to acknowledge His holiness. We can do that today with words of worship and reverence. Similarly, we can acknowledge His holiness by applying His truth to our lives. What better way is there to recognize who God is than by following His holy word?

The Thin Place: Ask, Answer, Pray.

Why do you think it is that so many today lack a proper fear of the Lord?
Does your worship, both private and corporate, reflect God's holiness?
How can you better express your understanding of God's holiness?

November 13
Pleasure in a Pine Cone

<u>**From Above**</u>: Luke 10:38-42

Focal Passage: "''Martha, Martha,'' the Lord answered, ''you are worried and upset about many things, but only one thing is needed. Mary has chosen what is better, and it will not be taken away from her.''"
–Luke 10:41-42

<u>**Here Below**</u>:

The other day I was taught another one of God's life lessons through the medium of my children. I went outside to find them fast at play, doing something that I remember doing myself as a child, but have long since forgotten. They were collecting the little seed pods that are found in the pine cones and on the ground surrounding the pine trees bordering our yard. As a child, I used to call them "helicopters". Well, they were collecting the helicopters and throwing them in the air and watching them spiral down to the ground. This cycle of flight, recovery and flight again had been going on for a while when I discovered them. They have a room full of toys, video games, bicycles, skateboards and multiple other forms of entertainment; yet, they had been playing with pine seed pods for nearly an hour. The irony of this scene was unmistakable and educational. Sometimes we are so busy filling our lives with other things that we miss out on the greater and simpler joys of life. I must admit that I joined with my kids in flying these little pine tree helicopters that day. What fun we had! It was the making of a great family memory.

I guess the complication of life is a natural tendency of our fallen human nature. We see the same happening in the above story. Martha was so busy with life that she was missing an opportunity to simply sit at the feet of Jesus as Mary was doing. What she was doing was not necessarily bad. On the contrary, she was taking care of her guests, which included the Savior. Yet, in her busyness she was missing out on a once in a lifetime opportunity. I am not too critical of Martha in this story, for I often find myself doing the same thing. Yet I have discovered that the greater pleasures, joys and blessings of life come when we simply stop and look at what is going on around us. Often *real* life is happening right under our nose and we do not see it. Don't let the hectic nature of life cause you to miss out on real joy! Instead of telling you to stop and smell the roses, I am going to leave you with this tidbit of wisdom. The next time you see a pine cone in your yard. Pick it up and pull the little seed pod loose from its prickly grasp. Then let your helicopter fly! You know you want too! A life with God is meant to be a life of joy! So have fun with it, just as God intended!

The Thin Place: Ask, Answer, Pray.

Would you say that you need to stop and look for the simpler pleasures of life more often?

What are some simple pleasures that you enjoy?

Has God ever used these moments to refresh and renew your spirit?

November 14
For His Glory and My Good

From Above: Isaiah 43:14-15; Hebrews 12:11-13

Focal Passage: "*No discipline seems pleasant at the time, but painful. Later on, however, it produces a harvest of righteousness and peace for those who have been trained by it.*" –Hebrews 12:11

Here Below:

What was I thinking? Have you ever asked this question of yourself? We all have. Looking back at our lives we sometimes question why we turned left when it so obvious now that we should have turned right. If only we knew then what we now know to be true. If we had this 20/20 hindsight then, perhaps many mistakes might have been avoided. Nevertheless, hindsight only comes after we make the mistakes. Unfortunately, we all make mistakes and with mistakes come the consequences. This is inevitably part of our human condition. But praise be to God, He is not limited by our human condition!

We serve a God that is so righteous, so loving and so powerful that he can even use our mess ups for good. Unlike men, God doesn't simply wash His hands of us when we fall short. He forgives and restores. In fact, He already knew of my mess ups when He set my life course in motion. This does not mean that my mistakes are part of His plan. It does mean that God's plan cannot be thwarted by them. He can use us despite our mistakes, if we have a repentant and willing heart. Do not misunderstand. His discipline is not always pleasant. Nevertheless, it is always for our good; that is, if we choose to learn from it. How we fulfill God's plan for our lives is often decided by how we respond to our own mistakes. If we ignore them, we go nowhere. Likewise, if we fail to let them go, we go nowhere. It is when we turn from them and take their teaching with us that we move forward in our walk. So do not let your mistake be the defining moment of your life. Instead, let your response to the mistake be the guiding principle that governs your future. Let God have your successes and your failures. Do this and you will find the mistakes coming fewer and farther between. Give it to God. He can use it for His glory and for your good.

The Thin Place: Ask, Answer, Pray.

Have you ever experienced the discipline of God? When?

Did you learn anything from the experience?

How can you apply lessons learned from the past to your future?

November 15
Good Company

<u>From Above</u>: Psalm 84

Focal Passage: *"Blessed are those who dwell in your house; they are ever praising you."* –Psalm 84:4

<u>Here Below</u>:

Abraham. Moses. Joseph. Samson. Gideon. Job. David. Daniel. Shadrach. Meshach. Abednego. Elijah. Ruth. Jonah. Mary. Joseph. Peter. Stephen. Paul. Silas. John. Etc... Etc... Etc... These people all have at least three things in common. First, none of them were perfect. Second, during at least one point in each of their lives they experienced a potentially overwhelming problem. Third, because of their faith, God was able to use that experience to do something astounding in their lives. These heroes of the faith and many others like them are heroes for this very reason. God was able to turn their crisis into an opportunity to show Himself faithful. Our faith leads to His faithfulness. God still works in our lives like this today.

In the above Psalm, the sons of Korah have written into this beautiful song a simple reminder for every child of faith. When they refer to "those who dwell in your house", they are referring to those within the family; in this case, the family of God. Those within that family have reason to praise in all times. This Psalm does not specify good or bad times. They are simply "ever praising". Why? Because genuine faith knows that God can take any circumstance and use it for His good and our good.

Did everyone mentioned in the above list always show strong faith? No. Unfortunately, it was sometimes slow in coming. Nevertheless, they each came around, and when they did, God revealed Himself in a mighty way. Sometimes they still had to go through the fire or face the stones of the enemy. Nevertheless, their faith won out and here we are still talking about their example thousands of years later. So just remember when you find yourself in a crisis that you are in very good company! Let God have His way with you today and He will show Himself faithful!

<u>The Thin Place</u>: Ask, Answer, Pray.

How has God shown Himself faithful in your life during a time of crisis?

How faithful are you in praising the Lord in the midst of life's problems?

What does our praise in times of crisis say to those around us about the Lord?

November 16
Two Birthdays and a Funeral

From Above: Ecclesiastes 7:1-2; I Corinthians 15:55-57

Focal Passage: *"A good name is better than fine perfume, and the day of death better than the day of birth." –Ecclesiastes 7:1*

Here Below:

My grandfather died. His funeral was the day following my daughter's fifth birthday, which was one day following mine. As a result, we had to travel out of town for the funeral and consequently our birthday party plans had to be readjusted. We were forced to spend the bulk of both of our birthdays at the funeral home. As an aging adult, not celebrating my birthday was just fine. However, it was my five year old daughter's disappointment that worried me. Thankfully, the family all joined together in an attempt to make my daughter's birthday special and we had probably the world's only recorded children's birthday party ever to take place at a funeral home. We pulled a table out in the parking lot and had cake, ice-cream, balloons and presents while just inside the building, my grandfather was lying in state. Ironically, as morbidly bizarre as this might sound, to date it is perhaps my daughter's favorite birthday memory. Looking back though, I see just how appropriate is truly was. Both gatherings were celebrations of life. Death was unable to rob us of the joy of life that day.

While this story is extremely unique and admittedly a little strange, it does illustrate a very biblical message. Death is not our enemy. It is not something to fear or dread, at least not for the child of God. On that day, we celebrated my grandfather's 97 years of life on this earth and we celebrated my daughter's 5 years. Two opposite ends of the spectrum and yet still the same. According to scripture, we are to view death as more of a cause for joy than sorrow. Sure, we are saddened at the loss of a loved one. Likewise, I do not wish to imply that we are to be excited about the prospects of our own demise either. Nevertheless, it is not something of which we are to be frightened. To fear death lessens the quality of life in the here and now. If you need convincing, just compare the response of a believer in Jesus Christ with that of a nonbeliever, upon facing their own mortality. As a pastor, I have counseled both. There is a definite difference. Without that shadow of death hanging over our hearts and minds, we are able to appreciate life more fully in spite of our circumstances. Don't let the shadow rob you of the light of life. Celebrate your life today! As for me and my daughter, I know we will never forget the day we had a birthday party at a funeral home.

The Thin Place: Ask, Answer, Pray.

How much time do you spend thinking of death?

How has your philosophy concerning death influenced your response to the loss of loved ones?

How does your philosophy of death affect your joy in life?

November 17
Cut the Bull!

From Above: Psalm 50; I Samuel 15:22

Focal Passage: *"I have no need of a bull from your stall or of goats from your pens, for every animal of the forest is mine, and the cattle on a thousand hills." –Psalm 50:9-10*

Here Below:

There is an old saying that goes something like this, "What's mine is mine and what's yours is yours." This trite expression is often twisted in a joking manner to say "What's mine is mine and what's yours is *mine!*" As funny as that might be, with God it is true! One thing we often forget is that everything we have and everything we see belongs to Him. He created it. It was His long before we took possession of it. It would be wise for all of us to remember this simple fact. In the above Psalm, we see God reminding us that He really does not *need* our sacrifices. He in actuality needs nothing. It is as if He is saying, "Not another bull...What I really want is you!" You see, God is not like man; in that, He does not have needs of which He cannot meet Himself. In all intellectual honesty, this fact is a little difficult for us to grasp. After all, even the wealthiest of men still have needs of some form. The need may be emotional, spiritual or relational, but it is still a need. This is not true of God. He has it all.

This Psalm was addressing the fact that the sacrifices offered to the Lord weren't due to His need for them, but His desire. He wanted a relationship with His children. The sacrifice would help our hearts be in proper standing with Him and enable us to be in a right relationship. You see, it wasn't need that led God to institute the sacrificial system; it was love for you and I. This truth would be ultimately displayed in the sacrifice of His Son on the cross, a sacrifice that God himself offered. This reference to the cattle on a thousand hills was reminding us that what God really wanted was our hearts, not our sacrifices. It is possible for our sacrifices to mean nothing if our hearts aren't right. However, if your heart is right, your sacrifice will be as well. As you read on down in this Psalm, you see God desiring to be an integral and caring part of our lives.

Well, you may be thinking that this is a no brainer. You may be right. However, I have seen many treat their service to and relationship with the Lord with an overabundance of self-assurance, as if God needed them to get something done. God doesn't need us. He wants us. In this sense, this relationship is unlike any earthly relationship. We cannot be codependent with God. We need Him, but He wants us. He wants you. For this reason, we need to make sure that our service and our sacrifices are given in the right spirit. Put simply, God desires less bull and more true devotion! He desires it and He deserves it.

<u>The Thin Place</u>: Ask, Answer, Pray.

What role does service and sacrifice play in your relationship with God? How important is it?

How does your service to the Lord reflect your need for Him?

How can your service and sacrifice be more pleasing to the Lord?

November 18
Go With What You Know!

<u>From Above</u>: Ephesians 1:17-23

Focal Passage: *"I pray also that the eyes of your heart may be enlightened in order that you may know the hope to which he has called you, the riches of his glorious inheritance in the saints, and his incomparably great power for us who believe. That power is like the working of his mighty strength," –Ephesians 1:18-19*

<u>Here Below</u>:

What a prayer! In the above letter, Paul tells the Ephesian church that his prayer for them is that their hearts would be enlightened in order that they might know the hope of their calling. He goes on to speak in reference to both eternal salvation as well as power for living in the here and now. He refers to this knowledge as a "mighty strength". Put simply, Paul was praying that his friends might come to know God's will for their lives. In discovering this will, they would be empowered, and so will we. There is strength in knowing God's will.

Knowing God's will is easier than we often make it out to be. God wants us to do His will. Therefore, doesn't it only make sense that it should be easy to discover. We do not have to climb a mountain and seek the advice of a wise old sage to find God's will. Nor do we have to go on some mythic spiritual quest in order to discover God's will. It is not a mystery to be unraveled. God wants you to find it! In fact, much of God's will for our lives is already revealed in His written word. The Bible contains many of the answers we seek. This combined with a sincere prayer life coming from a humbled and contrite heart will further reveal the guidance we seek. Once discovered, we gain strength from the knowing. We are stronger because we have the confidence to move forward in a direction that we know is pleasing to God. So when you are in doubt about God's will for your life, do that which you already know to be His will. Go with what you know! Live obediently in what you already know to be true and God will reveal the rest in His time and in His way. Don't complicate what is meant to be a simple matter with impatience. Live for God now and you will not be let down tomorrow.

The Thin Place: Ask, Answer, Pray.

Do you struggle with knowing the will of God?

What do you already know of God's will for your life?

What is still uncertain about God's will for your life and how do you pray for it?

November 19
The End of the Rope

From Above: Zechariah 4; I Corinthians 1:25

Focal Passage: *"Who despises the day of small things?..."* –Zechariah 4:10

Here Below:

Have you ever felt as if you were at the end of your rope? Isn't it interesting that God seems to be able to do the most with our lives when we are at the end of our rope? This is a theme we see very often in the New Testament. In one example we see Jesus feeding a crowd of thousands with a meager amount of fish and bread. Likewise, in several other instances we see Jesus healing people that the world had already written off. We even see Him reverse death, the ultimate end of the rope. It was in those moments, when there was nowhere else to turn, that God was able to do the most good. This was not a concept found only in the New Testament. It is found throughout the Old Testament as well. In the above chapter from the prophecy of Zechariah, we see this principle expressed. The above verse expresses the thought that it is on those days when we have seem to have little that we truly have the most, if our trust is in the Lord. Verse 6 says "'Not by might nor by power, but by my Spirit,' says the LORD Almighty." You see, when we come to the end of our rope, we need to remember that it is not our strength that matters, but God's. We do not need to fear the end of our rope.

The problem we often encounter with this principle and perhaps the reason God has placed so many examples in His word, is the fact that we all too often wait until we are at the end of our rope to seek His strength. We fail to turn to the One with limitless power and instead depend upon our own insufficient strength. God's strength is not just ours when we find ourselves coming up short. It is ours to depend upon at all times, even when our strength is firm. God is God in the day of small things as well as in the day of big. Our circumstances may change, but God does not. He is worthy of our praise and dependence in all circumstances. Don't wait until you have nowhere else to turn. Turn to God daily.

<u>**The Thin Place**</u>: Ask, Answer, Pray.

Have you ever felt as if you had nowhere to turn when facing a crisis?

At what point, if at all, did you turn to the Lord in this crisis?

How might this situation have been different if you had turned to the Lord sooner?

November 20

Disposable People

<u>**From Above**</u>: Luke 9:51-56; Luke 10:25-37

Focal Passage: "*And he sent messengers on ahead, who went into a Samaritan village to get things ready for him; but the people there did not welcome him, because he was heading for Jerusalem.*" –Luke 10:33

<u>Here Below</u>:

As you probably know, there was a definite two way prejudice that existed between the Jewish people of the Bible and the people then known as Samaritans. It is my understanding that this prejudice still exists to some small degree today. The Jews looked upon Samaritans as being impure, due to cultural and religious corruption. The Samaritans likewise had no love loss for Jews. This shared prejudice was so great that travelers from each side would travel by foot miles out of the way to avoid contact and contamination from the other. Of course, we do not have to travel the world over to find prejudice. It is everywhere. Perhaps the best place to look for it is in our own hearts.

In Luke 9, Jesus had planned on going to minister in a Samaritan village, but the Samaritans didn't want Him to come because He was on His way to Jerusalem. The disciples were so enraged by the attitude of the Samaritans that they were ready to dispose of them. They wanted to call down fire from heaven to destroy them. To the disciples, they were disposable people. Jesus rebuked their attitude. Ironically, in the very next chapter, Jesus tells the parable of the Good Samaritan. It was the Samaritan that exemplified the true Christian neighborly attitude in that story. This story was another rebuke to the existing prejudice. Jesus was reminding them with this story that there is no such thing as a disposable person as far as God is concerned. We are all important to Him. Regardless of our differences, we are equal in the eyes of the Lord. This fact is not only relevant to our social prejudices, but also our personal ones. You see, we can believe in social equality and still be prejudiced. We can think less of others due to their age, sex, family background and appearance. These are differences we cannot necessarily control. We can also look down upon others because of things they can control. Our prejudices can be directed toward the personalities, attitudes, mistakes or lifestyles of others. In these instances, it is important to remember that we are all fallen. While this does not excuse our behaviors, it does put us all on equal ground. After all, it was the "good" Samaritan that saved the day in Jesus' story, not the upright or religious. Don't let your prejudices get in the way of seeing in others what Jesus sees when He looks upon them. Dispose of no one. Instead, get to know your neighbor. Love them as yourself.

The Thin Place: Ask, Answer, Pray.

With what personal prejudices do you struggle? Why?

What possible blessings did you miss because of these prejudices?

What steps can you take to overcome these prejudices?

November 21

The View From My Chair

From Above: Ezekiel 3:15-21

Focal Passage: *"Then I came to them of the captivity at Telabib, that dwelt by the river of Chebar, and I sat where they sat, and remained there astonished among them seven days." –Ezekiel 3:15 (KJV)*

Here Below:

The above passage is one that testifies to the concept of accountability. According to this passage, we will be held accountable for the souls of others. Simply put, it is not enough to simply live and let live. The indifference of others to the things of the Lord does not excuse our indifference towards their spiritual condition. The prophet in this passage was going to be held accountable for the warnings he did or did not give to the wicked to which he was sent. However, notice what was required of the prophet prior to his warning the people of their sin. He had to sit where they sat. Before he could judge, he had to look at life from their perspective. I do not believe that God required this of him so that he might be more understanding of their choices. On the contrary, it was more likely to remind the prophet of the urgency of their situation and give him insight into how to bring the message more effectively. Looking at life from their chair would enable him to strengthen his message delivery. It would also strengthen his resolve to deliver it. Empathy creates a proper balance between judgment and compassion and results in a message that is more readily accepted.

Too often, we are quick to judge others for spiritual shortcomings. Sometimes these judgments are justified. Nevertheless, we very rarely gain any ground in the hearts of those with whom we carry a message of judgment until we at first try to see things from their point of view. In other words, when we deal with unbelievers, we need to remember what it is like to be where they are spiritually; in that, we have been there ourselves. We can do this without compromising our message. Again, it in fact strengthens our message when it is delivered with an empathetic heart. In this manner our intentions are not seen as authoritarian in nature, but more as a genuine concern felt by a friend who has been there themselves. Not to mention, this is more in line with the compassionate way Jesus seemed to handle these type confrontations. To win the lost, we must remember what it is like to be lost. To convince the sinner to repent, we must remember what it is like to struggle with a besetting sin. To persuade someone of the value of Christian living, we must understand their need for evidence. Empathy alone is good, but empathy along with integrity is a sure way to win others. So pull up a chair and change your point of view.

The Thin Place: Ask, Answer, Pray.

Have you ever been the recipient in a judgmental confrontation?

How did you accept the message? Did you dismiss it outright because of the approach?

How does this affect how you relate to others?

November 22
A Change of Clothes

<u>From Above</u>: Psalm 30; Romans 8:28

Focal Passage: *"You turned my wailing into dancing; you removed my sackcloth and clothed me with joy, that my heart may sing to you and not be silent. O LORD my God, I will give you thanks forever."* –Psalm 30:11-12

<u>Here Below</u>:

My favorite part of the day is when I come home and take off my work clothes, which for a Pastor is often a suit and tie; and don a pair of my favorite blue jeans and t-shirt. It is not that I do not like wearing a suit and tie. It is just that the blue jeans and t-shirt have come to represent home for me. When I change into them, regardless of what kind of day I have had, I feel at home and therefore I know it is all going to be all right. It is there that I can truly be comfortable. Of course, as nice as it might be, changing clothes doesn't always automatically change my attitude. There is no magic cure for a bad attitude this side of heaven. However, God is capable making that change in our hearts. How? Well, there is one thing we can do that might help make His job a little easier. It is simple actually. Just give thanks.

If we stop focusing on the things that haven't gone our way and instead think on the things that have, we will soon recognize a greater change of attitude. When we change our focus, God can really go to work in our hearts. Only then can we be a witness to his transformational miracles taking place. Only God is capable of taking our sackcloth and clothing us with joy. Only God can take a circumstance that might otherwise seem to be reason for despair and make something good come out of it. In fact, God has even taken the ultimate bringer of despair and fear and has pulled out its stinger. Even death itself has lost its meaning. That is how our God operates. If He can do that, doesn't it only make sense that He can work out your circumstances for good? If He can take the sting out of death, then can't He take my bad day and help me to see what is good about it? Hey, only He can! But God always works best in a willing heart. We have to be willing to see the good in our bad circumstances. When we are willing, He is more than able to show us. So take off that sackcloth and ashes and put on your old comfortable blue jeans. Wash your face and step back a moment. Now give thanks for the blessings in your life and let God do what He does best.

The Thin Place: Ask, Answer, Pray.

Do you find it difficult to look for good in all circumstances?

How can your attitude affect your circumstances in good or bad ways?

When has God caused something good to come from something bad in your life?

November 23
A Cycle of Thanks

From Above: 2 Corinthians 9:9-15

Focal Passage: *"You will be made rich in every way so that you can be generous on every occasion, and through us your generosity will result in thanksgiving to God." –2 Corinthians 9:11*

Here Below:

Let's make a pretend list of things of which we should be thankful. I imagine your list will be as mine. It will be lengthy, but it will still be insufficient, to say the least. This time of year we set aside time to thank God for the blessings of our life. This giving of thanks is in a very real sense a form of worship and something that should be a part of our lives 365 days out of the year. It should be a way of life. However, as we are reflecting on this list, let's remember the purpose behind the blessings. According to the verse above, one reason we are blessed is so that we might in turn be generous to others. In other words, we are blessed so that we might be a blessing to others. As a result, thanksgiving!

You see, everything God does is on purpose. The blessings He showers upon us are not simply a result of His love for us, they are given so that we might share that love with others. The above verse is not only referring to the material blessings of life, but the spiritual blessings as well. It reinforces the idea that the Christian life is more about what we give than what we receive. We are showered with blessings so that we might share them with others. The response is thanksgiving to God. It is a beautiful cycle of blessing, sharing, thanking, blessing, sharing and thanking. Once you find yourself in this cycle, you can add the corresponding feelings of joy and satisfaction to your list of blessings. This thankful spirit is at the heart of the healthy Christian life. Our lives should be a reflection of the gratitude we feel toward God. Think about it. Without a thankful heart, do we really have anything? Take time today to show your thankfulness to God by being generous to others. Let the cycle begin with you.

The Thin Place: Ask, Answer, Pray.

How are some ways in which God has blessed you?

How do you share your blessings with other people?

What is the result of this sharing?

November 24
Thank You...I Think

From Above: Ephesians 5:3-4; Acts 20:35

Focal Passage: *"Nor should there be obscenity, foolish talk or coarse joking, which are out of place, but rather thanksgiving." –Ephesians 5:3-4*

Here Below:

As a pastor, I am often given gifts, especially around the holiday season, from members of my congregation. There have been times when these gifts were obviously sacrificial in nature. In other words, they came from people who probably could not afford to give it to me; yet, they did so to honor their pastor and family. These gifts are difficult for me to take. Yet, I remember a professor telling me years ago to never deny one the blessing of giving a gift to their minister. Honor them by accepting it graciously. I didn't understand then what he meant by that. I do now. He was right. I have tried to turn gifts away only to see that in so doing I hurt the giver, even though my intentions were admirable. To honor them, it is best to accept graciously and return to them words of thankfulness and appreciation. Why is this so important? Because the giver of the gift is expressing love and the giver of thanks is expressing love in return. As a result, both are strengthened. Both gain from the experience. To deny either is to quench spirit of the gift and giver and to deny mutual encouragement. Ultimately, thanksgiving is more than just a holiday. It's a distinguishing call of the Christian life and it is part of our testimony.

Notice Paul's admonition from the above verse. Here we see a distinct difference drawn between those who know the Lord and those who do not. For the believer, there should be no inappropriate speech. This type speech takes on many forms, some of which need no explanation. However, it can be more than just an obscene joke. The Bible also refers to foolish talk. This is any unnecessary or offensive speech in which there is no purpose other than to fool, harm or shock the listener. In other words, it is selfish speech. Instead, the believer should be known for just the opposite. Out of his mouth should flow words of selfless thanksgiving. Truly giving thanks is perhaps one of the most unselfish expressions a person can make. Think about it. When thanking someone, we are acknowledging that some blessing or gift we have received has come from outside of ourselves and that it was received as intended, a gift. To return thanks is to acknowledge someone else's giving of themselves for our benefit and praising them for it. This principle is especially true when it comes to offering thanks to God. Therefore, our speech should be drenched with expressions of thankfulness. After all, Christians among all others, have the most reason to be thankful. We are forgiven. We are free. We are saved. And guess what, it was all a gift. So let your life and speech be a reflection of that gift.

The Thin Place: Ask, Answer, Pray.

Do you find it easy to thank others for the things they do for you? Why or why not?

How well do you receive when others are offering their thanks to you? How often do you thank the Lord for His blessings?

November 25
Happy Thanksgiving From Prison!

From Above: Colossians 4:1-6

Focal Passage: *"Devote yourselves to prayer, being watchful and thankful." –Colossians 4:2*

Here Below:

There is a clause found at the end of verse 3 in the above chapter that is very significant. It says "for which I am in chains". This is important. Paul is writing this passage while in prison. He is encouraging us to be devoted to prayer, be watchful and to be thankful from a prison cell. The devotion to prayer and watchful while in prison aspects we can understand. But thankful? How can one be thankful while imprisoned for doing God's will? Well, it is there. It must be possible.

If anything, this passage teaches us that thankfulness is to be more than just an occasional expression. In fact, I think it implies that is should be a regular habit of the Christian heart. It is not by accident that Paul includes the idea of thankfulness in this verse about prayer. Thankfulness is to be as common as prayer is for the Christian. It is to be like an exhale in breathing. After inhaling the blessings of God, expressing thankfulness is the natural response. It is an innate and healthy reaction. The giving of thanks should be a naturally reoccurring part of our lives.

Notice something else about this passage. He never asks them to pray for his release or complains about his chains. Again, he just tells them to be thankful. Put simply, our thankfulness is not dependent upon circumstances. What we do not have or what does not go our way has nothing to do with our thankfulness. Even in those times, we still have endless reasons to be thankful. Even in prison, we can find reasons to give thanks! The best way to maintain that kind of attitude during times of trial is to develop a habit of thankfulness beforehand. Let it become as much a part of your life as breathing. We do not wait until we are suffocating to try to breathe. Likewise, don't wait for a desired outcome to start giving thanks. Start right now. God will be honored and you will be blessed.

The Thin Place: Ask, Answer, Pray.

How easy does thankfulness come to you?

What are you the most thankful for today?

How can you express your thankfulness to God for his blessings?

November 26
The Black Friday Frenzy

From Above: Luke 12:13-31

Focal Passage: *"This is how it will be with anyone who stores up things for himself but is not rich toward God." –Luke 12: 21*

Here Below:

Perhaps one of the most dangerous places to be on "Black Friday" is in the local department store. The news has been filled in the last few years with stories of people literally fighting over toys, electronics and other desired Christmas gifts. I even recall from a year ago one shooting that took place not far from home over the latest video game equipment. Stores are having sales at one or two in the morning and people are lined up, sometimes even camping outside these department stores in order to be the first in the door. In another instance, I recall the story of a sales representative in one store being trampled to death upon the opening of their store on the day after Thanksgiving. This black Friday frenzy is materialism gone wild. It is the love of things at its absolute worst. It is otherwise normal people fighting over things. (Things I might add that our kids will have most likely discarded a week after Christmas!) The sad irony of it all is that it is all done in celebration of the birth of our Savior. Do not get me wrong. There is nothing necessarily wrong with the giving of gifts at Christmas. It becomes wrong when the Christmas gift itself takes prominence in our lives over the Christmas Child.

Of course, this principle not only applies to Christmas, but to all year round. Things are sometimes part of God's blessing. They are good to have. However, we must remember who owns whom! Do we own our things or do they own us? I would bet that the two moms carted off to jail on black Friday for fighting over the latest video game could answer that question! These crazy black Friday stories may seem extreme, but I'll bet it didn't start that way. It probably started with the best of intentions. A parent probably wanted their kids to have what they never did. They wanted their kids to be current with the popular trends and fads. At least, these were probably their justifications. That is the way sin works. It lies to us and takes us somewhere we could never have imagined. What started out as someone wanting something special for their kids turned into jail time and a reputation tarnished. What may start out as a harmless love of a certain thing can ultimately control your life. The remedy for this is to simply make sure that Jesus is always first. Don't let things take an inappropriate place in your life. Don't let the first day of the Christmas season be a "black" day! Take Christmas back today! Vow today to let the Child of Christmas stay first in your life this holiday season!

The Thin Place: Ask, Answer, Pray.

How much emphasis is placed on things during your Christmas celebrations?

Do you ever struggle with the sin of materialism?

How can take back the true meaning of Christmas in your life this season?

November 27
A Magnetic Me

__From Above__: Romans 8:1-14

Focal Passage: *"And if the Spirit of him who raised Jesus from the dead is living in you, he who raised Christ from the dead will also give life to your mortal bodies through his Spirit, who lives in you."* –Romans 8:11

__Here Below__:

Have you ever known anyone with what we call a "magnetic personality"? I have. They seem to make friends everywhere they go. Everyone likes them. They are popular and they make it look so easy. I would like to think that I am a likable guy, but I acknowledge the fact that I have to work at it. It just doesn't come that naturally for me. Perhaps you can relate to this social dilemma. Many times I have wished that I were more like someone else when it comes having that magnetic personality. It would definitely make my life as a pastor simpler. Nevertheless, there are those with that magnetic pull.

I believe Jesus was one such personality. Everywhere He went, there were crowds of people thronging about Him. Now I must acknowledge that Jesus was not an ordinary man. Being God and man, it can only be assumed that there would be some sort of supernatural magnetic pull. Yet, the Bible also goes to great lengths to point out that He was humble in nature. As far as His physical appearance goes, Isaiah 53:2 refers to Him by saying "He had no beauty or majesty to attract us to him, nothing in his appearance that we should desire him". As a result of these modest descriptions, we don't often picture Jesus as a loud and bubbly person bursting into the room and drawing a crowd. Don't get me wrong! He always seemed to be the life of the party, but it had more to do with the deeper things He exhibited than just a likable personality. He was compassionate. His attention was unconditional. He was always giving of Himself. As a result, people were drawn to Him.

According to scripture, the same Spirit that raised Jesus from the dead is living within us. In so doing, the Spirit has empowered us to be Christlike in our actions and behaviors. Our lives are to be lived in such a way as to draw people, not to ourselves, but to the One who lives within us. How do we do this? Well, first we allow the spirit to work through us. Second, we strive to be like Jesus. Christlikeness is still the number one way to win others to the Lord. This flies in the face of self-righteousness, which turns people away. Jesus was humble. Yet, He had a pull that cannot be denied. It is not about being the best me that I can be. It is about being like Jesus. Strive for that and others will see the difference.

The Thin Place: Ask, Answer, Pray.

Would you say that you have a magnetic personality?

How might you improve in this part of your personality?

What changes can you make to help you become more Christlike?

November 28
I'm Dreamin' of a Personal Christmas

From Above: 2 Corinthians 5:14-21

Focal Passage: *"For Christ's love compels us, because we are convinced that one died for all, and therefore all died." –2 Corinthians 5:14*

Here Below:

The holiday season is one filled with sentimental sights and sounds. One such heartwarming sound is the sound of the tinkling bell outside the department store. Likewise, within the church, the holiday season is filled with special offerings and giving is greater during the final two months of the year than any other time of the year. How appropriate it is that in celebration of the birth of our Savior that we should give! However, many give to these offerings for no other reason than a sense of pure seasonal sentiment! What do I mean by this? Well, many of us would eagerly drop some coins in the bucket as we enter the department store, because it is the Christmas thing to do; yet, we would never pick up the phone and call someone in our circle of acquaintances that might be in need and offer assistance. Similarly, we would be quick to drop off some old clothes at the local shelter's drop off site, yet we would never invite a needy person in the community for a meal or even invite them to join with us in a service at our church. These options are less anonymous and may require us to defy the cultural norms. In response, we are instead content to simply drop money in the bucket as we pass.

If anything, Christmas provides the easiest opportunity for us to share the love of Christ with others. It is a time of year when it is normal to discuss the implications of our Savior. With Christmas, we have the perfect backdrop for a discussion on the Lord and for helping others in the name of the Lord. It is the Christmas season! It is all about Jesus. Don't let the opportunities of this season slip by. Let your celebration of Christmas include the giving of yourself to others. After all, that is what the first Christmas was all about, right? Why not give that to someone else this season? The love of Christ is nothing if not personal and practical in its application. Don't let the sentiment of the season overpower the purpose of the season. Specifically share the love of the Bethlehem babe with someone today. Let's make Christmas personal again.

The Thin Place: Ask, Answer, Pray.

Would you say that you are a giving person? How so?

Why do you give?

How could you practically and personally give the message of Christmas to others this season?

November 29
When Life Isn't Fair

From Above: Isaiah 54:17; 2 Corinthians 5:10-12

Focal Passage: "*...What we are is plain to God, and I hope it is also plain to your conscience. We are not trying to commend ourselves to you again, but are giving you an opportunity to take pride in us, so that you can answer* *those who take pride in what is seen rather than in what is in the heart." –2 Corinthians 5:11b-12*

<u>**Here Below**</u>:

Let's be honest. When we are wronged, we want others to know about it. We want the vindication of having the truth revealed so that all might see and know. Unfortunately, it doesn't always happen that way. Sometimes we are wronged and no one else ever sees it from our point of view. This can create feelings of bitterness, anger and even thoughts of revenge in our hearts. After all, I am referring to those times when we are clearly in the right and still find ourselves holding the short end of the stick. It is not fair. Isn't it only right for us to seek vindication in such an instance? Doesn't God desire justice? Doesn't God want truth to prevail? Well, I have to think that the answer to those questions is a definite yes! However, that vindication, justice and truth is for God to deliver, not ourselves. You see, there is a very fine line between vindication and revenge. It is a line that is very easy for you and me to cross. However, God never crosses that line. He is able to administer these things in accordance with His will in just the right amounts, without compromising His nature. He is also able to deliver it in exactly the right time and way. This is why we must leave vindication to the Lord. We must be content in knowing that God knows the truth and the He will eventually sort it all out in a way that pleases Him.

What does this mean for us? Well, like Paul in the above letter, we need to come to a place in our lives where we are content in pleasing God above men. Notice the statement above in which Paul says "We are not trying to commend ourselves to you..." In other words, Paul wasn't overly concerned with what others thought of him. His main concern was what God thought of him. Sure reputation is important, but not nearly as important as being in right standing with the Lord. So, when we are wronged or thought wrongly of, we must make sure first that we are not wrong. Then we must make sure we are pleasing the Lord with our lives. Then we simply leave the rest to Him. We cannot risk ruining our witness by trying to convince those that more than likely will never be convinced anyway to see things our way. Only God can change hearts. Our task is to be genuine and let God work through us. Leave vindication in the hands of God.

The Thin Place: Ask, Answer, Pray.

When was the last time you felt as if you had been wronged and others failed to see it?

How does the need for vindication effect how we live?

How does waiting for the Lord to vindicate change the outcome as opposed to our own efforts?

November 30
Well, Whoop Ti Doo!

From Above: 2 Corinthians 10

Focal Passage: *"We do not dare to classify or compare ourselves with some who commend themselves. When they measure themselves by themselves and compare themselves with themselves, they are not wise."* –2 Corinthians 10:12

Here Below:

"Excuse me, but do you realize to whom you are speaking?" Wow! Or as one of my favorite expression says, "Well, whoop ti doo!" What a question! Thankfully, I have never heard this question asked in real life. I must admit I have only encountered this question on television. However, I have many times encountered the attitude that this question suggests. It is that attitude that I am someone that requires special attention and special recognition. I am something! Well, the truth is that we are all something! The question is more appropriately "What kind of something are we?"! Let's face the truth. Those with the above attitude usually gain no respect by that attitude. It usually has the opposite effect. To think more highly of oneself than appropriate is ultimately self destructive. By thinking too highly of ourselves, we are basically doing what Paul warns us to avoid in the above verse. We are foolishly measuring ourselves by ourselves. It really makes no sense. In the long run, it is those who practice humility that usually gain our admiration and respect. For this reason we must never fall into the trap of measuring ourselves by our own expectations or by those set by others or seen in others.

For the Christian, the measure of a person is found in following God's will. Whether it's someone serving of great notoriety or someone serving the Lord in quiet anonymity; as long as both are centered in God's will for their lives, both are at the top of the ladder of success. Some of the greatest men and women of faith will never have statues made of them or be quoted in books or other writings; yet, behind every one that has, you will find some anonymous hero of the faith that helped shape their lives. It must cause God to laugh when we pat ourselves on the back for having arrived at some socially respected station in life! In fact, in the New Testament, it was the regular Joes that Jesus seem to use the most. The socially respected leaders were instead of little use to Him. They were too sure of themselves to be used by God. The lesson in this is to not compare ourselves to others. God doesn't! The lesson is to simply live for the Lord with all our heart, soul, mind and spirit in humility. Then we are ready to make a real difference.

The Thin Place: Ask, Answer, Pray.

Do you ever struggle with feelings of inadequacy in comparison to others?

Are you ever envious of those who seem to have achieved more than you in life?

How do you think God feels concerning our achievements and accolades?

12

December

December 1
I Am that Man!

From Above: 2 Samuel 12:1-14; Psalm 32

Focal Passage: *"Then David said to Nathan, "I have sinned against the LORD." Nathan replied, "The LORD has taken away your sin. You are not going to die." –2 Samuel 12:13*

Here Below:

He used his influence to seduce and impregnate a married woman. He added to this sin with further abuse of his authority by covering his mistake by having her husband extinguished, a man devoted and dedicated to serving him. He was an adulterer. He was a murderer. In this instance, we can agree that he was a scoundrel. If he were alive today, we most likely would not allow him to serve in any leadership position in our churches. He would not pass our background checks! Yet, we mostly remember him as being a man after God's own heart. He wrote most of the Psalms and is probably the greatest King the nation of Israel has ever known. I am of course referring to David.

So, if all these terrible things are true of David, what made the difference? Why do we not remember him primarily as that scoundrel? Well, the above verse contains one key to understanding this phenomenon. When confronted with his sin, he immediately confessed. Keep in mind, some time had passed when Nathan brought this message from God to David. It wasn't that David had immediately repented after committing his sin that distinguishes him. In fact, he had maintained his lie for a while. However, what does set him apart is that when faced with the reality of what he had done, he did not place blame anywhere else. For the first time, someone had the nerve to confront the king with his sin. How did the king respond? You don't understand Nathan! She was naked and very beautiful! She seduced me! I am the king. I had to cover it up for the good of the nation! No. Instead, he said, "I have sinned against the Lord." Immediately, his sin was forgiven. You see, it wasn't that David was perfect that made him a man after God's own heart. It was that he understood just how far from perfect he was. In Psalm 32 we see how David regretted holding on to this sin and how liberating it is to finally confess it. The same is true for each of us. We find freedom from our sin when we confess it and turn toward the Lord. We only prolong the inevitable by hiding it. God knows. In sending Nathan, we see that God wants us to let go. Don't waste valuable time! Don't add to your sin by refusing to confess! Face the truth and let it go and watch God change your heart.

The Thin Place: Ask, Answer, Pray.

What are some reasons we might refuse to confess sin?

Have you ever held on to a particular sin for an extended period of time? If so, why?

What did it feel like when you finally confessed that sin before the Lord? Or have you?

December 2

I'm Finished!

From Above: James 1:1-4

Focal Passage: *"Perseverance must finish its work so that you may be mature and complete, not lacking anything."* *–James 1:4*

Here Below:

James begins his great epistle to the church by addressing the subject that was probably first and foremost on the minds of the believers. He begins by speaking of trials. While James was most likely speaking of persecution, we do know that trials can come in many forms. Sometimes they can even be the result of our own shortcomings. Regardless of the reasons, trials are an unfortunate part of life. Likewise, how we handle them can be the difference between a life that is pleasing to God and one that falls short.

There is a real irony in how the New Testament addresses the subject of trials. It teaches us that trials are not necessarily a bad thing; for it is often these trials that produce in us a maturity that we might not reach otherwise. It is not an easy process, but if faith is present, a trial can lead to genuine growth. However, this growth is conditional. Notice the above verse. In order for trials to produce maturity, it must be allowed to complete its work. More specifically, it's our perseverance throughout the trial that must be allowed to complete its transforming task in our hearts. Put simply, we must sometimes bare the trial to see the results.

This at first may not seem too encouraging. After all, who wants to bare a trial? We usually pray that God will take the trial away from us! I do not think this is necessarily wrong. We must pray honest prayers. If that is what we are feeling, then we must be honest with God. It is not wrong if in our heart we are trusting in God to do what is best when we pray to that end. It becomes wrong when we fail to see how God might be using it to shape and mold us. We must let it finish its task. Then we can be encouraged! How? Well, notice the end of the above verse. Once we reach the end of the trial, having persevered, we will be mature and complete and not lacking anything. That doesn't sound so bad, does it? You see, the Christian life is all about seeing past today and trusting in God to bring a bright tomorrow. That is in essence the definition of faith. So, be careful how you pray concerning your trials. It might just be that it is a trial for your benefit. Instead of letting your trials finish you, let them finish their task. You will be better for it.

The Thin Place: Ask, Answer, Pray.

What trials have you endured in your past?

Did any of these trials produce maturity in your heart?

How does reflecting on these past trials change how you might deal with current ones?

December 3
The Most Humble Man in the World

From Above: James 1:5-10

Focal Passage: *"The brother in humble circumstances ought to take pride in his high position." –James 1:9*

Here Below:

Here is another one of those spiritual ironies found throughout scripture. How can humble circumstances be considered a high position? Well, it must be possible, because there it is in James 1:9. This is of course not the only place where we see the roles of the least and the greatest reversed. It is a fundamental teaching of the scriptures; yet, it is a quality very much in danger of extinction in our day.

It is my belief that a truly humble person does not realize their own humility. Anyone who might look at themselves as humble probably isn't, or else they would not be satisfied with this description. They would, like Paul, consider themselves prime candidates for further humiliation. He considered himself the least of the apostles (I Corinthians 15:9), least of the saints (Ephesians 3:8) and the chief of sinners (I Timothy 1:15). You see, even imprisoned and persecuted Paul understood that he had not arrived at a place of complete humility. Perhaps it is not even possible this side of heaven. This is why we must continue to pick up our cross daily. It is when we realize our weaknesses and our complete and total dependence upon God that we can fully grasp the depth of God's love. In our complete and utter frailty, God still loved us enough to shower us with grace and forgiveness. You see, in contrast to my weakness, God's greatness and love seems even greater.

As I read this passage, I am reminded of the joke about a man recognized as the most humble man in the world. As a reward he was given a button to wear proclaiming his status as the most humble man in the world. However, when he put the button on his lapel for all to see, they had to take it away from him! He no longer fit the description. The point of this story is that is so easy to take pride in our position, whatever our station in life. Yet, to be used of God, for lack of a better expression, we must get over ourselves. There is no shame in our weakness. In fact, according to scripture it is a reason for a righteous pride. Don't be like the man in the above joke. Let your pride rest in simply knowing the Lord and knowing that He loves you in spite of your faults. Let His love be the source of your pride.

__The Thin Place__: Ask, Answer, Pray.

Do you ever struggle with pride? How so?

Who do you consider to be the most humble person you know? Why?

What are some ways in which you could show more humility?

December 4
The Dry Bones Dance

__From Above__: Ezekiel 37:1-14

Focal Passage: *"So I prophesied as he commanded me, and breath entered them; they came to life and stood up on their feet--a vast army." –Ezekiel 37:10*

__Here Below__:

As I read the above passage of scripture, I can't help but be reminded of the song called "The Dry Bones Dance" from years ago written and performed by the late great Mark Heard. In this song, reference is made to the "miraculous circumstance where the blind ones see and dry bones dance," an expression in which the life-giving nature of the Lord is illustrated. Only the Lord can bring life to something or someone that is by all descriptions dead. Only He can breathe life into one in which there is no life. From creation unto present day, this has always been God's desire and His specialty. Whether it is a couple close to 100 years of age having a child (Gen. 17) or a virgin teen giving birth (Luke 2), a blind eye given sight (Matt. 20) or the physically dead being raised to life (Mark 5), this truth remains. God can take what others may write off as dead or lifeless and give it meaning and purpose. He can give it breath.

My oldest son is a marathon runner. I always love to be at the finish line and watch how desperate many of the runners seem at the end. I might add, they are not nearly as desperate as I would be if I were to try to run 5k! Nevertheless, they are desperate for air. After running for miles, even the most fit are usually gasping for breath near the end. This is especially true on those days in which the weather is extreme. I am not sure which is worse, running in the hot steamy humidity or taking in the cold cutting winter air like a knife into our lungs. Regardless of which, the end is the same. We desperately need to breathe and the look on the faces of those runners reveals this desperation. Why? Because life is dependent upon breath!

The same is true of our spiritual lives. However, this need for breath can only be met in God. Only He can make our dry bones dance as we see in Ezekiel 37. Here is the beauty of it. If God can breathe life into a field of skeletons, can't He breathe life back into us spiritually? You see, when God is added to the equation, there does not have to be such a thing as a spiritually dead person or a dead church! To be spiritually dead is a choice. It is when we choose to ignore God's word, Spirit and leadership in our lives that we become dry bones. He is all about giving life and we are never so dead as to be beyond His ability to breathe life into us. Unlike that dead army in Ezekiel, we must first make the choice to breathe Him in. Then life begins anew.

The Thin Place: Ask, Answer, Pray.

Do you ever feel spiritually dead? How so?

Do you agree with the statement that we are never beyond God's ability to breathe life into us?

What then can you do to prevent spiritual death from occurring?

December 5
Avoiding the Cloudy Conversation

From Above: Matthew 5:33-37

Focal Passage: *"Simply let your 'Yes' be 'Yes,' and your 'No,' 'No'; anything beyond this comes from the evil one." –Matthew 5:37*

Here Below:

Cloudy conversation? What do I mean by this? Well, we have all heard it. We have all most likely participated in it ourselves. It is fairly easy to recognize. I am referring to that speech we often use that is filled with words like "but" and "if" and "maybe" and even "perhaps". These words are not inherently bad. It is when we use them to dodge a straight answer that they become dangerous. For example, "I would like too, but..." or "I'd love to help you tomorrow, if..." It is when we use them to "cloud" our speech instead of simply giving a clear and precise answer that we are in danger of breaking Jesus' commandment in the above verse. We often associate this verse as a reference to the sin of lying. This is definitely applicable. Yet, if you read it in its context, you will see that it is more appropriately referring to keeping our promises and vows both to the Lord and to others. You see, we often cloud our conversations with such types of speech to give the appearance of interest without ever truly making a commitment. This way we are free from obligation. While it may sound harmless, it is in reality a sign of selfishness, deceit and weakness. Put simply, we should not make promises or give the appearance of a promise if in our heart we have no intention of keeping it. As children of God, we are to be committed to the truth.

There are times when it may seem like it is best to cloud our conversation for the welfare of others. We may be trying to spare someone's feelings or prevent conflict. Yet, I do not believe this is what scripture teaches. We never see Jesus stretching the truth or clouding His speech for the benefit of the listener. He always deals with the truth, even when the truth may be hard to swallow. Likewise, we never see Him making "campaign promises" for the benefit of appearing committed. With Jesus, what you see is what you get! The same should be said of each of us. I am convinced that more harm is done to the cause of Christ by our hypocrisy than anything else, even our more innocent hypocrisies. The world needs to see integrity in the hearts of the children of God. A Christian with integrity will shine like a star in the dark world in which we live. Commit yourself to the truth in all circumstances and God is able to use you in a more effective way. Speak clearly and truthfully. Avoid the cloudy conversation.

The Thin Place: Ask, Answer, Pray.

Are you guilty of occasionally clouding your speech in the above manner?

If so, what reasons do you have for using this type of speech?

How do you think others see you as a result of less than straightforward speech? God?

December 6
Through the Dark Door

From Above: Deuteronomy 31:1- 8; Romans 8:31

Focal Passage: *"The LORD himself goes before you and will be with you; he will never leave you nor forsake you. Do not be afraid; do not be discouraged.""* –Deuteronomy 31:8

<u>Here Below</u>:

One of my favorite quotes is from the wise old sage named Moses Horowitz. (You probably know him better as Moe Howard from The Three Stooges!) He says with a trembling voice as he characteristically shoves his terrified buddies through a door into the dark unknown of the other side, "Don't be scared, I am right behind you!" I appreciate this joke because I have found myself there many times, scared to walk through a dark door into the unknown. Perhaps we all have. The uncertain future can be frightening. Yet, the children of God do not need to fear the uncertain future. According to the above scripture and many others, God does not push us from behind, forcing us into taking those frightening first steps. Nor is He simply there holding our hand as we move forward on our own initiative. He goes ahead of us! When God was leading the children of Israel into the fearsome Promised Land, He went ahead of them. This might explain the victories they experienced against such overwhelming odds. God had already been there and taken care of them, long before they had even arrived on the scene. God still does the same today.

When it comes to following the will of God, courage is vital; yet, we need to have a proper understanding of the true nature of courage. Courage is not simply a willingness to risk everything in hopes of success. Likewise, courage is not simply being willing to sacrifice for victory. In the keeping of God's will, courage is moving forward with the knowledge that God is one step ahead of you and that He is the one that ultimately brings the victory. It is not about our strength of spirit or will. It is about His. For the child of God, courage is directly tied to God's grace and mercy. When we surrender our lives to these aspects of God's nature, we can accomplish anything He asks of us. He will equip us and He will fight for us. How then can we lose? To fully comprehend this fact is to face the future with courage and faith instead of fear. Don't fear the other side of the open door! If God is leading you through that door, success waits for you on the other side! He is saying to you today, "Don't be scared, I'm going in ahead of you!"

The Thin Place: Ask, Answer, Pray.

What are your greatest fears?

Why do these things cause you to fear?

Is it possible that God might already be in these situations working for your victory? How so?

December 7
Family Matters

From Above: Luke 14:25-27; 2 Corinthians 6:17-18;

Focal Passage: *"I will be a Father to you, and you will be my sons and daughters, says the Lord Almighty." –2 Corinthians 6:18*

Here Below:

In Luke 14, we have one of the most difficult passages of Jesus' teaching. In verses 25- 27, we have Jesus telling us that we must hate our parents, spouses, children, siblings and even ourselves in order to be His disciple! Wow! That is pretty strong and it is a bitter pill to swallow, at least at first glance. Of course, no serious student of the Bible believes that this is a passage that is meant to be taken literally. We know this because Jesus Himself exemplified just the opposite. We see Jesus caring for His mother even as He was hanging on the cross. In addition, there are countless verses referring to the care and love of others, especially family. Instead, we must consider the principle behind this verse. Jesus is simply stating the case that God does not wish to be second place in our lives, even in relation to our closest and most intimate relationships. As we consider this passage, we must also consider those such as 2 Corinthians 6:17-18, which is in reference to several other Old Testament passages. Here we see why God wants first place in our lives. It is not out of some sense of pride, even though He would be just in feeling so. Instead, it is because He wants to be our Father. It is further evidence of His love for us! He wants the kind of intimacy with us that is found in family. This truth is especially important for those feeling rejected by those closest to them due to their faith.

It is my belief that a true disciple can expect some, if not all, of their family to question their faith. Those closest to us can more easily see the real us and it will be the same that will call us to account for any discrepancies. If those who know us best do not pick up on the differences faith has made in our lives, then it is a testimony to a lack of spiritual fruit. True devotion to Christ produces fruit and is inevitably going to cause others close to us to question themselves. It may produce repentance or it may produce bitterness in them as they deal with their own faith condition. Though it may not feel like it, this is a good thing. It shows that our life is making a difference. However, the point Jesus is making above is that we must also be content with the fact that those we love may never come to terms with our devotion to the Lord. This is why God wants to be our Father. This way, we receive the affirmation we need from Him, whether our earthly loved ones ever come around or not. For the child of God, this should be enough. Pray for the others to come to faith, but let God's love and acceptance be your number one concern.

<u>The Thin Place</u>: Ask, Answer, Pray.

Who are the most important people in your life?

Does your relationship with the Lord come before your relationship with these others?

How does your relationship with the Lord strengthen your relationship with those closest to you?

December 8
3D Vision

<u>From Above</u>: Proverbs 16:33, 20:24; Jeremiah 10:23

Focal Passage: *"A man's steps are directed by the LORD. How then can anyone understand his own way?" –Proverbs 20:24*

<u>Here Below</u>:

Recently while visiting a gift and novelty shop, one of my sons asked me to try on a pair of very unique sunglasses. These glasses had tiny mirrors affixed to the outside edges of the lenses. As a result, I could see both in front of me and behind me. With these glasses, I could see in two directions at the same time. I could see both my son in front of me and the one making faces behind my back. It was very disconcerting. Wouldn't it be nice if we had glasses that allowed us to see time in same way? Well, this may not be possible for us, but it is for the Lord. We can only see what has already passed and what is right in front of us; but God sees in all directions. For us, it is often difficult to simply comprehend the things we can see. For this reason, we've nothing left to do but trust in the One with perfect three-dimensional vision. He sees our past, present and future.

It has been my experience that it can sometimes take years of retrospection before I can fully understand how God might have been working in a particular past situation. At the time, we ask why? We want understanding right then. Yet, understanding often comes only after the fact. At the time, we are simply left with faith that God is in control of the situation. Isn't that the point? If God allowed us to see the future, we would have no reason to depend upon Him for guidance. Our faith would be limited to a simple head knowledge and would lack the quality of a trusting intimate heart relationship. It would also lack the adventure of trusting in the Lord.

Thankfully though, God has given us the ability to see His hand at work in the past. We can all see how our prayers were answered and how glad we are that they were not all answered in the way we thought they should have been at the time! We can look back and see how His hand was guiding our footsteps at times when we didn't even recognize it. Yet, He was there. This educational hindsight should give us courage as we face the future. God was there before and He is here today. Most importantly, He will be there tomorrow.

The Thin Place: Ask, Answer, Pray.

How has God answered specific prayers in your past?

Was it how you expected Him to answer? Why or why not?

What lessons did you learn along the way as you were waiting for His response?

December 9
No Take Backs

From Above: Proverbs 12:18; Colossians 3:12-14

Focal Passage: *"Reckless words pierce like a sword, but the tongue of the wise brings healing." –Proverbs 12:18*

Here Below:

We've all been there. We've all opened our mouth and inserted our size nine or whatever size your case may be. We've all spoken those words, that as soon as they left our lips we were filled with regret over saying them. To make it even worse, this usually happens within the context of our closest relationships. After all, in order to be hurt by the stinging words of an individual, that person's opinion must be important to us. We must care for them. We can usually dismiss the words of a stranger. However, when a friend cuts us with his tongue, it causes a wound that goes much deeper. To be on the giving end of that wound is a terrible place to be as well. It is usually done in the heat of the moment or in a moment of recklessness or weakness, as the above verse attests. Nevertheless, the damage is done. When a word is spoken, there are no take backs. Even if we try to take it back, the words are out there. They have been delivered and the hurt is real. There is no way around this reality. One heart is broken and one heart is filled with regret. For this reason, we must be very careful to guard our words. To guard them is to prevent the wound, the feelings of regret and a possible broken relationship from ever happening.

If there truly are no take backs, what do we do after we have been reckless with our words? Well, notice the last part of the above verse. Our words need to be words of healing. In other words, we need to recognize the wound caused by our recklessness and then speak words that might mend it. Put simply, we need to apologize. Too often we dismiss our carelessness by blaming it on the heat of the moment. I've even seen individuals blame the recipient of the harsh words for making them angry enough to speak them! Listen, there is never a justification for hurting anyone with our words. For this reason, we must seek forgiveness and be quick to offer forgiveness in the instance that we are the wounded party. If we do not seek to heal the wound right away, the words have a way of showing up again later in our relationships. A wound unattended has a way of becoming infected. We must be intentional in mending our relationships. Yes, we sometimes mess up and say things we can never take back. Yet, we can do our part to mend the rift. Those special friend and family type relationships do not just happen. We must care for them and help them to grow. In order to do this, we must not let any misspoken words remain unattended. Trust me, it is worth it. So swallow your pride, admit your fault if any, seek forgiveness and offer words of healing.

The Thin Place: Ask, Answer, Pray.

Have you ever spoken words in the heat of the moment that you later regretted?

Have you ever been on the receiving end of reckless and misspoken words?

How does knowing how it makes you feel affect your response when you are guilty of the same?

December 10
A Moment of Mimicry

<u>**From Above**</u>: 2 Timothy 1:1-10

Focal Passage: *"I have been reminded of your sincere faith, which first lived in your grandmother Lois and in your mother Eunice and, I am persuaded, now lives in you also."* –2 Timothy 1:5

<u>**Here Below**</u>:

For reasons I cannot remember, my two oldest children accompanied me to my church office one day. They were probably four and five years old at the time. While they played up and down the church halls, I was busy studying in my office. After a while I noticed that I no longer heard their chatter. I quickly left my office and began my search for the two possible trouble doers. I must admit that I was unprepared for what I would find. After hearing some noise coming from our sanctuary, I cracked open the door quietly in hopes of catching them in the act of whatever mischief they had found. However, I received a lesson that day. As I peeped through the crack in the door, I saw my oldest son standing behind the pulpit, which I might add was taller than he, with a Bible in his hand. He was telling the make believe congregation to turn in their Bibles to a book that doesn't even exist. After rambling on for a few seconds, he then called his brother to come up and lead the make believe congregation in a hymn. As they sang, I was overwhelmed with a sense of pride in them and an overwhelming sense of responsibility as I watched them mimic both myself and our worship leader. I became suddenly self aware of my influence over these two little men. I just stood there and watched for an indeterminate amount of time, not having the heart to break up their worship service.

The lesson I gleaned that day is that we all have the power to influence, whether we know it or not. People are watching and learning from us. This not only applies to those whom we would consider leaders. Anyone involved in a loving and caring relationship has the potential to influence. The Apostle Paul acknowledges the influence that Lois and Eunice had on Timothy and his ministry. Timothy's sincere faith was first seen in his grandmother and mother. Timothy must have been watching them and was now mimicking their attitude of selflessness. Their lives shaped Timothy. Sometimes we get discouraged, thinking that we are not making a difference. Never underestimate the power of your influence. You may not realize who is watching you! We may not always see our influence right away. Nevertheless, it exists. Here is the catch though; we can influence both for the good and the bad. So take care of your witness. Others are watching, like it or not! For this reason, we must strive to be an influence that honors God.

The Thin Place: Ask, Answer, Pray.

Who would you say had the greatest influence in your life?

Over whom would you say that you have the greatest influence?

How can you be a better influence for that person on others like them?

December 11
Not Good

From Above: Genesis 2:18-25

Focal Passage: *"The LORD God said, "It is not good for the man to be alone. I will make a helper suitable for him."" –Genesis 2:18*

Here Below:

In Genesis 2:18, we get a glimpse of a universal truth. In this one verse we see part of the purpose for which we were created. God looked upon the crown jewel of His creation and saw that something was still missing. "It is not good for man to be alone." God said. Man was created to be in relationship, with God first and then other people. This truth can be proven from a spiritual, social and scientific perspective. Anyone forced to live in extreme isolation can only do so for a limited amount of time. To do otherwise can lead to deep psychological problems. At the very least, isolation can lead to the development of socially inadequate behaviors, only furthering the problem. Simply put, we are not meant to live alone on this earth.

Many of us struggle with the concept of letting others get too close. Relationships are risky. Friends, lovers and even family can let us down at times. While we are created in God's image and therefore created to be relational beings, we are also fallen and imperfect. Our fallen nature does not negate our need for others. In fact, it might increase our need for others. We need others to lean upon in times of struggle. We need the shoulders of others to cry upon from time to time. Without others, we have no outlet for both our sorrows and our joys. God recognized this fact. Out of love for His creation he gave us each other. Do not neglect the gift God has given you in others. Our relationships can be a valuable resource to aid us in dealing with life. Cherish them. Nurture them. Build upon them. You were not meant to be alone.

The Thin Place: Ask, Answer, Pray.

Apart from your relationship with God, what are your most important relationships in life?

How have those relationships aided you in life?

How do you care for these relationships to ensure they are healthy?

December 12
Eating the Aha!

From Above: Psalm 70; Ephesians 3:20-21

Focal Passage: *"May those who say to me, "Aha! Aha!" turn back because of their shame." –Psalm 70:3*

Here Below:

In Psalm 70, David sings a song of deliverance. He was in the midst of a trial and yet he understood something that we would all do well to remember. God delights in doing the unexpected! In verse 3, we see that David realized that his enemies were expecting him to fall. To them, David's demise was certain. Yet, he prayed that God might cause them to eat their "aha's"! He prayed that his enemies would be forced to walk away ashamed and confused. This psalm contains two very important ingredients for a prayer of deliverance. First, David acknowledges his own weakness and subsequent need for God's help. Second, he praises God for His faithfulness, recognizing God's ability to deliver on His promises to His children. Though the world may have written David off at this point, he knew God could still do the unexpected and deliver him from his enemies. And deliver him he did!

Often we are frightened of the unexpected. We too quickly forget that God works best through the unexpected circumstances of life. It is there that we are most likely to turn to Him for help. Likewise, it is there that He is most likely to surprise us with the unpredictable answers to our heartfelt concerns. It is when we are out of answers that God is able to do "immeasurably more than we can ask or imagine" (Ephesians 3:20). It is there that God can turn the "aha" moments of others and of ourselves into the "wow" moments. Never underestimate God's ability to surprise you. Leave the unknown to God and just trust in Him. Trust God in the unexpected. Trust God to do the unexpected.

<u>**The Thin Place**</u>: Ask, Answer, Pray.

How has God surprised you in the past?

What future uncertainties are of concern to you at the moment?

Is there any reason to believe that God will not be faithful to you in these situations?

December 13
39 and Holding

<u>**From Above**</u>: Job 32:6-9; Isaiah 46:3-4;

Focal Passage: *"I thought, 'Age should speak; advanced years should teach wisdom.' But it is the spirit in a man, the breath of the Almighty, that gives him understanding." –Job 32:7-8*

<u>**Here Below**</u>:

It was the night before my 39th birthday and the only word I can use to describe how I was feeling is surreal. My children were teasing me about my age and I responded by telling them that I was going to remind them of this evening when they turn 39! My eleven year old son replied by saying "Yeah, if you are still alive!" We all laughed at his quick witted sense of humor, but I must admit that there was just enough truth in his statement to cause me some reflection later on in the evening. When I was his age and even somewhat older, the age of 39 seemed almost ancient to me. The thought that I would one day reach that age myself seemed so far in the distant future that it seemed almost impossible to imagine. Yet, here I am and suddenly 39 still seems pretty young. As children and adolescents, we feel as if we own the world and time has no power over us. If only we could have the same perspective on aging as we now have when we are younger. Perhaps a greater appreciation of life and the things that really matter, the things that truly make it special, would occur and we would likewise have fewer regrets. Perhaps it is for this reason that God has given us eternity. Through the eyes of eternity, aging is meaningless. To borrow from a worn out and over used cliché, which is nonetheless true, we are only as old as we feel. This truth however takes on a whole special and new meaning when taken into consideration with eternity.

With aging should come wisdom. Our life experiences should promote growth and understanding in our hearts. However, as Job 32 attests, this is not always the case. Nevertheless, the opportunity for wisdom is there, if we allow our life experiences to speak to us. If done, we can view aging as an opportunity to face the challenges of life better equipped. I know I am smarter than I was thirty, twenty, ten and even five years ago. I'm older, but in a better position to find fulfillment and happiness in life. Of course, this goal can never be achieved outside of the will of God. To age gracefully, we must accept His *grace* on a daily basis. So if you find yourself like me, feeling your age, don't let it get you down. Look at it as though greater possibilities still lie ahead in which you can be used of God. They do! And you are better prepared than ever before to reach your full potential!

The Thin Place: Ask, Answer, Pray.

Would you say that you consider yourself to be older or younger in attitude?

Do you agree that as long as you are alive that you are in a position to be used of God?

What life lessons have you attained over the years that might make your future brighter?

December 14
Trust Me On This One!

From Above: Romans 11:33-36

Focal Passage: *"Oh, the depth of the riches of the wisdom and knowledge of God! How unsearchable his judgments, and his paths beyond tracing out!"* *–Job 32:7-8*

Here Below:

Have you ever had anyone say to you, "Just trust me on this one!"? By asking this question, they are asking us to accept their direction in a situation in which most likely we cannot see the outcome as they see it. They are asking us to put aside our worries and fears and to trust in their judgment. It is easier said than done for most of us. Most of us do not like giving up the driver's seat. We like to be in control of our own destinies. Yet, I would say that the idea of being in control of our own destinies is a myth. It only takes one unexpected event in our lives to send all of our plans and dreams to the recycle bin. It may be an unexpected illness, tragedy or even a moral failure by either ourselves or someone close to us. It can be something as simple as an auto accident or a loss of income. Nevertheless, as much as we might like to think that we are in control, it is really a myth. Everything can change in an instant. In the course of a day, the entire direction of a person's life can be totally redirected and there may be absolutely nothing that can be done about it. For this reason, it only makes sense to trust in someone that truly does have control over our destinies.

I've often wondered as to how God must feel as He watches us struggle to direct our own lives; when He knows all along the changes that might be coming ahead. Do our futile efforts cause Him to laugh? Or do they cause Him to cry? I would think that watching your children fight for control over something which they can never truly control must cause the Lord great grief and frustration. If only we would trust and follow His direction! Perhaps you are in one of those life changing periods in your life. Maybe you are facing some tough decisions ahead. Well, if that is you today, He may be asking you to "Just trust me on this one!" The reason we often dismiss His direction is that it doesn't always make sense. That's right. We can't always understand His direction. Guess what? We are not supposed to! We are to simply trust in the Lord! We are to have simple faith! We can do this knowing that His unsearchable judgments and untraceable paths are always the best and that they would never lead in the wrong direction or in a direction that might cause us harm. So stop trying to take the wheel away from the only One that knows where you are going! Let God direct your paths and you will never go wrong. Just trust Him on this one!

<u>**The Thin Place**</u>: Ask, Answer, Pray.

Has there ever been a time when God's will didn't make sense until later on down the road?

Did you follow His will or try to change your circumstances as you thought best?

How might this situation have differed if you would have simply followed God's guidance first?

December 15
Getting You Nowhere...

From Above: Job 32:21-22; Psalm 5:9, 12:2

Focal Passage: *"I will show partiality to no one, nor will I flatter any man; for if I were skilled in flattery, my Maker would soon take me away."* –Job 32:22

Here Below:

One thing experience has taught me is that a person quick to flatter is not a person to be trusted. That is a terrible thing for someone to say, especially a pastor, but I believe it to be nonetheless true. It is especially true coming from someone that barely knows you. Beware! That same mouth may later come back to bite you! This is not meant to be critical. It is a biblical warning. Scripture is filled with warnings against using flattery and accepting flattery. This is once again a testimony to the power of our words to heal, harm or just plain confuse the listener. Flattery is especially dangerous. As the old saying goes, "Flattery will get you nowhere!"

However, we must be careful to not confuse flattery with words of encouragement. We are called to be encouragers. The difference between flattery and encouragement lies in the motive of the speaker. Both may be truthful, but they are spoken for totally different reasons. The flatterers words are spoken for their own benefit, for selfish reasons. On the other hand, the words of the encourager are spoken for the benefit of the recipient. I do believe though that not all flatterers have sinister reasons behind their words. Many do it for the simple hope of being liked. As innocent as that might seem, the motive is still selfish in nature and it is basically less than honest manipulation. This is why the best policy is always complete honesty. Being honest is more than just not telling lies. It also means not saying things that deep down we really do not feel.

Thankfully the believer is not left to the mercy of his own emotions. We have the Holy Spirit of God to guide us and to give us the right words at the right time. Likewise, He can instill in us the gift of true encouragement. Flattery only harms both the giver and the receiver. It usually promotes a false image of both. Conversely, when encouragement is given, both sides win. So watch out for flattering words coming both from others and from your own mouth. Let your words be genuine just as you are called to be genuine.

The Thin Place: Ask, Answer, Pray.

Have you ever been flattered by someone only to later discover selfish motives?

Are you quick to recognize flattery for what it really is or are you quick to fall victim?

Have you ever been guilty of using flattery yourself?

December 16
The Siren Snooze

From Above: Proverbs 20:13; 24:30-34

Focal Passage: *"Do not love sleep or you will grow poor; stay awake and you will have food to spare." –Proverbs 20:13*

Here Below:

Every morning of my life begins with a battle. Each day, I start my day off with an epic struggle of resistance against the siren like call of the glowing red light by my bedside. Sometimes I win. Most times I lose. You know the call. We all hear it! That glowing red temptress is of course the snooze button on my alarm clock. Each day, it becomes harder and harder to resist. The more often I give in, the harder it becomes. This is especially true on these cold winter mornings, when that bed is so warm and inviting. Nevertheless, I cannot live life from under a heavy comforter. We cannot snooze our lives away! There is always work to be done.

I am of course exaggerating the issue. There is nothing wrong with the occasional hitting of the snooze button. Sleeping in every now and then, if possible, can be a treat and a much needed respite. However, the problem lies in the fact that for many of us, if not careful, it can become a way of life. The Bible is very explicit in its warnings against slothfulness, even though we rarely hear sermons preached on the subject. The book of Proverbs is especially filled with these real life applications warning us of the dangers of a lazy spirit. Put simply, God seems to be against it! Perhaps this is another reason why our lives are limited to 70 or 80 years upon this earth. We do not have time to waste. With time being our most precious commodity, we simply cannot afford to waste it by pulling the covers back over our heads and putting off life for another ten minutes, again figuratively speaking. We must be diligent in our use of time. We must make the most of what time we have. The funny thing about time is that while it is our most precious belonging, we really do not know how much of it we have. In fact, it could be said that the only time we have is right now! With that in mind, push back the covers, turn off the alarm and put your feet to the floor. God has work for you to do today! Don't put off His tasks any longer! It is time to rise and shine!

The Thin Place: Ask, Answer, Pray.

Are you ever tempted to be lazy? How so?

How do you fight the temptation to be slothful?

Is there anything right now that God has called you to do that you have put off until later? Why?

December 17
Eyes Wide Shut

From Above: 2 Peter 1:1-11; Romans 3:23

Focal Passage: *"For if you possess these qualities in increasing measure, they will keep you from being ineffective and unproductive in your knowledge of our Lord Jesus Christ. But if anyone does not have them, he is nearsighted and blind, and has forgotten that he has been cleansed from his past sins." –2 Peter 1:8-9*

Here Below:

I wish I could buy back some of the precious time of my life that I have wasted looking for my glasses. Each night, I take my contacts out of my eyes. If I was careless in the morning when I was putting them in and did not place my eye glasses in a convenient place, I find myself very close to blind and in need of my wife's vision to help me find my glasses. I also often find myself too proud to ask for her help, until I have wasted a considerable amount of time feeling my way around the house in the desperate hope of finding them, without anyone knowing of my mistake. It is not until I can't find my glasses that I remember just how poor my vision is without them.

Many of us are often guilty of making the same mistake spiritually as well. We watch as others stumble in the darkness of their own sins and shortcomings, which we often see with crystal clarity; yet, we forget that our heart is just as prone to sin as theirs. Sure, we are all at differing levels of spiritual maturity and growth and therefore able to deal with temptation in differing ways. However, this truth remains; we are all still sinners (Romans 3:23)! All means all! Without the grace of God, we would *all* be blind in our sin. We are never beyond stumbling ourselves. If we ever forget this, we are denying the truth that is right in front of our eyes and are setting the stage for our own fall. This truth should lead us to greater compassion toward those that are stumbling. Similarly, it should lead us to a greater appreciation for God's grace and love. Never become so confident in yourself that you are blind to the possibility of sin in your life. Instead, place your confidence in God's grace and forgiveness. Let God open your eyes to His truth.

The Thin Place: Ask, Answer, Pray.

How quick are you to recognize the sins of others?

How quick are you to acknowledge your own sin?

What sins are you more apt to overlook in your own life?

December 18
Put on Your Glad Pants

<u>From Above</u>: Psalm 100

Focal Passage: *"Serve the Lord with gladness: come before his presence with singing." –Psalm 100:2*

<u>Here Below</u>:

I can remember as a child throwing a temper tantrum, only to be told very matter of factly "You can just get glad in the same pants you got mad in!" Sound familiar? Well, this trite and somewhat humorous expression implies that you and I have a certain amount of control over our attitude. This does seem to be true. It is especially true concerning our attitude over spiritual matters such as worship, devotion and service. Unfortunately, with these matters as well as many others, we do not always exercise our control. Instead, we let our emotions lead us. The problem with following our emotions is that they do not always lead us in the same direction as God's will.

Just as important as following God's will is following it with the right attitude. We are told in the above verse that we are to serve God with gladness. While there is a lot to be said about our responsibilities as children of God, we must remember that our service to Him is not meant to be performed out of obligation or duty so much as it is to be done out of love and appreciation. In fact, in the remainder of this short psalm, the writer reminds us that we are God's creation, not simply of ourselves, and that we have great reason to be thankful. What an understatement of an epic truth! Think of the cross. That alone is reason enough to serve the Lord with a glad heart. If God chose to never give us another blessing, our salvation would still be reason enough to serve with gladness. Yet, He continually gives us even more. His mercy is everlasting (vs. 5). In other words, his supply of mercy is endless. So if you find yourself with a poor attitude, count your blessings, starting with your salvation. Soon you will find your mad pants exchanged for glad pants. Let your attitude be an act of worship.

The Thin Place: Ask, Answer, Pray.

Do you ever find yourself serving or worshiping out of duty rather than love?

Why do you think this sometimes happens?

How can you approach these differently in order to better express your love for God?

December 19
The Social Network Shocker

From Above: Psalm 138

Focal Passage: *"Though the LORD is on high, he looks upon the lowly, but the proud he knows from afar." –Psalm 138:6*

Here Below:

With my embracing of the social network technology now available to us, I have been forced to come to terms with certain truths about myself. I have been able to see some friends that I have not seen in years. At first, I was shocked to see how much they have aged since I last saw them. How did they age so much and I did not? Well, this arrogance was quickly brought low. After looking at some old pictures of myself, I was forced to recognize that I have aged just as much as the others, if not more in most instances. Our self perception is often jaded by our own personal prejudices and misconceptions about ourselves. We often have a hard time seeing ourselves as we really are. We may see ourselves as strong, when we are in reality weak. We may see ourselves as independent, when in fact we are in need of help. We may see youth, when in fact the opposite is closer to the truth. This form of pride is dangerous; in that, reality can bring a sudden and sometimes painful lesson in truth. Just look at the whole "midlife crisis" phenomenon so prevalent in our day. It is nothing but people struggling to come to terms with their real selves. While I laugh (mostly) about the above lesson I received, it is nevertheless a reminder of the importance of being truthful with ourselves and most importantly with the God.

Pride in our self is sin. Scripture repeatedly teaches this truth. Likewise, it is a sin that God seems to hate the most. When we have an unhealthy appreciation for our own accomplishments or attributes, whether real or products of self delusion, we are putting our self in a position that only God deserves. Put simply, there is no room for worship of the Lord in the heart of the proud. That is why He says in the above verse that He knows the proud "from afar". This doesn't mean that we should look at ourselves as nothing or that we should not strive to better ourselves. On the contrary, we are special; in that God loves us as He does. However, we must remember why God loves us. He loves us because it is His nature to do so! It is not because of anything we've done or deserve. If we can grasp that, then we are in a position for God to really work in our lives. Otherwise, He will not compete for control of our lives. If we in our pride think we know best, He may leave us to find out the truth for ourselves. So if you must take pride in something, take pride in the fact that you serve a God who does not see men as the world does. See yourself as you really are, as He sees you. You are someone loved by a great God.

The Thin Place: Ask, Answer, Pray.

Have you ever struggled with a certain truth about yourself?

Why do you think we often have a difficult time coming to terms with the "real" us?

How comforting is it to you to know that God knows the real you, and He loves you anyway?

December 20
The Leap

From Above: Luke 1:26-57

Focal Passage: *"When Elizabeth heard Mary's greeting, the baby leaped in her womb, and Elizabeth was filled with the Holy Spirit."* –Luke 1:41

<u>Here Below</u>:

This is always an exciting time of year around my house. The children are beside themselves with excitement in anticipation of Christmas. There are presents under the tree and school is now officially out for Christmas break. There is nothing now to do but to look forward to that joy filled day. The youngest of my children are especially excited. I remember being that age and the feelings that I had as well. I am excited for them. I must admit, I too can hardly wait! Yet, wait we must.

I can't help but wonder how it must have been for those who were waiting for that first Christmas. For centuries Israel had been awaiting their Messiah. For years they have been praying for His arrival. Yet, most would not recognize Him when He did arrive. Nevertheless, John recognized Him even before He was born. His cousin acknowledged Jesus before anyone else would be able too. Did I mention that John was still in the womb at the time?! Of course, we don't fully understand what is happening in the above story when John "leaps" for joy in the presence of Mary and the unborn Jesus. There are many theories, but most commentators acknowledge that it must have been being in the presence of the Savior which set him to moving in his mother's womb. That baby Baptist couldn't wait for Christmas either it seems! He couldn't wait to start praising the Lord for what He was doing. That unborn child in Mary's womb would be a world changer. Everything known was about to be different. The anticipation was more than John could bear. How about you? Do you get excited when you think about the Lord? Sure, we are looking at His birth from the other side of history; nonetheless, we have just as much reason to be excited. Don't let the hectic nature of this season rob you of that joyful anticipation. Don't let the holiday humbugs rob you of your leap! Just like John, we have the presence of God in our midst in His Holy

Spirit. Let His presence bring you the joy that is intended this Christmas!

The Thin Place: Ask, Answer, Pray.

Do you look forward to Christmas or do you dread its coming? Be honest.

Why do you think so many people get depressed this time of year?

How can you approach this time of year differently as to avoid the humbugs?

December 21
Thinking of You

From Above: Matthew 1:1-25

Focal Passage: *"All this took place to fulfill what the Lord had said through the prophet: 'The virgin will be with child and will give birth to a son, and they will call him Immanuel' --which means, 'God with us.'..."* –Matthew 1:22-23

Here Below:

Perhaps one of the most overlooked passages of scripture among Christians is that of Matthew 1 just prior to the birth account. The genealogy of Jesus is one of those passages that many believers pass over in their daily reading of scripture. Often this is done with the assumption that it simply does not apply to me. Nothing could be farther from the truth. The genealogy of Jesus is all about me and it is all about you. It is a historical record of God's attempt to reach you with His love. The genealogies show us specifically the great lengths that God will go to in order to have a relationship with you. It is further evidence of God's divine fingerprints throughout history and His deep love for you and me. Furthermore, to understand this is to have a greater appreciation for Christmas.

The genealogical account of Jesus and even the Christmas story itself shows God's rearranging of history to fulfill His sacred purpose. He is putting the right people in the right place in exactly the right time, so that hundreds, if not thousands of years later, a special baby might be born in Bethlehem. Think about it. Even the political situation in the Christmas story had to be specifically arranged. This could not have been an easy task. Yet, God designed it all so that we might find redemption and have intimacy with Him, with Immanuel. In fact, all of scripture and biblical history could be examined in the same light. It all points to Jesus and it all points to you. The birth of Christ is the climax of history, or at least the beginning of it. It might better be said that the empty tomb is the climax of all history. Yet, it all began long before Easter and long before Christmas. Put simply, God went to great trouble to see that it all occurred just as it was supposed to occur. Most importantly, He did it all for you. Don't let the message of this passage pass you by this Christmas. It is at the very heart of Christmas. Just as we send Christmas cards to let others know we are thinking about them, God has sent this message to let us know the same. It is God's Christmas card to you!

The Thin Place: Ask, Answer, Pray.

How hard is it to miss the real meaning of the Christmas holiday?

Have you ever really considered your role in God's divine history?

How has God arranged events in your own life so that you might know Him better?

December 22
Born to Die

From Above: Luke 2:1-7; John 1:14

Focal Passage: *"From Above became flesh and made his dwelling among us. We have seen his glory, the glory of the One and Only, who came from the Father, full of grace and truth." –John 1:14*

Here Below:

I once heard it said that the moment we take our first breath, we begin to die. I suppose this statement is true in a very realistic physiological sense. However, most of us do not look at birth as the beginning of death. We look at babies, especially newborns, as an affirmation of life. This is perhaps why babies have a way of bringing joy to even the most cynical of souls. They can bring a smile to even the hardest of hearts. Yet, in the case of the Bethlehem babe, we must remember the purpose for which He was born. He was literally born to die.

Often we think of the sacrifice of Jesus as being that of His offering Himself on the cross. However, that is only the beginning of His sacrifice. His sacrifice really began in Bethlehem. He sacrificed all the glories of Heaven and the comforts His divinity allowed Him to be born in the most humble of means. He did not even allow Himself the comforts that most human beings enjoyed at the time of their birth. There were no doctors, nurses, midwives and not even the comfort of having Grandma nearby. He was literally born in a barn or cave. To deepen the significance of this sacrifice, He stepped into humanity with full understanding that it would ultimately result in His death on the cross. Old Testament prophecy had already foretold of this reality. He knew what was coming; yet, He chose to be born. He was born for the sole purpose of pursuing the cross and our redemption. He was born to die for you and for me. Don't let the reality of what Christmas must have meant to God slip by you this season. Nevertheless, because Jesus was born to die for our sins, His birth is still an affirmation of life, of real life. Let the purpose behind Christmas be the source of your joy this season! Celebrate life in Christ!

<u>The Thin Place</u>: Ask, Answer, Pray.

How does Christmas provide affirmation of your importance to the Lord?

How should knowing the purpose behind Christmas affect our relationships with others?

How can you make this purpose more apparent in your celebration this year?

December 23
From Counting Sheep to Counting Angels

<u>**From Above**</u>: Luke 2:8-18

Focal Passage: *"When the angels had left them and gone into heaven, the shepherds said to one another, "Let's go to Bethlehem and see this thing that has happened, which the Lord has told us about."" –Luke 2:15*

<u>**Here Below**</u>:

Perhaps my favorite characters in the Christmas story, aside from Christ himself, are the shepherds. They were not very important people in the grand scheme of things. They had a job to do. It was a hard job and a messy job. Their job required months of wandering the Judean hillsides as they followed the green pasture and clean water supply. They often lived in seclusion, sleeping in open fields or damp caves, with no one but sheep to keep them company. As a result, they were probably socially inept, at least in comparison with most others. I would bet that they even smelled like sheep! Yet, it was these ancient blue collar workers with which God first chose to share the greatest news mankind would ever hear. He didn't share it with Herod or Caesar. He didn't go to the religious elite or socially influential to find the recipients of this message. Instead, He chose these regular guys! Instead of counting sheep tonight, they would be counting the host of the heavenly beings! Soon these men would be telling the world of its Savior! And here we are two thousand years later still talking about these simple men and how God revealed Himself to them and used them to reveal Himself to others!

This aspect of the Christmas story is really at the heart of the Christmas gospel. Jesus came for all, regardless of our station in life. Furthermore, it is a reminder that God sees people differently than we often do. Where we may have seen smelly sheep herders, God saw those whom would in reality be the first Christian missionaries. Not only should this story influence how we view others, but it should remind us that He sees us differently than we probably see ourselves.

God sees past our social inadequacies and into our hearts. Never sell yourself or others short. God sees someone of great value, so much so that He gave His Son. Let these truths influence how you relate to others this Christmas season. He may want to use you to share His message of hope and love much as He used the shepherds. Never underestimates God desire to use a willing heart!

The Thin Place: Ask, Answer, Pray.

Do you ever struggle to find worth in others? With whom in particular?

Do you ever struggle to appreciate your own worth in the eyes of God?

How can Christmas be an opportunity to show appreciation for the worth of others?

December 24
Gold, Frankincense, Myrrh and other Dollar Store Treasures

From Above: Matthew 2:1-11

Focal Passage: *"On coming to the house, they saw the child with his mother Mary, and they bowed down and worshiped him. Then they opened their treasures and presented him with gifts of gold and of incense and of myrrh." –Matthew 2:11*

Here Below:

We all have those extra special Christmas memories that we cherish. One of my favorites revolves around some gifts given to my wife and to me by our five-year-old son. His school had set up a little shop in December in which students could buy Christmas gifts for their parents. In all honesty, the gifts were not much. Not one of them cost over a dollar. They consisted of pens, candles and other knick knacks that you might find at the local $1.00 store. The school also provided gift wrapping for these gifts. Well, unbeknownst to us, my son Carlos had taken his birthday money to school and bought over thirty dollars worth of these little treasures, each one gift-wrapped and proudly placed under our Christmas tree. To say he was eager to see us unwrap his gifts on Christmas day is an understatement. He sat with his big brown eyes glued to our every move, intently watching us unwrap each one, awaiting our thanks and hug. What made these trinkets so special was that he had spent every dollar he had on them! He had saved the money he had received as birthday gifts in October for the sole purpose of spending it on us in December. Instead of spending it on himself, he gave his all for his parents! He kept none for himself. We still have these gifts on proud display in our home and offices. I do not see them as the dust collectors that others may see when they view them on my office desk. To me, they are part of my son. They will always be in a place of prominence. I will never get rid of them.

Christmas has always been about giving. First, it was about God giving of Himself to mankind. Second, it was about mankind returning the gesture by giving our lives back to God. The wise man brought God gifts of worldly value to the baby Jesus, but they also gave of themselves. This trip had cost months, if not years of their lives. They had even put their lives at risk with Herod, just for a glimpse of Jesus. In their willingness to give of themselves, they met the Savior of the world. I am guessing that this probably meant more to the Lord than their gifts. What are you willing to give to the Lord this Christmas? However big or small your gift may be, a dollar store trinket or gold, frankincense or myrrh, if it comes from the heart, God will honor it. When you give of yourself to the Lord or to others for the Lord, God will take your gift and place it in His place of prominence. Give of yourself this Christmas and see for yourself the joy it brings!

The Thin Place: Ask, Answer, Pray.

What is your most precious Christmas memory? What is your favorite gift?

What makes these things so special to you?

How might you give of yourself to others this holiday season?

December 25
Star Light, Star Bright

<u>**From Above**</u>: Matthew 2:1-11

Focal Passage: "*After they had heard the king, they went on their way, and the star they had seen in the east went ahead of them until it stopped over the place where the child was. When they saw the star, they were over-joyed.*" –*Matthew 2:9-10*

<u>**Here Below**</u>:

As we take another look at the wise men angle of the Christmas story, we see another very important player in the scene. In fact, the wise men might have never found Jesus without this player. I am of course referring to the star that hung over Bethlehem. We can only assume that it was brighter than the others and new to the Bethlehem skyscape. The wise men had been following it and it had brought them finally to Jesus. Herod had seen the star. Others must have seen it as well. Yet, only the wise men followed it. One thing that I have always found interesting about the Christmas story is the people that did not come to see the baby Jesus. This bright star was right above them pointing the way. The town was filled to capacity with those whom had come for the census, leaving not even enough room for one man and his pregnant wife. Yet, aside from the shepherds and wise men, no one comes to see the Savior. The long awaited Messiah was right there in the next stable and He goes virtually unnoticed. Even the starlit sky was pointing to Him, and everyone missed Him.

I do not wish to seem overly critical of those Bethlehem residents for missing the great event. After all, we are often guilty of the same thing. They were probably busy. Their lives were probably filled with activities and chores. There were meals to prepare, people to see and children and animals to tend. Besides, there was this census thing for which they had to worry! Let's face it, they had some valid excuses! Sound familiar? Well, I have discovered that one excuse is as good as another. Whatever the reason, the outcome was the same. They missed the greatest even of all history! Jesus was right there and they went on about their business as if it were just another day. I would bet that looking back, there were some that would give anything to be able to go back and stop what they were doing long enough to get a glimpse of baby Jesus. Again, how often do we do the same thing? Could it be that God is working right under our nose and we are missing it because we are so preoccupied with other things? The wise men saw the star for what it was because they were looking for it! Perhaps that is what distinguished them from everyone else in Bethlehem. They were looking for the Lord. Don't let your life become so busy that you miss the star shining right over your head. Don't miss the miracles of God.

The Thin Place: Ask, Answer, Pray.

Do you agree that we often do not see God at work because we are not really looking?

What are some things with which we fill our lives that might distract us from spiritual matters?

What can we do to assure that we do not miss God at work in the world around us?

December 26
The Intercessor

From Above: Romans 8:26; Hebrews 7:22-25

Focal Passage: *"Therefore he is able to save completely those who come to God through him, because he always lives to intercede for them." –Hebrews 7:25*

Here Below:

I was once awarded a great honor. I was asked by a member of my congregation to assume power of attorney over him as he was facing a very serious surgery. I was given the responsibility that would usually fall to the next of kin. However, this man wanted his pastor to assume this role. It was a tremendous compliment and implied that he held a deep trust in me. This responsibility meant that I would be his advocate in the event he was unconscious or unable to answer possible life and death medical questions for himself. For him, it was comforting to know that someone he trusted would be interceding on his behalf. What a comfort this is in times of uncertainty! Guess what? You and I have an advocate as well. According to scripture, we have both the Holy Spirit of God and Jesus Himself standing up for us in those instances when we either don't know what to say for ourselves or don't know how to pray. Think about it. Not only do we often have other people praying for us, but the Holy Spirit and Jesus are praying for us!

Hebrews 7:25 tells us that Jesus lives to intercede for us. Of course, this has many implications toward our salvation and the nature of the Trinity, but it also implies a relationship that we have with God from the point of salvation forward. Jesus lives to speak up on our behalf to our Heavenly Father. Being our High Priest, we literally have access to the ear of God! What assurance comes from knowing that Jesus is praying for us! We can trust that Jesus is going to seek the best for His children. We can trust Him fully as our intercessor. With Jesus as our intercessor, we can face whatever comes with a courage unlike any other. I could have failed my friend above as his advocate. Still, he trusted me. Yet, Jesus will never fail us. How much more can we trust in Him?

The Thin Place: Ask, Answer, Pray.

Has there ever been a time when you didn't know how to pray for a certain situation?

Have you ever been the subject of someone else's intercessory prayer?

How has God answered in both of these situations?

December 27
How Many Times?

From Above: Matthew 18:21-22

Focal Passage: *"Then Peter came to Jesus and asked, "Lord, how many times shall I forgive my brother when he sins against me? Up to seven times? Jesus answered, "I tell you, not seven times, but seventy-seven times."* –Matthew 18:21-22

Here Below:

The rabbis of Peter's day had been teaching that we should be willing to forgive those whom have hurt us up to three times. This teaching was based on the tradition found in the writings of the Old Testament Prophet Amos which speaks of God forgiving the enemies of Israel three times before casting judgment upon them. In usual fashion, good old eager Peter seems to want to impress Jesus in this passage by going over and above what is traditionally expected. Probably thinking pretty highly of himself, Peter instead offers the number seven as the ideal number of times in which to offer forgiveness. However, Jesus responds with an answer Peter most likely did not expect. He says "not seven, but seventy-seven times"! Of course, most people agree that this number was figurative. Jesus was simply teaching that we should always be willing to forgive others of their mistakes. There should be no limit to our forgiveness. After all, God had forgiven Israel for their sins more times than we can count!

This concept of forgiveness is at the heart of the gospel message. It is not only at the heart of our salvation, but at the heart of daily Christian living. We must be willing to forgive others if we expect to be in a right relationship with them and with God. Contrary to popular belief and human nature, our forgiveness of others is not based upon their apology or their repentance. In fact, the above verse implies that we are to repeatedly forgive those who repeatedly hurt us! Now this does not mean we just sit back and let someone abuse us! On the contrary, sin sometimes demands a response. Forgiveness doesn't mean turning a blind eye to the transgression. Nevertheless, even in that we are to have a spirit of forgiveness in our hearts, understanding that it is most likely a matter of spiritual weakness on behalf of the guilty party. Your undeserved forgiveness might be the instrument by which God heals their heart and changes their attitude. Besides, we have all been in need of undeserved forgiveness. Likewise, to withhold forgiveness is to prolong the pain and to prohibit the beginnings of peace and reconciliation for both parties involved. Put simply, we're only hurting ourselves by withholding forgiveness. Yes, forgiving seventy times seven may be easier said than done. Nevertheless, there it is. Jesus said it and with His help it can be done. So start counting and start forgiving!

The Thin Place: Ask. Answer. Pray.

Have you ever had to forgive someone else more than once for the same sin?

If so, did you find it difficult to do? Why or why not?

Has God ever forgiven you more than once for the same sin?

December 28
We Cater to Cowards

From Above: I John 4:15-21

Focal Passage: *"There is no fear in love. But perfect love drives out fear, because fear has to do with punishment. The one who fears is not made perfect in love." –I John 4:18*

Here Below:

There was a sign outside a local dentist office that read "We Cater to Cowards!" I am tempted to change dentists. I like that sign. I think they had me in mind when they put it out in front of that office. The thought of drills and needles in my mouth definitely brings out the coward in me. To make it even worse, this is a fear that I must face again and again every few months. Even though I have only had mostly positive experiences with my dentistry in the past, it is still a fear I cannot shake. Perhaps you can relate. For you it may not be something as trivial as going to the dentist, but we all have those things in life that cause us to tremble a little. Fear is an overwhelming emotion. Thankfully, fear does not have to be our master.

We are told that "perfect loves drives out fear". Does this mean we never experience fear or that we are weak in faith if we are afraid? Of course not, as my dentist can attest. However, it does mean that fear has only the control over us that we allow. God's love has eradicated the power of fear over our lives. God's grace, mercy and eternal life is the cure for life's fears. Even in the worst-case scenarios that life can throw at us, God's love and protection will eventually win out. We can face them knowing that in the end God will take care of us. So, if you find yourself trembling with a white-knuckle grasp on your dentist examination chair, look to God. Instead of dwelling on the object of your fear, reflect instead on the love of God. Let His love drive away your fears. God caters to cowards like you and me!

The Thin Place: Ask, Answer, Pray.

What are your greatest fears?

Why do these things cause you to fear?

How has God calmed your fears in the past?

December 29
Filthy Rags

From Above: Isaiah 64:1-9; Romans 3:22

Focal Passage: *"All of us have become like one who is unclean, and all our righteous acts are like filthy rags; we all shrivel up like a leaf, and like the wind our sins sweep us away." –Isaiah 64:6*

Here Below:

As we come to the end of another year, we often find ourselves doing an annual spiritual inventory of our lives. We reflect on the successes and failures of the past year with the hopes that next year might be better. This is healthy; in that, we can learn from both. However, one thing I have discovered in my own spiritual journey, is that we are often inclined to overemphasize our successes and deemphasize our mistakes. We must recognize both, but in an appropriate and spiritually honest manner. Do not misunderstand! We are not intended to keep harboring feelings of shame and guilt over the moral and spiritual shortcomings of times past! In Christ, we are set free from those debilitating conditions. By His grace, we have no reason to keep punishing ourselves for something of which God has forgiven us. Remembering this fact and remembering from where this grace derives should also help us to remember from where our righteousness comes. It comes from Christ.

When it comes to our spiritual victories of the past year, we must likewise be careful to give credit where credit is due. Isaiah teaches us that our righteousness is as filthy rags. In the original language of this scripture, Isaiah is suggesting that compared to that of God, our righteousness is more than just weak and more than just dirty. It's disgusting! Now Isaiah is not implying a futility in living for the Lord, nor is he suggesting that it is impossible to achieve a righteous life or a spiritually successful life. He is implying that it is impossible to achieve it on our own strength. We must depend upon His! All the great heroes of the faith understood this simple yet life-changing principle. The prophets of old, David, Paul, Peter and almost anyone else you can think of seemed to understand this truth. This understanding didn't always come to them easily. Sometimes it took a period of trials, failures and difficult self examination to help them see it. When we come to terms with the reality of our own strength in relation to that of God, it opens the door for Him to work through us, thus bringing the victories we desire. It also frees us from the burden of never measuring up. In Christ, we do measure up, just not because of anything we've done. It is all about what He can do in us. So, recognize your sin for what it is. Most importantly, recognize His grace for what it is. Now let Him have your future.

The Thin Place: Ask, Answer, Pray.

What successes have you experienced over the past year?

What failures have you experienced over the past year?

What has God taught you through these experiences and how might they affect the coming year?

December 30
Explain Yourself!

__From Above__: Psalm 40; I Peter 3:15

Focal Passage: *"I do not hide your righteousness in my heart; I speak of your faithfulness and salvation. I do not conceal your love and your truth from the great assembly." –Psalm 40:10*

__Here Below__:

There are two verses in the above Psalm that are of special interest as we approach the beginning of a new year. They are especially important when you take them in the proper biblical context. This song is a prayer for deliverance. David is crying out to God for release from his current situation and for victory over his enemies. Yet in the midst of these trials, notice verse 10. David is determined to not hold God's righteousness in! In spite of his circumstances, David is declaring his intent to make His relationship with the Lord known! He doesn't seem to think of his faith as something to keep to himself, but something he is compelled to make known. Likewise, verse 16 tells us why. His purpose for this attitude is not so that David might be exalted. His desire is that God be exalted. As we approach a new year, what better resolution could we desire than to live a life in which God is exalted? In order for this to happen, we must let our faith show! We cannot keep it to ourselves! We must let it out!

One of the ironies of the times in which we live is in our willingness to let others into some very private areas of our lives, while we often keep that which is most important to ourselves. For example, we use various social networks, internet and media to share personal facts about ourselves with complete strangers, sometimes to our own detriment; yet, we are reluctant to even talk to our own family about our faith. Why is that? Are we ashamed? Are we scared? Well, whatever the reason, genuine faith is not meant to be a secret. Our faith should be such that it demands an explanation. A life of faith that demands explanation is a life in which God can be exalted. There is no other way. Resolve to live your life in such a way in the coming year to demand explanation. Let God be your answer.

The Thin Place: Ask, Answer, Pray.

Would you say that your life has exalted God in the past year?

Would you say that your faith is obvious to others?

In what ways can you better exalt God with your life in the year to come?

December 31
Tomorrow's Yesterday

From Above: Psalm 103

Focal Passage: "*The LORD is compassionate and gracious, slow to anger, abounding in love. He will not always accuse, nor will he harbor his anger forever; he does not treat us as our sins deserve or repay us according to our iniquities.*" *–Psalm 103:8-10*

Here Below:

Today is the last day of the year. It is hard to believe, but nonetheless true. Hopefully, for you the past year was a good one. For many, it may not have been. With each new year comes new challenges. Some are positive in nature, others are not. Some challenges are self inflicted. Some are unavoidable. Such is the nature of the human experience. Thankfully, we have a God that is not governed by the limits of the human experience! And thankfully tomorrow brings with it a new year, a new day and a new opportunity to experience life as God meant it to be!

Psalm 103 is a good reading in which to conclude a year. It reminds us that God is not overly concerned with our calendars. First, in the above verses, we are basically told that God does not carry a grudge from this day to the next. He doesn't hold our past mistakes against us, even when we think we may deserve it. When He forgives, He truly forgives and forgets. If God can let go of the past, shouldn't we? Secondly, we are reminded that God was with us in the past and He will be with us in the future. Verse 17 contains a beautiful and poetic truth about the love of God. It is from everlasting to everlasting. In other words, God's love extends back as far as we can remember and it goes forward beyond what we can see. Everlasting to everlasting! Wow! With that in mind, the next year doesn't seem so uncertain. God will be there in full strength!

There is an old saying that often gets quoted this time of year. It says that today is the first day of the rest of your life. How true! However, I like to take this statement one step further. Today is also the last day of your past! It is tomorrow's yesterday! Everything from here on out is your future! Scripture seems to teach us that the future is that of which God seems to be most concerned. So give both your past and your future to Him. Maybe this past year wasn't what you had hoped for, or maybe it was much more! Nonetheless, tomorrow is a new opportunity for it to be even greater! Don't let the disappointments of the past determine your future. Remember, the human calendar is just that, human in origin. From God's perspective, every day begins a new year. Let this new one be one that you will talk about years from now as the year in which God did something amazing with your life. It begins today! It begins right now! Happy New Year!

The Thin Place: Ask, Answer, Pray.

What would you do differently if you could relive this past year?

Are there any sins of the past year in which you have not repented and sought forgiveness?

How can you approach life differently in this new year?

Scripture Index

Jonah
4 – (June 1)
Micah
7:18-19 – (June 2)
Nahum
Habakkuk
3 – (July 24)
Zephaniah
1:12 – (July 11)
Haggai
Zechariah
4 – (Nov 19)
8:16-17 – (Aug 29)
Malachi
1:6-14 – (Oct 28)
4:2 – (Feb 4)
6:3-10 – (July 22)
Matthew
1:1-25 – (Dec 21)
2:1-11 – (Dec 24, Dec 25)
3:1-3 – (Jan 8)
4:17 – (Jan 8)
4:23-25 – (Feb 4)
5:1-12 – (Jan 24, Mar 10)
5:1-16 – (Mar 6)
5:9 – (June 16)
5:13-16 – (Apr 14)
5:13-17 – (Feb 9)
5:33-37 – (Dec 5)
5:43-48 – (July 8)
6:1-4 – (July 14, Sept 23)
6:1-8 – (Mar 5)
6:19-20 – (Jan 4)
6:19-21 – (May 22)
6:19-34 – (Jan 14)
6:24-34 – (Oct 25)
6:25-34 – (Feb 27)
6:33-34 – (July 26)
7:1-5 – (Feb 28, July 7, July 25)
7:1-15 – (Sept 14)
7:7-8 – (Aug 11, Nov 11)

5:16-26 – (June 6)

5:22-26 – (Feb 6, Sept 6)

6:12-18 – (Apr 16)

Ephesians

1:17-23 – (July 20, Nov 18)

2:1-5 – (Jan 15)

2:1-13 – (Jan 28)

2:10 – (Feb 7)

2:13-22 (Mar 15)

2:14-15 – (Feb 19)

2:17-18 – (Sept 1)

3 – (Jan 20)

3:12 – (Feb 3)

3:14-21 – (Feb 16)

3:16-21 – (Feb 14)

3:20-21 – (Oct 13, Dec 12)

4:21-24 – (Feb 8)

4:22-27 – (Feb 17)

4:22-32 – (Oct 29)

4:26-27 – (June 26)

4:28-32 – (Feb 23)

4:31-32 – (Feb 24)

5:3-4 – (Nov 24)

5:8-10 – (Mar 18)

5:12 – (Jan 18)

6:1-4 – (June 20)

6:6-8 – (July 2)

6:11-18 – (Mar 22)

Philippians

1:6 – (July 25)

1:1-11 – (Apr 13)

1:1-14 – (July 31)

1:21-26 – (May 14)

2:1-2 – (Jan 12)

2:1-8 – (Jan 26)

2:1-11 – (Aug 13)

2:5-8 – (June 24)

2:5-11 – (Mar 29)

2:17-24 – (Oct 30)

3:7-9 – (Apr 15)

3:17-20 – (June 10)

1 Peter
1:1-9 – (July 13)
1:13-16 – (Feb 23)
2:1-5 – (Jan 19)
2:21-25 – (July 12)
3:15 – (Sept 8, Dec 30)
3:15-16 – (May 24)
3:18-22 – (Feb 12)
2 Peter
1:1-8 – (Mar 6)
1:1-11 – (Mar 27, Dec 17)
1:10-21 – (May 26)
1:16-21 – (Aug 6)
3:9, 15 – (Mar 24)
3:17-18 – (Mar 2)
1 John
1:5-10 – (Jan 22)
2:14-17 – (May 31)
3:1-3 – (Feb 13, June 8)
3:1-11 – (June 5)
3:16 – (Feb 12)
3:21-22 – (Nov 3)
4 – (May 9)
4:1-3 – (Feb 25)
4:1-6 – (Sept 9)
4:1-11 – (May 1)
4:15-21 – (Dec 28)
5:1-5 – (Mar 2)
5:14-15 – (Mar 5, Aug 31)
2 John
1 – (Oct 9)
3 John
Jude
1-25 – (Mar 16)
17-25 – (July 28)
Revelation
1:1-6 – (May 30)
3:13-22 – (Oct 21)
3:14-22 – (July 1, July 11)
4 – (Nov 12)

Topic Index

About the Author

Dr. Rodney Peavy is a native of the state of Georgia. He and his family currently reside in Adel, Georgia, where he serves as pastor of Lakeview Baptist Church. He has served on staff in church ministry since the age of eighteen in varying capacities, including youth ministry, and in both associate and senior pastor positions in churches across the central and north Georgia area. For these many years, his passion has been to fulfill God's vocational call in his life.

Reverend Peavy's educational background includes a master's degree in Theological Studies from Liberty Baptist Theological Seminary, a bachelor's degree in Christian Education, and an Associate's Degree of Divinity from the Baptist College of Florida (formerly called Florida Baptist Theological College), and an associate's degree from Truett McConnell College. Also, among his educational achievements, his most personal and most treasured recognition came in the form of an Honorary Doctor of Divinity Degree from Grace Bible Institute in his hometown of Buford, Georgia, in 2011.

It was in Graceville, Florida, while attending Florida Baptist Theological College, that Rodney met the woman who would become his wife: Beverly Messer. Rodney and Beverly were married on August

2, 1997. She is a special-education schoolteacher currently serving at Connections Academy in Duluth, Georgia.

The Peavy's have four adopted children, three of which are grown and out of the house. They are Christian, Carlos, Tosha, and Joshua respectively. They also have several grandkids.

Prior to this, Rev. Peavy also wrote a book called *Filling the Quiver: Is Adoption God's Will for My Family?* and *Killing My Old Man: Being the Person God Sees in Me.* These books are available through Covenant Books, Amazon or other usual major retail book avenues.

To learn more about the author and his family and ministry, or to sample other writings, please go to www.gospelfoot.com.

Other Works by the Author

Killing My Old Man: Being the Person God Sees in Me

"Knowing this, that our old man is crucified with him, that the body of sin might be destroyed, that henceforth we should not serve sin. For he that is dead is freed from sin. Now if we be dead with Christ, we believe that we shall also live with him:" -Romans 6:6-8

As a Christian, do you ever wonder why you still struggle with sin? Are you tired of repeating the same old mistakes? Have you found yourself in a seemingly never-ending cycle of habitual sin and shame? Are you tired of the feelings of defeat and long for the freedom, peace, and victory promised in being a new creation?

Then it's time to face him. He is called the old man, the old self, or our old nature. We all have one. Are you ready to look him in the eye? Are you ready to fight him? Are you ready to live free? Let it begin today. It's time to kill your old man and be the person God sees in you.

Killing My Old Man is available at Convenantbooks.com, Amazon, Barnes and Noble, and other major book retailers.

Also, check out www.gospelfoot.com for more info...

Filling the Quiver: Is Adoption God's Will for My Family?

"As arrows are in the hand of a mighty man; so are children of thy youth. Happy is the man that hath his quiver full of them: they shall not be ashamed, but they shall speak with the enemies in the gate" (Ps. 127:4–5).

Have you ever considered adopting but been fearful because of the many questions flooding your mind? Could I love an adopted child as I would one born to me? What if there are emotional issues? Would my family accept my adopted children? These are all real questions and not easy to ask.

In Filling the Quiver; Is Adoption God's Will for My Family? author and adoptive father Rodney Peavy holds nothing back as he answers the questions you are afraid to ask in a way that is genuine, practical, and heartwarming. He shares his family's personal testimony of the many challenges they faced in adopting their children, as well as the many blessings they have received. From there, Peavy takes on the questions he and his wife have been asked since adoption first became part of their family history. To the Peavy's, adoption is more than just a family decision; it is a faith decision. Filling the Quiver approaches the decision to adopt from the perspective that God is—and should be—involved in the process.

This testimony seeks to offer those who have considered adoption a deeper understanding of the impact and spiritual implications of adoption. If you are still wondering about adoption as an option, this book can help you discover this answer for yourself, with God's guidance.

To purchase, go to covenantbooks.com, Amazon, Barnes and Noble or other major book retailers....

Also, check out www.gospelfoot.com for more info...

The Lonely Moon

Courage is not the absence of fear or a willingness to fight. Sometimes true courage is found in surrender. *The Lonely Moon* is an adventure story that will appeal to readers of all ages. Anyone who has ever struggled with feelings of shame, doubt and loneliness will find themselves in this story. Follow the epic adventure of a rogue wolf as he searches for true meaning while navigating life under the lonely moon.

This story is an allegorical Christian fiction writing that will inspire you to step out of your comfort zone into the unknown aadventure of faith. Follow along with our hero as he battles enemies from without and within along the way. Sound familiar?

This story is the story of all who have ever heard the call of the wild life of faith. Come along, but know this...it is not for the tame of heart.

The Lonely Moon is available on Amazon, Barnes and Noble and other major book retailers.

Also, check out www.gospelfoot.com for more info...